CHILTON'S
REPAIR & TUNE-UP GUIDE

CHEVROLET MID-SIZE 1964-84

Chevelle 1964-77 • Laguna S-3 1974-77 • Malibu 1978-84 Monte Carlo 1970-84 • El Camino 1964-84

Vice President and General Manager JOHN P. KUSHNERICK
Managing Editor KERRY A. FREEMAN, S.A.E.
Senior Editor RICHARD J. RIVELE, S.A.E.
Editor A. LINDSAY BROOKE

CHILTON BOOK COMPANY
Radnor, Pennsylvania
19089

SAFETY NOTICE

Proper service and repair procedures are vital to the safe, reliable operation of all motor vehicles, as well as the personal safety of those performing repairs. This book outlines procedures for servicing and repairing vehicles using safe, effective methods. The procedures contain many NOTES, CAUTIONS and WARNINGS which should be followed along with standard safety procedures to eliminate the possibility of personal injury or improper service which could damage the vehicle or compromise its safety.

It is important to note that repair procedures and techniques, tools and parts for servicing motor vehicles, as well as the skill and experience of the individual performing the work vary widely. It is not possible to anticipate all of the conceivable ways or conditions under which vehicles may be serviced, or to provide cautions as to all of the possible hazards that may result. Standard and accepted safety precautions and equipment should be used when handling toxic or flammable fluids, and safety goggles or other protection should be used during cutting, grinding, chiseling, prying, or any other process that can cause material removal or projectiles.

Some procedures require the use of tools specially designed for a specific purpose. Before substituting another tool or procedure, you must be completely satisfied that neither your personal safety, nor the performance of the vehicle will be endangered.

Although information in this guide is based on industry sources and is as complete as possible at the time of publication, the possibility exists that the manufacturer made later changes which could not be included here. While striving for total accuracy, Chilton Book Company cannot assume responsibility for any errors, changes, or omissions that may occur in the compilation of this data.

PART NUMBERS

Part numbers listed in this reference are not recommendations by Chilton for any product by brand name. They are references that can be used with interchange manuals and aftermarket supplier catalogs to locate each brand supplier's discrete part number.

ACKNOWLEDGMENTS

The Chilton Book Company expresses its appreciation to the Chevrolet Motor Division, General Motors Corporation, Detroit, Michigan for their generous assistance.

Information has been selected from Chevrolet shop manuals, owners manuals, service bulletins, and technical training manuals.

Copyright © 1984 by Chilton Book Company
All Rights Reserved
Published in Radnor, Pennsylvania 19089, by Chilton Book Company

Manufactured in the United States of America
1234567890   3210987654

Chilton's Repair & Tune-Up Guide: Chevrolet Mid-Size 1964–84
ISBN 0-8019-7456-9 pbk.
Library of Congress Catalog Card No. 83-45299

CONTENTS

Quick Reference
Specifications For Your Vehicle

Fill in this chart with the most commonly used specifications for your vehicle. Specifications can be found in Chapters 1 through 3 or on the tune-up decal under the hood of the vehicle.

 # Tune-Up

Firing Order_____

Spark Plugs:

    Type_____

    Gap (in.)_____

Point Gap (in.)_____

Dwell Angle (°)_____

Ignition Timing (°)_____

    Vacuum (Connected/Disconnected)_____

Valve Clearance (in.)

    Intake_____   Exhaust_____

Capacities

Engine Oil (qts)

    With Filter Change_____

    Without Filter Change_____

Cooling System (qts)_____

Manual Transmission (pts)_____

    Type_____

Automatic Transmission (pts)_____

    Type_____

Front Differential (pts)_____

    Type_____

Rear Differential (pts)_____

    Type_____

Transfer Case (pts)_____

    Type_____

FREQUENTLY REPLACED PARTS
Use these spaces to record the part numbers of frequently replaced parts.

PCV VALVE

Manufacturer_____

Part No._____

OIL FILTER

Manufacturer_____

Part No._____

AIR FILTER

Manufacturer_____

Part No._____

General Information and Maintenance

HOW TO USE THIS BOOK

This book is divided into ten easy to follow chapters, avoiding "mechanic's jargon" and highlighting important procedures with illustrations wherever possible. As time goes by, you'll probably find that some chapters such as Chapter 2 (Tune Up) naturally accumulate more dirty fingerprints than others, but everything from engine rebuilding to waxing the car is covered here. Of course, even professional mechanics won't attempt a repair without the proper tools and a thorough knowledge of the work required. This is why operations like rebuilding your transmission or rear axle assembly are not covered here—they require a range of special tools which are too expensive, and a technical knowledge too extensive to be useful to you, the owner/mechanic.

Before loosening a single nut, read through the entire section you are dealing with and make sure you have the time, tools, and replacement parts necessary to do the job. This will save you much frustration, many hassles, and possibly a walk to the bus stop Monday morning because you needed a part or were without a tool Saturday afternoon. Remember, too, that auto parts stores sometimes have to order certain parts, so it's wise to run through a procedure and make a couple phone calls to be sure a part will be available when you need it.

Each section begins with a brief description of the particular system and the basic theory behind it. When repairs involve a level of technical know-how beyond most owner/mechanics, we tell you how to remove the part and replace it with a new or rebuilt unit. This way you can at least save the cost of labor, and the percentage that is often placed on top of the retail cost of new parts.

There are a few basic mechanic's rules that should be followed when working on any car:

1. Left side of the car means the driver's side; right side is the passenger's side;
2. Most screws, bolts, and nuts are "right handed"—they are tightened by turning clockwise and removed by turning counterclockwise.
3. *Never* crawl under a vehicle supported only by a jack—jack up the car, then support it with jackstands!
4. *Never* smoke or position an exposed flame near the battery or any part of the fuel system;
5. *Never* operate an engine in a closed room;
6. Use common sense during all operations.

TOOLS AND EQUIPMENT

The following list contains the basic tools needed to perform most of the maintenance and repair work covered in this book. The nut, bolts and thread sizes in your Chevrolet are mostly standard U.S. sizes (S.A.E.) in the 1964 through '76 models, and a combination of standard U.S. sizes (S.A.E.) and metric sizes in the 1977 and later models. Most of the later models covered here use metric fasteners and thread sizes exclusively on their engines, transmissions and drive axles. It's a good idea to check your particular model for the types of fasteners used on various assemblies.

1. One set each of both metric and S.A.E. sockets, including a ⅝ in. spark plug socket. Various length socket drive extensions and universals are also very helpful, but you'll probably acquire these as you need them. Ratchet handles are available in ¼, ⅜ and ½ in. drives, and will fit both metric and S.A.E. sockets (just make sure that your sockets are the proper drive size for the ratchet handle you buy);
2. One set each of metric and S.A.E. "combination" (one end open and one end box) wrenches;

FROM TOP: BATTERY
TERMINAL TOOL;
FEELER GAUGES;
OIL SPOUT; FILTER
WRENCH

ALLEN WRENCHES

JACKSTAND

BEAM-TYPE TORQUE WRENCH

DWELL TACHOMETER

DWELL/TACHOMETER

VACUUM GAUGE

COMPRESSION GAUGE

TIMING LIGHT

You need only a basic assortment of hand tools and test instruments for most maintenance and repair jobs

3. Wire-type spark plug feeler gauge;

4. Blade-type feeler gauge for ignition and valve settings;

5. Slot and Phillips head screwdrivers in various sizes;

6. Oil filter strap wrench, necessary for removing oil filters (*never* used, though, for installing the filters);

7. Oil can filler spout, for pouring fresh oil from quart oil cans;

8. Pair of slip-lock pliers;

9. Pair of vise-type pliers;

10. Adjustable wrench;

11. At least two sturdy jackstands for working underneath the car—any other type of support (bricks, wood and especially cinderblocks) is just plain dangerous;

12. Timing light, preferably a DC battery hookup type, and preferably an inductive type for use on cars with electronic ignition.

This is an adequate set of tools, and the more work you do yourself on your car, the larger you'll find the set growing—a pair of pliers here, a wrench or two there. It makes more sense to have a comprehensive set of basic tools as listed above, and then to acquire more along the line as you need them, than to go out and plunk down big money for a professional size set you may never use. In addition to these basic tools, there are several other tools and gauges you may find useful.

Special Tools

• A hydraulic floor jack of at least 1½ ton capacity. If you are serious about maintaining your own car, then a floor jack is as necessary as a spark plug socket. The greatly increased utility, strength, and safety of a hydraulic floor jack makes it pay for itself many times over through the years.

• A compression gauge. The screw-in type is slower to use but it eliminates the possibility of a faulty reading due to escaping pressure.

• A manifold vacuum gauge, very useful in troubleshooting ignition and emissions problems.

• A drop light, to light up the work area (make sure yours is Underwriter's approved, and has a shielded bulb).

• A volt/ohm meter, used for determining whether or not there is current in a wire. These are handy for use if a wire is broken somewhere and are especially necessary for working on today's electronics-laden vehicles.

As a final note, a torque wrench is necessary for all but the most basic work—it should even be used when installing spark plugs. The more common beam-type models are perfectly adequate and are usually much less expensive than

the more precise "click" type (on which you pre-set the torque and the wrench "clicks" when that setting arrives on the fastener you are torquing).

NOTE: *Chevrolet special tools referred to in this guide are available through the Service Tool Division, Kent-Moore Corporation, 29784 Little Mack, Roseville, MI 48066-2298. In Canada, contact Kent-Moore of Canada, Ltd., 2395 Cawthra Mississauga, Ontario, Canada L5A 3P2.*

SERVICING YOUR CAR SAFELY

It is virtually impossible to anticipate all of the hazards involved with automotive maintenance and service, but care and common sense will prevent most accidents.

The rules of safety for mechanics range from "don't smoke around gasoline," to "use the proper tool for the job." The trick to avoiding injuries is to develop safe work habits and take every possible precaution.

Dos

• Do keep a fire extinguisher and first aid kit within easy reach.

• Do wear safety glasses or goggles when cutting, drilling, grinding or prying, even if you have 20-20 vision. If you wear glasses for the sake of vision, they should be made of hardened glass that can serve also as safety glasses, or wear safety goggles over your regular glasses.

• Do shield your eyes whenever you work around the battery. Batteries contain sulphuric acid. In case of contact with the eyes or skin, flush the area with water or a mixture of water and baking soda and get medical attention immediately.

• Do use safety stands for any undercar service. Jacks are for raising vehicles; safety stands are for making sure the vehicle stays raised until you want it to come down. Whenever the car is raised, block the wheels remaining on the ground and set the parking brake.

• Do use adequate ventilation when working with any chemicals or hazardous materials. Like carbon monoxide, the asbestos dust resulting from brake lining wear can be poisonous in sufficient quantities.

• Do disconnect the negative battery cable when working on the electrical system. The secondary ignition system can contain up to 40,000 volts.

• Do follow manufacturer's directions whenever working with potentially hazardous materials. Both brake fluid and antifreeze are poisonous if taken internally.

Always use jackstands when supporting the car; never use cinder blocks or tire changing jacks

• Do properly maintain your tools. Loose hammerheads, mushroomed punches and chisels, frayed or poorly grounded electrical cords, excessively worn screwdrivers, spread wrenches (open end), cracked sockets, slipping ratchets, or faulty droplight sockets can cause accidents.

• Likewise, keep your tools clean; a greasy wrench can slip off a bolt head, ruining the bolt and often ruining your knuckles in the process.

• Do use the proper size and type of tool for the job being done.

• Do when possible, pull on a wrench handle rather than push on it, and adjust your stance to prevent a fall.

• Do be sure that adjustable wrenches are tightly closed on the nut or bolt and pulled so that the face is on the side of the fixed jaw.

• Do select a wrench or socket that fits the nut or bolt. The wrench or socket should sit straight, not cocked.

• Do strike squarely with a hammer; avoid glancing blows.

• Do set the parking brake and block the drive wheels if the work requires the engine running.

Don'ts

• Don't run the engine in a garage or anywhere else without proper ventilation—EVER! Carbon monoxide is poisonous; it takes a long time to leave the human body and you can build up a deadly supply of it in your system by simply breathing in a little every day. You may not realize you are slowly poisoning yourself. Always use power vents, windows, fans or open the garage doors.

• Don't work around moving parts while wearing a necktie or other loose clothing. Short sleeves are much safer than long, loose sleeves; hard-toed shoes with neoprene soles protect your toes and give a better grip on slippery surfaces. Jewelry such as watches, fancy belt buckles, beads or body adornment of any kind

is not safe working around a car. Long hair should be tied back under a hat or cap.

• Don't use pockets for toolboxes. A fall or bump can drive a screwdriver deep into your body. Even a wiping cloth hanging from the back pocket can wrap around a spinning shaft or fan.

• Don't smoke when working around gasoline, cleaning solvent or other flammable material.

• Don't smoke when working around the battery. When the battery is being charged, it gives off explosive hydrogen gas.

• Don't use gasoline to wash your hands; there are excellent soaps available. Gasoline may contain lead, and lead can enter the body through a cut, accumulating in the body until you are very ill. Gasoline also removes all the natural oils from the skin so that bone dry hands will suck up oil and grease.

• Don't service the air conditioning system unless you are equipped with the necessary tools and training. The refrigerant, R-12, is extremely cold when compressed, and when released into the air will instantly freeze any surface it contacts, including your eyes. Although the refrigerant is normally non-toxic, R-12 becomes a deadly poisonous gas in the presence of an open flame. One good whiff of the vapors from burning refrigerant can be fatal.

• Don't use screwdrivers for anything other than driving screws! A screwdriver used as a prying tool can snap when you least expect it, causing injuries. At the very least, you'll ruin a good screwdriver.

• Don't use a bumper jack (that little ratchet, scissors, or pantograph jack supplied with the car) for anything other than changing a flat! These jacks are only intended for emergency use out on the road; they are NOT designed as a maintenance tool. If you are serious about maintaining your car yourself, invest in a hydraulic floor jack of at least 1½ ton capacity, and at least two sturdy jackstands.

SERIAL NUMBER IDENTIFICATION

Vehicle Identification Number
(VIN) PLATE

The 1964–67 vehicle serial number is stamped on a vehicle identification plate, attached to the left front door hinge pillar. On 1968 and later cars, the Vehicle Identification Number (VIN) is stamped on a plate located on the top left-hand side of the instrument panel, so it can be seen by looking through the windshield.

Vehicle serial number for 1964–67, found on left front door pillar

VIN location on 1968 and later cars

The VIN is a thirteen digit (1968–80) or seventeen digit (1981 and later) sequence of numbers and letters important for ordering parts and for servicing.

NOTE: *Model years appear in the VIN as the last digit of each particular year (6 is 1976, 8 is 1978, etc.), until 1980 (which is A). This is the final year under the thirteen digit code. The seventeen digit VIN begins with 1981 (B) and continues 1982 (C), 1983 (D), etc.*

Engine Serial Number

The engine serial number shows the manufacturing plant signified by a letter (F for Flint, T for Tonawanda, etc.), the month of manufacture, the day of manufacture, and the transmission and engine type represented by a two or

Body number plate—Canadian models

Body number plate—U.S. models

three-letter code. A typical engine serial number would be F1005FA. The F represents the manufacturing plant (Flint), the 10 signifies the month of manufacture (October), 05 signifies the day of manufacture, and FA signifies the engine and transmission type. Beginning with 1968 models, a VIN is stamped on the cylinder block next to the engine serial number. The VIN (up to 1971) is the same as the vehicle serial number stamped on the instrument panel except that it does not include the four numbers representing body style.

In 1972, the VIN changed somewhat. A typ-

VIN code, 1968–71

Thirteen digit VIN, 1972–80

Seventeen digit VIN, 1981 and later

ENGINE V.I.N. (L.H. FRONT)

Engine VIN location, V6 and V8 Diesels

LABEL LOCATION

ENGINE UNIT NUMBER

Some 305 and 350 V8s have VIN codes here

VIN label (decal) locations, 231 V6

ical VIN for a 1972 Chevelle might be: IQ87F2F000001 identifying this particular car as the first (000001) 1972 Chevelle to roll off the Flint assembly line. It includes the manufacturer's identity number (number 1 representing Chevrolet products), a series code letter (Q representing Camaro in this particular instance), a two-digit body style number (87 representing 2 dr. Sport Coupe), an engine code letter (letters listed below), a one-digit model year number (2 representing 1972), an assembly plant letter (F signifying Flint), and a unit number signifying order of production. According to the VIN, this car had a 307 cu in. engine with two-barrel carburetor represented by the engine code letter "F."

This basic format is utilized through the 1981 model year, although specific letter/number designations may change from year to year.

INLINE 6 CYLINDER ENGINES (1964–79)

On six-cylinder engines, the serial number is found on a pad at the front right-hand side of the cylinder block, just to the rear of the distributor.

Engine serial number location—inline six cylinder engine

V8 AND V6 ENGINES (1967–84)

On the 229 V6 and all V8 engines, the serial number is found on a pad at the front right-

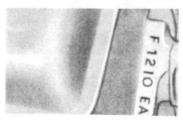

229 V6 and all V8 engine serial number location— just below right-hand valve cover, stamped on engine block

ENGINE V.I.N.

231 V6 engine serial number—at extreme left rear of cylinder block

hand side of the cylinder block, just below the cylinder head. On the 231 V6, the number can be found on a pad on the left side of the cylinder block, where it meets the transmission.

Transmission Serial Number

A transmission serial number is stamped on each transmission. Beginning with 1968 models, a VIN is stamped on each cylinder block and on every transmission, in addition to the serial number. The VIN is the same as the vehicle serial number stamped on the instrument panel except that it does not include the four numbers representing body style. The location of the transmission serial number on each transmission is as follows:

Serial number location-Saginaw 3 and 4 speed (© Chevrolet Motor Division)

Serial number location-Muncie 4 speed (© Chevrolet Motor Division)

Serial number location on the Powerglide

Serial number location-Turbo Hydra-Matic (© Chevrolet Motor Division)

Manual transmission serial number location—1979–81

V.I.N. LOCATION

V.I.N. LOCATION
(OPTIONAL)

Serial number location on the Turbo Hydra-Matic 350 and 350C

V.I.N. LOCATION
(OPTIONAL)

V.I.N. LOCATION

Serial number location on the Turbo Hydra-Matic 200 and 250

Vehicle Emission Control Information Label

The Vehicle Emission Control Information Label is located in the engine compartment (fan shroud, radiator support, hood underside, etc.) of every vehicle produced by General Motors. The label contains important emission specifications and setting procedures, as well as a vacuum hose schematic with various emissions components identified.

When servicing your Chevrolet, this label should always be checked for up-to-date information pertaining specifically to your car.

NOTE: *Always follow the timing procedures on this label when adjusting ignition timing.*

ROUTINE MAINTENANCE

Air Cleaner

The air cleaner has a dual purpose. It not only filters the air going to the carburetor, but also acts as a flame arrester if the engine should backfire through the carburetor. If an engine maintenance procedure requires the temporary removal of the air cleaner, remove it; otherwise, never run the engine without it. Operating a car without its air cleaner results in some throaty sounds from the carburetor giving the impression of increased power but will only cause trouble. Unfiltered air to the carburetor will eventually result in a dirty, inefficient carburetor and engine. A dirty carburetor increases the chances of carburetor backfire and, without the protection of an air cleaner, fire becomes a probable danger. The air cleaner assembly consists of the air cleaner itself, which is the large metal container that fits over the carburetor, the element (paper or polyurethane) contained within, and the flame arrester located in the base of the air cleaner. If your car

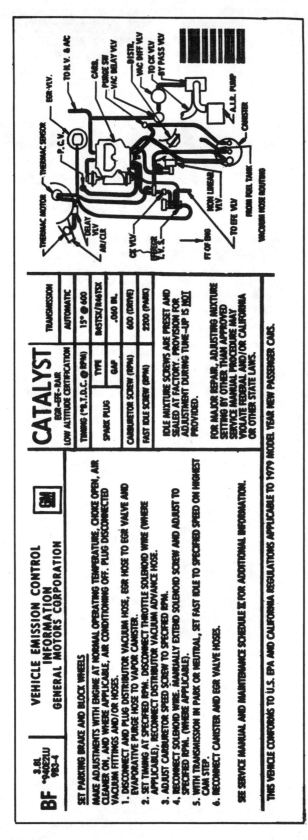

Typical emissions decal, 1979 231 V6 shown. Located under hood

Unscrew the wing nut and remove the cover

Using a clean rag or paper towel, wipe out the inside of the air cleaner

Remove and discard the old filter

Check the small crankcase breather

is equipped with the paper element, it should be inspected at its first 12,000 miles, rechecked every 6,000 miles thereafter, and replaced after 24,000 miles. 1975 and later air cleaners should be replaced at 30,000 mile intervals if the paper type (V6 and V8), and 15,000 miles if the oil wetted type (inline six). Inspections and replacements should be more frequent if the car is operated in a dirty, dusty environment. When inspecting the element, look for dust leaks, holes or an overly dirty appearance. If the element is excessively dirty, it

may cause a reduction in clean air intake. If air has trouble getting through a dirty element, the carburetor fuel mixture will become richer (more gas, less air), the idle will be rougher, and the exhaust smoke will be noticeably black. To check the effectiveness of your paper element, remove the air cleaner assembly and, if the idle increases, then the element is restricting airflow and should be replaced. If a polyurethane element is installed, clean or replace it every 12,000 miles. If you choose to clean it, do so with kerosene or another suitable solvent. Squeeze out all of the solvent, soak in engine oil, and then squeeze out the oil using a clean, dry cloth to remove the excess. The flame arrester, located at the base of the carburetor, should be cleaned in solvent (kerosene) once every 12,000 miles.

Positive Crankcase Ventilation Valve (PCV)

The crankcase ventilation system (PCV) must be operating properly in order to allow evaporation of fuel vapors and water from the crankcase. This system should be checked at every oil change and serviced after one year or 12,000 miles. The PCV valve is replaced after 2 years or 24,000 miles. For 1975 and later cars, the service interval has been upgraded to one year or 15,000 miles, with PCV valve replacement scheduled for two years or 30,000 miles. Normal service entails cleaning the passages of the system hoses with solvent, inspecting them for cracks and breaks, and replacing them as necessary. The PCV valve contains a check valve and, when working properly, this valve will make a rattling sound when the outside case is tapped. If it fails to rattle, then it is probably stuck in a closed position and needs to be replaced.

The PCV system is designed to prevent the emission of gases from the crankcase. It does

PCV system schematic; V8 engine (others similar)

Pulling out the PCV valve from the rocker cover

Checking PCV valve for vacuum

this by connecting a crankcase outlet (valve cover, oil filler tube, back of engine) to the intake manifold with a hose. The crankcase gases travel through the hose to the intake manifold where they are returned to the combustion chamber to be burned. If maintained properly, this system reduces condensation in the crank-

case and the resultant formation of harmful acids and oil dilution. A clogged PCV valve will often cause a slow or rough idle due to a richer fuel mixture. A car equipped with a PCV system has air going through a hose to the intake manifold from an outlet at the valve cover, oil filler tube, or rear of the engine. To compensate for this extra air going to the manifold, carburetor specifications require a richer (more gas) mixture at the carburetor. If the PCV valve or hose is clogged, this air doesn't go to the intake manifold and the fuel mixture is too rich. A rough, slow idle results. The valve should be checked before making any carburetor adjustments. Disconnect the valve from the engine or merely clamp the hose shut. If the engine speed decreases less than 50 rpm, the valve is clogged and should be replaced. If the engine speed decreases much more than 50 rpm, then the valve is good. The PCV valve is an inexpensive item and it is suggested that it be replaced. If the new valve doesn't noticeably improve engine idle, the problem might be a restriction in the PCV hose. For further details on PCV valve operation see Chapter 4.

Crankcase Depression Regulator and Flow Control Valve

V8 AND V6 DIESEL ENGINES

The Crankcase Depression Regulator (CDR), found on 1981 and later diesels, and the flow control valve, used from 1978 to 1980, are designed to scavenge crankcase vapors in basically the same manner as the PCV valve on gasoline engines. The valves are located either on the left rear corner of the intake manifold (CDR), or on the rear of the intake crossover pipe (flow control valve). On each system there are two ventilation filters, one per valve cover.

The filter assemblies should be cleaned every

V8 diesel crankcase ventilation system, 1978–80

V8 diesel crankcase ventilation system, 1981 and later

V6 diesel crankcase ventilation system, 1982 and later

15,000 miles by simply prying them carefully from the valve covers (be aware of the grommets underneath), and washing them out in solvent. The ventilation pipes and tubes should also be cleaned. Both the CDR and flow control valves should also be cleaned every 30,0000 miles (the cover can be removed from the CDR;

the flow control valve can simply be flushed with solvent). Dry each valve, filter, and hose with compressed air before installation.

NOTE: *Do not attempt to test the crankcase controls on these diesels. Instead, clean the valve cover filter assembly and vent pipes and check the vent pipes.*

Replace the breather cap assembly every 30,000 miles. Replace all rubber fittings as required every 15,000 miles.

Evaporative Emissions Control System

This system, standard since 1970, eliminates the release of unburned fuel vapors into the atmosphere. The only periodic maintenance required is an occasional check of the connecting lines of the system for kinks or other damage and deterioration. Lines should only be replaced with quality fuel line or special hose marked "evap." On 1970 and 1971 vehicles, every 12,000 miles or 12 months, the filter in the bottom of the carbon canister which is located in the engine compartment should be removed and replaced. On 1972–1976 vehicles, this service interval is 24,000 miles or 24 months. For 1977 and later vehicles, the mileage interval has been increased to 30,000 miles, while the time interval remains the same. For further details on the Evaporative Emission Control System please refer to Chapter 4.

FILTER REPLACEMENT

1. Tag and disconnect all hoses connected to the charcoal canister.

2. Loosen the retaining clamps and then lift out the canister.

3. Grasp the filter in the bottom of the canister with your fingers and pull it out. Replace it with a new one.

DIESEL CRANKCASE VENTILATION SYSTEM   **CRANKCASE DEPRESSION REGULATOR**

Diesel crankcase ventilation and crankcase depression regulator cutaway, 1980 and later

Typical evaporation canister

4. Installation of the remaining components is in the reverse order of removal.

Battery

SPECIFIC GRAVITY (EXCEPT "MAINTENANCE FREE" BATTERIES)

At least once a year, check the specific gravity of the battery. It should be between 1.20 and 1.26 at room temperature.

The specific gravity can be checked with the use of an hydrometer, an inexpensive instrument available from many sources, including auto parts stores. The hydrometer has a squeeze

u
g
the
cific
than
shoul

It is
in this
batteries
top of the
signs of ba
is dark, the
If the indica
low, and the
placed.

CABLES AND

Once a year, the
ble clamps shoul
clamps and remove
first. On batteries w
a puller specially ma
ommended. These are
able in auto parts store
cables are secured with

Clean the cable clamp
minal with a wire brush,
grease, etc. is removed and
It is especially important to
the clamp thoroughly, since
foreign material or oxidation wi
electrical connection and inhib
or charging. Special tools are
cleaning these parts, one type for
batteries and another type for s
batteries.

Before installing the cables, loose

Specific gravity can be checked with an hydrometer

Pullers make clamp removal easier

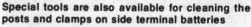

he posts with a wire brush, or a terminal
made for the purpose (shown)

Special tools are also available for cleaning the
posts and clamps on side terminal batteries

tery hold-down clamp or strap, remove the
battery and check the battery tray. Clear it of
any debris, and check it for soundness. Rust
should be wire brushed away, and the metal
given a coat of anti-rust paint. Replace the battery and tighten the hold-down clamp or strap
securely, but be careful not to overtighten,
which will crack the battery case.

After the clamps and terminals are clean,
reinstall the cables, negative cable last; do not
hammer on the clamps to install. Tighten the
clamps securely, but do not distort them. Give
the clamps and terminals a thin external coat of
grease after installation, to retard corrosion.

Check the cables at the same time that the
terminals are cleaned. If the cable insulation is
cracked or broken, or if the ends are frayed,
the cable should be replaced with a new cable
of the same length and gauge.

NOTE: *Keep flame or sparks away from the
battery; it gives off explosive hydrogen gas.
Battery electrolyte contains sulphuric acid.
If you should splash any on your skin or in
your eyes, flush the affected area with plenty
of clear water; if it lands in your eyes, get
medical help immediately.*

REPLACEMENT

When it becomes necessary to replace the battery, select a battery with a rating equal to or

Clean the inside of the clamps with a wire brush, or
the special tool

greater than the battery originally installed. Deterioration, embrittlement and just plain aging of the battery cables, starter motor, and associated wires makes the battery's job harder in successive years. The slow increase in electrical resistance over time makes it prudent to install a new battery with a greater capacity than the old. Details on battery removal and installation are covered in Chapter 3.

Manifold Heat Control Valve (Heat Riser) 1964–74

This valve is located in the exhaust manifold under the carburetor on in-line engines, and in either the right or left side exhaust manifold on V engines. It can be identified by looking for an external thermostatic spring and weight, and hinge pins that run through the walls of the manifold. Check the valve for free operation every 6,000 miles and, if it binds or is frozen, free it up with a solvent.

Typical heater riser valve (six cylinder shown) (© Chevrolet Motor Div.)

NOTE: *Certain early engines had the heat riser built into the manifold and could only be repaired by replacing the entire manifold.*

Early Fuel Evaporation (EFE) System 1975 and Later

This is a more effective form of heat riser which is vacuum actuated. It is used on all models built in 1975 and later. It heats incoming mixture during the engine warm-up process, utilizing a ribbed heat exchanger of thin metal that is located in the intake manifold. This pre-heating allows the choke to open more rapidly, thus reducing emissions. Problems in this sytem might be indicated by poor engine operation during warm-up.

This valve should be checked initially at 6 months/7,500 miles, and, thereafter, at 18 months/22,500 mile intervals.

EFE valve

To check, move the valve through its full stroke by hand, making sure that the linkage does not bind and is properly connected. If the valve sticks, free it with a solvent. Also check that all vacuum hoses are properly connected and free of cracks or breaks. Replace hoses or broken or bent linkage parts as necessary.

Belts

TENSION CHECKING AND ADJUSTMENT

Check the drive belts every 7,500 miles or six months for evidence of wear such as cracking, fraying, and incorrect tension. Determine belt tension at a point halfway between the pulleys by pressing on the belt with moderate thumb pressure. If the distance between the pulleys (measured from the center of each pulley) is 13–16 in., the belt should deflect ½ in. at the halfway point or ¼ in. if the distance is 7–10 in. If the deflection is found to be too much or too little, loosen the mounting bolts and make the adjustments.

Before you attempt to adjust any of your engine's belts, you should take an old rag soaked in solvent and clean the mounting bolts of any road grime which has accumulated there. On some of the harder-to-reach bolts, an application of penetrating oil will make them easier to loosen. When you're adjusting belts, especially on late model V8's with air conditioning and power steering, it would be especially helpful to have a variety of socket extensions and universals to get to those hard-to-reach bolts.

NOTE: *When adjusting the air pump belt, if you are using a pry bar, make sure that you pry against the cast iron end cover and not against the aluminum housing. Excessive force on the housing itself will damage it.*

HOW TO SPOT WORN V-BELTS

V-Belts are vital to efficient engine operation—they drive the fan, water pump and other accessories. They require little maintenance (occasional tightening) but they will not last forever. Slipping or failure of the V-belt will lead to overheating. If your V-belt looks like any of these, it should be replaced.

Cracking or weathering

This belt has deep cracks, which cause it to flex. Too much flexing leads to heat build-up and premature failure. These cracks can be caused by using the belt on a pulley that is too small. Notched belts are available for small diameter pulleys.

Softening (grease and oil)

Oil and grease on a belt can cause the belt's rubber compounds to soften and separate from the reinforcing cords that hold the belt together. The belt will first slip, then finally fail altogether.

Glazing

Glazing is caused by a belt that is slipping. A slipping belt can cause a run-down battery, erratic power steering, overheating or poor accessory performance. The more the belt slips, the more glazing will be built up on the surface of the belt. The more the belt is glazed, the more it will slip. If the glazing is light, tighten the belt.

Worn cover

The cover of this belt is worn off and is peeling away. The reinforcing cords will begin to wear and the belt will shortly break. When the belt cover wears in spots or has a rough jagged appearance, check the pulley grooves for roughness.

Separation

This belt is on the verge of breaking and leaving you stranded. The layers of the belt are separating and the reinforcing cords are exposed. It's just a matter of time before it breaks completely.

7" TO 10"
1/4" DEFLECTION

13" TO 16"
1/2" DEFLECTION

A gauge is recommended, but you can check belt tension with thumb pressure (© Chevrolet Motor Div.)

To adjust belt tension or to replace belts, first loosen the component's mounting and adjusting bolts slightly

Push the component toward the engine and slip off the belt

Slip the new belt over the pulley

Pull outward on the component and tighten the mounting bolts

Hoses

Upper and lower radiator hoses and all heater hoses should be checked for deterioration, leaks and loose hose clamps every 15,000 miles. To remove the hoses:

1. Drain the radiator as detailed later in this chapter.

2. Loosen the hose clamps at each end of the hose to be removed.

3. Working the hose back and forth, slide it off its connection and then install a new hose if necessary.

4. Position the hose clamps at least ¼ in. from the end of the hose and tighten them.

NOTE: *Always make sure that the hose clamps are beyond the bead and placed in the center of the clamping surface before tightening them.*

Cooling System

Dealing with the cooling system can be a dangerous matter unless the proper precautions are

HOW TO SPOT BAD HOSES

Both the upper and lower radiator hoses are called upon to perform difficult jobs in an inhospitable environment. They are subject to nearly 18 psi at under hood temperatures often over 280°F., and must circulate nearly 7500 gallons of coolant an hour—3 good reasons to have good hoses.

Swollen hose

A good test for any hose is to feel it for soft or spongy spots. Frequently these will appear as swollen areas of the hose. The most likely cause is oil soaking. This hose could burst at any time, when hot or under pressure.

Cracked hose

Cracked hoses can usually be seen but feel the hoses to be sure they have not hardened; a prime cause of cracking. This hose has cracked down to the reinforcing cords and could split at any of the cracks.

Frayed hose end (due to weak clamp)

Weakened clamps frequently are the cause of hose and cooling system failure. The connection between the pipe and hose has deteriorated enough to allow coolant to escape when the engine is hot.

Debris in cooling system

Debris, rust and scale in the cooling system can cause the inside of a hose to weaken. This can usually be felt on the outside of the hose as soft or thinner areas.

observed. It is best to check the coolant level in the radiator when the engine is cold. On early models this is accomplished by carefully removing the radiator cap and checking that the coolant is within 2 in. of the bottom of the filler neck. On later models, the cooling system has, as one of its components, a coolant recovery tank. If the coolant level is at or near the "FULL COLD" line (engine cold) or the "FULL HOT" line (engine hot), the level is satisfactory. Always be certain that the filler caps on both the radiator and the recovery tank are closed tightly.

In the event that the coolant level must be checked when the engine is hot on engines without a coolant recovery tank, place a thick rag over the radiator cap and slowly turn the cap counterclockwise until it reaches the first detent. Allow all hot steam to escape. This will allow the pressure in the system to drop gradually, preventing an explosion of hot coolant. When the hissing noise stops, remove the cap the rest of the way.

If the coolant level is found to be low, add a 50/50 mixture of ethylene glycol-based antifreeze and clean water. On older models, coolant must be added through the radiator filler

Some radiator caps have pressure release levers

neck. On newer models with the recovery tank, coolant may be added either through the filler neck on the radiator or directly into the recovery tank.

CAUTION: *Never add coolant to a hot engine unless it is running. If it is not running you run the risk of cracking the engine block.*

If the coolant level is chronically low or rusty, refer to Chapter 11 for diagnosis of the problem.

The radiator hoses and clamps and the radiator cap should be checked at the same time as the coolant level. The radiator cap gasket should be checked for any obvious tears, cracks or swelling, or any signs of incorrect seating in the radiator filler neck.

Air Conditioning

Regular maintenance for the air conditioning system includes periodic checks of the drive belt tension. In addition, the system should be operated for at least five minutes every month. This ensures an adequate supply of lubricant to the bearings and also helps to prevent the seals and hoses from drying out. To do this comfortably in the winter months, turn the air conditioning on, the temperature control lever to the WARM or HI position and turn the blower fan to its highest setting. This will engage the compressor, circulating lubricating oils within the system, but prevent the discharge of cold air. The system should also be checked for proper refrigerant charge using the procedure given below.

SYSTEM CHECKS

CAUTION: *Do not attempt to charge or discharge the refrigerant system unless you are thoroughly familiar with its operation and the hazards involved. The compressed refrigerant used in the air conditioning system expands and evaporates (boils) into the atmosphere at a temperature of* $-21.7°F$

On models without a coolant recovery tank, the coolant level should be about 2 in. below the filler neck (engine cold)

If the engine is hot, cover the radiator cap with a rag

The coolant recovery tank is mounted on the right fender skirt

Air conditioning VIR assembly showing sight glass and connections

(−29.8°C) or less. This will freeze any surface that it comes in contact with, including your eyes. In addition, the refrigerant decomposes into a poisonous gas in the presence of flame.

1964–77 cars with factory installed air conditioners have a sight glass for checking the refrigerant charge. The sight glass is on top of the VIR (valves-in-receiver) which is located in the front of the engine compartment, usually on the left side of the radiator.

1978 and later models utilize a different system which does not include a sight glass.

NOTE: *If your car is equipped with an aftermarket air conditioner, the following system checks may not apply. Contact the manufacturer of the unit for instructions on system checks.*

1964–77

This test works best if the outside air temperature is warm (above 70°F).

1. Place the automatic transmission in Park or the manual in Neutral. Set the parking brake.

2. With the help of a friend, run the engine at a fast idle (about 1500 rpm).

3. Set the controls for maximum cold with the blower on high.

4. Look at the sight glass on top of the VIR. If a steady stream of bubbles is present in the sight glass, the system is low on charge. Very likely there is a leak in the system.

5. If no bubbles are present, the system is either fully charged or completely empty. Feel the high and low pressure lines at the compressor, if no appreciable temperature difference is felt, the system is empty or nearly so.

6. If one hose is warm (high pressure) and the other is cold (low pressure), the system may be OK. However, you are probably making these tests because there is something wrong with the air conditioner, so proceed to the next step.

7. Either disconnect the compressor clutch wire or have a friend in the car turn the fan control on and off to operate the compressor clutch. Watch the sight glass.

8. If bubbles appear when the clutch is disengaged and disappear when it is engaged, the system is properly charged.

9. If the refrigerant takes more than 45 seconds to bubble when the clutch is disengaged, the system is more than likely overcharged. This condition will usually result in poor cooling at low speeds.

NOTE: *If it is determined that the system has a leak, it should be repaired as soon as possible. Leaks may allow moisture to enter the system, causing an expensive rust problem.*

1978 and Later

The air conditioning system on these cars has no sight glass.

1. Run the engine until it reaches normal operating temperature.

2. Open the hood and all doors.

3. Turn the air conditioning on, move the temperature selector to the first detent to the right of COLD (outside air) and then turn the blower on HI.

4. Idle the engine at 1000 rpm.

5. Feel the temperature of the evaporator inlet and the accumulator outlet with the compressor clutch engaged.

6. Both lines should be cold. If the inlet pipe

is colder than the outlet pipe, the system is low on charge. Do not attempt to charge the system yourself.

Windshield Wipers

For maximum effectiveness and longest element life, the windshield and wiper blades should be kept clean. Dirt, tree sap, road tar and so on will cause streaking, smearing and blade deterioration if left on the glass. It is advisable to wash the windshield carefully with a commercial glass cleaner at least once a month. Wipe off the rubber blades with the wet rag afterwards. Do not attempt to move the wipers back and forth by hand; damage to the motor and drive mechanism will result.

If the blades are found to be cracked, broken or torn, they should be replaced immediately. Replacement intervals will vary with usage, although ozone deterioration usually limits blade life to about one year. If the wiper pattern is smeared or streaked, or if the blade chatters across the glass, the blades should be replaced. It is easiest and most sensible to replace them in pairs.

There are basically three different types of wiper blade refills, which differ in their method of replacement. One type has two release buttons, approximately one-third of the way up from the ends of the blade frame. Pushing the buttons down releases a lock and allows the rubber blade to be removed from the frame. The new blade slides back into the frame and locks in place.

The second type of refill has two metal tabs which are unlocked by squeezing them together. The rubber blade can then be withdrawn from the frame jaws. A new one is installed by inserting it into the front frame jaws and sliding it rearward to engage the remaining frame jaws. There are usually four jaws; be certain when installing that the refill is engaged in all of them. At the end of its travel, the tabs will lock into place on the front jaws of the wiper blade frame.

The third type is a refill made from polycarbonate. The refill has a simple locking device at one end which flexes downward out of the groove into which the jaws of the holder fit, allowing easy release. By sliding the new refill through all the jaws and pushing through the slight resistance when it reaches the end of its travel, the refill will lock into position.

Regardless of the type of refill used, make sure that all the frame jaws are engaged as the refill is pushed into place and locked. The metal blade holder and frame will scratch the glass if allowed to touch it.

Checking the evaporator inlet and the accumulator outlet line temperatures—1978 and later

TRICO

BLADE FRAME LEVER

RUBBER BLADE ELEMENT ASSY.

SQUEEZE SIDES OF RETAINER

LEVER JAWS

LATCH LOCK RELEASE

METAL BACKING IS WIDER

HOLD FRAME FROM TWISTING

METAL BACKING STRIP

RETAINING TABS

METAL BACKING STRIP

FRAME

INSERT SCREWDRIVER BEHIND TAB AND PUSH HANDLE DOWN.

ANCO

LATCH-PIN

YOKE JAWS

RUBBER BLADE ELEMENT ASSY.

YOKE JAWS

POLYCARBONATE

UNLOCKED

LOCKED

The three types of wiper blade retention

Fluid Level Checks

ENGINE OIL

Every time you stop for fuel, check the engine oil as follows:

1. Make sure the car is parked on level ground.

2. When checking the oil level it is best for the engine to be at normal operating temperature, although checking the oil immediately after stopping will lead to a false reading. Wait a few minutes after turning off the engine to allow the oil to drain back into the crankcase.

3. Open the hood and locate the dipstick which will be on either the right or left side depending upon your particular engine. Pull the dipstick from its tube, wipe it clean and then reinsert it.

4. Pull the dipstick out again and, holding it horizontally, read the oil level. The oil should be between the "FULL" and "ADD" marks on the dipstick. If the oil is below the "ADD" mark, add oil of the proper viscosity through the

The oil level is checked with the dipstick

The oil level should be between the 'ADD' and 'FULL' marks on the dipstick

Automatic transmission dipstick marks; the proper level is within the shaded area

capped opening in the top of the cylinder head cover. See the "Oil and Fuel Recommendations" chart in this chapter for the proper viscosity and rating of oil to use.

5. Replace the dipstick and check the oil level again after adding any oil. Be careful not to overfill the crankcase. Approximately one quart of oil will raise the level from the "ADD" mark to the "FULL" mark. Excess oil will generally be consumed at an accelerated rate.

TRANSMISSION

Manual

The oil in the manual transmission should be checked at least every 6,000 miles for 1964–74 models or every 7,500 miles for all 1975 and later models.

1. With the car parked on a level surface, remove the filler plug from the side of the transmission housing.

2. If the lubricant begins to trickle out of the hole, there is enough and you need not go any further. Otherwise, carefully insert your finger (watch out for sharp threads) and check to see if the oil is up to the edge of the hole.

3. If not, add oil through the hole until the level is at the edge of the hole. Most gear lubricants come in a plastic squeeze bottle with a nozzle; making additions simple. You can also use a common kitchen baster. Use only standard GL-5 hypoid-type gear oil—SAE 80W or SAE 80W/90.

4. Replace the filler plug, run the engine and check for leaks.

Automatic

Check the automatic transmission fluid level at least every 6,000 miles (7,500 miles for 1975 and later models). The dipstick can be found in the rear of the engine compartment. The fluid level should be checked only when the transmission is hot (normal operating temperature). The transmission is considered hot after about 20 miles of highway driving.

1. Park the car on a level surface with the engine idling. Shift the transmission into Neutral and set the parking brake.

2. Remove the dipstick, wipe it clean and then reinsert it firmly. Be sure that it has been pushed all the way in. Remove the dipstick again

Add automatic transmission fluid through the dipstick tube

and check the fluid level while holding it horizontally. With the engine running, the fluid level should be between the second notch and the "FULL HOT" line. If the fluid must be checked when it is cool, the level should be between the first and second notches.

3. If the fluid level is below the second notch (engine hot) or the first notch (engine cold), add DEXRON® (1964–75) or DEXRON® II (1976 and later) automatic transmission fluid through the dipstick tube. This is easily done with the aid of a funnel. Check the level often as you are filling the transmission. Be extremely careful not to overfill it. Overfilling will cause slippage, seal damage and overheating. Approximately one pint of ATF will raise the fluid level from one notch/line to the other.

NOTE: *Always use DEXRON® or DEXRON® II AFT. The use of AFT Type F or any other fluid will cause severe damage to the transmission.*

The fluid on the dipstick should always be a bright red color. If it is discolored (brown or black), or smells burnt, serious transmission troubles, probably due to overheating, should be suspected. The transmission should be inspected by a qualified technician to locate the cause of the burnt fluid.

BRAKE MASTER CYLINDER

The brake master cylinder is located under the hood, in the left rear section of the engine compartment. It is divided into two sections (reservoirs) and the fluid must be kept within ¼ in. of the top edge of both reservoirs. The level should be checked at least every 6,000 miles (7,500 miles for 1975 and later models).

Pry the retaining bail from the master cylinder reservoir cap to check the fluid level

The fluid level in the master cylinder reservoir should be within ¼ in. of the top edge

NOTE: *Any sudden decrease in the level of fluid indicates a possible leak in the system and should be checked out immediately.*

To check the fluid level, simply pry off the retaining bar and then lift off the top cover of the master cylinder. When making additions of brake fluid, use only fresh, uncontaminated brake fluid which meets or exceeds DOT 3 standards. Be careful not to spill any brake fluid on painted surfaces, as it eats paint. Do not allow the brake fluid container or the master cylinder reservoir to remain open any longer than necessary; brake fluid absorbs moisture from the air, reducing its effectiveness and causing corrosion in the lines.

NOTE: *The reservoir cover on some later models (1978 and later) may be without a retaining bail. If so, simply pry the cover off with your fingers.*

RADIATOR COOLANT

It's a good idea to check the coolant level every time that you stop for fuel. If the engine is hot, let it cool for a few minutes and then check the level following the procedure given earlier in this chapter.

Check the freezing protection rating at least once a year, preferably just before the winter

Coolant protection can be checked with a simple, float-type tester

The system should be pressure tested at least once a year

sets in. This can be done with an antifreeze tester (most service stations will have one on hand and will probably check it for you, if not, they are available at an auto parts store). Maintain a protection rating of at least −20°F (−29°C) to prevent engine damage as a result of freezing and to assure the proper engine operating temperature.

REAR AXLE

The oil in the differential should be checked at least every 6,000 miles (7,500 miles for 1975 and later models).

1. With the car on a level surface, remove the filler plug from the front side of the differential.

2. If the oil begins to trickle out of the hole,

FILLER PLUG

Remove the filler plug to check the lubricant level in the rear axle

there is enough. Otherwise, carefully insert your finger (watch out for sharp threads) into the hole and check that the oil is up to the bottom edge of the filler hole.

3. If not, add oil through the hole until the level is at the edge of the hole. Most gear oils come in a plastic squeeze bottle with a nozzle; making additions is simple. You can also use a common kitchen baster. Use only standard GL-5 hypoid-type gear oil—SAE 80W or SAE 80W/90.

NOTE: *On all models equipped with the positraction/limited slip rear axle, GM recommends that you use only the special lubricant which is available at your local Chevrolet parts department.*

POWER STEERING RESERVOIR

Power steering fluid level should be checked at least once every 6,000 miles (7,500 miles for 1975 and later models). To prevent possible overfilling, check the fluid level only when the fluid has warmed to operating temperatures and the wheels are turned straight ahead. If the level is low, fill the pump reservoir with DEXRON® Automatic Transmission Fluid on 1976 and earlier cars. 1977 and later cars require GM

"HOT" MARK

"COLD" MARK

COLD

"ADD"

Use the dipstick to check the power steering fluid

power steering fluid, until the fluid level measures "full" on the reservoir dipstick. Low fluid level usually produces a moaning sound as the wheels are turned (especially when standing still or parking) and increases steering wheel effort.

BATTERY

Check the battery fluid level (except in Maintenance Free batteries) at least once a month, more often in hot weather or during extended periods of travel. The electrolyte level should be up to the bottom of the split ring in each cell. All batteries are equipped with an "eye" in the cap of one cell. If the "eye" glows or has an amber color to it, this means that the level is low and only distilled water should be added. Do not add anything else to the battery. If the "eye" has a dark appearance the battery electrolyte level is high enough. It is also wise to check each cell individually.

At least once a year, check the specific gravity of the battery. It should be between 1.20–1.26. Clean and tighten the clamps and apply a thin coat of petroleum jelly to the terminals. This will help to retard corrosion. The terminals can be cleaned with a stiff wire brush or with an inexpensive terminal cleaner designed for this purpose.

If water is added during freezing weather, the car should be driven several miles to allow the electrolyte and water to mix. Otherwise the battery could freeze.

If the battery becomes corroded, a solution of baking soda and water will neutralize the corrosion. This should be washed off after making sure that the caps are securely in place. Rinse the solution off with cold water.

Some batteries were equipped with a felt terminal washer. This should be saturated with engine oil approximately every 6,000 miles. This will also help to retard corrosion.

If a "fast" charger is used while the battery is in the car, disconnect the battery before connecting the charger.

NOTE: *Keep flame or sparks away from the battery; it gives off explosive hydrogen gas.*

RING BOTTOM

Fill each battery cell to the bottom of the split ring with distilled water

The specific gravity of the battery can be checked with a simple float-type hydrometer

Battery State of Charge at Room Temperature

Specific Gravity Reading	Charged Condition
1.260–1.280	Fully Charged
1.230–1.250	¾ Charged
1.200–1.220	½ Charged
1.170–1.190	¼ Charged
1.140–1.160	Almost no Charge
1.110–1.130	No Charge

Testing the Maintenance-Free Battery

All later model cars are equipped with maintenance-free batteries, which do not require normal attention as far as fluid level checks are concerned. However, the terminals require periodic cleaning, which should be performed at least once a year.

The sealed-top battery cannot be checked for charge in the normal manner, since there is no provision for access to the electrolyte. To check the condition of the battery:

1. If the indicator eye on top of the battery is dark, the battery has enough fluid. If the eye is light, the electrolyte fluid is too low and the battery must be replaced.

2. If a green dot appears in the middle of the eye, the battery is sufficiently charged. Proceed to Step 4. If no green dot is visible, charge the battery as in Step 3.

3. Charge the battery at this rate:

Charging Rate Amps	Time
75	40 min
50	1 hr
25	2 hr
10	5 hr

BATTERY TOP	BATTERY TOP	BATTERY TOP
DARKENED INDICATOR (WITH GREEN DOT)	DARKENED INDICATOR (NO GREEN DOT)	LIGHT YELLOW OR BRIGHT INDICATOR
MAY BE JUMP STARTED	MAY BE JUMP STARTED	DO NOT JUMP START

Maintenance-free batteries contain their own built in hydrometer

CAUTION: *Do not charge the battery for more than 50 amp/hours. If the green dot appears, or if electrolyte squirts out of the vent hole, stop the charge and proceed to Step 4.*

It may be necessary to tip the battery from side to side to get the green dot to appear after charging.

4. Connect a battery load tester and a voltmeter across the battery terminals (the battery cables should be disconnected from the battery). Apply a 300 amp load to the battery for 15 seconds to remove the surface charge. Remove the load.

5. Wait 15 seconds to allow the battery to recover. Apply the appropriate test load, as specified in the following chart:

Battery	Test Load
Y85-4	130 amps
R85-5	170 amps
R87-5	210 amps
R89-5	230 amps

Apply the load for 15 seconds while reading the voltage. Disconnect the load.

6. Check the results against the following chart. If the battery voltage is at or above the

Temperature (°F)	Minimum Voltage
70 or above	9.6
60	9.5
50	9.4
40	9.3
30	9.1
20	8.9
10	8.7
0	8.5

specified voltage for the temperature listed, the battery is good. If the voltage falls below what's listed, the battery should be replaced.

Tires

Tires should be checked weekly for proper air pressure. A chart, located either in the glove compartment or on the driver's or passenger's door, gives the recommended inflation pressures. Maximum fuel economy and tire life will result if the pressure is maintained at the highest figure given on the chart. Pressures should be checked before driving since pressure can increase as much as six pounds per square inch (psi) due to heat buildup. It is a good idea to have your own accurate pressure gauge, because not all gauges on service station air pumps can be trusted. When checking pressures, do not neglect the spare tire. Note that some spare tires require pressures considerably higher than those used in the other tires.

While you are about the task of checking air pressure, inspect the tire treads for cuts, bruises and other damage. Check the air valves to be

A penny works as well as anything for checking tire tread depth; when you can see the top of Lincoln's head, it's time for a new tire

Tread wear indicators will appear when the tire is worn out

Tread depth can be checked with an inexpensive gauge

sure that they are tight. Replace any missing valve caps.

Check the tires for uneven wear that might indicate the need for front end alignment or tire rotation. Tires should be replaced when a tread wear indicator appears as a solid band across the tread.

When buying new tires, give some thought to the following points, especially if you are considering a switch to larger tires or a different profile series:

1. All four tires must be of the same construction type. This rule cannot be violated. Radial, bias, and bias-belted tires must not be mixed.

2. The wheels should be the correct width for the tire. Tire dealers have charts of tire and rim compatibility. A mismatch will cause sloppy handling and rapid tire wear. The tread width should match the rim width (inside bead to inside bead) within an inch. For radial tires, the rim should be 80% or less of the tire (not tread) width.

3. The height (mounted diameter) of the new tires can change speedometer accuracy, engine speed at a given road speed, fuel mileage, acceleration, and ground clearance. Tire manufacturers furnish full measurement specifications.

4. The spare tire should be usable, at least for short distance and low speed operation, with the new tires.

5. There shouldn't be any body interference when loaded, on bumps, or in turns.

TIRE ROTATION

Tire rotation is recommended every 6,000 miles or so, to obtain maximum tire wear. The pattern you use depends on whether or not your car has a usable spare. Radial tires should not be cross-switched (from one side of the car to the other); they last longer if their direction of rotation is not changed. Snow tires sometimes have directional arrows molded into the side of

Tire rotation diagrams; note that radials should not be cross-switched

the carcass; the arrow shows the direction of rotation. They will wear very rapidly if the rotation is reversed. Studded tires will lose their studs if their rotational direction is reversed.

NOTE: *Mark the wheel position or direction of rotation on radial tires or studded snow tires before removing them.*

STORAGE

Store the tires at the proper inflation pressure if they are mounted on wheels. Keep them in a cool dry place, laid on their sides. If the tires are stored in the garage or basement, do not let them stand on a concrete floor; set them on strips of wood.

Fuel Filter

Gasoline Engines

The carburetor inlet fuel filter should be replaced every 12,000 miles (15,000 miles for 1975 and later models) or more often if necessary. Two types of fuel filters are used in the carburetor body, a bronze type and a paper element type. Either one may be encountered at any given time. However, the replacement filter should be of the same type as the one removed. Inline fuel filters may be used on some engines and should be changed at the same time as the filter in the line between the pump and the carburetor. It may be made of either plastic or metal. To replace the filter:

1. Place some absorbent rags under the filter; remember, it will be full of gasoline when removed.

2. Use a pair of pliers to expand the clamp on one end of the filter, then slide the clamp down past the point to which the filter pipe extends in the rubber hose. Do the same with the other clamp.

3. Gently twist and pull the hoses free of the filter pipes. Remove and discard the old filter.

FUEL LINE

The fuel filter is located behind the large fuel line inlet nut on the carburetor

FUEL FILTER UNSCREWS

Remove the retaining nut and the filter will pop out under spring pressure

NEW
GASKET

Install the new filter and spring. Certain early models use a bronze filter element, but most are made of paper

INSTALL&REMOVE
JUMPER HERE

ENGINE
TEMPERATURE
SWITCH

HDCA solenoid connection, diesels

4. Install the new filter into the hoses, slide the clamps back into place, and check for leaks with the engine idling.

Diesel Engines

The diesel fuel filter is mounted on the rear of the inake manifold, and is larger than that on a gasoline engine because diesel fuel generally is "dirtier" (has more suspended particles) than gasoline.

The diesel fuel filter should be changed every 30,000 miles or two years.

To install a new filter:

1. With the engine cool, place absorbent rags underneath the fuel line fittings at the filter.

2. Disconnect the fuel lines from the filter.

3. Unbolt the filter from its bracket.

4. Install the new filter. Start the engine and check for leaks. Run the engine for about two minutes, then shut the engine off for the same amount of time to allow any trapped air in the injection system to bleed off.

The GM diesel cars also have a fuel filter inside the fuel tank which is maintenance-free.

NOTE: *If the filter element ever becomes clogged, the engine will stop. This stoppage is usually preceded by a hesitation or sluggish running. General Motors recommends*

that after changing the diesel fuel filter, the Housing Pressure Cold Advance be activated manually, if the engine temperature is above 125°F. Activating the H.P.C.A. will reduce engine cranking time.

To activate the H.P.C.A. solenoid, disconnect the two-lead connector at the engine temperature switch and bridge the connector with a jumper. After the engine is running, remove the jumper and reconnect the connector to the engine temperature switch. When the new filter element is installed, start the engine and check for leaks.

LUBRICATION

Oil and Fuel Recommendations

OIL

The SAE (Society of Automotive Engineers) grade number indicates the viscosity of the engine oil and thus its ability to lubricate at a given temperature. The lower the SAE grade number, the lighter the oil; the lower the viscosity,

18 N·m
(13 FT. LBS.)

FUEL LINE

TO FUEL SOLENOID FEED

FUEL LINE HEATER
(OPTIONAL)

CLIP

VIEW A

FUEL FILTER

CLIP
FUEL LINE

27 N·m
(20 FT. LBS.)
BOTH ENDS OF
FUEL LINE

Diesel fuel filter and lines

RECOMMENDED SAE VISCOSITY GRADES

30
20W-20, 20W-40, 20W-50
10W-30, 10W-40
10W
5W-30
5W-20

| °F | -20 | | 0 | | 20 | 40 | 60 | 80 | 100 |
| °C | -30 | -20 | -10 | 0 | 10 | 20 | 30 | 40 |

TEMPERATURE RANGE ANTICIPATED BEFORE NEXT OIL CHANGE

NOTICE: Do not use SAE 5W-20 oils for continuous high-speed driving.

Oil viscosity chart

the easier it is to crank the engine in cold weather.

Oil viscosities should be chosen from those oils recommended for the lowest anticipated temperatures during the oil change interval.

Multi-viscosity oils (10W-30, 20W-50 etc.) offer the important advantage of being adaptable to temperature extremes. They allow easy starting at low temperatures, yet they give good protection at high speeds and engine temperatures. This is a decided advantage in changeable climates or in long distance touring.

The API (American Petroleum Institute) designation indicates the classification of engine oil used under certain given operating conditions. Only oils designated for use "Service SE" should be used. Oils of the SE type perform a variety of functions inside the engine in addition to their basic function as a lubricant. Through a balanced system of metallic detergents and polymeric dispersants, the oil prevents the formation of high and low temperature deposits and also keeps sludge and particles of dirt in suspension. Acids, particularly sulfuric acid, as well as other byproducts of combustion, are neutralized. Both the SAE grade number and the API designation can be found on top of the oil can.

For recommended oil viscosities, refer to the chart.

NOTE: *As of late 1980, the API has come out with a new designation of motor oil, SF. Oils designated for use "Service SF" are equally acceptable in your car.*

CAUTION: *Non-detergent or straight mineral oils should not be used in your car.*

SYNTHETIC OIL

There are excellent synthetic and fuel-efficient oils available that, under the right circumstances, can help provide better fuel mileage and better engine protection. However, these advantages come at a price, which can be three or four times the price per quart of conventional motor oils.

Before pouring any synthetic oils into your car's engine, you should consider the condition of the engine and the type of driving you do. Also, check the car's warranty conditions regarding the use of synthetics.

Generally, it is best to avoid the use of synthetic oil in both brand new and older, high mileage engines. New engines require a proper break-in, and the synthetics are so "slippery" that they can prevent this; most manufacturers recommend that you wait at least 5,000 miles before switching to a synthetic oil. Conversely, older engines are looser and tend to "use" more oil; synthetics will slip past worn parts more readily than regular oil, and will be used up

faster. If your car already leaks and/or "uses" oil (due to worn parts and bad seals or gaskets), it will leak and use more with a slippery synthetic inside.

Consider your type of driving. If most of your accumulated mileage is on the highway at higher, steadier speeds, a synthetic oil will reduce friction and probably help deliver better fuel mileage. Under such ideal highway conditions, the oil change interval can be extended, as long as the oil filter will operate effectively for the extended life of the oil. If the filter can't do its job for this extended period, dirt and sludge will build up in your engine's crankcase, sump, oil pump and lines, no matter what type of oil is used. If using synthetic oil in this manner, you should continue to change the oil filter at the recommended intervals.

Cars used under harder, stop-and-go, short hop circumstances should always be serviced more frequently, and for these cars synthetic oil may not be a wise investment. Because of the necessary shorter change interval needed for this type of driving, you cannot take advantage of the long recommended change interval of most synthetic oils.

Finally, most synthetic oils are not compatible with conventional oils and cannot be added to them. This means you should always carry a couple of quarts of synthetic oil with you while on a long trip, as not all service stations carry this oil.

FUEL

Gasoline

All 1964–74 models are designed to run on either regular or premium grade fuel depending upon the particular engine's compression ratio. All engines having a compression ratio of 9.0:1 or less can run efficiently on regular gasoline, while any engines with a higher ratio must use premium fuel. All 1975 and later models have been designed to run on unleaded fuel. The use of a leaded fuel in a car requiring unleaded fuel will plug the catalytic converter and render it inoperative. It will also increase exhaust backpressure to the point where engine output will be severely reduced. In all cases, the minimum octane rating of the unleaded fuel being used must be at least 91 RON (87 CLC). All unleaded fuels sold in the U.S. ae required to meet this minimum rating.

The use of a fuel too low in octane (a measurement of anti-knock quality) will result in spark knock. Since many factors such as altitude, terrain, air temperature and humidity affect operating efficiency, knocking may result even though the recommended fuel is being used. If persistent knocking occurs, it may be necessary to switch to a higher grade of fuel. Continuous or heavy knocking may result in engine damage.

NOTE: *Your engine's fuel requirement can change with time, mainly due to carbon buildup, which will in turn change the compression ratio. If your engine pings, knocks, or diesels (runs with the ignition off) switch to a higher grade of fuel. Sometimes just changing brands will cure the problem. If it becomes necessary to retard the timing from the specifications, don't change it more than a few degrees. Retarded timing will reduce power output and fuel mileage, in addition to making the engine run hotter.*

Diesel Fuel

Fuel makers produce two grades of diesel fuel, No. 1 and No. 2, for use in automotive diesel engines. Generally speaking, No. 2 fuel is recommended over No. 1 for driving in temperatures above 20°F. In fact, in many areas, No. 2 diesel is the only fuel available. By comparison, No. 2 diesel fuel is less volatile than No. 1 fuel, and gives better fuel economy. No. 2 fuel is also a better injection pump lubricant.

Two important characteristics of diesel fuel are its cetane number and its viscosity.

The cetane number of a diesel fuel refers to the ease with which a diesel fuel ignites. High cetane numbers mean that the fuel will ignite with relative ease or that it ignites well at low temperatures. Naturally, the lower the cetane number, the higher the temperature must be to ignite the fuel. Most commercial fuels have cetane numbers that range from 35 to 65. No. 1 diesel fuel generally has a higher cetane rating than No. 2 fuel.

Viscosity is the ability of a liquid, in this case diesel fuel, to flow. Using straight No. 2 diesel fuel below 20°F can cause problems, because this fuel tends to become cloudy, meaning wax crystals begin forming in the fuel (20°F is often called the "cloud point" for Nol. 2 fuel). In extreme cold weather, No. 2 fuel can stop flowing altogether. In either case, fuel flow is restricted, which can result in a "no start" condition or poor engine performance. Fuel manufacturers often "winterize" No. 2 diesel fuel by using various fuel additives and blends (No. 1 diesel fuel, kerosene, etc.) to lower its winter-time viscosity. Generally speaking, though, No. 1 diesel fuel is more satisfactory in extremely cold weather.

NOTE: *No. 1 and No. 2 diesel fuels will mix and burn with no ill effects, although the engine manufacturer will undoubtedly recommend one or the other. Consult the owner's manual for information.*

Depending on local climate, most fuel manufacturers make winterized No. 2 fuel available seasonally.

Many automobile manufacturers (Oldsmobile, for example) publish pamphlets giving the locations of diesel fuel stations nationwide. Contact the local dealer for information.

NOTE: *Do not substitute home heating oil for automotive diesel fuel.*

While in some cases, home heating oil refinement levels equal those of diesel fuel, many times they are far below diesel engine requirements. The result of using "dirty" home heating oil will be a clogged fuel system, in which case the entire system may have to be dismantled and cleaned.

One more word on diesel fuels. Don't thin diesel fuel with gasoline in cold weather. The lighter gasoline, which is more explosive, will cause rough running at the very least, and may cause extensive damage if enough is used.

Fluid Changes

ENGINE OIL AND FILTER

The oil should be changed every four months or 6,000 miles on all 1964–74 models. On 1975–78 models, the interval is six months or 7,500 miles. 1979 and later models increased the time interval to 12 months while keeping the mileage (7,500) the same (Diesel interval is 5,000 miles). Make sure that you change the oil based on whichever interval comes first.

The oil drain plug is located on the bottom of the oil pan (bottom of the engine, underneath the car). The oil filter is located on the right side of the inline six cylinder engine and on the left side of all other engines.

The mileage figures given are the Chevrolet recommended intervals assuming normal driving and conditions. If your car is used under dusty, polluted or off-road conditions, change the oil and filter more often than specified. The same goes for cars driven in stop-and-go traffic or only for short distances at a time. Always drain the engine oil after the engine has been running long enough to bring it up to normal operating temperature. Hot oil will flow easier and more contaminants will be removed along with the oil than if it were drained cold. To change the oil and filter:

1. Run the engine until it reaches normal operating temperature.

2. Jack up the front of the car and support it on safety stands.

3. Slide a drain pan of at least 6 quarts capacity under the oil pan.

4. Loosen the drain plug. Turn the plug out by hand. By keeping an inward pressure on the plug as you unscrew it, oil won't escape

By keeping an inward pressure on the plug as you unscrew it, oil won't escape past the threads

Coat the new oil filter gasket with clean oil

past the threads and you can remove it without being burned by hot oil.

5. Allow the oil to drain completely and then install the drain plug. Don't overtighten the plug, or you'll be buying a new pan or a trick replacement plug for stripped threads.

6. Using a strap wrench, remove the oil filter. Keep in mind that it's holding about one quart of dirty, hot oil.

7. Empty the old filter into the drain pan and dispose of the filter.

8. Using a clean rag, wipe off the filter adapter on the engine block. Be sure that the rag doesn't leave any lint which could clog an oil passage.

9. Coat the rubber gasket on the filter with fresh oil. Spin it onto the engine *by hand;* when the gasket touches the adapter surface, give it another ½–¾ turn. No more, or you'll squash the gasket and it will leak.

10. Refill the engine with the correct amount of fresh oil. See the "Capacities" chart.

11. Check the oil level on the dipstick. It is normal for the level to be a bit above the full mark. Start the engine and allow it to idle for a few minutes.

CAUTION: *Do not run the engine above idle speed until it has built up oil pressure, indicated when the oil light goes out.*

12. Shut off the engine, allow the oil to drain for a minute, and check the oil level. Check around the filter and drain plug for any leaks, and correct as necessary.

Install the new oil filter by hand

Add oil through the capped opening in the cylinder head cover

MANUAL TRANSMISSION

There is no recommended interval for the manual transmission but it is always a good idea to change the fluid if you have purchased the car used or if it has been driven in water high enough to reach the axles.

1. The oil must be hot before it is drained. Drive the car until the engine reaches normal operating temperature.

2. Remove the filler plug to provide a vent.

3. Place a large container underneath the transmission and then remove the drain plug.

4. Allow the oil to drain completely. Clean off the drain plug and replace it; tighten it until it is just snug.

Remove the oil filter with a strap wrench

5. Fill the transmission with the proper lubricant as detailed earlier in this chapter. Refer to the "Capacities" chart for the correct amount of lubricant.

6. When the oil level is up to the edge of the filler hole, replace the filler plug. Drive the car for a few minutes, stop, and check for any leaks.

AUTOMATIC TRANSMISSION

The procedures for automatic transmission fluid drain and refill, filter change and band adjustment are all detailed in Chapter 6.

REAR AXLE

There is no recommended change interval for the rear axle but it is always a good idea to change the fluid if you have purchased the car used or if it has been driven in water high enough to reach the axle.

1. Park the car on a level surface and set the parking brake.
2. Remove the filler plug.
3. Place a large container underneath the rear axle.
4. Unscrew the retaining bolts and remove the rear cover. This will allow the lubricant to drain out into the container.
5. Install the rear cover using a new gasket and sealant. Tighten the retaining bolts in a crosswise pattern.
6. Refill with the proper grade and quantity of lubricant as detailed earlier in this chapter. Replace the filler plug, run the car and then check for any leaks.

RADIATOR COOLANT

The cooling system should be drained, thoroughly flushed and then refilled at least every 30,000 miles. This should be done with the engine cold.

1. Remove the radiator cap and the expansion tank cap (if so equipped).
2. With the caps removed, run the engine until the upper radiator hose is hot. This means that the thermostat is open and the coolant is flowing through the system.
3. Turn off the engine, place a large container underneath the radiator and open the drain valve at the bottom of the radiator.

NOTE: *Drainage may be speeded by removing the drain plugs on the sides of the cylinder block.*

4. Close the drain valve and add water until the system is filled.
5. Repeat Steps 3 and 4 several times until the drained liquid is nearly colorless.
6. Tighten the drain valve and then fill the radiator with a 50/50 mixture of ethylene glycol and water.

7. With the radiator cap still removed, run the engine until the upper radiator hose is hot. Add coolant if necessary, replace the caps and check for any leaks.

Chassis Greasing

Chassis greasing can be performed with a pressurized grease gun or it can be performed at home by using a hand-operated grease gun. Wipe the grease fittings clean before greasing in order to prevent the possibility of forcing any dirt into the component.

Body Lubrication

TRANSAXLE SHIFT LINKAGE

Lubricate the manual transaxle shift linkage contact points with the EP grease used for chassis greasing, which should meet G.M. specification 6031M. The automatic transaxle linkage should be lubricated with clean engine oil.

HOOD LATCH AND HINGES

Clean the latch surfaces and apply clean engine oil to the latch pilot bolts and the spring anchor. Use the engine oil to lubricate the hood hinges as well. Use a chassis grease to lubricate all the pivot points in the latch release mechanism.

DOOR HINGES

The gas tank filler door, car door, and rear hatch or trunk lid hinges should be wiped clean and lubricated with clean engine oil. Silicone spray also works well on these parts, but must be applied more often. Use engine oil to lubricate the trunk or hatch lock mechanism and the lock bolt and striker. The door lock cylinders can be lubricated easily with a shot of silicone spray or one of the many dry penetrating lubricants commercially available.

PARKING BRAKE LINKAGE

Use chassis grease on the parking brake cable where it contacts the guides, links, levers, and pulleys. The grease should be a water resistant one for durability under the car.

ACCELERATOR LINKAGE

Lubricate the carburetor stud, carburetor lever, and the accelerator pedal lever at the support inside the car with clean engine oil.

Wheel Bearings

Once every 12 months or 12,000 miles, clean and repack wheel bearings with a wheel bear-

Capacities

Year	Engine No. Cyl Displacement (cu in.)	Engine Crankcase Add 1 qt for New Filter	Transmission Pts to Refill After Draining — Manual 3-Speed	4-Speed	Automatic●	Drive Axle (pts)	Gasoline Tank (gals)	Cooling System (qts) With Heater	With A/C
1964	6-194 6-230	4	2	—	15.2①	3.5	20	11.5	12
	8-283	4	2	2.5	15.2①	3.5	20	17	18
	8-327	4	2	2.5	15.2①	3.5	20	16②	18②
1965	6-194 6-230	4	2	—	15.2①	4	20	12	12
	8-283	4	2	2.5	15.2①	4	20	17	18
	8-327	4	2	2.5	15.2①	4	20	16②	18②
1966	6-194	4	2	—	6③	3.5	20	12	12
	6-230	4	2	2.5	6③	3.5	20	12	12
	8-283	4	2	2.5	6③	3.5	20	16	18
	8-327	4	3④	3	6.5③	3.5⑤	20	15	17⑥
	8-396	4	3④	3	6.5③	3.5⑤	20	23	23
1967	6-230	4	3④	3④	6③	3.5	20	14	14
	6-250	4	3④	3④	6③	3.5	20	13	14
	8-283	4	3④	3④	6③	3.5	20	16	17
	8-327	4	3④	3④	6③	3.5	20	15	18
	8-396	4	3④	3④	6③	3.5	20	23	23
1968	6-230	4	3④	3④	6③	3.5	20	12	12
	6-250	4	3④	3④	6③	3.5	20	12	12
	8-307	4	3④	3④	6③	3.5	20	17	17
	8-327	4	2.5	3④	6③	3.5	20	16	16
	8-350	4	2.5	3④	6③	3.5	20	16	16
	8-396	4	2.5	3④	6⑦③	3.5	20	23	23
1969	6-230	4	3④	—	6⑧③	3.5⑤	20	13	13
	6-250	4	3④	—	6⑧③	3.5⑤	20	13	13
	8-307	4	3④	3④	6⑧③	3.5⑤	20	17	18
	8-350	4	3④	3④	6⑧③	3.5⑤	20	16	17
	8-396	4	3④	3④	8③	3.5⑤	20	23	24
1970	6-230	4	3	—	6⑧③	3.75⑨	20⑩	12	13
	6-250	4	3	—	6⑧③	3.75⑨	20⑩	12	13
	8-307	4	3	—	6⑧③	3.75⑨	20⑩	15	16
	8-350	4	3	3	6.5⑧⑪③	3.75⑨	20⑩	16	16
	8-400	4	3	3	8③	3.75⑨	20⑩	16	16
	8-396	4	3	3	8③	3.75⑨	20⑩	23	24
	8-402	4	3	3	8③	3.75⑨	20⑩	23	24
	8-454	4	3	3	8③	3.75⑨	20⑩	22	23
1971	6-250	4	3	—	6③	3.75	19⑩	12	—
	8-307	4	3	—	6⑧③	3.75	19⑩	15	16

Capacities (cont.)

Year	Engine No. Cyl Displacement (cu in.)	Engine Crankcase Add 1 qt for New Filter	Transmission Pts to Refill After Draining			Drive Axle (pts)	Gasoline Tank (gals)	Cooling System (qts)	
			Manual					With Heater	With A/C
			3-Speed	4-Speed	Automatic ●				
1971	8-350	4	3	3	6.5 ⑧ ③	3.75	19 ⑩	16	16
	8-402	4	3	3	8 ③	3.75	19 ⑩	23	23
	8-454	4	—	3	8 ③	3.75	19 ⑩	22	23
1972	6-250	4	3	—	6 ⑧ ③	4.25	19 ⑩	12	—
	8-307	4	3	—	6 ⑧ ③	4.25	19 ⑩	15	16
	8-350	4	3	3	6.5 ⑧ ③	4.25	19 ⑩	16	16
	8-402	4	—	3	8 ③	4.25 ⑫	19 ⑩	24	24
	8-454	4	—	3	8 ③	4.25 ⑫	19 ⑩	23	24
1973	6-250	4	3	—	6 ⑧ ③	4.25	22	12.5	—
	8-307	4	3	—	5 ③	4.25	22	16	17
	8-350	4	3	3	5 ③	4.25	22	16	17
	8-454	4	—	3	8 ③	4.25 ⑫	22	23	24
1974	6-250	4	3	—	8 ③	4.25	22	12.5	—
	8-350	4	3	3	8 ③	4.25	22	16	17
	8-400	4	—	—	8 ③	4.25 ⑫	22	16	17
	8-454	4	—	3	9 ③	4.9	22	23	24
1975	6-250	4	3	—	8 ③	4.25	22	14	16
	8-350	4	3	3	8 ③	4.25	22	17	18
	8-400	4	—	—	8 ③	4.25 ⑫	22	17 ⑬	18
	8-454	4	—	3	9 ③	4.9	22	23	23
1976–77	6-250	4	3	—	8 ③	4.25	22	15	17
	8-305	4	3	—	8 ③	4.25	22	17	18
	8-350	4	—	3	8 ③	4.25	22	17	18
	8-400	4	—	—	8 ③	4.25	22	17	18
1978	V6-200	4	3	—	6 ③	3.5	⑯	16.8	18.8
	V6-231	4 ⑮	3	3	6 ③	3.5	⑯	14.7	14.7
	6-250	4	3	—	6 ③	3.5	⑯	14.6	14.6
	8-305	4	—	3	6 ③	3.5 ⑭	⑯	19.2	19.2
	8-350	4	—	3	6 ③	3.5 ⑭	⑯	19.2	19.2
1979	V6-200	4	3	—	8 ③	3.25	18	18.5	18.5
	V6-231	4 ⑮	3	—	8 ③	3.25	18	15.5	15.5
	8-267	4	—	3.4	8 ③	3.25	18	19.2	19.2
	8-305	4	—	3.4	8 ③	3.5 ⑭	18	19.2	19.2
	8-350	4	—	3.4	8 ③	3.5 ⑭	18	19.2	19.2
1980–81	V6-229	4 ⑮	3	—	8 ③ ⑰	3.25	18	18.5	18.5
	V6-231	4 ⑮	3	—	8 ③ ⑰	3.25	18	15.5	15.5
	8-267	4	—	—	8 ③ ⑱	3.25	18	21	21
	8-305	4	—	3.4	8 ③ ⑱	3.5 ⑭	18	19	19

Capacities (cont.)

Year	Engine No. Cyl Displacement (cu in.)	Engine Crankcase Add 1 qt for New Filter	Transmission Pts to Refill After Draining			Drive Axle (pts)	Gasoline Tank (gals)	Cooling System (qts)	
			Manual		Automatic●			With Heater	With A/C
			3-Speed	4-Speed					
1982–84	V6-229	4 ⑮	—	—	7 ⑲	3.5 ⑭	⑬⑳	12 ㉑	13 ㉑
	V6-231	4 ⑮	—	—	7 ⑲	3.5 ⑭	⑬⑳	12 ㉑	13 ㉑
	8-267	4	—	—	7 ⑲	3.5 ⑭	⑬⑳	16.75	16.75 ㉒
	8-305	4	—	—	7 ⑲	3.5 ⑭	⑬⑳	15.5	15.5 ㉒
	8-350	4	—	—	7 ⑲	3.5 ⑭	⑬⑳	19.2	19.2
	V6-263 Diesel	6	—	—	7 ⑲	3.5 ⑭	⑳	13.4	14.4
	V8-350 Diesel	6	—	—	7 ⑲	3.5 ⑭	⑳	18.3	19.3

● Specifications do not include torque converter
① Figure given is for dry refill
② 18 qts—300 hp eng., 19 qts—350 hp eng.
③ Figure given is for drain and refill
④ 3.5 pts with heavy duty trans.
⑤ 4 pts with 8.875 in. ring gear
⑥ 16 qts— 350 hp eng.
⑦ 8 pts—THM 400
⑧ 5 pts—THM 350
⑨ 4.25 pts with 8.875 in. ring gear
⑩ 18 gals—station wagon
⑪ 8 pts—360 hp eng.
⑫ 4.9 pts with 8.875 in. ring gear
⑬ 18 gals—Monte Carlo
⑭ 4.25 pts—8.5 in. ring gear; 5.4 pts. with 8.75 in. ring gear
⑮ Figure is the same with or without a filter change
⑯ 18.1—Malibu, El Camino
    18.2—Malibu station wagon
    17.5—Monte Carlo
⑰ 7.0 pts—1981
⑱ 6.0 pts—1981
⑲ 6.0 pts—THM 350
⑳ 25 gals—Malibu
    22 gals—Malibu station wagon
    27 gals—Diesel coupe
    22 gals—Diesel station wagon
㉑ Chevrolet-built V6; 15 qts. (heater) and 16 qts. (A/C) with Buick V6
㉒ Monte Carlo 21 qts, 267 V8; 19 qts 305 V8

ing grease. Use only enough grease to completely coat the rollers. Remove any excess grease from the exposed surface of the hub and seal.

It is important that wheel bearings be properly adjusted after installation. Improperly adjusted wheel bearings can cause steering instability, front-end shimmy and wander, and increased tire wear. For complete lubrication and adjustment procedures, see the "Wheel Bearing" section in Chapter 9.

PUSHING AND TOWING

Push Starting

This is the last recommended method of starting a car and should be used only in an extreme case. Chances of body damage are high, so be sure that the pushcar's bumper does not override your bumper. If your Chevrolet has an automatic transmission it cannot be push started. In an emergency, you can start a manual transmission car by pushing. With the bumpers evenly matched, get in your car, switch on the ignition, and place the gearshift in Second or Third géar—do not engage the clutch. Start off slowly. When the speed of the car reaches about 15–20 mph, release the clutch.

Towing

The car can be towed safely (with the transmission in Neutral) from the front at speeds of 35 mph or less. The car must either be towed with the rear wheels off the ground or the driveshaft

Lubricate every 6000 miles
Replace every 24,000 miles
Check for grease leakage every 36,000 miles

GL—Multi-purpose Gear Lubricant*
WB—Wheel Bearing Lubricant
CL—Chassis Lubricant
AT —DEXRON® Automatic Transmission Fluid
BF —Hydraulic Brake Fluid
SG —Steering Gear Lubricant

* Refill Positraction Rear Axle with Special Positraction Rear Axle Lubricant Only.

1. Front suspension
2. Steering linkage
3. Steering gear
4. Air cleaner
5. Front wheel bearings
6. Transmission
7. Rear axle
8. Oil filter
9. Battery
10. Parking brake
11. Brake master cylinder

Chassis lubrication—1972–74

Recommended Lubricants

Item	Lubricant
Engine Oil (Gasoline)	API "SE", "SF/CC" or "SF/CD"
Engine Oil (Diesel)	API "SF/CC", "SF/CD" or "SE/CC"
Manual Transmission	SAE 80W GL-5 or SAE 80W/90 GL-5
Automatic Transmission	DEXRON® or DEXRON® II ATF
Rear Axle–Standard	SAE 80W GL-5 or SAE 80W/90 GL-5
Positraction/Limited Slip	GM Part #1052271 or 1052272
Power Steering Reservoir	DEXRON® ATF—1964–76 Power Steering Fluid—1977 and later
Brake Fluid	DOT 3
Antifreeze	Ethylene Glycol
Front Wheel Bearings	GM Wheel Bearing Grease
Clutch Linkage	Engine Oil
Hood and Door Hinges	Engine Oil
Chassis Lubrication	NLGI #1 or NLGI #2
Lock Cylinders	WD-40 or Powdered Graphite

JUMP STARTING A DEAD BATTERY

The chemical reaction in a battery produces explosive hydrogen gas. This is the safe way to jump start a dead battery, reducing the chances of an accidental spark that could cause an explosion.

Jump Starting Precautions

1. Be sure both batteries are of the same voltage.
2. Be sure both batteries are of the same polarity (have the same grounded terminal).
3. Be sure the vehicles are not touching.
4. Be sure the vent cap holes are not obstructed.
5. Do not smoke or allow sparks around the battery.
6. In cold weather, check for frozen electrolyte in the battery.
7. Do not allow electrolyte on your skin or clothing.
8. Be sure the electrolyte is not frozen.

Jump Starting Procedure

1. Determine voltages of the two batteries; they must be the same.
2. Bring the starting vehicle close (they must not touch) so that the batteries can be reached easily.
3. Turn off all accessories and both engines. Put both cars in Neutral or Park and set the handbrake.
4. Cover the cell caps with a rag—do not cover terminals.
5. If the terminals on the run-down battery are heavily corroded, clean them.
6. Identify the positive and negative posts on both batteries and connect the cables in the order shown.
7. Start the engine of the starting vehicle and run it at fast idle. Try to start the car with the dead battery. Crank it for no more than 10 seconds at a time and let it cool off for 20 seconds in between tries.
8. If it doesn't start in 3 tries, there is something else wrong.
9. Disconnect the cables in the reverse order.
10. Replace the cell covers and dispose of the rags.

Side terminal batteries occasionally pose a problem when connecting jumper cables. There frequently isn't enough room to clamp the cables without touching sheet metal. Side terminal adaptors are available to alleviate this problem and should be removed after use.

Make certain vehicles do not touch

This hook-up for negative ground cars only

○ Lubricate every 6000 miles

◉ Replace every 12,000 miles

◎ Replace every 24,000 miles

GL —Multi-purpose Gear Lubricant*
WB —Wheel Bearing Lubricant
CL —Chassis Lubricant

☐ Check for grease leakage every 36,000 miles

*Refill Positraction Rear Axle with Special Posi-
traction Rear Axle Lubricant Only.

AT —DEXRON® Automatic Transmission Fluid
BF —Hydraulic Brake Fluid
SG —Steering Gear Lubricant

1. Front suspension
2. Steering linkage
3. Steering gear
4. Air cleaner
5. Front wheel bearings
6. Transmission
7. Rear axle
8. Oil filter
9. Battery
10. Parking brake
11. Brake master cylinder

Chassis lubrication—1975 and later

disconnected if: towing speeds are to be over 35 mph, or towing distance is over 50 miles, or transmission or rear axle problems exist.

When towing the car on its front wheels, the steering wheel must be secured in a straight-ahead position and the steering column unlocked. Tire-to-ground clearance should not exceed 6 in. during towing.

JACKING

The standard jack utilizes slots in the bumper to raise the car. The jack supplied with the car should never be used for any service operation other than tire changing. Never get under the car while it is supported by only a jack. Always block the wheels when changing tires.

The service operations in this book often require that one end or the other, or both, of the car be raised and safely supported. The ideal

method, of course, would be a hydraulic hoist. Since this is beyond both the resource and requirement of the do-it-yourselfer, a small hydraulic, screw or scissors jack will suffice for the procedures in this guide. Two sturdy jackstands should be acquired if you intend to work under the car at any time. An alternate method of raising the car would be drive-on ramps. These are available commercially or can be fabricated from heavy boards or steel. Be sure to block the wheels when using ramps. Never use concrete blocks to support the car. They may break if the load is not evenly distributed.

Regardless of the method of jacking or hoisting the car, there are only certain areas of the undercarriage and suspension you can safely use to support it. See the illustration below, and make sure that only the shaded areas are used. In addition, be especially careful on vehicles built after 1974 that you do not damage the catalytic converter. Remember that various cross

Gasoline-Engined Cars
1970–76 Maintenance Intervals

Interval At Which Services Are To Be Performed	Service
LUBRICATION AND GENERAL MAINTENANCE	
Every 6 months or 7,500 miles	*CHASSIS-Lubricate ●*FLUID LEVELS-Check *ENGINE OIL-Change
At first oil change-then every 2nd	*ENGINE OIL FILTER-Replace (V-6 Replace each oil change)
See Explanation of Maintenance Schedule	TIRES-Rotate DIFFERENTIAL
Every 12 months	AIR CONDITIONING SYSTEM-Check charge & hose condition. TEMPMATIC AIR FILTER-Replace every other year.
Every 12 months or 15,000 miles	*COOLING SYSTEM-See Explanation of Maintenance Schedule
Every 30,000 miles	WHEEL BEARINGS-Clean and repack *AUTOMATIC TRANS.-Change fluid and service filter MANUAL STEERING GEAR-Check seals CLUTCH CROSS SHAFT-Lubricate
SAFETY MAINTENANCE	
Every 6 months or 7,500 miles	TIRES AND WHEELS-Check condition *EXHAUST SYSTEM-Check condition of system *DRIVE BELTS-Ck. cond. & adjustment. Replace every 30,000 miles FRONT AND REAR SUSPENSION & STEERING SYSTEM-Ck. cond. BRAKES AND POWER STEERING-Check all lines and hoses
Every 12 months or 15,000 miles	DRUM BRAKES AND PARKING BRAKE-Check condition of linings; adjust parking brake THROTTLE LINKAGE-Check operation and condition UNDERBODY-Flush and check condition BUMPERS-Check condition
EMISSION CONTROL MAINTENANCE	
At 1st 6 months or 7,500 miles-then at 18 month/22,500 mile Intervals Thereafter	THERMOSTATICALLY CONTROLLED AIR CLEANER-Check operation CARBURETOR CHOKE-Check operation ENGINE IDLE SPEED ADJUSTMENT EFE VALVE-Check operation CARBURETOR-Torque attaching bolts or nuts to manifold
Every 12 months or 15,000 miles	CARBURETOR FUEL INLET FILTER-Replace VACUUM ADVANCE SYSTEM AND HOSES-Check oper. PCV SYSTEMS-See Explanation of Maintenance Schedule
Every 18 months or 22,500 miles	IDLE STOP SOLENOID OR DASHPOT-Check operation SPARK PLUG AND IGNITION COIL WIRES-Inspect and clean
Every 22,500 miles	SPARK PLUGS-Replace ENGINE TIMING ADJUSTMENT & DISTRIBUTOR CHECK
Every 24 months or 30,000 miles	ECS SYSTEM-See Explanation of Maintenance Schedule FUEL CAP, TANK AND LINES-Check condition
Every 30,000 miles	AIR CLEANER ELEMENT-Replace

*Also Required Emission Control Maintenance
●Also a Safety Service

Gasoline-Engined Cars
1977 and Later Maintenance Intervals

When to Perform Services (Months or Miles, Whichever Occurs First)	Services
LUBRICATION AND GENERAL MAINTENANCE	
Every 12 months or 7,500 miles (12 000 km)	●CHASSIS-Lubricate ●FLUID LEVELS-Check CLUTCH PEDAL FREE TRAVEL-Check/Adjust
See Explanation of Maintenance Schedule	*ENGINE OIL-Change *ENGINE OIL FILTER-Replace TIRES-Rotation (Radial Tires) REAR AXLE OR FINAL DRIVE-Check lube
Every 12 months or 15,000 miles (24 000 km)	*COOLING SYSTEM-See Explanation of Maintenance Schedule
Every 30,000 miles (48 000 km)	WHEEL BEARINGS-Repack CLUTCH CROSS SHAFT-Lubricate
See Explanation	AUTOMATIC TRANSMISSION-Change fluid and service filter
SAFETY MAINTENANCE	
Every 12 months or 7,500 miles (12 000 km)	TIRES, WHEELS AND DISC BRAKES-Check condition *EXHAUST SYSTEM-Check condition SUSPENSION & STEERING SYSTEM-Check condition BRAKES AND POWER STEERING-Check all lines and hoses
Every 12 months or 15,000 miles (24 000 km)	*DRIVE BELTS-Check condition and adjustment (1) DRUM BRAKES AND PARKING BRAKE-Check condition of linings; adjust parking brake THROTTLE LINKAGE-Check operation and condition BUMPERS-Check condition *FUEL CAP, TANK AND LINES-Check
EMISSION CONTROL MAINTENANCE	
At first 6 MOnths or 7,500 Miles (12 000 km)–Then at 24-Month/ 30,000 Mile (48 000 km) Intervals as Indicated in Log, Except Choke Which Requires Service at 45,000 Miles (72 000 km)	CARBURETOR CHOKE & HOSES-Check (2) ENGINE IDLE SPEED-Check adjustment (2) EFE SYSTEM-Check operation (If so equipped) CARBURETOR-Torque attaching bolts or nuts to manifold (2)
Every 30,000 miles (48 000 km)	THERMOSTATICALLY CONTROLLED AIR CLEANER-Check operation VACUUM ADVANCE SYSTEM AND HOSES-Check (3) SPARK PLUG WIRES-Check IDLE STOP SOLENOID AND/OR DASH POT OR ISC-Check operation SPARK PLUGS-Replace (2) ENGINE TIMING ADJUSTMENT AND DISTRIBUTOR-Check AIR CLEANER AND PCV FILTER ELEMENT-Replace (2) PCV VALVE-Replace EGR VALVE-Service

●Also a Safety Service
*Also an Emission Control Service
(1) In California, a separately driven air pump belt check is recommended but not required at 15,000 miles (24 000 km) and 45,000 miles (72 000 km).
(2) Only these emission control maintenance items are considered to be required maintenance as defined by the California Air Resources Board (ARB) regulation and are, according to such regulation, the minimum maintenance an owner in California must perform to fulfill the minimum requirements of the emission warranty. All other emission maintenance items are recommended maintenance as defined by such regulation. General Motors urges that all emission control maintenance items be performed.
(3) Not applicable on vehicles equipped with electronic spark timing (EST).

Diesel Maintenance Intervals

When to Perform Services (Months or Miles, Whichever Occurs First)	Services
LUBRICATION AND GENERAL MAINTENANCE	
Every 5,000 Miles (8 000 km)	*ENGINE OIL-Change *OIL FILTER-Change ●CHASSIS-Lubricate ●FLUID LEVELS-Check
See Explanation	TIRES-Rotation REAR AXLE OR FINAL DRIVE-Check lube
Every 12 months or 15,000 miles (24 000 km) Every 30,000 miles (48 000 km)	*COOLING SYSTEM-Check *CRANKCASE VENTILATION-Service WHEEL BEARINGS-Repack
See Explanation	AUTOMATIC TRANSMISSION-Change fluid and filter
SAFETY MAINTENANCE	
At first 5,000 miles (8 000 km) Then at 15,000/30,000/45,000 miles	*EXHAUST SYSTEM-Check condition
Every 12 months or 10,000 miles (16 000 km)	TIRES, WHEEL AND DISC BRAKE-Check SUSPENSION AND STEERING-Check BRAKES AND POWER STEERING-Check
Every 5,000 Miles (8 000 km)	*DRIVE BELTS-Check condition and adjustment
Every 12 months or 15,000 miles (24 000 km)	DRUM BRAKES AND PARKING BRAKE-Check THROTTLE LINKAGE-Check operation BUMPERS-Check condition
EMISSION CONTROL MAINTENANCE	
At first 5,000 miles (8 000 km) Then at 15,000/30,000/45,000 miles	EXHAUST PRESSURE REGULATOR VALVE
At first 5,000 miles (8 000 km) Then at 30,000 miles (48 000 km)	ENGINE IDLE SPEED-Adjust
Every 30,000 miles (48 000 km)	AIR CLEANER-Replace FUEL FILTER-Replace

●Also a Safety Service
*Also on Emission Control Service

braces and supports on a lift can sometimes contact lowhanging parts of the car.

HOW TO BUY A USED CAR

Many people believe that a two or three year old used car is a better buy than a new car. This may be true; the new car suffers the heaviest depreciation in the first two years, but is not old enough to present a lot of costly repair problems. Whatever the age of the used car you might want to buy, this section and a little patience will help you select one that should be safe and dependable.

TIPS

1. First decide what model you want, and how much you want to spend.
2. Check the used car lots and your local newspaper ads. Privately owned cars are usually less expensive, however you will not get a warranty that, in most cases, comes with a used car purchased from a lot.
3. Never shop at night. The glare of the lights make it easy to miss faults on the body caused by accident or rust repair.
4. Try to get the name and phone number of the previous owner. Contact him/her and ask about the car. If the owner of the lot refuses this information, look for a car somewhere else.

A private seller can tell you about the car and maintenance. Remember, however, there's no law requiring honesty from private citizens selling used cars. There is a law that forbids the tampering with or turning back the odometer mileage. This includes both the private citizen and the lot owner. The law also requires that the seller or anyone transferring ownership of the car must provide the buyer with a signed

DRIVE ON HOIST

 FLOOR JACK OR JOIST LIFT: DO NOT LIFT AT REAR AXLE WHEN EQUIPPED WITH REAR STABILIZER.

Vehicle hoisting and jacking points

statement indicating the mileage on the odometer at the time of transfer.

5. Write down the year, model and serial number before you buy any used car. Then dial 1-800-424-9393, the toll free number of the National Highway Traffic Safety Administration, and ask if the car has ever been included on any manufacturer's recall list. If so, make sure the needed repairs were made.

6. Use the "Used Car Checklist" in this section and check all the items on the used car you are considering. Some items are more important than others. You know how much money you can afford for repairs, and, depending on the price of the car, may consider doing any needed work yourself. Beware, however, of trouble in areas that will affect operation, safety or emission. Problems in the "Used Car Checklist" break down as follows:

1-8: Two or more problems in these areas indicate a lack of maintenance. You should beware.

9-13: Indicates a lack of proper care, however, these can usually be corrected with a tune-up or relatively simple parts replacement.

14-17: Problems in the engine or transmission can be very expensive. Walk away from any car with problems in both of these areas.

7. If you are satisfied with the apparent con-

dition of the car, take it to an independent diagnostic center or mechanic for a complete check. If you have a state inspection program, have it inspected immediately before purchase, or specify on the bill of sale that the sale is conditional on passing state inspection.

8. Road test the car—refer to the "Road Test Checklist" in this section. If your original evaluation and the road test agree—the rest is up to you.

USED CAR CHECKLIST

NOTE: *The numbers on the illustrations refer to the numbers on this checklist.*

1. *Mileage:* Average mileage is about 12,000 miles per year. More than average mileage may indicate hard usage. 1975 and later catalytic converter equipped models may need converter service at 50,000 miles.

2. *Paint:* Check around the tailpipe, molding and windows for overspray indicating that the car has been repainted.

3. *Rust:* Check fenders, doors, rocker panels, window moldings, wheelwells, floorboards, under floormats, and in the trunk for signs of rust. Any rust at all will be a problem. There is no way to check the spread of rust, except to replace the part or panel.

4. *Body appearance:* Check the moldings,

bumpers, grille, vinyl roof, glass, doors, trunk lid and body panels for general overall condition. Check for misalignment, loose holdown clips, ripples, scratches in glass, rips or patches in the top. Mismatched paint, welding in the trunk, severe misalignment of body panels or ripples may indicate crash work.

5. *Leaks:* Get down and look under the car. There are no normal "leaks", other than water from the air conditioning condenser.

6. *Tires:* Check the tire air pressure. A common trick is to pump the tire pressure up to make the car roll easier. Check the tread wear, open the trunk and check the spare too. Uneven wear is a clue that the front end needs alignment. See the troubleshooting chapter for clues to the causes of tire wear.

7. *Shock absorbers:* Check the shock absorbers by forcing downward sharply on each corner of the car. Good shocks will not allow the car to bounce more than twice after you let go.

8. *Interior:* Check the entire interior. You're looking for an interior condition that agrees with the overall condition of the car. Reasonable wear is expected, but be suspicious of new seatcovers on sagging seats, new pedal pads, and worn armrests. These indicate an attempt to cover up hard use. Pull back the carpets and look for evidence of water leaks or flooding. Look for missing hardware, door handles, control knobs etc. Check lights and signal operations. Make sure all accessories (air conditioner, heater, radio etc.) work. Check windshield wiper operation.

9. *Belts and Hoses:* Open the hood and check all belts and hoses for wear, cracks or weak spots.

10. *Battery:* Low electrolyte level, corroded terminals and/or cracked case indicate a lack of maintenance.

11. *Radiator:* Look for corrosion or rust in the coolant indicating a lack of maintenance.

12. *Air filter:* A dirty air filter usually means a lack of maintenance.

13. *Ignition Wires:* Check the ignition wires for cracks, burned spots, or wear. Worn wires will have to be replaced.

14. *Oil level:* If the oil level is low, chances are the engine uses oil or leaks. Beware of water in the oil (cracked block), excessively thick oil (used to quiet a noisy engine), or thin, dirty oil with a distinct gasoline smell (internal engine problems).

15. *Automatic Transmission:* Pull the transmission dipstick out when the engine is running. The level should read "Full", and the fluid should be clear or bright red. Dark brown or black fluid that has distinct burnt odor, signals a transmission in need of repair or overhaul.

16. *Exhaust:* Check the color of the exhaust smoke. Blue smoke indicates, among other problems, worn rings; black smoke can indicate burnt valves or carburetor problems. Check the exhaust system for leaks; it can be expensive to replace.

17. *Spark Plugs:* Remove one of the spark plugs (the most accessible will do). An engine in good condition will show plugs with a light tan or gray deposit on the firing tip. See the

You should check these points when buying a used car. The "Used Car Checklist" gives an explanation of the numbered items

color Tune-Up tips section for spark plug conditions.

ROAD TEST CHECK LIST

1. *Engine Performance:* The car should be peppy whether cold or warm, with adequate power and good pickup. It should respond smoothly through the gears.

2. *Brakes:* They should provide quick, firm stops with no noise, pulling or brake fade.

3. *Steering:* Sure control with no binding, harshness, or looseness and no shimmy in the wheel should be expected. Noise or vibration from the steering wheel when turning the car means trouble.

4. *Clutch (Manual Transmission):* Clutch action should give quick, smooth response with easy shifting. The clutch pedal should have about 1–1½ inches of free-play before it disengages the clutch. Start the engine, set the parking brake, put the transmission in first gear and slowly release the clutch pedal. The engine

should begin to stall when the pedal is one-half to three-quarters of the way up.

5. *Automatic Transmission:* The transmission should shift rapidly and smoothly, with no noise, hesitation, or slipping.

6. *Differential:* No noise or thumps should be present. Differentials have no "normal" leaks.

7. *Driveshaft, Universal Joints:* Vibration and noise could mean driveshaft problems. Clicking at low speed or coast conditions means worn U-joints.

8. *Suspension:* Try hitting bumps at different speeds. A car that bounces has weak shock absorbers. Clunks mean worn bushings, or ball joints.

9. *Frame:* Wet the tires and drive in a straight line. Tracks should show two straight lines, not four. Four tire tracks indicate a frame bent by collision damage. If the tires can't be wet for this purpose, have a friend drive along behind you and see if the car appears to be traveling in a straight line.

2

TUNE-UP PROCEDURES

In order to extract the full measure of performance and economy from your engine it is essential that it is properly tuned at regular intervals. A regular tune-up will keep your car's engine running smoothly and will prevent the annoying breakdowns and poor performance associated with an untuned engine.

NOTE: *All models used a conventional breaker point ignition system through 1974. In 1975, Chevrolet switched to a fully electronic ignition system known as HEI.*

A complete tune-up should be performed at least every 15,000 miles (12,000 miles for early models) or twelve months, whichever comes first.

NOTE: *1981 and later models have increased their interval to 30,000 miles.*

This interval should be halved if the car is operated under severe conditions such as trailer towing, prolonged idling, start-and-stop driving, or if starting or running problems are noticed. It is assumed that the routine maintenance described in Chapter 1 has been kept up, as this will have a decided effect on the results of a tune-up. All of the applicable steps of a tune-up should be followed in order, as the result is a cumulative one.

If the specifications on the underhood tune-up sticker in the engine compartment of your car disagree with the "Tune-Up Specifications" chart in this chapter, the figures on the sticker must be used. The sticker often reflects changes made during the production run.

Spark Plugs

A typical spark plug consists of a metal shell surrounding a ceramic insulator. A metal electrode extends downward through the center of the insulator and protrudes a short distance.

Located at the end of the plug and attached to the side of the outer metal shell is the side electrode. This side electrode bends in at 90° so its tip is even with, and parallel to, the tip

THE SHORTER THE PATH, THE FASTER THE HEAT IS DISSIPATED AND THE COOLER THE PLUG

THE LONGER THE PATH, THE SLOWER THE HEAT IS DISSIPATED AND THE HOTTER THE PLUG

HEAVY LOADS, HIGH SPEEDS

SHORT TRIP STOP-AND-GO

SHORT Insulator Tip
Fast Heat Transfer
LOWER Heat Range
COLD PLUG

LONG Insulator Tip
Slow Heat Transfer
HIGHER Heat Range
HOT PLUG

Spark plug heat range

PORCELAIN INSULATOR

INSULATOR CRACKS OFTEN OCCUR HERE

SHELL

ADJUST FOR PROPER GAP

SIDE ELECTRODE (BEND TO ADJUST GAP)

CENTER ELECTRODE; FILE FLAT WHEN ADJUSTING GAP; DO NOT BEND!

Cross section of a spark plug

of the center electrode. This distance between these two electrodes (measured in thousandths of an inch) is called spark plug gap. The spark plug in no way produces a spark but merely provides a gap across which the current can arc. The coil produces 20,000–25,000 V (the HEI transistorized ignition produces considerably more voltage than the standard type, approximately 50,000 volts), which travels to the distributor where it is distributed through the spark plug wires to the plugs. The current passes along the center electrode and jumps the gap to the side electrode and, in so doing, ignites the air/fuel mixture in the combustion chamber. All plugs used since 1969 have a resistor built into the center electrode to reduce interference to any nearby radio and television receivers. The resistor also cuts down on erosion of plug electrodes caused by excessively long sparking. Resistor spark plug wiring is original equipment on all models.

Spark plug life and efficiency depend upon the condition of the engine and the temperatures to which the plug is exposed. Combustion chamber temperatures are affected by many factors such as compression ratio of the engine, fuel/air mixtures, exhaust emission equipment, and the type of driving you do. Spark plugs are designed and classified by number according to the heat range at which they will operate most efficiently. The amount of heat that the plug absorbs is determined by the length of the lower insulator. The longer the insulator (it extends farther into the engine), the hotter the plug will operate; the shorter it is, the cooler it will operate. A plug that has a short path for heat transfer and remains too cool will quickly accumulate deposits of oil and carbon since it is not hot enough to burn them off. This leads to plug fouling and consequently to misfiring. A plug that has a long path for heat transfer will have no deposits but, due to the excessive heat, the electrodes will burn away quickly and, in some instances, pre-ignition may result. Pre-ignition takes place when plug tips get so hot that they glow sufficiently to ignite the fuel/air mixture before the spark does. This early ignition will usually cause a pinging (sounding much like castanets) during low speeds and heavy loads. In severe cases, the heat may become enough to start the fuel/air mixture burning throughout the combustion chamber rather than just to the front of the plug as in normal operation. At this time, the piston is rising in the cylinder making its compression stroke. The burning mass is compressed and an explosion results producing tremendous pressure. Something has to give, and it does—pistons are often damaged. Obviously, this detonation (explosion) is a destructive condition that can be avoided by installing a spark plug designed and specified for your particular engine.

A set of spark plugs usually requires replacement after 10,000 to 12,000 miles depending on the type of driving (this interval has been increased to 22,500 miles for all 1975–79 models and 30,000 miles for all 1980–and later models). The electrode on a new spark plug has a sharp edge but, with use, this edge becomes rounded by erosion causing the plug gap to increase. In normal operation, plug gap increases about 0.001 in. in every 1,000–2,000 miles. As the gap increases, the plug's voltage requirement also increases. It requires a greater voltage to jump the wider gap and about two to three times as much voltage to fire a plug at high speeds and acceleration than at idle.

The higher voltage produced by the HEI ignition coil is one of the primary reasons for the prolonged replacement interval for spark plugs in 1975 and later cars. A consistently hotter spark prevents the fouling of plugs for much longer than could normally be expected; this spark is also able to jump across a larger gap more efficiently than a spark from a conventional system. However, even plugs used with the HEI system wear after time in the engine.

Worn plugs become obvious during acceleration. Voltage requirement is greatest during acceleration and a plug with an enlarged gap may require more voltage than the coil is able to produce. As a result, the engine misses and sputters until acceleration is reduced. Reducing acceleration reduces the plug's voltage requirement and the engine runs smoother. Slow, city driving is hard on plugs. The long periods of idle experienced in traffic creates an overly rich gas mixture. The engine isn't running fast enough to completely burn the gas and, consequently, the plugs are fouled with gas deposits and engine idle becomes rough. In many cases, driving under the right conditions can effectively clean these fouled plugs.

NOTE: *There are several reasons why a spark plug will foul and you can usually learn which is at fault by just looking at the plug. A few of the most common reasons for plug fouling, and a description of the fouled plug's appearance, can be found in the color insert in this book.*

Accelerate your car to the speed where the engine begins to miss and then slow down to the point where the engine smooths out. Run at this speed for a few minutes and then accelerate again to the point of engine miss. With each repetition this engine miss should occur at increasingly higher speeds and then disappear altogether. Do not attempt to shortcut this procedure by hard acceleration. This approach will compound problems by fusing deposits into

Gasoline Engine Tune-Up Specifications

When analyzing the compression test results, look for uniformity among cylinders rather than specific pressures.

| Year | Engine No. Cyl Displacement (cu in.) | hp | Spark Plugs | | Distributor | | Ignition Timing ▲(deg)■● | | ●Valves■ Intake Opens (deg) | Fuel Pump Pressure (psi) | ●Idle Speed▲* | |
			Type	Gap (in.)	Point Dwell (deg)	Point Gap (in.)	Man Trans	Auto Trans			Man Trans	Auto Trans
1964	6-194	120	46N	0.035	31–34	0.019	8B	8B	62	4½–6	500②	500②
	6-230	155	46N	0.035	31–34	0.019	4B	4B	62	4½–6	500②	500②
	8-283	195, 220	45	0.035	28–32	0.019	4B	4B	32½	5¼–6½	500②	500②
	8-327	250, 300	44	0.035	28–32	0.019	8B	8B	32½	5¼–6½	500②	500②
1965	6-194	120	46N	0.035	31–34	0.019	8B	8B	62	4½–6	500②	500②
	6-230	140	46N	0.035	31–34	0.019	4B	4B	62	4½–6	500②	500②
	8-283	195, 280	45	0.035	28–32	0.019	4B	4B	32½	5¼–6½	500②	500②
	8-327	250, 300	44	0.035	28–32	0.019	8B	8B	32½	5¼–6½	500②	500②
	8-327	350	44	0.035	28–32	0.019	10B	—	54	5–6½	750②	750②
1966	6-194	120	46N	0.035	31–45	0.019	8B	8B	62	4½–6	500②	500②
	6-194①	120	46N	0.035	31–34	0.019	3B	8B	62	4½–6	700②	600②
	6-230	140	46N	0.035	31–34	0.019	4B	4B	62	4½–6	500②	500②
	6-230①	140	46N	0.035	28–32	0.019	4B	4B	62	4½–6	700②	600②
	8-283	195	45	0.035	28–32	0.019	4B	4B	32½	5¼–6½	500②	500②
	8-283①	220	45	0.035	28–32	0.019	4B	4B	32½	5¼–6½	700②	600②
	8-327	275	44	0.035	28–32	0.019	8B	8B	32½	5¼–6½	500②	500②
	8-327①	275	44	0.035	28–32	0.019	8B	2A	32½	5–6½	700②	600②
	8-327	350	44	0.035	28–32	0.019	10B	—	54	5–6½	750②	—
	8-396	325	43N	0.035	28–32	0.019	4B	4B	40	5–6½	500②	500②

Year	Engine											
	8-396	360	43N	0.035	28-32	0.019	4B	4B	56	5-6½	550②	550②
	8-396	375	R-43N	0.035	28-32	0.019	4B	—	44	5-8½	750	—
1967	6-230	140	46N	0.035	31-34	0.019	4B	4B	62	3½-4½	500②	500②
	6-230①	140	46N	0.035	31-34	0.019	4B	4B	62	3½-4½	700	500
	6-250	155	46N	0.035	31-34	0.019	4B	4B	62	3½-4½	500②	500②
	6-250①	155	46N	0.035	31-34	0.019	4B	4B	62	3½-4½	700	500
	8-283	195	45	0.035	28-32	0.019	4B	4B	38	5-6½	500②	500②
	8-283①	195	45	0.035	28-32	0.019	TDC	4B	38	5-6½	700	600
	8-327	275	44	0.035	28-32	0.019	8B	8B	38	5¼-6½	500②	500②
	8-327①	275	44	0.035	28-32	0.019	6B	6B	38	5¼-6½	700	600
	8-327	325	44	0.035	28-32	0.019	10B	—	54	5-6½	700②	—
	8-327①	325	44	0.035	28-32	0.019	10B	—	54	5-6½	750②	—
	8-396	325	43N	0.035	28-32	0.019	4B	4B	40	5-6½	500②	500②
	8-396①	325	43N	0.035	28-32	0.019	4B	4B	40	5-6½	700	500②
	396	350	43N	0.035	28-32	0.019	4B	4B	56	7¼-8½	550②	550②
	396①	350	43N	0.035	28-32	0.019	4B	4B	56	7¼-8½	700②	500②
	8-396	375	R-43N	0.035	28-32	0.019	4B	—	44	5-8½	750	—
1968	6-230	140	46N	0.035	31-34	0.019	TDC	4B	16	3½-4½	700	500②/400
	6-250	155	46N	0.035	31-34	0.019	TDC	4B	16	3½-4½	700	500②/400
	8-307	200	45S	0.035	28-32	0.019	2B	2B	28	5-6½	700	600
	8-327	275	44	0.035	28-32	0.019	TDC	4B	28	5-6½	700	600
	8-327	325	44	0.035	28-32	0.019	4B	—	40	5-6½	750②	—
	8-396	325	43N	0.035	28-32	0.019	4B	4B	28	5-6½	700②	600②
	8-396	350	43N	0.035	28-32	0.019	TDC	4B	40	7¼-8½	700	600
	8-396	375	R-43N	0.035	28-32	0.019	4B	—	44	5-8½	750	—
1969	6-230	140	R-46N	0.035	31-34	0.019	TDC	4B	16	3-4½	700	550/400

Gasoline Engine Tune-Up Specifications (cont.)

When analyzing the compression test results, look for uniformity among cylinders rather than specific pressures.

Year	Engine No. Cyl Displacement (cu in.)	hp	Spark Plugs Type	Gap (in.)	Distributor Point Dwell (deg)	Point Gap (in.)	Ignition Timing ▲ (deg) ■● Man Trans	Auto Trans	Valves ■ Intake Opens (deg)	Fuel Pump Pressure (psi)	●Idle Speed ▲* Man Trans	Auto Trans
1969	6-250	155	R-46N	0.035	31–34	0.019	TDC	4B	16	3–4½	700	550/400 ②
	8-307	200	R-45S	0.035	28–32	0.019	2B	2B	28	5–6½	700	600
	8-350	250	R-44	0.035	28–32	0.019	TDC	4B	28	5–6½	700	600
	8-350	300	R-44	0.035	28–32	0.019	TDC	4B	28	5–6½	700	600
	8-396	325	R-44N	0.035	28–32	0.019	4B	4B	28	5–8½	800	600
	8-396	350	R-43N	0.035	28–32	0.019	TDC	4B	56	5–8½	800	600
	8-396	375	R-43N	0.035	28–32	0.019	4B	4B	44	5–8½	750	750/400
1970	6-250	155	R-46T	0.035	31–34	0.019	TDC	4B	16	3–4½	750	600/400
	8-307	200	R-43	0.035	28–32	0.019	2B	8B	28	5–6½	700	600/450
	8-350	250	R-44	0.035	28–32	0.019	TDC	4B	28	5–6½	750	600/450
	8-350	300	R-44	0.035	28–32	0.019	TDC	4B	28	5–6½	700	600
	8-396	350	R-44T	0.035	28–32	0.019	TDC	4B	56	5–8½	700	600
	8-396	375	R-43T	0.035	28–32	0.019	4B	4B	NA	5–8½	750	700
	8-400	265	R-44	0.035	28–32	0.019	4B	8B	28	5–8½	700	600/450
	8-402	330	R-44T	0.035	28–32	0.019	4B	4B	28	5–8½	700	600
	8-454	360	R-43T	0.035	28–32	0.019	6B	6B	56	5–8½	700	600
	8-454	390	R-43T	0.035	28–32	0.019	6B	6B	NA	5–8½	700	600
	8-454	450	R-43T	0.035	28–32	0.019	4B	4B	NA	5–8½	700	700

Year	Engine											
1971	6-250	145	R-46TS	0.035	31–34	0.019	4B	4B	16	3½–4½	550	500
	8-307	200	R-45TS	0.035	29–31	0.019	4B	8B	28	5–6½	600	550
	8-350	245	R-45TS	0.035	29–31	0.019	2B	6B	28	7–8½	600	550
	8-350	270	R-44TS	0.035	29–31	0.019	4B	8B	28	7–8½	600	550
	8-400	255	R-44TS	0.035	29–31	0.019	4B	8B	28	7–8½	600	550
	8-402	300	R-44TS	0.035	29–31	0.019	8B	8B	28	7–8½	600	600
	8-454	365	R-42TS	0.035	29–31	0.019	8B	8B	56	7–8½	600	600
	8-454	425	R-42TS	0.035	29–31	0.019	8B	12B	44	7–8½	700	700
1972	6-250	110	R-46TS	0.035	31–34	0.019	4B	4B	16	3½–4½	700	600
	8-307	130	R-44T	0.035	29–31	0.019	4B	8B	28	5–6½	900	600
	8-350	165	R-44T	0.035	29–31	0.019	6B	6B	28	7–8½	900	600
	8-350	175	R-44T	0.035	29–31	0.019	4B	8B	28	7–8½	800	600
	8-402	240	R-44T	0.035	29–31	0.019	8B	8B	30	7–8½	750	600
	8-454	270	R-44T	0.035	29–31	0.019	8B	8B	56	7–8½	750	600
1973	6-250	100	R-46T	0.035	31–34	0.019	6B	6B	16	3½–4½	700/450	600/450
	8-307	115	R-44T	0.035	29–31	0.019	4B	8B	28	5–6½	900/450	600/450
	8-350	145	R-44T	0.035	29–31	0.019	8B	8B	28	7–8½	900/450	600/450
	8-350	175	R-44T	0.035	29–31	0.019	8B	12B	28	7–8½	900/450	600/450
	8-454	245	R-44T	0.035	29–31	0.019	10B	10B	55	7–8½	900/450	600/450
1974	6-250	100	R-46T	0.035	31–34	0.019	6B	6B	16	4–5	800/450	600/450
	8-350	145	R-44T	0.035	29–31	0.019	4B	8B	28	7½–9	900/450	600/450
	8-350	160	R-44T	0.035	29–31	0.019	4B	8B	44	7½–9	900/450	600/450

Gasoline Engine Tune-Up Specifications (cont.)

When analyzing the compression test results, look for uniformity among cylinders rather than specific pressures.

Year	Engine No. Cyl Displacement (cu in.)	hp	Spark Plugs Type	Gap (in.)	Distributor Point Dwell (deg)	Point Gap (in.)	Ignition Timing ▲(deg)■● Man Trans	Auto Trans	●Valves■ Intake Opens (deg)	Fuel Pump Pressure (psi)	●Idle Speed▲* Man Trans	Auto Trans
1974	8-400	150	R-44T	0.035	29–31	0.019	—	8B	28	7½–9	—	600/450
	8-400	180	R-44T	0.035	29–31	0.019	—	8B	44	7½–9	—	600/450
	8-454	235	R-44T	0.035	29–31	0.019	10B	10B	55	7½–9	800/450	600/450
1975	6-250	105	R-46TX	0.060	Electronic		10B	10B	16	4–5	850/425	550/425 (600/425)
	8-350	145	R-44TX	0.060	Electronic		6B	6B	28	7½–9	800	600
	8-350	155	R-44TX	0.060	Electronic		—	6B	28	7½–9	—	600
	8-400	175	R-44TX	0.060	Electronic		—	8B	28	7½–9	—	600
	8-454	215	R-44TX	0.060	Electronic		—	16B	55	7½–9	—	600/500
1976	6-250	105	R-46TS	0.035	Electronic		6B	6B	16	3½–4½	850	550 (600)
	8-305	140	R-45TS	0.045	Electronic		—	8B (TDC)	28	7–8½	—	600
	8-350	145	R-45TS	0.045	Electronic		—	6B	28	7–8½	—	600
	8-350	165	R-45TS	0.045	Electronic		—	8B (6B)	28	7–8½	—	600
	8-400	175	R-45TS	0.045	Electronic		—	8B	28	7–8½	—	600
1977	6-250	110	R-46TS	0.035	Electronic		6B @ 850	8B @ 600	16	4–5	750	550

8-305	145	R-45TS	0.045	Electronic	—	8B @ 500	28	7½-9	—	500
8-350	170	R-45TS	0.045	Electronic	—	8B @ 500	28	7½-9	—	500
1978										
6-200	95	R-45TS	0.045	Electronic	8B	8B	28	7.5-9	700	600
6-231	105	R46TSX	0.060	Electronic	15B	15B	17	6-7	600	500
8-305	145	R-45TS	0.045	Electronic	4B	④	28	7.5-9	600	500
8-350	170	R-45TS	0.045	Electronic	—	8B	2B	7.5-9	—	500
1979										
6-200	all	R-45TS	0.045	Electronic	8B	14B	34	4.5-6.0	700	600
6-231	all	R-46TSX	0.060	Electronic	15B	15B	16	4.2-5.7	600	500
8-267	all	R-45TS	0.045	Electronic	4B	10B	2B	7.5-9.0	600	500
8-305	all	R-43TS	0.045	Electronic	4B	4B	28	7.5-9.0	600	500
8-350	all	R-43TS	0.045	Electronic	—	8B	2B	7.5-9.0	—	500
1980										
6-229	115	R-T5TS ⑤	0.045	Electronic	8B	12B	42	4.5-6.0	700	600
6-231	110	R-45TSX	0.060	Electronic	—	15B	16	4.25-5.75	—	560 (600)
6-231 Turbo	170	R-45TSX	0.060	Electronic	—	15B	16	4.25-5.75	—	550 (600)
8-267	120	R-45TS	0.045	Electronic	—	4B	28	7.5-9.0	—	500
8-305	155	R-45TS	0.045	Electronic	4B	4B	28	7.5-9.0	700	500 (550)
1981										
6-229	110	R-45TS	0.045	Electronic	6B	6B	42	4.5-6.0	⑥	⑥
6-231	110	R-45TS8	0.080	Electronic	—	15B	16	4.25-5.75	—	⑥
6-231 Turbo	170	R-45TS	0.040	Electronic	—	15B	16	4.25-5.75	—	⑥
8-267	115	R-45TS	0.045	Electronic	—	6B	28	7.5-9.0	—	500
8-305	150	R-45TS	0.045	Electronic	6B	6B	28	7.5-9.0	700	500
1982-84										
6-229	110	R-45TS	0.045	Electronic	—	6B ⑥	42	4.5-6.0	—	⑥
6-231	110	R-45TS	0.045	Electronic	—	15B ⑥	16	4.5-6.0	—	⑥

Gasoline Engine Tune-Up Specifications (cont.)

When analyzing the compression test results, look for uniformity among cylinders rather than specific pressures.

| Year | Engine No. Cyl Displacement (cu in.) | hp | Spark Plugs | | Distributor | | Ignition Timing ▲(deg)■● | | Valves■ Intake Opens (deg) | Fuel Pump Pressure (psi) | Idle Speed ▲* | |
			Type	Gap (in.)	Point Dwell (deg)	Point Gap (in.)	Man Trans	Auto Trans			Man Trans	Auto Trans
1982–84	8-267	115	R-45TS	0.045	Electronic		—	6B ⑥	44	7.5–9.0	—	⑥
	8-305	145⑦	R-45TS	0.045	Electronic		—	6B ⑥	44	7.5–9.0	—	⑥

NOTE: The underhood specification sticker often reflects tune-up specification changes made in production. Sticker figures must be used if they disagree with those in this chart.

▲ See text for procedure
● Figures in parentheses indicate California
■ All figures Before Top Dead Center
* When two idle speed figures are separated by a slash, the lower figure is with the idle speed solenoid disconnected
NA Not Available
① Equipped with the Air Injection Reactor system
② A/C on
③ Lower figure is with idle solenoid disconnected
④ 49 states—4B
   Calif.—6B
   High alt.—8B
⑤ With A/T—R-45TS
⑥ See underhood specifications sticker
⑦ 150 hp, 1983 and later

a hard permanent glaze. Dirty, fouled plugs may be cleaned by sandblasting. Many shops have a spark plug sandblaster. After sandblasting, the electrode should be filed to a sharp, square shape and then gapped to specifications. Gapping a plug too close will produce a rough idle while gapping it too wide will increase its voltage requirement and cause missing at high speeds and during acceleration.

The type of driving you do may require a change in spark plug heat range. If the majority of your driving is done in the city and rarely at high speeds, plug fouling may necessitate changing to a plug with a heat range one number higher than that specified by the car manufacturer. For example, a 1970 Chevelle with a 350 cu in. (300 hp) engine requires an R44 plug. Frequent city driving may foul these plugs making engine operation rough. An R45 is the next hottest plug in the AC heat range (the higher the AC number, the hotter the plug) and its insulator is longer than the R44 so that it can absorb and retain more heat than the shorter R44. This hotter R45 burns off deposits even at low city speeds but would be too hot for prolonged turnpike driving. Using this plug at high speeds would create dangerous preignition. On the other hand, if the aforementioned Chevelle were used almost exclusively for long distance high speed driving, the specified R44 might be too hot resulting in rapid electrode wear and dangerous preignition. In this case, it might be wise to change to a colder R43. If the car is used for abnormal driving (as in the examples above), or the engine has been modified for higher performance, then a change to a plug of a different heat range may be necessary. For a modified car it is always wise to go to a colder plug as a protection against preignition. It will require more frequent plug cleaning, but destructive detonation during acceleration will be avoided.

REMOVAL

When you're removing spark plugs, you should work on one at a time. Don't start by removing the plug wires all at once because unless you number them, they're going to get mixed up. On some models though, it will be more convenient for you to remove all the wires before you start to work on the plugs. If this is necessary, take a minute before you begin and number the wires with tape before you take them off. The time you spend here will pay off later on.

1. Twist the spark plug boot and remove the boot from the plug. You may also use a plug wire removal tool designed especially for this purpose. *Do not pull on the wire itself.* When

Twist and pull on the rubber boot to remove the spark plug wires; never pull on the wire itself

the wire has been removed, take a wire brush and clean the area around the plug. Make sure that all the grime is removed so that none will enter the cylinder after the plug has been removed.

2. Remove the plug using the proper size socket, extensions, and universals as necessary. For all engines through 1969, and all V8s through 1971, use a 13/16 in. spark plug socket. Six-cylinder engines from 1970 and V8s from 1972 are equipped with tapered seat plugs which require a 5/8 in. socket.

3. If removing the plug is difficult, drip some penetrating oil on the plug threads, allow it to work, then remove the plug. Also, be sure that the socket is straight on the plug, especially on those hard to reach plugs.

INSPECTION

Check the plugs for deposits and wear. If they are not going to be replaced, clean the plugs thoroughly. Remember that any kind of deposit will decrease the efficiency of the plug. Plugs can be cleaned on a spark plug cleaning machine, which can sometimes be found in service stations, or you can do an acceptable job of cleaning with a stiff brush. If the plugs are cleaned, the electrodes must be filed flat. Use an ignition points file, not an emory board or the like, which will leave deposits. The electrodes must be filed perfectly flat with sharp edges; rounded edges reduce the spark plug voltage by as much as 50%.

Check spark plug gap before installation. The ground electrode (the L-shaped one connected

Plugs that are in good condition can be filed and re-used

Always use a wire gauge to check the electrode gap

Adjust the electrode gap by bending the side electrode

to the body of the plug) must be parallel to the center electrode and the specified size wire gauge (see "Tune-Up Specifications") should pass

through the gap with a slight drag. Always check the gap on new plugs, too; they are not always set correctly at the factory. Do not use a flat feeler gauge when measuring the gap, because the reading will be inaccurate. Wire gapping tools usually have a bending tool attached. Use that to adjust the side electrode until the proper distance is obtained. *Absolutely never bend the center electrode.* Also, be careful not to bend the side electrode too far or too often; it may weaken and break off within the engine, requiring removal of the cylinder head to retrieve it.

INSTALLATION

1. Lubricate the threads of the spark plugs with a drop of oil. Install the plugs and tighten them hand-tight. Take care not to cross-thread them.
2. Tighten the spark plugs with the socket. Do not apply the same amount of force you would use for a bolt; just snug them in. If a torque wrench is available, tighten to 11–15 ft. lbs.
3. Install the wires on their respective plugs. Make sure the wires are firmly connected. You will be able to feel them click into place.

CHECKING AND REPLACING SPARK PLUG WIRES

Every 15,000 miles, inspect the spark plug wires for burns, cuts, or breaks in the insulation. Check the boots and the nipples on the distributor cap. Replace any damaged wiring.

Every 45,000 miles or so, the resistance of the wires should be checked with an ohmmeter. Wires with excessive resistance will cause misfiring, and may make the engine difficult to start in damp weather. Generally, the useful life of the cables is 45,000–60,000 miles.

To check resistance, remove the distributor cap, leaving the wires in place. Connect one lead of an ohmmeter to an electrode within the cap; connect the other lead to the corresponding spark plug terminal (remove it from the spark plug for this test). Replace any wire which shows a resistance over 30,000 ohms. A chart in Chapter 11 gives resistance values as function of length. Generally speaking, however, resistance should not be over 25,000 ohms, and 30,000 ohms must be considered the outer limit of acceptability.

It should be remembered that resistance is also a function of length; the longer the wire, the greater the resistance. Thus, if the wires on your car are longer than the factory originals, resistance will be higher, quite possibly outside these limits.

When installing new wires, replace them one at a time to avoid mixups. Start by replacing the longest one first. Install the boot firmly over the spark plug. Route the wire over the same path as the original. Insert the nipple firmly onto the tower on the distributor cap, then install the cap cover and latches to secure the wires.

Breaker Points and Condenser

The points function as a circuit breaker for the primary circuit of the ignition system. The ignition coil must boost the 12 volts of electrical pressure supplied by the battery to as much as 25,000 volts in order to fire the plugs. To do this, the coil depends on the points and the condenser to make a clean break in the primary circuit.

The coil has both primary and secondary circuits. When the ignition is turned on, the battery supplies voltage through the coil and onto the points. The points are connected to ground, completing the primary circuit. As the current passes through the coil, a magnetic field is created in the iron center core of the coil. When the cam in the distributor turns, the points open, breaking the primary circuit. The magnetic field in the primary circuit of the coil then collapses and cuts through the secondary circuit windings around the iron core. Because of the physical principle called "electromagnetic induction," the battery voltage is increased to a level sufficient to fire the spark plugs.

When the points open, the electrical charge in the primary circuit tries to jump the gap created between the two open contacts of the points. If this electrical charge were not transferred elsewhere, the metal contacts of the points would start to change rapidly.

The function of the condenser is to absorb excessive voltage from the points when they open and thus prevent the points from becoming pitted or burned.

If you have ever wondered why it is necessary to tune-up your engine occasionally, consider the fact that the ignition system must complete the above cycle each time a spark plug fires. On a four-cylinder, four-cycle engine, two of the four plugs must fire once for every engine revolution. If the idle speed of your engine is 800 revolutions per minute (800 rpm), the breaker points open and close two times for each revolution. For every minute your engine idles, your points open and close 1,600 times ($2 \times 800 = 1,600$). And that is just at idle. What about at 60 mph?

There are two ways to check breaker point gap: with a feeler gauge or with a dwell meter.

Either way you set the points, you are adjusting the amount of time (in degrees of distributor rotation) that the points will remain open. If you adjust the points with a feeler gauge, you are setting the maximum amount the points will open when the rubbing block on the points is on a high point of the distributor cam. When you adjust the points with a dwell meter, you are measuring the number of degrees (of distributor cam rotation) that the points will remain closed before they start to open as a high point of the distributor cam approaches the rubbing block of the points.

If you still do not understand how the points function, take a friend, go outside, and remove the distributor cap from your engine. Have your friend operate the starter (make sure that the transmission is not in gear) as you look at the exposed parts of the distributor.

There are two rules that should always be followed when adjusting or replacing points. *The points and condenser are a matched set; never replace one without replacing the other. If you change the point gap or dwell of the engine, you also change the ignition timing. Therefore, if you adjust the points, you must also adjust the timing.*

REMOVAL AND INSTALLATION
Through 1974

The usual procedure is to replace the condenser each time the point set is replaced. Although this is not always necessary, it is easy to do at this time and the cost is negligible. Every time you adjust or replace the breaker points, the ignition timing must be checked and, if necessary, adjusted. No special equipment other than a feeler gauge is required for point replacement or adjustment, but a dwell meter is strongly advised. A magnetic screwdriver is handy to prevent the small points and condenser screws from falling down into the distributor.

Point sets using the push-in type wiring terminal should be used on those distributors equipped with an R.F.I. (Radio Frequency Interference) shield (1970–74). Points using a lockscrew-type terminal may short out due to contact between the shield and the screw.

1. Push down on the spring-loaded V8 distributor cap retaining screws and give them a half-turn to release. Unscrew the captive six-cylinder cap retaining screws. Remove the cap. You might have to unclip or detach some or all of the plug wires to remove the cap. If so, number the wires and the cap from removal.

2. Clean the cap inside and out with a clean rag. Check for cracks and carbon paths. A car-

The six cylinder distributor cap is retained by two captive screws

The eight cylinder distributor cap has spring latches

bon path shows up as a dark line, usually from one of the cap sockets or inside terminals to a ground. Check the condition of the carbon button inside the center of the cap and the inside terminals. Replace the cap as necessary. Carbon paths cannot usually be successfully scraped off. It is better to replace the cap.

3. Pull the six-cylinder rotor up and off the shaft. Remove the two screws and lift the round V8 rotor off. There is less danger of losing the screws if you just back them out all the way and lift them off with the rotor. Clean off the metal outer tip if it is burned or corroded. Don't file it. Replace the rotor as necessary or if one came with your tune-up kit.

4. Remove the radio frequency interference shield if your distributor has one. Watch out for those little screws! The factory says that the points don't need to be replaced if they are only slightly rough or pitted. However, sad experience shows that it is more economical and reliable in the long run to replace the point set while the distributor is open, than to have to do this at a later (and possibly more inconvenient) time.

5. Pull of the two wire terminals from the point assembly. One wire comes from the condenser and the other comes from within the distributor. The terminals are usually held in place by spring tension only. There might be a

clamp screw securing the terminals on some older versions. There is also available a one-piece point/condenser assembly for V8s. The radio frequency interference shield isn't needed with this set. Loosen the point set hold-down screw(s). Be very careful not to drop any of these little screws inside the distributor. If this happens, the distributor will probably have to be removed to get at the screw. If the hold-down screw is lost elsewhere, it must be replaced with one that is no longer than the original to avoid interference with the distributor workings. Remove the point set, even if it is to be reused.

6. If the points are to be reused, clean them with a few strokes of a special point file. This is done with the points removed to prevent tiny metal filings from getting into the distributor. Don't use sandpaper or emery cloth; they will cause rapid point burning.

7. Loosen the condenser hold-down screw and slide the condenser out of the clamp. This will save you a struggle with the clamp, condenser, and the tiny screw when you install the new one. If you have the type of clamp that is permanently fastened to the condenser, remove the screw and the condenser. Don't lose the screw.

8. Attend to the distributor cam lubricator. If you have the round kind, turn it around on its shaft at the first tune-up and replace it at

Pull the six cylinder rotor straight up to remove it

The eight cylinder rotor is held on by two screws

the second. If you have the long kind, switch ends at the first tune-up and replace it at the second.

NOTE: *Don't oil or grease the lubricator. The foam is impregnated with a special lubricant.*

If you didn't get any lubricator at all, or if it looks like someone took it off, don't worry. You don't really need it. Just rub a matchhead size dab of grease on the cam lobes.

9. Install the new condenser. If you left the clamp in place, just slide the new condenser into the clamp.

10. Replace the point set and tighten the screws on a V8. Leave the screw slightly loose on a six. Replace the two wire terminals, making sure that the wires don't interfere with anything. Some V8 distributors have a ground wire that must go under one of the screws.

11. Check that the contacts meet squarely. If they don't, bend the tab supporting the fixed contact.

NOTE: *If you are installing preset points on a V8, go ahead to Step 16. If they are preset, it will say so on the package. It would be a good idea to make a quick check on point gap, anyway. Sometimes those preset points aren't.*

12. Turn the engine until a high point on the cam that opens the points contacts the rub-

The points are retained by screws; use a magnetic screwdriver to avoid losing them

The condenser is held in place by a screw and a clamp

Install the point set on the breaker plate and then attach the wires

LATERAL MISALIGNMENT   PROPER LATERAL ALIGNMENT

CORRECT LATERAL MISALIGNMENT BY BENDING FIXED CONTACT SUPPORT NEVER BEND BREAKER LEVER

Check the points for proper alignment after installation

bing block on the point arm. You can turn the engine by hand if you can get a wrench on the crankshaft pulley nut, or you can grasp the fan belt and turn the engine with the spark plugs removed.

CAUTION: *If you try turning the engine by hand, be very careful not to get your fingers pinched in the pulleys.*

On a stick-shift you can push it forward in High gear. Another alternative is to bump the starter switch or use a remote starter switch.

13. On a six, there is a screwdriver slot near the contacts. Insert a screwdriver and lever the points open or closed until they appear to be at about the gap specified in the "Tune-Up Specifications." On a V8, simply insert a 1/8 in. allen wrench into the adjustment screw and turn. The wrench sometimes comes with a tune-up kit.

14. Insert the correct size feeler gauge and adjust the gap until you can push the gauge in and out between the contacts with a slight drag, but without disturbing the point arm. This operation takes a bit of experience to obtain the correct feel. Check by trying the gauges 0.001–0.002 larger and smaller than the setting size. The larger one should disturb the point arm, while the smaller one should not drag at all. Tighten the six-cylinder point set hold-down screw. Recheck the gap, because it often changes when the screw is tightened.

Use a screwdriver to lever the points closer together or farther apart on the six cylinder models

You will need an Allen wrench to adjust the point gap on the V8 engine

The arrow indicates the feeler gauge used to check the point gap

15. After all the point adjustments are complete, pull a white index card through (between) the contacts to remove any traces of oil. Oil will cause rapid contact burning.

NOTE: *You can adjust six-cylinder dwell at this point, if you wish. Refer to Step 18.*

16. Replace the radio frequency interfer-

ence shield, if any. You don't need it if you are installing the one-piece point/condenser set. Push the rotor firmly down into place. It will only go on one way. Tighten the V8 rotor screws. If the rotor is not installed properly, it will probably break when the starter is operated.

17. Replace the distributor cap.

18. If a dwell meter is available, check the dwell. The dwell meter hookup is shown in the "Troubleshooting" chapter.

NOTE: *This hookup may not apply to electronic, capacitive discharge, or other special ignition systems. Some dwell meters won't work at all with such systems.*

1975 and Later

These engines use the breakerless HEI (High Energy Ignition) system. Since there is no mechanical contact, there is no wear or need for periodic service. There is an item in the distributor that resembles a condenser; it is a radio interference suppression capacitor which requires no service.

Dwell Angle

Dwell angle is the amount of time (measured in degrees of distributor cam rotation) that the contact points remain closed. Initial point gap determines dwell angle. If the points are set too wide they open gradually and dwell angle (the time they remain closed) is small. This wide gap causes excessive arcing at the points and, because of this, point burning. This small dwell doesn't give the coil sufficient time to build up maximum energy and so coil output decreases. If the points are set too close, the dwell is increased but the points may bounce at higher speeds and the idle becomes rough and starting is made harder. The wider the point opening, the smaller the dwell and the smaller the

To set the dwell on a V8, lift the window and then turn the adjusting screw

Inspection points for the distributor, rotor, cap and coil

gap, the larger the dwell. Adjusting the dwell by making the initial point gap setting with a feeler gauge is sufficient to get the car started but a finer adjustment should be made. A dwell meter is needed to check the adjustment.

Connect the red lead (positive) wire of the meter to the distributor primary wire connection on the positive (+) side of the coil, and the black ground (negative) wire of the meter to a good ground on the engine. The dwell angle may be checked either with the engine cranking or running, although the reading will be more accurate if the engine is running. With the engine cranking, the reading will fluctuate between zero degrees dwell and the maximum figure for that angle. While cranking, the maximum figure is the correct one.

Dwell angle is permanently set electronically on HEI distributors, requiring no adjustment or checking.

ADJUSTMENT

1964-74

Dwell can be checked with the engine running or cranking. Decrease dwell by increasing the point gap; increase by decreasing the gap. Dwell angle is simply the number of degrees of distributor shaft rotation during which the points stay closed. Theoretically, if the point gap is correct, the dwell should also be correct or nearly so. Adjustment with a dwell meter produces more exact, consistent results since it is a dynamic adjustment. If dwell varies more than 3 degrees from idle speed to 1,750 engine rpm, the distributor is worn.

1. To adjust dwell on a six, trial and error point adjustments are required. On a V8, simply open the metal window on the distributor and insert a 1/8 in. allen wrench. Turn until the meter shows the correct reading. Be sure to snap the window closed.

2. An approximate dwell adjustment can be made without a meter on a V8. Turn the adjusting screw clockwise until the engine begins to misfire, then turn it out 1/2 turn.

3. If the engine won't start, check:

a. That all the spark plug wires are in place.

b. That the rotor has been installed.

c. That the two (or three) wires inside the distributor are connected.

d. That the points open and close when the engine turns.

e. That the gap is correct and the hold-down screw (on a six) is tight.

4. After the first 200 miles or so on a new set of points, the point gap often closes up due to initial rubbing block wear. For best performance, recheck the dwell (or gap) at this time. This quick initial wear is the reason the factory recommends 0.003 in. more gap on new points.

5. Since changing the gap affects the ignition timing, the timing should be checked and adjusted as necessary after each point replacement or adjustment.

1975 and Later

The dwell angle on these models is preset at the factory and not adjustable.

High Energy Ignition (HEI) System

The General Motors HEI system is a pulse-triggered, transistor-controlled, inductive discharge ignition system. Except on inline six-cylinder models through 1977, the entire HEI system is contained within the distributor cap. Inline six-cylinder engines through 1977 have an external coil. Otherwise, the systems are the same.

The distributor, in addition to housing the mechanical and vacuum advance mechanisms, contains the ignition coil (except on some inline six engines), the electronic control module, and the magnetic triggering device. The magnetic pick-up assembly contains a permanent magnet, a pole piece with internal "teeth," and a pick-up coil (not to be confused with the ignition coil).

For 1981 and later an HEI distributor with Electronic Spark Timing is used (for more information on EST, refer to Chapter 4). This system uses a one piece distributor with the ignition coil mounted in the distributor cap, similar to 1980.

All spark timing changes in the 1981 and later distributors are done electronically by the Electronic Control Module (ECM) which moniters information from various engine sensors, computes the desired spark timing and then signals the distributor to change the timing accordingly. No vacuum or mechanical advance systems are used whatsoever.

In the HEI system, as in other electronic

Early six cylinder engines with the HEI distributor had an external coil

ignition systems, the breaker points have been replaced with an electronic switch—a transistor—which is located *within* the control module. This switching transistor performs the same function the points did in a conventional ignition system; it simply turns coil primary current on and off at the correct time. Essentially then, electronic and conventional ignition systems operate on the same principle.

The module which houses the switching transistor is controlled (turned on and off) by a magnetically generated impulse induced in the pick-up coil. When the teeth of the rotating

V8 HEI distributor components—1975–80 (1978–80 6-cyl. similar)

timer align with the teeth of the pole piece, the induced voltage in the pick-up coil signals the electronic module to open the coil primary circuit. The primary current then decreases, and a high voltage is induced in the ignition coil secondary windings which is then directed through the rotor and high voltage leads (spark plug wires) to fire the spark plugs.

In essence then, the pick-up coil module system simply replaces the conventional breaker points and condenser. The condenser found within the distributor is for radio suppression purposes only and has nothing to do with the ignition process. The module automatically controls the dwell period, increasing it with increasing engine speed. Since dwell is automatically controlled, it cannot be adjusted. The module itself is non-adjustable and non-repairable and must be replaced if found defective.

HEI SYSTEM PRECAUTIONS

Before going on to troubleshooting, it might be a good idea to take note of the following precautions:

Timing Light Use

Inductive pick-up timing lights are the best kind to use with HEI. Timing lights which connect between the spark plug and the spark plug wire occasionally (not always) give false readings.

Spark Plug Wires

The plug wires used with HEI systems are of a different construction than conventional wires. When replacing them, make sure you get the correct wires, since conventional wires won't carry the voltage. Also, handle them carefully to avoid cracking or splitting them and *never* pierce them.

Tachometer Use

Not all tachometers will operate or indicate correctly when used on a HEI system. While some tachometers may give a reading, this does not necessarily mean the reading is correct. In addition, some tachometers hook up differently from others. If you can't figure out whether or not your tachometer will work on your car,

All HEI circuitry is contained within the distributor body (1980 shown)

HEI EST distributor components—1981 (note absence of vacuum advance unit)

BATTERY TERMINAL
CONNECTED TO IGNITION SWITCH

TACHOMETER TERMINAL
CONNECT TACHOMETER FROM
THIS TERMINAL TO GROUND
(SOME TACHOMETERS
MUST CONNECT FROM
THIS TERMINAL TO
ENERGIZER POSITIVE +.
CONSULT TACHOMETER
MANUFACTURER.)

B + TERMINAL

GROUND
TERMINAL

C-TERMINAL

CONNECTOR

LATCH (4)

Typical HEI distributor connections

check with the tachometer manufacturer. Dwell readings, or course, have no significance at all.

HEI System Testers

Instruments designed specifically for testing HEI systems are available from several tool manufacturers. Some of these will even test the module itself. However, the tests given in the following section will require only an ohmmeter and a voltmeter.

TROUBLESHOOTING THE HEI SYSTEM

The symptoms of a defective component within the HEI system are exactly the same as those you would encounter in a conventional system. Some of these symptoms are:

• Hard or no Starting
• Rough Idle
• Poor Fuel Economy
• Engine misses under load or while accelerating

If you suspect a problem in your ignition system, there are certain preliminary checks which you should carry out before you begin to check the electronic portions of the system. First, it is extremely important to make sure the vehicle battery is in a good state of charge. A defective or poorly charged battery will cause the various components of the ignition system to read incorrectly when they are being tested. Second, make sure all wiring connections are clean and tight, not only at the battery, but also at the distributor cap, ignition coil, and at the electronic control module.

Since the only change between electronic and conventional ignition systems is in the distributor component area, it is imperative to check the secondary ignition circuit first. If the secondary circuit checks out properly, then the engine condition is probably not the fault of the ignition system. To check the secondary ignition system, perform a simple spark test. Remove one of the plug wires and insert some sort of extension in the plug socket. An old spark plug with the ground electrode removed makes a good extension. Hold the wire and extension about ¼ in. away from the block and crank the engine. If a normal spark occurs, then the problem is most likely *not* in the ignition system. Check for fuel system problems, or fouled spark plugs.

If, however, there is no spark or a weak spark, then further ignition system testing will have to be done. Troubleshooting techniques fall into two categories, depending on the nature of the problem. The categories are (1) Engine cranks, but won't start or (2) Engine runs, but runs rough or cuts out. To begin with, let's consider the first case.

Engine Fails to Start

If the engine won't start, perform a spark test as described earlier. This will narrow the problem area down considerably. If no spark occurs, check for the presence of normal battery voltage of the battery (BAT) terminal in the distributor cap. The ignition switch must be in the "on" position for this test. Either a voltmeter or a test light may be used for this test. Connect the test light wire to ground and the probe end to the BAT terminal at the distributor. If the light comes on, you have voltage to the distributor. If the light fails to come on, this indicates an open circuit in the ignition primary writing leading to the distributor. In this case, you will have to check wiring continuity back to the ignition switch using a test light. If there is battery voltage at the BAT terminal, but no spark at the plugs, then the problem lies within the distributor assembly. Go on to the distributor components test section.

Engine Runs, But Runs Rough or Cuts Out

1. Make sure the plug wires are in good shape first. There should be no obvious cracks or breaks. You can check the plug wires with an ohmmeter, but *do not* pierce the wires with a probe. Check the chart for the correct plug wire resistance.

2. If the plug wires are OK, remove the cap assembly and check for moisture, cracks, chips, or carbon tracks, or any other high voltage leaks or failures. Replace the cap if any defects are found. Make sure the timer wheel rotates when

HEI Plug Wire Resistance Chart

Wire Length	Minimum	Maximum
0–15 inches	3000 ohms	10,000 ohms
15–25 inches	4000 ohms	15,000 ohms
25–35 inches	6000 ohms	20,000 ohms
Over 35 inches		25,000 ohms

the engine is cranked. If everything is all right so far, go on to the distributor components test section following.

DISTRIBUTOR COMPONENTS TESTING

If the trouble has been narrowed down to the units within the distributor, the following tests can help pinpoint the defective component. An ohmmeter with both high and low ranges should be used. These tests are made with the cap assembly removed and the battery wire disconnected. If a tachometer is connected to the TACH terminal, disconnect it before making these tests.

1. Connect an ohmmeter between the TACH and BAT terminals in the distributor cap. The primary coil resistance should be less than one ohm.

2. To check the coil secondary resistance, connect an ohmmeter between the rotor button and the BAT terminal. Note the reading.

Connect the ohmmeter between the rotor button and the TACH terminal. Note the reading. The resistance in both cases should be between 6,000 and 30,000 ohms. Be sure to test between the rotor button and both the BAT and TACH terminals.

3. Replace the coil *only* if the readings in Step 1 and Step 2 are infinite.

NOTE: *These resistance checks will not disclose shorted coil windings. This condition can only be detected with scope analysis or a suitably designed coil tester. If these instruments are unavailable, replace the coil with a known good coil as a final coil test.*

4. To test the pick-up coil, first disconnect the white and green module leads. Set the ohmmeter on the high scale and connect it between a ground and either the white or green lead. Any resistance measurement *less* than infinity requires replacement of the pick-up coil.

5. Pick-up coil continuity is tested by connecting the ohmmeter (on low range) between the white and green leads. Normal resistance is between 650 and 850 ohms, or 500 and 1500 ohms on 1977 and later models. Move the vacuum advance arm while performing this test.

The coil on all but the 1975–77 six cylinder engine is accessible by removing the four attaching screws

Ohmmeter 1 shows the primary coil resistance connection. Ohmmeter 2 shows the secondary resistance connection (1980 shown, most models similar)

Check the condition of the arc seal under the coil

Ohmmeter 1 shows the connections for testing the pickup coil. Ohmmeter 2 shows the connections for testing the pickup coil continuity (1980 shown, most models similar)

Pickup coil removal (1981 and later models have no vacuum advance unit)

This will detect any break in coil continuity. Such a condition can cause intermittent misfiring. Replace the pick-up coil if the reading is outside the specified limits.

6. If no defects have been found at this time, you still have a problem, then the module will have to be checked. If you do not have access to a module tester, the only possible alternative is a substitution test. If the module fails the substitution test, replace it.

HEI SYSTEM MAINTENANCE

Except for periodic checks of the spark plug wires, and an occasional check of the distribu-

tor cap for cracks (see Steps 1 and 2 under "Engine Runs, But Runs Rough or Cuts Out" for details), no maintenance is required on the HEI System. No periodic lubrication is necessary; engine oil lubricates the lower bushing, and an oil-filled reservoir lubricates the upper bushing.

COMPONENT REPLACEMENT

Integral Ignition Coil

1. Disconnect the feed and module wire terminal connectors from the distributor cap.
2. Remove the ignition set retainer.
3. Remove the 4 coil cover-to-distributor cap screws and the coil cover.
4. Remove the 4 coil-to-distributor cap screws.
5. Using a blunt drift, press the coil wire spade terminals up out of distributor cap.
6. Lift the coil up out of the distributor cap.
7. Remove and clean the coil spring, rubber seal washer and coil cavity of the distributor cap.
8. Coat the rubber seal with a dielectric lubricant furnished in the replacement ignition coil package.
9. Reverse the above procedures to install.

Distributor Cap

1. Remove the feed and module wire terminal connectors from the distributor cap.
2. Remove the retainer and spark plug wires from the cap.
3. Depress and release the 4 distributor cap-to-housing retainers and lift off the cap assembly.
4. Remove the 4 coil cover screws and cover.
5. Using a finger or a blunt drift, push the spade terminals up out of the distributor cap.
6. Remove all 4 coil screws and lift the coil, coil spring and rubber seal washer out of the cap coil cavity.
7. Using a new distributor cap, reverse the above procedures to assemble being sure to clean and lubricate the rubber seal washer with dielectric lubricant.

Rotor

1. Disconnect the feed and module wire connectors from the distributor.
2. Depress and release the 4 distributor cap-to-housing retainers and lift off the cap assembly.
3. Remove the two rotor attaching screws and rotor.
4. Reverse the above procedure to install.

Vacuum Advance (1975–80)

1. Remove the distributor cap and rotor as previously described.

2. Disconnect the vacuum hose from the vacuum advance unit.

3. Remove the two vacuum advance retaining screws, pull the advance unit outward, rotate and disengage the operating rod from its tang.

4. Reverse the above procedure to install.

Module

1. Remove the distributor cap and rotor as previously described.

2. Disconnect the harness connector and pick-up coil spade connectors from the module. Be careful not to damage the wires when removing the connector.

3. Remove the two screws and module from the distributor housing.

4. Coat the bottom of the new module with dielectric lubricant supplied with the new module. Reverse the above procedure to install.

Module replacement, be sure to coat the mating surfaces with silicone lubricant

HEI SYSTEM TACHOMETER HOOKUP

There is a terminal marked TACH on the distributor cap. Connect one tachometer lead to this terminal and the other lead to a ground. On some tachometers, the leads must be connected to the TACH terminal and to the battery positive terminal.

CAUTION: *Never ground the TACH terminal; serious module and ignition coil damage will result. If there is any doubt as to the correct tachometer hookup, check with the tachometer manufacturer.*

1975–77 models with a six cylinder engine utilize an HEI distributor with an external coil. For these particular vehicles, connect one tachometer lead to the TACH terminal on the ignition coil and connect the other one to a suitable ground.

Ignition Timing

Ignition timing is the measurement, in degrees of crankshaft rotation, of the point at which the spark plugs fire in each of the cylinders. It is measured in degrees before or after Top Dead Center (TDC) of the compression stroke.

Because it takes a fraction of a second for the spark plug to ignite the mixture in the cylinder, the spark plug must fire a little before the piston reaches TDC. Otherwise, the mixture will not be completely ignited as the piston passes TDC and the full power of the explosion will not be used by the engine.

The timing measurement is given in degrees of crankshaft rotation before the piston reaches TDC (BTDC). If the setting for the ignition timing is 5° BTDC, the spark plug must fire 5° before each piston reaches TDC. This only holds true, however, when the engine is at idle speed.

As the engine speed increases, the pistons go faster. The spark plugs have to ignite the fuel even sooner if it is to be completely ignited when the piston reaches TDC. To do this, the distributor has two means to advance the timing of the spark as the engine speed increases. This is accomplished by centrifugal weights within the distributor, and a vacuum diaphragm mounted on the side of the distributor.

If the ignition is set too far advanced (BTDC), the ignition and expansion of the fuel in the cylinder will occur too soon and tend to force the piston down while it is still traveling up. This causes engine ping. If the ignition spark is set too far retarded, after TDC (ATDC), the piston will have already passed TDC and started on its way down when the fuel is ignited. This will cause the piston to be forced down for only a portion of its travel. This will result in poor engine performance and lack of power.

Timing marks consist of a notch on the rim of the crankshaft pulley and a scale of degrees attached to the front of the engine. The notch corresponds to the position of the piston in the number 1 cylinder. A stroboscopic (dynamic) timing light is used, which is hooked into the

Typical ignition timing marks

circuit of the No. 1 cylinder spark plug. Every time the spark plug fires, the timing light flashes. By aiming the timing light at the timing marks, the exact position of the piston within the cylinder can be read, since the stroboscopic flash makes the mark on the pulley appear to be standing still. Proper timing is indicated when the notch is aligned with the correct number on the scale.

There are three basic types of timing lights available. The first is a simple neon bulb with two wire connections (one for the spark plug and one for the plug wire, connecting the light in series). This type of light is quite dim, and must be held closely to the marks to be seen, but it is quite inexpensive. The second type of light operates from the car's battery. Two alligator clips connect to the battery terminals, while a third wire connects to the spark plug with an adapter. This type of light is more expensive, but the xenon bulb provides a nice bright flash which can even be seen in sunlight. The third type replaces the battery source with 110 volt house current. Some timing lights have other functions built into them, such as dwell meters, tachometers, or remote starting switches. These are convenient, in that they reduce the tangle of wires under the hood, but may duplicate the functions of tools you already have.

If your car has electronic ignition, you should use a timing light with an inductive pickup. This pickup simply clamps onto the No. 1 spark plug wire, eliminating the adapter. It is not susceptible to crossfiring or false triggering, which may occur with a conventional light, due to the greater voltages produced by electronic ignition.

CHECKING AND ADJUSTMENT

1. Warm the engine to normal operating temperature. Shut off the engine and connect the timing light to the No. 1 spark plug (left front on V8, front on a six). Do not, under any circumstances, pierce a wire to hook up a light.

2. Clean off the timing marks and mark the pulley or damper notch and the timing scale with white chalk or paint. The timing notch on the damper or pulley can be elusive. Bump the engine around with the starter or turn the crankshaft with a wrench on the front pulley bolt to get it to an accessible position.

3. Disconnect and plug the vacuum advance hose at the distributor, to prevent any distributor advance. The vacuum line is the rubber hose connected to the metal cone-shaped canister on the side of the distributor. A short screw, pencil, or a golf tee can be used to plug the hose.

NOTE: *1981 models with Electronic Spark Timing have no vacuum advance, therefore you may skip the previous step, but you must disconnect the four terminal EST connector before going on.*

4. Start the engine and adjust the idle speed to that specified in the "Tune-Up Specifications" chart. Some cars require that the timing be set with the transmission in Neutral. You can disconnect the idle solenoid, if any, to get the speed down. Otherwise, adjust the idle speed screw. This is to prevent any centrifugal advance of timing in the distributor.

The tachometer hookup for cars through 1974 is the same as that shown for the dwell meter in the "Tune-Up" section. On 1975–77 HEI systems, the tachometer connects to the TACH terminal on the distributor for V8s, or on the coil for sixes, and to a ground. For 1978 and later models, all tachometer connections are to the TACH terminal. Some tachometers must connect to the TACH terminal and to the positive battery terminal. Some tachometers won't work at all with HEI. Consult the tachometer manufacturer if the instructions supplied with the unit do not give the proper connection.

CAUTION: *Never ground the HEI TACH terminal; serious system damage will result, including module burnout.*

5. Aim the timing light at the timing marks. Be careful not to touch the fan, which may appear to be standing still. Keep your clothes and hair, and the light's wires clear of the fan, belts, and pulleys. If the pulley or damper notch isn't aligned with the proper timing mark (see the "Tune-Up Specifications" chart), the timing will have to be adjusted.

NOTE: *TDC or Top Dead Center corresponds to 0 degrees; B, or BTDC, or Before Top Dead Center, may be shown as BEFORE; A, or ATDC, or After Top Dead Center, may be shown as AFTER.*

6. Loosen the distributor base clamp locknut. You can buy special wrenches which make this task a lot easier on V8s. Turn the distributor slowly to adjust the timing, holding it by the body and not the cap. Turn the distributor in the direction of rotor rotation (found in the "Firing Order" illustration in Chapter 3) to retard, and against the direction to advance.

NOTE: *The 231 V6 engine has two timing marks on the crankshaft pulley. One timing mark is 1/8 in. wide and the other, four inches away, is 1/16 in. wide. The smaller mark is used for setting the timing with a hand-held timing light. The larger mark is used with the magnetic probe and is only of use to a dealer or garage. Make sure you set the timing using the smaller mark.*

7. Tighten the locknut. Check the timing,

in case the distributor moved as you tightened it.

8. Replace the distributor vacuum hose, if removed. Correct the idle speed.

9. Shut off the engine and disconnect the light.

Valve Lash

Hydraulic valve lifters rarely require adjustment, and are not adjusted as part of a normal tune-up. All adjustment procedures concerning them will be found in Chapter 3. The procedures listed here are for solid lifters only. Before adjusting solid lifters, thoroughly warm the engine. The solid lifters are generally found on certain high-performance engines.

SOLID LIFTERS

Engine Running

1. Run the engine to reach normal operating temperature.

2. Remove the valve covers and gaskets by tapping the end of the cover rearward. Do not attempt to pry the cover off.

3. To avoid being splashed with hot oil, use oil deflector clips. Place one each oil hole in the rocker arm.

4. Measure between the rocker arm and the valve stem with a flat feeler gauge, then adjust the rocker arm stud nut until clearance agrees with the specifications in the chart.

5. After adjusting all the valves, stop the engine, clean the gasket surfaces, and install the valve covers with new gaskets.

Oil deflector clips will prevent splatter when adjusting the valves with the engine running

Engine Not Running

These are initial adjustments usually required after assembling an engine or doing a valve job. They should be followed up by an adjustment with the engine running as described above.

Adjusting the solid valve lifters

1. Set the engine to the No. 1 firing position.

2. Adjust the clearance between the valve stems and the rocker arms with a feeler gauge. Check the Chart for the proper clearance. Adjust the following valves in the No. 1 firing position: Intake No. 2, 7, Exhaust No. 4, 8.

3. Turn the crankshaft one-half revolution clockwise. Adjust the following valves: Intake No. 1, 8, Exhaust No. 3, 6.

4. Turn the crankshaft one-half revolution clockwise to No. 6 firing position. Adjust the following valves in the No. 6 firing position: Intake No. 3, 4, Exhaust No. 5, 7.

5. Turn the crankshaft one-half revolution clockwise. Adjust the following valves: Intake No. 5, 6, Exhaust No. 1, 2.

6. Run the engine until the normal operating temperature is reached. Reset all clearances, using the procedure listed above under "Engine Running."

HYDRAULIC LIFTERS

All models, with the exception of those few already discussed, use a hydraulic tappet system with adjustable rocker mounting nuts to obtain zero lash. No periodic adjustment is necessary.

Carburetor

Idle mixture and speed adjustments are critical aspects of exhaust emission control. It is important that all tune-up instructions be carefully followed to ensure satisfactory engine performance and minimum exhaust pollution. The different combinations of emission systems application on the different engine models have resulted in a great variety of tune-up specifications. See the "Tune-Up Specifications" at the beginning of this section. Beginning in 1968, all models have a decal conspicuously placed in the engine compartment giving tune-up specifications.

When adjusting a carburetor with two idle mixture screws, adjust them alternately and evenly, unless otherwise stated.

IDLE SPEED AND MIXTURE ADJUSTMENT

See Chapter 4 for illustrations and adjustment specifications of Carter and Rochester carburetors. In the following adjustment procedures the term "lean roll" means turning the mixture adjusting screws in (clockwise) from optimum setting to obtain an obvious drop in engine speed (usually 20 rpm).

1964–66

Turn the idle screw(s) slightly *in* to seat, and then back out 1½ turns (3 when equipped with A.I.R.). Do not turn the idle mixture screws tightly against their seats or you could damage them. With the engine idling at operating temperature (air cleaner on, preheater valve and choke valve wide open), adjust the idle speed to the specified rpm (automatic transmission in Drive; manual in Neutral).

Adjust the mixture screw to obtain the highest steady idle speed, then adjust the idle speed screw to the specificed rpm. Adjust the mixture screw *in* to obtain a 20 rpm drop, then back the screw out ¼ turn. Repeat this operation on the second mixture, if so equipped. Readjust the idle speed screw as necessary until the specified rpm is reached.

1967 Without Air

Adjust with air cleaner removed.

1. Remove the air cleaner.
2. Connect a tachometer and vacuum gauge to the engine, set the parking brake, and place the transmission in Neutral.
3. Turn in the idle mixture screws until they *gently* seat, then back out 1½ turns.
4. Start the engine and allow it to come to the normal operating temperature. Make sure the choke is fully open, then adjust the idle speed screw to obtain the specified idle speed (automatic in Drive, manual in Neutral).
5. Adjust the idle mixture screw(s) to obtain the highest steady vacuum at the specified idle speed, except for the Rochester BV. For this carburetor, adjust the idle mixture screw out ¼ turn from lean "drop-off," the point where a

20–30 rpm drop is achieved by leaning the mixture.

NOTE: *On carburetors having a hot idle compensator valve (A/C models), hold the brass valve down with a pencil while making the mixture adjustment.*

6. Repeat Steps four and five if necessary.
7. Turn off the engine, remove the gauges, and install the air cleaner.

1967 With Air

Adjust with the air cleaner removed.

NOTE: *During this adjustment, air conditioning should be turned off on 327 and 350 cu in. engines.*

1. Remove the air cleaner.
2. Connect a tachometer and a vacuum gauge to the engine, set the parking brake, and place the transmission in Neutral.
3. Turn in the idle mixture screw(s) until they *gently* seat, then back them out three turns.
4. Start the engine and allow it to reach normal operating temperature. Make sure the choke is fully open, then adjust the idle speed screw(s) to obtain the specified idle speed (automatic in Drive, manual in Neutral).
5. Turn the idle mixture screw(s) clockwise (in) to the point where a 20–30 rmp drop in speed is achieved—this is the lean "drop off" point. Back out the screws ¼ turn from this point.
6. Repeat Steps four and five if necessary.
7. Turn off the engine, remove the gauges, and install the air cleaner.

1968–69

Adjust with the air cleaner installed.

NOTE: *Turn off the air conditioner (if applicable) unless your car is a 1968 model with the 6 cylinder engine and automatic transmission. These cars should have the air conditioner turned on when setting the idle.*

1. Turn in the idle mixture screw(s) until they seat gently, then back them out three turns.
2. Start the engine and allow it to reach operating temperature. Make sure the choke is fully open and the preheater valve is open, then adjust the idle speed screw to obtain the specified idle speed (automatic in Drive, manual in Neutral).
3. Adjust the idle mixture screw(s) to obtain the highest steady idle speed, then readjust the idle speed screw to obtain the specified speed. On cars with an idle stop solenoid adjust as follows:

   a. Adjust the idle speed to 500 RPM (6) or 600 rpm (1968 V8) by turning the hex on the solenoid plunger. Refer to the tune-up decal in the engine compartment for 1969 idle speeds.

Idle speed and mixture screw location—1964-72

b. Disconnect the wire at the solenoid. This allows the throttle lever to seat against the idle screw.

c. Adjust the idle screw to obtain 400 rpm (1968), then reconnect the wire. On 1969 models, adjust the idle to that specified on the tune-up decal in the engine compartment.

4. Adjust one mixture screw to obtain a 20 rpm drop in idle speed, and back out the screw ¼ turn from this point.

5. Repeat Steps three and four for the second mixture screw (if so equipped).

6. Readjust the idle speed to obtain the specified idle speed.

1970—Initial Adjustments

Adjust with the air cleaner installed.

1. Disconnect the fuel tank line from the vapor canister (EEC).

2. Connect a tachometer to the engine, start the engine and allow it to reach operating temperature. Make sure the choke and preheater valves are fully open.

3. Turn off the air conditioner and set the parking brake. Disconnect and plug the distributor vacuum line.

4. Make the following adjustments:

6-250

1. Turn in the mixture screw until it *gently* seats, then back out the screw four turns.

2. Adjust the solenoid screw to obtain 830 rpm for manual transmissions (in Neutral) or 630 rpm for automatic transmissions (in Drive).

3. Adjust the mixture screw to obtain 750 rpm for manual transmissions (in Neutral) or 600 rpm for automatic transmissions (in Drive).

4. Disconnect the solenoid wire and set the idle speed to 400 rpm, then reconnect it.

5. Reconnect the distributor vacuum line.

V8-307, 400

1. Turn in the mixture screws until they seat *gently*, then back them out four turns.

2. Adjust the carburetor idle speed screw to obtain 800 rpm for manual transmissions (in Neutral), or adjust the solenoid screw to obtain 630 rpm for automatic transmissions (in Drive).

3. Adjust both mixture screws equally inward to obtain 700 rpm for manual transmis-

sions, 600 rpm for automatic transmissions (in Drive).

4. On cars with automatic transmissions, disconnect the solenoid wire, set the carburetor idle screw to obtain 450 rpm and reconnect the solenoid.

5. Reconnect the distributor vacuum line.

V8-350 (250 HP)

1. Turrn in the mixture screws until they *gently* seat, then back them out four turns.

2. Adjust the solenoid screw to obtain 830 rpm for manual transmissions (in Neutral), or 630 rpm for automatic transmissions (in Drive).

3. Adjust both mixture screws equally inward to obtain 750 rpm for manual transmissions or 600 rpm for automatics (in Drive).

4. Disconnect the solenoid wire, set the carburetor idle screw to obtain 450 rpm, and reconnect the solenoid.

5. Reconnect the distributor vacuum line.

V8-350 (300 HP), 402 (330 HP)

1. Turn in both mixture screws until they *gently* seat, then back them out four turns.

2. Adjust the carburetor idle screw to obtain 775 rpm for manual transmissions, 630 rpm for automatics (in Drive).

3. Adjust the mixture screws equally to obtain 700 rpm for manual transmissions, 600 rpm for automatics (in Drive).

4. Reconnect the distributor vacuum line.

V8-402 (350 HP), 454

1. Turn in both mixture screws until they *gently* seat, then back them out four turns.

2. Adjust the carburetor idle screw to obtain 700 rpm for manual transmissions or 630 rpm for automatics (in Drive).

3. For cars with automatic transmissions: adjust the mixture screws equally to obtain 600 rpm with the transmission in Drive.

4. For cars with manual transmissions: turn in *one* mixture screw until the speed drops to 400 rpm, then adjust the carburetor idle screw to obtain 700 rpm. Turn in the *other* mixture screw until the speed drops 400 rpm, then regain 700 rpm by adjusting the carburetor idle screw.

5. Reconnect the distributor vacuum line.

1971–72—Initial Adjustments

Adjust with air cleaner installed. The following initial idle adjustments are part of the normal engine tune-up. There is a tune-up decal placed conspicuously in the engine compartment outlining the specific procedure and settings for each engine application. Follow all of the instructions when adjusting the idle. These tuning procedures are necessary to obtain the del-icate balance of variables for the maintenance of both reliable engine performance and efficient exhaust emission control.

NOTE: *All engines have limiter caps on the mixture adjusting screws. The idle mixture is preset and the limiter caps installed at the factory in order to meet emission control standards. Do not remove these limiter caps unless all other possible causes of poor idle condition have been thoroughly checked out. The solenoid used on 1971 carburetors is different from the one used on earlier models. The Combination Emission Control System (C.E.C.) solenoid valve regulates distributor vacuum as a function of transmission gear position.*

CAUTION: *The C.E.C. solenoid is adjusted only after: 1) replacement of the solenoid, 2) major carburetor overhaul, or 3) after the throttle body is removed or replaced.*

All initial adjustments described below are made:

1. With the engine warmed up and running.

2. With the choke fully open.

3. With the fuel tank line disconnected from the Evaporative Emission canister on all models.

4. With the vacuum hose disconnected at the distributor and plugged.

Be sure to reconnect the distributor vacuum hose and to connect the fuel tank-to-evaporative emission canister line or install the gas cap when idle adjustments are complete.

6-250

1. Adjust the carburetor idle speed screw to obtain 550 rpm (700 rpm for 1972) for manual transmissions (in Neutral) or 500 rpm (600 rpm for 1972) for automatics (in Drive). *Do not adjust the solenoid screw.* Using the solenoid screw to set idle or incorrectly adjusting it may result in a decrease in engine braking.

2. Reconnect the vapor line and distributor vacuum advance line.

V8-307 AND 350 (2-BBL)

1. On 1971 models, adjust the carburetor idle speed screw to obtain 600 rpm for manual transmission (in Neutral) with the air conditioning turned off, or 550 rpm for automatic transmissions (in Drive) with the air conditioning turned on. *Do not adjust the solenoid screw.* On 1972 models, turn the air conditioning off and adjust the idle stop solenoid screw to obtain 900 rpm for manual transmissions (in Neutral) or 600 rpm for automatics (in Drive). Place the transmission in Park or Neutral and adjust the fast idle cam screw to get 1,850 rpm on 307 engines and 2,200 rpm on 350 engines.

ROCHESTER CARBURETORS

Idle speed and mixture screw location—1973–75

2. Reconnect the vapor line and distributor vacuum advance line.

V8-350 (4-BBL)

1. On 1971 models, adjust the carburetor idle speed screw to obtain 600 rpm for manual transmissions (in Neutral) with the air conditioning turned off, or 550 rpm for automatics (in Drive) with the air conditioning turned on. *Do not adjust the solenoid screw.* On 1972 models, turn the air conditioning off and adjust the idle stop solenoid screw to get 800 rpm for manual transmissions (in Neutral) or 600 rpm for automatic transmissions (in Drive).

2. For both 1971 and 1972 models, place the fast idle cam follower on the second step of the fast idle cam, turn the air conditioning off and adjust the fast idle to 1,350 rpm for manual transmissions (in Neutral) or 1,500 rpm for automatics (in Park).

IDLE MIXTURE
SCREW

IDLE SPEED
SOLENOID SCREW

Idle speed and mixture screw location—1972 Holley 4150

3. Reconnect the vapor line and the distributor vacuum advance line on all models.

V8-402, 454

1. On 1971 models, turn off the air conditioner and adjust the carburetor idle speed screw to obtain 600 rpm with manual transmissions in Neutral and automatics in Drive. *Do not adjust the solenoid screw.* On 1972 cars, turn off the air conditioning and adjust the idle stop solenoid screw to 800 rpm (in Neutral) for manual transmissions and 600 rpm (in Drive) for automatics.

2. On both 1971 and 1972 cars, place the fast idle cam follower on the second step of the fast idle cam, turn off the air conditioner and adjust the fast idle to 1,350 rpm for manual transmissions (in Neutral) or 1,500 rpm for automatics (in Park).

3. Reconnect the vapor line and the distributor vacuum line on 1971 and 1972 cars.

1973—Initial Adjustments

All models are equipped with idle limiter caps and idle solenoids. Disconnect the fuel tank line from the evaporative canister. The engine must be running at operating temperature, choke off, parking brake on, and rear wheels blocked. Disconnect the distributor vacuum hose and plug it. After adjustment, reconnect the vacuum and evaporative hoses.

6-250

Adjust the idle stop solenoid for 700 rpm on manual transmission models or 600 rpm on automatics (in Drive). On manual models, make no attempt to adjust the CEC solenoid (the larger of the two carburetor solenoids) or a decrease in engine braking could result.

V8-307 & 350, 400 (2-BBL)

1. With the air conditioning Off, adjust the idle stop solenoid screw for a speed of 900 rpm on manual models; 600 rpm for automatics in Drive.

2. Disconnect the idle stop solenoid electrical connector and adjust the idle speed screw (screw resting on lower step of the cam) for 450 rpm on all 307 cu in. engines, 400 rpm on 350 and 400 engines with automatic transmissions, or 500 rpm on 350 and 400 cu in. engine with manual transmissions.

V8-350, 400 (4-BBL)

1. Adjust the idle stop solenoid screw for 900 rpm on manual, 600 rpm on automatic (in Drive).

2. Connect the distributor vacuum hose and position the fast idle cam follower on the top step of the fast idle cam (turn air conditioning off) and adjust the fast idle to 1300 rpm on manual transmission 350 engines; 1600 rpm for all automatics in Park.

V8-454

1. With the air conditioning off, adjust the idle stop solenoid screw to 900 rpm for the manual transmission; 700 rpm with the automatic transmission in Drive.

2. Connect the distributor vacuum hose and place fast idle cam follower on the top step of the fast idle cam. Adjust the fast idle to 1300 rpm for manual transmission; and 1600 rpm for automatic transmissions (in Park).

1974

The same preliminary adjustments as for 1973 apply.

6-250

1. Using the hex nut on the end of the solenoid body, turn the entire solenoid to get 850 rpm for the manual transmission; 600 rpm for automatic transmissions in Drive.

V8-350, 400 (2-BBL)

1. Turn the air conditioning off. Adjust the idle stop solenoid screw for 900 rpm on manual; 600 rpm on automatic (in Drive).

2. De-energize the solenoid and adjust the carburetor idle cam screw (on low step of cam) for 400 rpm on automatic models (in Drive); 500 rpm on 350 engines with manual transmission.

V8-350, 400 (4-BBL)

1. Turn the air conditioning off. Adjust the idle stop solenoid screw for 900 rpm on manual transmission models; 600 rpm on automatic (in Drive).

2. Connect the distributor vacuum hose. Position the fast idle cam follower on the top step of the fast idle cam and adjust the fast idle speed to 1300 rpm on manual; 1600 on automatic (in Park).

V8-454

1. With the air conditioning off, adjust the idle stop solenoid screw for 800 rpm with the manual transmission; 600 with the automatic transmission in Drive.

2. Reconnect the distributor vacuum advance hose and place the fast idle cam follower on the top step of the fast idle cam. With the air conditioning off, adjust the fast idle to 1600 rpm for manual transmissions; 1500 rpm for all automatics in Park.

1975-76

6-250 (1-BBL)

1. Idle speed is adjusted with the engine at normal operating temperature, air cleaner on, choke open, and air conditioning off (air conditioning on—1976 automatic transmission models). Hook up a tachometer to the engine.

2. Block the rear wheels and apply the parking brake.

3. Disconnect the fuel tank hose from the evaporative canister.

4. Disconnect and plug the distributor vacuum advance hose.

5. Start the engine and check the ignition timing. Adjust if necessary. Reconnect the vacuum hose. To adjust the idle speed, turn the solenoid in or out to obtain the higher of the two specifications listed on the decal. With the automatic transmission in Drive or the manual transmission in Neutral, disconnect the solenoid electrical connector and turn the 1/8 in. allen screw in the end of the solenoid body to the lower idle speed.

Idle mixture screw location—1976-77 2GC

6. Place the shift lever in Drive on cars with automatic transmissions and have an assistant apply the brakes. On cars with manual transmissions, put it into Neutral.

7. Cut the tab off the mixture limiter cap, but don't remove the cap. Turn the screw counterclockwise until the highest idle speed is reached.

8. Set the idle speed to the higher of the two listed idle speeds by turning the solenoid in or out.

9. Check the tachometer and turn the mixture screw clockwise until the idle speed is at the lower of the two listed idle speeds.

10. Shut off the engine, remove the tachometer, and reconnect the carbon canister hose.

V8-350; 1975 (2-BBL)
V8-305; 1976 (2-BBL)

1. Idle speed is adjusted with the engine at normal operating temperature, air cleaner on, choke open, and air conditioning off. Hook up a tachometer to the engine.

2. Block the rear wheels and apply the parking brake.

3. Disconnect the fuel tank hose from the evaporative canister.

4. Disconnect and plug the distributor vacuum advance hose.

5. Start the engine and check the ignition timing. Adjust if necessary. Reconnect the vacuum hose.

6. Adjust the idle speed screw to the specified rpm. If the figures given in the "Tune-Up Specifications" chart differ from those on the tune-up decal, those on the decal take precedence. Automatic transmissions should be in Drive, manual transmissions should be in Neutral.

CAUTION: *Make doubly sure that the rear wheels are blocked and the parking brake applied.*

Adjust the idle speed to the higher of the two figures on the tune-up decal. Back out the two mixture screws equally until the highest idle is reached. Reset the speed if necessary to the higher one on the tune-up decal. Next, turn the screws in equally until the lower of the two figures on the decal is obtained.

7. Shut off engine, reconnect hose to evaporative canister, and remove blocks from wheels.

V8-350, 400, 454

1975 four-barrel carburetors are equipped with idle stop solenoids. There are two idle speeds, one with the solenoid engergized and second with the solenoid de-energized. Both are set with the solenoid. The slower speed (solenoid de-energized) is necessary to prevent dieseling by allowing the throttle plates to close further than at a normal idle speed.

1. Idle speed is set with the engine at normal operating temperature, air cleaner on, choke open, and air conditioning off. Hook up a tachometer to the engine.

2. Block the rear wheels and apply the parking brake.

3. Disconnect the fuel tank hose from the evaporative canister.

4. Disconnect and plug the distributor vacuum advance hose.

5. Start the engine and check the ignition timing. Adjust if necessary. Reconnect the vacuum hose.

6. Disconnect the electrical connector at the idle solenoid.

7. Set the transmission in Drive. Adjust the low idle speed screw for the lower of the two figures given for idle speed.

CAUTION: *Make sure that the drive wheels are blocked and the parking brake is applied.*

8. Reconnect the idle solenoid and open the throttle slightly to extend the solenoid plunger.

9. Turn the solenoid plunger screw in or out to obtain the higher of the two idle speed figures (this is normal curb-idle).

To adjust the mixture, break off the limiter caps. Make sure that the idle is at the higher of the two speeds listed on the decal. Turn the mixture screws out equally to obtain the highest idle. Reset the idle speed with the plunger screw if necessary. Turn the mixture screws in until the lower of the two figures on the decal is obtained.

10. Shut off engine, remove blocks from drive wheels, and reconnect hose to evaporative canister.

For 1976, the idle solenoid has been dropped. To adjust the idle, follow the preceding Steps 1–5. Skip Steps 6, 7, and 8, then follow Steps 9 and 10, adjusting the idle speed screw.

1977

1. First satisfy all the following requirements:

A. Set parking brake and block drive wheels.

B. Bring the engine to operating temperature.

C. Remove the air cleaner for access, but make sure all hoses stay connected.

D. Consult the Emission Control Information label under the hood, and disconnect and plug hoses as reequired by the instructions there.

E. Connect an accurate tach to the engine.

2. Set ignition timing as described above.

**Idle speed adjustment screw location—1976-79
1 BBL**

3. Remove the cap(s) from the idle mixture screw(s). Remove caps carefully, to prevent bending these screws.

4. Turn in the screw(s) till they seat *very lightly,* then back screw(s) out just far enough to permit the engine to run.

5. Put automatic transmission in Drive.

6. Back out screw(s) ⅛ turn at a time, going alternately from screw to screw after each ⅛ turn where there are two screws, until the highest possible idle speed is achieved. Then, set the idle speed as follows: 250 CID engine with manual transmission—950; with automatic—575; with automatic in California—640; with automatic used in higher altitude area—650; 305 V8 with manual transmission—650; with automatic—550; standard 350 V8, manual transmission—800; standard 350 V8 with automatic—550; 350 V8 used at high altitudes—650.

7. After setting the idle speed, repeat the mixture adjustment to ensure that mixture is at the point where highest idle speed is obtained.

Idle speed adjustment for the six cylinder engine—1976-78

Idle speed adjustment for the the V8, 4 BBL with solenoid—1977

Idle speed adjustment for the V8, 4 BBL without solenoid—1977

Idle speed adjustment for the 2 BBL with solenoid—1978–79

Then, if idle speed has increased, repeat idle speed adjustment of Step 6.

8. Now, turn screw(s) in, going evenly in ⅛ turn increments where there are two, until the following idle speeds are obtained: 250 CID engine with manual transmission—750; with automatic—550; with automatic in California—600; with automatic used in high altitude areas—600; 305 V8 with manual transmission—600; with automatic—500; standard 350 V8, manual transmission—700; standard 350 V8 with automatic—500; 350 V8 used at high altitudes—600.

9. Reset idle speed to the value shown on the engine compartment sticker, if that differs from the final setting in the step above.

10. Check and adjust fast idle as described on the engine compartment sticker. See Chapter 4.

11. Reconnect any vacuum hoses that were disconnected for the procedure, and install the air cleaner.

12. If idle speed has changed, reset according to the engine compartment sticker. Disconnect tach.

1978 and Later

1978 and later models have sealed idle mixture screws; in most cases these are concealed under staked-in plugs. Idle mixture is adjustable only during carburetor overhaul, and requires

Idle speed adjustment for the 2 BBL without solenoid—1978–79

the addition of propane as an artificial mixture enrichener.

See the emission control label in the engine compartment for procedures and specifications not supplied here. Prepare the car for adjustment (engine warm, choke open, fast idle screw off the fast idle cam) as per the label instructions.

1 BBL

1. Run the engine to normal operating temperature.

2. Make sure that the choke is fully opened.

3. Turn the A/C Off and disconnect the vacuum line at the vapor canister. Plug the line.

4. Set the parking brake, block the drive wheels and place the transmission in Drive (AT) or Neutral (MT). Connect a tachometer to the engine according to the manufacturer's instructions.

5. Turn the solenoid assembly to achieve the solenoid-on speed.

6. Disconnect the solenoid wire and turn the ⅛ inch hex screw in the solenoid end, to achieve the solenoid-off speed.

7. Remove the tachometer, connect the canister vacuum line and shut off the engine.

2 BBL AND 4 BBL (ALL BUT V8-350)

1. Run the engine to normal operating temperature.

2. Make sure that the choke is fully opened, turn the A/C Off, set the parking brake, block the drive wheels and connect a tachometer to the engine according to the manufacturer's instructions.

3. Disconnect and plug the vacuum hoses at the EGR valve and the vapor canister.

4. Place the transmission in Park (AT) or Neutral (MT).

5. Disconnect and plug the vacuum advance hose at the distributor. Check and adjust the timing.

6. Connect the distributor vacuum line.

7. Manual transmission cars without A/C and without solenoid: place the idle speed screw on

② TURN IDLE SPEED SCREW TO SET CURB IDLE SPEED TO SPECIFICATIONS – A / C OFF (SEE EMISSION LABEL)

① PREPARE VEHICLE FOR ADJUSTMENTS – SEE EMISSION LABEL ON VEHICLE. NOTE: IGNITION TIMING SET PER LABEL.

1979 and later 4BBL adjustment without solenoid

③ SOLENOID ENERGIZED – A/C COMPRESSOR LEAD DISCONNECTED AT A/C COMPRESSOR, A/C ON, A/T TRANSMISSION IN DRIVE, M/T IN NEUTRAL

① PREPARE VEHICLE FOR ADJUSTMENTS – SEE EMISSION LABEL ON VEHICLE. NOTE: IGNITION TIMING SET PER LABEL.

⑤ TURN SOLENOID SCREW TO ADJUST TO SPECIFIED RPM. (RECONNECT A/C COMPRESSOR LEAD AFTER ADJUSTMENT)

ELECTRICAL CONNECTION

④ OPEN THROTTLE SLIGHTLY TO ALLOW SOLENOID PLUNGER TO FULLY EXTEND

② TURN IDLE SPEED SCREW TO SET CURB IDLE SPEED TO SPECIFICATIONS – A/C OFF (SEE EMISSION LABEL)

1979 and later 4BBL adjustment with solenoid

① DISCONNECT ELECTRICAL LEAD FROM IDLE SPEED SOLENOID (IF SO EQUIPPED).

③ RECONNECT ELECTRICAL LEAD TO IDLE SPEED SOLENOID.

② ADJUST BASE IDLE SPEED SCREW TO R.P.M. SPECIFIED ON EMISSION LABEL (AUTOMATIC TRANSMISSION IN DRIVE OR MANUAL TRANSMISSION IN NEUTRAL).

Idle speed adjustment with solenoid—1980 2 BBL

A/C IDLE SPEED ADJUSTMENT (ON VEHICLE)

③ SOLENOID ENERGIZED - A/C COMPRESSOR LEAD DISCONNECTED AT A/C COMPRESSOR , A/C ON, A/T TRANSMISSION IN DRIVE, M/T IN NEUTRAL

① PREPARE VEHICLE FOR ADJUSTMENTS - SEE EMISSION LABEL ON VEHICLE. NOTE: IGNITION TIMING SET PER LABEL.

⑤ TURN SOLENOID SCREW TO ADJUST TO SPECIFIED RPM. (RECONNECT A/C COMPRESSOR LEAD AFTER ADJUSTMENT)

ELECTRICAL CONNECTION

TURN IDLE SPEED SCREW TO SET CURB IDLE SPEED TO

④ OPEN THROTTLE SLIGHTLY TO ALLOW SOLENOID PLUNGER TO FULLY EXTEND

② SPECIFICATIONS - A/C OFF (SEE EMISSION LABEL)

Idle speed adjustment without solenoid—1980 2 BBL

the low step of the fast idle cam and turn the screw to achieve the specified idle speed.

Cars with A/C: set the idle speed screw to the specified rpm. Disconnect the compressor clutch wire and turn the A/C On. Open the throttle momentarily to extend the solenoid plunger. Turn the solenoid screw to obtain the specified rpm.

Automatic transmission cars without A/C; manual transmission cars without A/C, solenoid-equipped carburetor: momentarily open the throttle to extend the solenoid plunger. Turn the solenoid screw to obtain the specified rpm. Disconnect the solenoid wire and turn the idle speed screw to obtain the slow engine idle speed.

V8-350

1. Run the engine to normal operating temperature.
2. Set the parking brake and block the drive wheels.
3. Connect a tachometer to the engine according to the manufacturer's instructions.
4. Disconnect and plug the purge hose at the vapor canister. Disconnect and plug the EGR vacuum hose at the EGR valve.
5. Turn the A/C Off.
6. Place the transmission in Park (AT) or Neutral (MT).
7. Disconnect and plug the vacuum advance line at the distributor. Check and adjust the timing.
8. Connect the vacuum advance line. Place the automatic transmission in Drive.
9. Manual transmission cars without A/C: adjust the idle stop screw to obtain the specified rpm. Cars with A/C: with the A/C off, adjust the idle stop screw to obtain the specified rpm. Disconnect the compressor clutch wire and turn the A/C on. Open the throttle slightly to allow the solenoid plunger to extend. Turn the solenoid screw to obtain the solenoid rpm listed on the underhood emission sticker.
10. Connect all hoses and remove the tachometer.

Diesel Fuel Injection

NOTE: *GM diesel engines are equipped with Roosa-Master, CAV Lucas, or Stanodyne injection pumps. The Roosa-Master and Stanodyne pumps are nearly identical.*

IDLE SPEED ADJUSTMENT

A special tachometer with an RPM counter suitable for the 263 V6 and 350 V8 diesels is necessary for this adjustment; a standard tach suitable for gasoline engines will not work.

ENGINE TEMPERATURE SWITCH

INSTALL&REMOVE JUMPER HERE V6

Fast idle temperature switch, V6 diesel

CAV-Lucas injection pump slow idle screw

Roosa-Master injection pump slow idle screw

1. Place the transmission in Park, block the rear wheels and firmly set the parking brake.

2. If necessary, adjust the throttle linkage as described in Chapter 6.

3. Start the engine and allow it to warm up for 10–15 minutes.

4. Shut off the engine and remove the air cleaner assembly.

5. Clean off any grime from the timing probe holder on the front cover; also clean off the crankshaft balancer rim.

6. Install the magnetic probe end of the tachometer fully into the timing probe holder. Complete the remaining tachometer connections according to the tach manufacturer's instructions.

7. On the V6 diesel, disconnect the A/C compressor clutch lead at the compressor (if equipped with A/C).

8. Make sure all electrical accessories are OFF.

NOTE: *At no time should either the steering wheel or brake pedal be touched.*

Fast idle temperature switch (V8 diesel)

9. Start the engine and place the transmission in Drive (after first making sure the parking brake is firmly applied).

10. Check the slow idle speed reading against the one printed on the underhood emissions sticker. Reset if necessary.

Diesel Tune-Up Specifications

Year	Eng V.I.N. Code	Engine No. Cyl. Displacement (Cu. in.)	Eng. Mfg.	Fuel Pump Pressure (psi)	Compression (lbs)▲	Ignition Timing (deg) Auto. Trans.	Intake Valve Opens (deg)	Idle Speed● (rpm)
'80	N	8-350	Olds.	5.5–6.5	275 min.	5B ②	16	750/600
'81	N	8-350	Olds.	5.5–6.5	275 min.	①	16	①
'82	V	V6-263	Olds.	5.5–6.5	275 min.	①	16	①
	N	8-350	Olds.	5.5–6.5	275 min.	①	16	①
'83–'84	V	V6-263	Olds.	5.5–6.5	275 min.	①	16	①
	N	8-350	Olds.	5.5–6.5	275 min.	①	16	①

NOTE: The underhood specifications sticker often reflects changes made in production. Sticker figures must be used if they disagree with those in this chart.
① See underhood specifications sticker.
② Static.
● Where two idle speed figures appear separated by a slash, the first is idle speed with solenoid energized; the second is with solenoid disconnected.
▲ The lowest cylinder reading should not be less than 70% of the highest cylinder reading.

FAST IDLE
SOLENOID

ADJUST HERE

8 N·m
(6 FT. LBS.)

V6 diesel fast idle solenoid

11. Unplug the connector from the fast idle cold advance (engine temperature) switch, and install a jumper wire between the connector terminals.

NOTE: *DO NOT allow the jumper to ground.*

12. Check the fast idle speed and reset if necessary according to the specification printed on the underhood emissions sticker.

13. Remove the jumper wire and reconnect it to the temperature switch.

14. Recheck the slow idle speed and reset if necessary.

15. Shut off the engine.

16. Reconnect the leads at the generator and A/C compressor.

17. Disconnect and remove the tachometer.

18. If the car is equipped with cruise control, adjust the servo throttle rod to minimum slack, then put the clip in the first free hole closest to the bellcrank or throttle lever.

19. Install the air cleaner assembly.

Engine and Engine Rebuilding

3

UNDERSTANDING THE ENGINE ELECTRICAL SYSTEM

The engine electrical system can be broken down into three separate and distinct systems—(1) the starting system; (2) the charging system; (3) the ignition system.

Battery and Starting System

The battery is the first link in the chain of mechanisms which work together to provide cranking of the automobile engine. In most modern cars, the battery is a lead-acid electro-chemical device consisting of six two-volt (2 V) subsections connected in series so the unit is capable of producing approximately 12 V of electrical pressure. Each subsection, or cell, consists of a series of positive and negative plates held a short distance apart in a solution of sulfuric acid and water. The two types of plates are of dissimilar metals. This causes a chemical reaction to be set up, and it is this reaction which produces current flow from the battery when its positive and negative terminals are connected to an electrical appliance such as a lamp or motor. The continued transfer of electrons would eventually convert the sulfuric acid in the electrolyte to water, and make the two plates identical in chemical composition. As electrical energy is removed from the battery, its voltage output tends to drop. Thus, measuring battery voltage and battery electrolyte composition are two ways of checking the ability of the unit to supply power. During the starting of the engine, electrical energy is removed from the battery. However, if the charging circuit is in good condition and the operating conditions are normal, the power removed from the battery will be replaced by the generator (or alternator) which will force electrons back through the battery, reversing the normal flow, and restoring the battery to its original chemical state.

The battery and starting motor are linked by very heavy electrical cables designed to minimize resistance to the flow of current. Generally, the major power supply cable that leaves the battery goes directly to the starter, while other electrical system needs are supplied by a smaller cable. During the starter operaton, power flows from the battery to the starter and is grounded through the car's frame and the battery's negative ground strap.

The starting motor is a specially designed, direct current electric motor capable of producing a very great amount of power for its size. One thing that allows the motor to produce a great deal of power is its tremendous rotating speed. It drives the engine through a tiny pinion gear (attached to the starter's armature), which drives the very large flywheel ring gear at a greatly reduced speed. Another factor allowing it to produce so much power is that only intermittent operation is required of it. Thus, little allowance for air circulation is required, and the windings can be built into a very small space.

The starter solenoid is a magnetic device which employs the small current supplied by the starting switch circuit of the ignition switch. This magnetic action moves a plunger which mechanically engages the starter and electrically closes the heavy switch which connects it to the battery. The starting switch circuit consists of the starting switch contained within the ignition switch, a transmission neutral safety switch or clutch pedal switch, and the wiring necessary to connect these with the starter solenoid or relay.

A pinion, which is a small gear, is mounted to a one-way drive clutch. This clutch is splined to the starter armature shaft. When the ignition switch is moved to the "start" position, the solenoid plunger slides the pinion toward the flywheel ring gear via a collar and spring. If the teeth on the pinion and flywheel match properly, the pinion will engage the flywheel immediately. If the gear teeth butt one another, the spring will be compressed and will force the gears to mesh as soon as the starter turns far enough to allow them to do so. As the solenoid plunger reaches the end of its travel, it closes the contacts that connect the battery and starter and then the engine is cranked.

As soon as the engine starts, the flywheel ring gear begins turning fast enough to drive the pinion at an extremely high rate of speed. At this point, the one-way clutch begins allowing the pinion to spin faster than the starter shaft so that the starter will not operate at excessive speed. When the ignition switch is released from the starter position, the solenoid is de-energized, and a spring contained within the solenoid assembly pulls the gear out of mesh and interrupts the current flow to the starter.

Some starters employ a separate relay, mounted away from the starter, to switch the motor and solenoid current on and off. The relay thus replaces the solenoid electrical switch, but does not eliminate the need for a solenoid mounted on the starter used to mechanically engage the starter drive gears. The relay is used to reduce the amount of current the starting switch must carry.

The Charging System

The automobile charging system provides electrical power for operation of the vehicle's ignition and starting systems and all the electrical accessories. The battery serves as an electrical surge or storage tank, storing (in chemical form) the energy originally produced by the engine-driven generator. The system also provides a means of regulating generator output to protect the battery from being overcharged and to avoid excessive voltage to the accessories.

The storage battery is a chemical device incorporating parallel lead plates in a tank containing a sulfuric acid-water solution. Adjacent plates are slightly dissimilar, and the chemical reaction of the two dissimilar plates produces electrical energy when the battery is connected to a load such as the starter motor. The chemical reaction is reversible, so that when the generator is producing a voltage (electrical pressure) greater than that produced by the battery, electricity is forced into the battery, and the battery is returned to its fully charged state.

The vehicle's generator is driven mechanically, through V belts, by the engine crankshaft. It consists of two coils of fine wire, one stationary (the "stator"), and one movable (the "rotor"). The rotor may also be known as the "armature," and consists of fine wire wrapped around an iron core which is mounted on a shaft. The electricity which flows through the two coils of wire (provided initially by the battery in some cases) creates an intense magnetic field around both rotor and stator, and the interaction between the two fields creates voltage, allowing the generator to power the accessories and charge the battery.

There are two types of generators; the earlier is the direct current (DC) type. The current produced by the DC generator is generated in the armature and carried off the spinning armature by stationary brushes contacting the commutator. The commutator is a series of smooth metal contact plates on the end of the armature. The commutator plates, which are separated from one another by a very short gap, are connected to the armature circuits so that current will flow in one direction only in the wires carrying the generator output. The generator stator consists of two stationary coils of wire which draw some of the output current of the generator to form a powerful magnetic field and create the interaction of fields which generates the voltage. The generator field is wired in series with the regulator.

Newer automobiles use alternating current generators or "alternators" because they are more efficient, can be rotated at higher speeds, and have fewer brush problems. In an alternator, the field rotates while all the current produced passes only through the stator windings. The brushes bear against continuous slip rings rather than a commutator. This causes the current produced to periodically reverse the direction of its flow. Diodes (electrical one-way switches) block the flow of current from traveling in the wrong direction. A series of diodes is wired together to permit the alternating flow of the stator to be converted to a pulsating, but unidirectional flow at the alternator output. The alternator's field is wired in series with the voltage regulator.

The regulator consists of several circuits. Each circuit had a core, or magnetic coil of wire, which operates a switch. Each switch is connected to ground through one or more resistors. The coil of wire responds directly to system voltage. When the voltage reaches the required level, the magnetic field created by the winding of wire closes the switch and inserts a resistance into the generator field circuit, thus reducing the output. The contacts of the switch cycle open and close many times each second to precisely control voltage.

While alternators are self-limiting as far as maximum current is concerned, DC generators employ a current regulating circuit which responds directly to the total amount of current flowing through the generator circuit rather than to the output voltage. The current regulator is similar to the voltage regulator except that all system current must flow through the energizing coil on its way to the various accessories.

SAFETY PRECAUTIONS

Observing these precautions will ensure safe handling of the electrical system components, and will avoid damage to the vehicle's electrical system:

a. Be *absolutely* sure of the polarity of a booster battery before making connections. Connect the cables positive to positive, and negative to negative. Connect positive cables first and then make the last connection to a ground on the body of the booster vehicle so that arcing cannot ignite hydrogen gas that may have accumulated near the battery. Even momentary connection of a booster battery with the polarity reversed will damage alternator diodes.

b. Disconnect both vehicle battery cables before attempting to charge a battery.

c. Never ground the alternator or generator output or battery terminal. Be cautious when using metal tools around a battery to avoid creating a short circuit between the terminals.

d. Never ground the field circuit between the alternator and regulator.

e. Never run an alternator or generator without load unless the field circuit is disconnected.

f. Never attempt to polarize an alternator.

g. Keep the regulator cover in place when taking voltage and current limiter readings.

h. Use insulated tools when adjusting the regulator.

i. Whenever DC generator-to-regulator wires have been disconnected, the generator *must* be repolarized. To do this with an externally grounded, light duty generator, momentarily place a jumper wire between the battery terminal and the generator terminal of the regulator. With an internally grounded heavy duty unit, disconnect the wire to the regulator field terminal and touch the regulator battery terminal with it.

ENGINE ELECTRICAL

High Energy Ignition (HEI) Distributor

The Delco-Remy High Energy Ignition (HEI) System is a breakerless, pulse triggered, transistor controlled, inductive discharge ignition system available as an option in 1974 and standard in 1975.

There are only nine external electrical connections; the ignition switch feed wire, and the eight spark plug leads. On eight cylinder models through 1977, and all 1978 and later models, the ignition coil is located with the distributor cap, connecting directly to the rotor.

The magnetic pick-up assembly located inside the distributor contains a permanent magnet, a pole piece with internal teeth, and a pick-up coil. When the teeth of the rotating timer core and pole piece align, an induced voltage in the pick-up coil signals the electronic module to open the coil primary circuit. As the primary current decreases, a high voltage is induced in the secondary windings of the ignition coil, directing a spark through the rotor and high voltage leads to fire the spark plugs. The dwell period is automatically controlled by the electronic module and is increased with increasing engine rpm. The HEI System features a longer spark durection which is instrumental in firing lean and EGR diluted fuel/air mixtures. The condenser (capacitor) located within the HEI distributor is provided for noise (static) suppression purposes only and is not a regularly replaced ignition system component.

As already noted in Chapter 2, 1981 models continue to use the HEI distributor although it now incoprorates an Electronic Spark Timing System (for more information on EST, please refer to Chapter 4). With the new EST system, all spark timing changes are performed electronically by the Electronic Control Module (ECM) which moniters information from various engine sensors, computes the desired spark timing and then signals the distributor to change the timing accordingly. Because all timing changes are controlled electronically, no vacuum or mechanical advance systems are used whatsoever.

Distributor

REMOVAL AND INSTALLATION

Points-Type Ignition—1964–74

1. Remove the distributor cap and position it out of the way.

2. Disconnect the primary coil wire and the vacuum advance hose.

3. Scribe a mark on the distributor body and the engine block showing their relationship. Mark the distributor housing to show the direction in which the rotor is pointing. Note the positioning of the vacuum advance unit.

4. Remove the hold-down bolt and clamp and remove the distributor.

To install the distributor with the engine undisturbed:

CAP

CONDENSOR

ROTOR

POINT UNIT

LUBRICATOR

BRACKET

PLATE

PLATE

SPRING

WEIGHT

CAM AND
BREAKER

PIN

MAINSHAFT

SEAL

SCREW

CONTROL

HOUSING

GEAR

Exploded view of the six cylinder points-type distributor

5. Reinsert the distributor into its opening, aligning the previously made marks on the housing and the engine block.

6. The rotor may have to be turned either way a slight amount to align the rotor-to-housing marks.

7. Install the retaining clamp and bolt. Install the distributor cap, primary wire or electrical connector, and the vacuum hose.

8. Start the engine and check the ignition timing.

To install the distributor with the engine disturbed:

9. Turn the engine to bring the No. 1 piston to the top of its compression stroke. This may be determined by inserting a rag into the No. 1 spark plug hole and slowly turning the engine over. When the timing mark on the crankshaft pulley aligns with the 0 on the timing scale and the rag is blown out by compression, the No. 1 piston is at top dead center (TDC).

NOTE: *On Mark IV (big block) V8 engines there is a punch mark on the distributor drive gear which indicates the rotor position. Thus, the distributor may be installed with the cap in place. Align the punch mark 2° clockwise from the No. 1 cap terminal, then rotate the distributor body ⅛ turn counterclockwise and push the distributor down into the block.*

10. Install the distributor to the engine block so that the vacuum advance unit points in the correct direction.

11. Turn the rotor so that it will point to the No. 1 terminal in the cap.

12. Install the distributor into the engine

CAP

ROTOR

RADIO FREQUENCY
INTERFERENCE
SHIELD

WEIGHT SPRINGS

MAINSHAFT

ADVANCE WEIGHTS

CAM WEIGHT
BASE ASSEMBLY

CONDENSER

CONTACT POINT
ASSEMBLY

RETAINING RING

BREAKER PLATE

VACUUM ADVANCE UNIT

FELT WASHER

PLASTIC SEAL

HOUSING

TANGED WASHER

SHIM WASHER

DRIVE GEAR

DRIVE PIN

Exploded view of the V8 points-type distributor

CIRCLIP

POLE PIECE

AMPLIFIER MODULE
CAPACITOR

VACUUM CONTROL UNIT

HOUSING

GASKET

CONNECTOR

GEAR

PIN

WASHER

COVER

LEAD WIRE

COIL

SEAL

CAP

ROTOR

ADVANCE SPRING

Exploded view of the HEI distributor (1981 models have no vacuum advance unit)

block. It may be necessary to turn the rotor a little in either direction in order to engage the gears.

13. Tap the starter a few times to ensure that the oil pump shaft is mated to the distributor shaft.

14. Bring the engine to No. 1 TDC again and check to see that the rotor is indeed pointing toward the No. 1 terminal of the cap.

15. After correct poisitioning is assured, turn the distributor housing so that the points are just opening. Tighten the retaining clamp.

16. Install the cap and primary wire. Check the ignition timing. Install the vacuum hose.

HEI Distributor 1975—and later

1. Disconnect the ground cable from the battery.

2. Tag and disconnect the feed and module terminal connectors from the distributor cap.

3. Disconnect the hose at the vacuum advance (1975–80 only).

4. Depress and release the 4 distributor cap-to-housing retainers and lift off the cap assembly.

5. Using crayon or chalk, make locating marks on the rotor and module and on the distributor housing and engine for installation purposes.

6. Loosen and remove the distributor clamp bolt and clamp, and lift the distributor out of the engine. Nothing the relative position of the rotor and module alignment marks, make a second mark on the rotor to align it with the mark on the module.

7. With a new O-ring on the distributor housing and the second mark on the rotor aligned with the mark on the module, install the distributor, taking care to align the mark on the housing with the one on the engine. It may be necessary to lift the distributor and turn the rotor slightly to align the gears and the oil pump driveshaft.

8. With the respective marks aligned, install the clamp and bolt finger-tight.

9. Install and secure the distributor cap.

10. Connect the feed and module connectors to the distributor cap.

11. Connect a timing light to the engine and plug the vacuum hose.

12. Connect the ground cable to the battery.

13. Start the engine and set the timing.

14. Turn the engine off and tighten the distributor clamp bolt. Disconnect the timing light and unplug and connect the hose to the vacuum advance.

FIRING ORDER

To avoid confusion, replace spark plug wires one at a time.

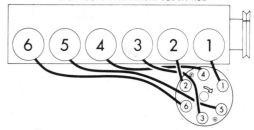

ENGINE FIRING ORDER: 1-5-3-6-2-4
DISTRIBUTOR ROTATION: CLOCKWISE

1964–74 inline six cylinder firing order

ENGINE FIRING ORDER: 1-5-3-6-2-4
DISTRIBUTOR ROTATION: CLOCKWISE

1975–79 inline six cylinder firing order

ENGINE FIRING ORDER: 1-6-5-4-3-2
DISTRIBUTOR ROTATION: CLOCKWISE

1978–79 200 and 1980 and later 229 V6 firing order

ENGINE FIRING ORDER: 1-6-5-4-3-2
DISTRIBUTOR ROTATION: CLOCKWISE

1980 and later 231 V6 firing order

ENGINE FIRING ORDER: 1-8-4-3-6-5-7-2
DISTRIBUTOR ROTATION: CLOCKWISE

1967–74 V8 firing order

ENGINE FIRING ORDER: 1-8-4-3-6-5-7-2
DISTRIBUTOR ROTATION: CLOCKWISE

1975 and later V8 firing order

Alternator

The alternating current generator (alternator) supplies a continuous output of electrical energy at all engine speeds. The alternator generates electrical energy and recharges the battery by supplying it with electrical current. This unit consists of four main asemblies: two end frame assemblies, a rotor assembly, and a stator assembly. The rotor assembly is supported in the drive end frame by a ball bearing and at the other end by a roller bearing. These bearings are lubricated during asembly and require no maintenance. There are six diodes in the end frame assembly. These diodes are electrical check valves that also change the alternating current developed within the stator windings to a direct (DC) current at the output (BAT) terminal. Three of these diodes are negative and are mounted flush with the end frame while the other three are positive and are mounted

into a strip called a heat sink. The positive diodes are easily identified as the ones within small cavities or depressions.

ALTERNATOR PRECAUTIONS

To prevent serious damage to the alternator and the rest of the charging system, the following precautions must be observed:

1. When installing a battery, make sure that the positive cable is connected to the positive terminal and the negative to the negative.

2. When jump-starting the car with another battery, make sure that like terminals are connected. This also applies when using a battery charger.

3. Never operate the alternator with the battery disconnected or otherwise on an uncontrolled open circuit. Double-check to see that all connections are tight.

4. Do not short across or ground any alternator or regulator terminals.

5. Do not try to polarize the alternator.

6. Do not apply full battery voltage to the field (brown) connector.

7. Always disconnect the battery ground cable before disconnecting the alternator lead.

REMOVAL

1. Disconnect the battery ground cable to prevent diode damage.

2. Tag and disconnect the alternator wiring.

3. Remove the alternator brace bolt. If the car is equipped with power steering loosen the pump brace and mount nuts. Detach the drive belt(s).

4. Support the alternator and remove the mount bolt(s). Remove the unit from the vehicle.

INSTALLATION AND BELT ADJUSTMENT

To install, reverse the above removal procedure. Alternator belt tension is quite critical. A belt that is too tight may cause alternator bearing failure; one that is too loose will cause a gradual battery discharge. For details on correct belt adjustment, see "Drive Belts" in Chapter One.

Regulator

The voltage regulator combines with the battery and alternator to comprise the charging system. Just as the name implies, the voltage regulator regulates the alternator voltage output to a safe amount. A properly working regulator prevents excessive voltage from burning out wiring, bulbs, or contact points, and prevents overcharging of the battery. Mechanical adjustments (air gap, point opening) must be

VIEW A

VIEW B

VIEW C

Typical alternator mounting—inline six cylinder (top), V6 and small-block V8 (center) and big-block V8 (bottom)

followed by electrical adjustments and not vice versa.

Since 1973 all GM cars have been equipped with alternators which have built-in solid state voltage regulators. The regulator is in the end frame (inside) of the alternator and requires no adjustment. The following adjustments apply to pre-1973 units.

NOTE: *Although standard since 1973, this integral alternator/regulator has been available as an option since 1969.*

REMOVAL AND INSTALLATION

1. Disconnect the battery ground dable.
2. Disconnect the writing harness from the regulator.
3. Remove the mounting screws and remove the regulator.

Non-integral voltage regulator charging system schematic

Checking the field relay point opening

Integral voltage regulator charging system schematic

4. Make sure that the regulator base basket is in place before installation.

5. Clean the attaching area for proper grounding.

6. Install the regulator. Do not overtighten the mounting screws, as this will cancel the cushioning effect of the rubber grommets.

ADJUSTMENT—1964–72

The standard voltage regulator is the conventional double-contact type; however, an optional transistorized regulator was available from 1964–68. Voltage adjustment procedures are the same for both except for the adjustment points. The double-contact adjustment screw is under the regulator cover (also on the 1964 transistorized regulator); the 1965–68 transistorized regulator is adjusted externally after removing an allen screw from the adjustment hole.

Field Relay Adjustments (Mechanical Adjustment)

As explained earlier, mechanical adjustments must be made first and then followed by electrical adjustments.

Point Opening

Using a feeler gauge, check the point opening as illustrated. To change the opening, carefully bend the armature stop. The point opening for all regulators should be 0.014 in.

Air Gap

Check the air gap with the points just touching. The gap should be 0.067 in. If the point opening setting is correct, then the relay will

Schematic for testing the regulator voltage setting

Checking the air gap on the field relay

Voltage setting adjustment

operate OK even if the air gap is off. To adjust air gap, bend the flat contact spring.

Voltage Adjustment (Electrical Adjustment)

1. Connect a ¼ ohm 25 watt fixed resistor (a knife blade switch using a ¼ ohm resistor) into the charging circuit (as illustrated) at the battery positive terminal. One end of the resistor connects to the battery positive terminal while the other connects to the voltmeter.

2. Operate the engine at 1,500 rpm or more for at least 15 minutes. Disconnect and reconnect the regulator connector and read the voltage on the voltmeter. If the regulator is functioning properly, the reading should be 13.5–15.2V. If the reading is not within this range, keep the engine running at 1,500 rpm and do the following:

a. Disconnect the terminal connector (four terminal connector) and remove the regulator cover. Reconnect the connector and adjust the voltage to 14.2–14.6 by turning the adjusting screw.
CAUTION: *When removing the regulator cover ALWAYS disconnect the connector first*

to prevent regulator damage by short circuits.

b. Disconnect the connector, install the cover, and reconnect the connector.

c. Increase the regulator temperature by running the engine at 1,500 rpm for 10 more minutes.

d. Disconnect and reconnect the connector and read the voltmeter. A reading of 13.5–15.2 indicates a good regulator.

Starter

REMOVAL AND INSTALLATION

NOTE: *The starters on some engines require the addition of shims to provide proper clearance between the starter pinion gear and the flywheel. These shims are available in .015 in. sizes from Pontiac dealers. Flat washers can be used if shims are unavailable.*

1. Disconnect the battery cable.
2. Raise the car to a convenient working height.
3. Disconnect all wiring from the starter solenoid. Replace each nut as the connector is removed, as thread sizes differ from connector to connector. Note or tag the wiring positions for installation.

Chilton Time Saver

Starter removal on certain models may necessitate the removal of the frame support. This support runs from the corner of the frame to the front crossmember. To remove:
1. Loosen the mounting bolt that attaches the support to the corner of the frame.
2. Loosen and remove the mounting bolt that attaches the support to the front crossmember and then swing the support out of the way.
3. Installation is in the reverse order of removal.

---

4. Remove the front bracket from the starter and the two mounting bolts. On engines with a solenoid heat shield, remove the front bracket upper bolt and detach the bracket from the starter.
5. Remove the front bracket bolt or nut. Lower the starter front end first, and then remove the unit from the car.
6. Reverse the removal procedures to install the starter. Torque the two mounting bolts to 25–35 ft. lbs.

SHIMMING THE STARTER

Starter noise during cranking and after the engine fires is often a result of too much or too little distance between the starter pinion gear and the flywheel. A high pitched whine during

1. Frame—commutator end
2. Brush and holder pkg.
3. Brush
4. Brush holder
5. Housing—drive end
6. Frame and field asm.
7. Solenoid switch
8. Armature
9. Drive asm.
10. Plunger
11. Shift lever
12. Plunger return springer
13. Shift lever shaft
14. Lock washer
15. Screw—brush attaching
16. Screw—field lead to switch
17. Screw—switch attaching
18. Washer—brake
19. Thru bolt
20. Bushing—commutator end
21. Bushing—drive end
22. Pinion stop collar
23. Thrust collar
24. Grommet
25. Grommet
26. Plunger pin
27. Pinion stop retainer ring
28. Lever shaft retaining ring

Exploded view of the starter

Cross section of a typical starter

| 1 | USE SHIMS AS REQUIRED |
| 2 | SHIELD |

STARTER NOISE DIAGNOSTIC PROCEDURE

1. STARTER NOISE DURING CRANKING: REMOVE 1 – .015" DOUBLE SHIM OR ADD SINGLE .015" SHIM TO <u>OUTER</u> BOLT ONLY.
2. HIGH PITCHED WHINE AFTER ENGINE FIRES: ADD .015" DOUBLE SHIMS UNTIL NOISE DISAPPEARS.

SEE TEXT FOR COMPLETE PROCEDURE.

Starter motor mounting; V6 at left, diesel at right. Others similar

A .015" SHIM WILL INCREASE THE CLEARANCE APPROXIMATELY .005". MORE THAN ONE SHIM MAY BE REQUIRED.

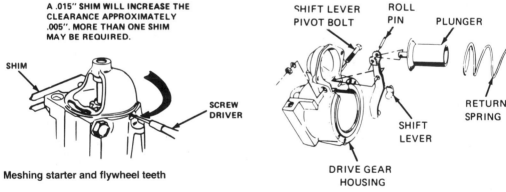

Meshing starter and flywheel teeth

Removing shaft lever and plunger from starter

Flywheel-to-pinion clearance

Starter and drive assembly removed

cranking (before the engine fires) can be caused by the pinion and flywheel being too far apart. Likewise, a whine after the engine starts (as the key is released) is often a result of the pinion-flywheel relationship being too close. In both cases flywheel damage can occur. Shims are available in .015 in. sizes to properly adjust the starter on its mount. You will also need a flywheel turning tool, available at most auto parts stores or from any auto tool store or salesperson.

If your car's starter emits the above noises, follow the shimming procedure below:

1. Disconnect the negative battery cable.
2. Remove the flywheel inspection cover on the bottom of the bellhousing.
3. Using the flywheel turning tool, turn the flywheel and examine the flywheel teeth. If damage is evident, the flywheel should be replaced.
4. Insert a screwdriver into the small hole in the bottom of the starter and move the starter pinion and clutch assembly so the pinion and flywheel teeth mesh. If necessary, rotate the flywheel so that a pinion tooth is directly in the center of the two flywheel teeth and on the centerline of the two gears, as shown in the accompanying illustration.
5. Check the pinion-to-flywheel clearance by using a .020 in. wire gauge (a spark plug wire gauge may work here, or you can make your own). Make sure you center the pinion tooth between the flywheel teeth and the gauge—NOT in the corners, as you may get a false reading. If the clearance is *under* this minimum, shim the starter *away* from the flywheel by adding shim(s) one at a time to the starter mount. Check clearance after adding each shim.
6. If the clearance is a good deal *over* .020 in. (in the vicinity of .050 plus), shim the starter *towards* the flywheel. Broken or severely mangled flywheel teeth are also a good indicator that the clearance here is too great. Shimming the starter towards the flywheel is done by adding shims to the outboard starter mounting pad only. Check the clearance after each shim is added. A shim of .015 in. at this location will decrease the clearance about .010 in.

STARTER OVERHAUL

Drive Replacement

1. Disconnect the field coil straps from the solenoid.
2. Remove the thru-bolts, and separate the commutator end frame, field frame assembly, drive housing, and armature assembly from each other.

NOTE: *On diesel starters, remove the insu-*

Use a piece of pipe to drive the retainer toward the snap-ring

Snap-ring installation

lator from the end frame. The armature on the diesel starter remains in the drive end frame.

On diesel starters, remove the shift lever pivot bolt. On the diesel 25 MT starter only, remove the center bearing screws and remove the drive gear housing from the armature shaft. The shift lever and plunger assembly will now fall away from the starter clutch.

3. Slide the two piece thrust collar off the end of the armature shaft.
4. Slide a suitably sized metal cylinder, such as a standard half-inch pipe coupling, or an old pinion, onto the shaft so that the end of the coupling or pinion butts up against the edge of the pinion retainer:
5. Support the lower end of the armature

securely on a soft surface, such as a wooden block, and tap the end of the coupling or pinion, driving the retainer towards the armature end of the snap ring.

6. Remove the snap ring from the groove in the armature shaft with a pair of pliers. Then, slide the retainer and starter drive from the shaft.

7. To reassemble, lubricate the drive end of the armature shaft with silicone lubricant, and then slide the starter drive onto the shaft *with the pinion facing outward.* Slide the retainer onto the shaft *with the cupped surface facing outward.*

8. Again support the armature on a soft surface, with the pinion at the upper end. Center the snap ring on the top of the shaft (use a new snap ring if the original was damaged during removal). Gently place a block of wood flat on top of the snap ring so as not to move it from a centered position. Tap the wooden block with a hammer in order to force the snap ring around the shaft. Then, slide the ring down into the snap ring groove.

9. Lay the armature down flat on the surface you're working on. Slide the retainer close up on to the shaft and position it and the thrust collar next to the snap ring. Using two pairs of pliers on opposite sides of the shaft, squeeze the thrust collar and the retainer together until the snap ring is forced into the retainer.

10. Lube the drive housing bushing with a silicone lubricant. Then, install the armature and the clutch assembly into the drive housing, engaging the solenoid shift leveryoke with the clutch, and positioning the front of the armature shaft into the bushing.

NOTE: *On non-diesel starters the shift lever may be installed in the drive gear housing first.*

On the 25 MT diesel starter only, install the center bearing screws and the shift lever pivot bolt, and tighten securely.

11. Apply a sealing compound approved for this application onto the drive housing; then position the field frame around the armatures shaft and against the drive housing. *Work slowly and carefully to prevent damaging the starter brushes.*

12. Lubricate the bushing in the commutator end frame with a silicone lubricant, place the leather brake washer onto the armature shaft, and then slide the commutator end frame over the shaft and into position against the field frame. Line up the bolt holes, and then install and tighten the thru-bolts.

13. Reconnect the field coil straps to the "motor" terminal of the solenoid.

NOTE: *If replacement of the starter drive fails to cure improper engagement of starter pinion to flywheel, there are probably defective parts in the solenoid and/or shift lever. The best procedure would probably be to take the assembly to a shop where a pinion clearance check can be made by energizing the solenoid on a test bench. If the pinion clearance is incorrect, disassemble the solenoid and shift lever, inspect, and replace worn parts.*

Brush Replacement

1. Disassemble the starter by following Steps 1 and 2 of the "Drive Replacement" procedure above.

2. Replace the brushes one at a time to avoid having the mark wiring. For each brush; remove the brush holding screw; remove the old brush and position the new brush in the same direction (large end toward center of field frame), position wire connector on top of brush, line up holes, and reinstall screw. Make sure screw is snug enough to ensure good contact.

3. Reassemble starter according to Steps 10–13 above.

Solenoid Replacement

1. Remove the screw and washer from the motor connector strap terminal.

2. Remove the two solenoid retaining screws.

3. Twist the solenoid housing clockwise to remove the flange key from the keyway in the housing. Then remove the housing.

4. To re-install the unit, place the return spring on the plunger and place the solenoid body on the drive housing. Turn counterclockwise to engage the flange key. Place the two retaining screws in position and install the screw and washer which secures the strap terminal. Install the unit on the starter.

ENGINE MECHANICAL

Design

All Chevrolet engines, whether inline sixes (L6), V6 or V8, are water-cooled, overhead valve powerplants. Most engines use cast iron blocks and heads, with the exception of some high-performance 454s, which use aluminum heads.

The crankshaft in the 230 and 250 cu. in. inline six cylinder engines is supported in seven main bearings, with the thrust being taken by the No. 7 bearing. The camshaft is low in the block and is gear-driven. Relatively long pushrods actuate the valves through ball-jointed rocker arms.

The small-block family of V8 engines, which has included the 267, 283, 305, 307, 327, 350 and 400 cu. in. blocks, have all evolved from the design of the 1955 265 cu. in. V8. It was

Battery and Starter Specifications

Year	Engine No. Cyl Displacement (cu in.)	Battery			Starter							Brush Spring Tension (oz)
		Ampere Hour Capacity	Volts	Terminal Grounded	Lock Test		Torque (ft. lbs.)	No-Load Test			
					Amps	Volts		Amps	Volts	RPM	
1964–65	ALL	44	12	Neg	Not Recommended			49–76	10.6	7,800	35
1966–67	6, 8-283	44	12	Neg	Not Recommended			49–76	10.6	7,800	35
	8-327, 396	61	12	Neg	Not Recommended			65–100	10.6	4,200	35
1968–69	6, 8-307	45	12	Neg	Not Recommended			—	10.6	—	35
	8-302, 327, 350, 396	61	12	Neg	Not Recommended			—	9	—	35
1970–71	6, 8-307	45	12	Neg	Not Recommended			50–80	9	5,500–10,500	35
	8-350	61	12	Neg	Not Recommended			55–80	9	3,500–6,000	35
	8-402 (396)	61	12	Neg	Not Recommended			65–95	9	7,500–10,500	35
	8-454	62	12	Neg	Not Recommended			65–95	9	7,500–10,500	35
1972	6-250	45	12	Neg	Not Recommended			50–80	9	5,500–10,500	35
	8-307, 350, 402	61	12	Neg	Not Recommended			50–80 ①	9	5,500–10,500	35
	8-454	76	12	Neg	Not Recommended			65–95	9	7,500–10,500	35
1973	6-250	45	12	Neg	Not Recommended			50–80	9	5,500–10,500	35
	8-307	61	12	Neg	Not Recommended			50–80	9	5,500–10,500	35
	8-350, 454	76	12	Neg	Not Recommended			65–95	9	7,500–10,500	35
1974	6-250	2300 ②	12	Neg	Not Recommended			50–80	9	5,500–10,500	35
	8-350, 400	2900 ②	12	Neg	Not Recommended			65–95	9	7,500–10,500	35
	8-454	3750 ②	12	Neg	Not Recommended			65–95	9	7,500–10,500	35
1975–76	6-250	2500 ②	12	Neg	Not Recommended			50–80	9	5,500–10,500	35
	8-350, 400	3200 ②	12	Neg	Not Recommended			65–95	9	7,500–10,000	35
	8-454	4000 ②	12	Neg	Not Recommended			65–95	9	7,500–10,000	35
1977–78	6-250	275 ③	12	Neg	Not Recommended			50–80	9	5,500–10,500	35
	8-305	350 ③	12	Neg	Not Recommended			50–80	9	5,500–10,500	35
	8-350	350 ③	12	Neg	Not Recommended			65–95	9	7,500–10,500	35

Battery and Starter Specifications (cont.)

Year	Engine No. Cyl Displacement (cu in.)	Battery			Starter							Brush Spring Tension (oz)
		Ampere Hour Capacity	Volts	Terminal Grounded	Lock Test		Torque (ft. lbs.)	No-Load Test			
					Amps	Volts		Amps	Volts	RPM	
1979	6-250	275 ③	12	Neg	Not Recommended			60–88	10.6	6,500–10,100	35
	6-231	350 ③	12	Neg	Not Recommended			50–80	10.6	7,500–11,400	35
	6-200	350 ③	12	Neg	Not Recommended			50–80	10.6	7,500–11,400	35
	8-305	350 ③	12	Neg	Not Recommended			50–80	10.6	7,500–11,400	35
	8-350	350 ③	12	Neg	Not Recommended			65–95	10.6	7,500–10,500	35
1980–81	6-229	350 ③	12	Neg	Not Recommended			50–80	10.6	7,500–11,400	35
	6-231	350 ③	12	Neg	Not Recommended			50–80	10.6	7,500–11,400	35
	8-267	350 ③	12	Neg	Not Recommended			50–80	10.6	7,500–11,400	35
	8-305	350 ③	12	Neg	Not Recommended			50–80	10.6	7,500–11,400	35
1982–84	6-229	350 ③ ④	12	Neg	Not Recommended			60–80	10.6	7,500–11,400	35
	6-231	350 ③ ④	12	Neg	Not Recommended			60–80	10.6	7,500–11,400	35
	6-263	465 ③ ⑥	12	Neg	Not Recommended			160–220	10.6	4,000–5,500	35
	8-267	350 ③	12	Neg	Not Recommended			45–70	10.6	7,500–11,400	35
	8-305	350 ③	12	Neg	Not Recommended			45–70	10.6	7,500–11,400	35
	8-350	465 ③ ⑥	12	Neg	Not Recommended			160–220	10.6	4,000–5,500	35

① 350 & 402 use 454 starter
② Cranking power in watts @ 0°F
③ Cranking power in amps @ 0°F
④ 80 minute reserve capacity
⑤ 75 minute reserve capacity
⑥ 115 minute reserve capacity; 2 batteries used

this engine that introduced the ball-joint type rocker arm design which is now used by many car makers. The Chevrolet-built 229 V6 is also similar.

This line of engines features a great deal of interchangeability, and later parts may be utilized on earlier engines for increased reliability and/or performance. For example, in 1968 the 283 was dropped and replaced by the 307, which is in effect a 327 crankshaft in a 283 block. And the 267, 305 and 350 V8s all share the same stroke crankshaft, bore dimensions being the main difference between the engines.

The 396, 402 and 454 engines are known as the big-blocks, or less frequently, the Mark IV

engines. They were available in the high-performance SS versions of the Chevelle, and feature many tuning modifications such as high-lift camshafts, solid lifters (in some cases), high compression ratios and large carburetors. These big-block engines are similar to their small-block little brothers in basic design.

The 350 V8 diesel is derived from the 350 gasoline engine, except that the cylinder block, cranksahft and main bearings, connecting rods and wrist pins are heavier duty in the diesel (due to the much higher compression ratio). The 263 V6 diesel is nearly a six-cylinder copy of the 350 V8, sharing the same bore and stroke and many engine components. Both V8 and V6

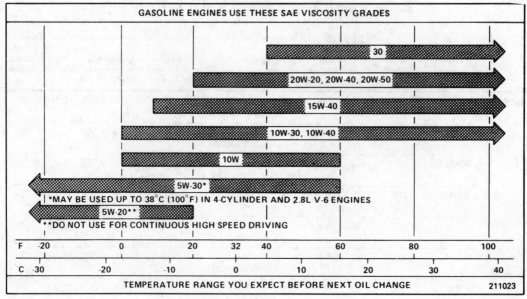

Gasoline engine oil viscosity chart

Diesel oil viscosity chart

Alternator and Regulator Specifications

	Alternator			Regulator					
				Field Relay			Regulator		
Year	Part No. or Manufacturer	Field Current @ 12 V	Output (amps)	Air Gap (in.)	Point Gap (in.)	Volts to Close	Air Gap (in.)	Point Gap (in.)	Volts @ 75°
1964	1100668	1.9–2.3	42	0.15	0.30	2.3–3.7	0.067	0.014	13.5–14.4
	1100669	1.9–2.3	40	0.15	0.30	2.3–3.7	0.067	0.014	13.5–14.4
	1100670	1.9–2.3	37	0.15	0.30	2.3–3.7	0.067	0.014	13.5–14.4
	1117765	3.7–4.4	62	0.15	0.30	2.3–3.7	0.067	0.014	①
1965–67	1100693	2.2–2.6	37	0.15	0.30	2.3–2.7	0.067	0.014	13.5–14.4
	1100695	2.2–2.6	32	0.15	0.30	2.3–2.7	0.067	0.014	13.5–14.4

Alternator and Regulator Specifications (cont.)

Year	Part No. or Manufacturer	Field Current @ 12 V	Output (amps)	Air Gap (in.)	Point Gap (in.)	Volts to Close	Air Gap (in.)	Point Gap (in.)	Volts @ 75°
		Alternator			Field Relay			Regulator	
1965–67	1100794	2.2–2.6	37	0.15	0.30	2.3–2.7	0.067	0.014	13.5–14.4
1968	1100813	2.2–2.6	37	0.15	0.30	2.3–2.7	0.067	0.014	13.5–14.4
	1100693	2.2–2.6	37	0.15	0.30	2.3–2.7	0.067	0.014	13.5–14.4
1969	1100834	2.2–2.6	37	0.15	0.30	2.3–2.7	0.067	0.014	13.5–14.4
	1100836	2.2–2.6	37	0.15	0.30	2.3–2.7	0.067	0.014	13.5–14.4
1970	1100834	2.2–2.6	37	0.15	0.30	2.3–2.7	0.067	0.014	13.5–14.4
	1100837	2.2–2.6	37	0.15	0.30	2.3–2.7	0.067	0.014	13.5–14.4
1971	1100838	2.2–2.6	37	0.15	0.30	2.3–2.7	0.067	0.014	13.5–14.4
	1100839	2.2–2.6	37	0.15	0.30	2.3–2.7	0.067	0.014	13.5–14.4
1972	1100566	2.2–2.6	35	0.15	0.30	1.5–3.2	0.067	0.014	13.8–14.8
	1100917	2.8–3.2	59	0.30	0.30	1.5–3.2	0.067	0.014	13.8–14.8
	1100843	2.8–3.2	58	Integrated with Alternator					13.8–14.8
1973	1100497	2.8–3.2	36	Integrated with Alternator					13.8–14.8
	1100934	2.8–3.2	37	Integrated with Alternator					13.8–14.8
1974	1100934	4–4.5	37	Integrated with Alternator					13.8–14.8
	1102347	4–4.5	61	Integrated with Alternator					13.8–14.8
	1100497	4–4.5	37	Integrated with Alternator					13.8–14.8
	1100573	4–4.5	42	Integrated with Alternator					13.8–14.8
	1100597	4–4.5	61	Integrated with Alternator					13.8–14.8
	1100560	4–4.5	55	Integrated with Alternator					13.8–14.8
	1100575	4–4.5	55	Integrated with Alternator					13.8–14.8
1975	1100497	4–4.5	37	Integrated with Alternator					13.8–14.8
	1102397	4–4.5	37	Integrated with Alternator					13.8–14.8
	1102483	4–4.5	37	Integrated with Alternator					13.8–14.8
	1100560	4–4.5	55	Integrated with Alternator					13.8–14.8
	1100575	4–4.5	55	Integrated with Alternator					13.8–14.8
	1100597	4–4.5	61	Integrated with Alternator					13.8–14.8
	1102347	4–4.5	61	Integrated with Alternator					13.8–14.8
1976–79	1102491	4–4.5	37	Integrated with Alternator					13.8–14.8
	1102480	4–4.5	61	Integrated with Alternator					13.8–14.8
	1102486	4–4.5	61	Integrated with Alternator					13.8–14.8
	1102394	4–4.5	37	Integrated with Alternator					13.8–14.8
1980–81	1103161	4–4.5	37	Integrated with Alternator					13.8–14.8
	1103118	4–4.5	37	Integrated with Alternator					13.8–14.8
	1103043	4–4.5	42	Integrated with Alternator					13.8–14.8
	1103162	4–4.5	37	Integrated with Alternator					13.8–14.8
	1103092	4–4.5	55	Integrated with Alternator					13.8–14.8
	1103088	4–4.5	55	Integrated with Alternator					13.8–14.8

Alternator and Regulator Specifications (cont.)

Year	Part No. or Manufacturer	Field Current @ 12 V	Output (amps)	Field Relay			Regulator		
				Air Gap (in.)	Point Gap (in.)	Volts to Close	Air Gap (in.)	Point Gap (in.)	Volts @ 75°
1980–81	1103100	4–4.5	55	Integrated with Alternator					13.8–14.8
	1103085	4–4.5	55	Integrated with Alternator					13.8–14.8
	1103044	4–4.5	63	Integrated with Alternator					13.8–14.8
	1103091	4–4.5	63	Integrated with Alternator					13.8–14.8
	1103169	4–4.5	63	Integrated with Alternator					13.8–14.8
	1103102	4–4.5	63	Integrated with Alternator					13.8–14.8
	1103122	4–4.5	63	Integrated with Alternator					13.8–14.8
	1101044	4–4.5	70	Integrated with Alternator					13.8–14.8
	1101071	4–4.5	70	Integrated with Alternator					13.8–14.8
1982–84	1103161	4–4.5	37	Integrated with Alternator					13.8–14.8
	1103118	4–4.5	37	Integrated with Alternator					13.8–14.8
	1103043	4–4.5	42	Integrated with Alternator					13.8–14.8
	1103162	4–4.5	37	Integrated with Alternator					13.8–14.8
	1103092	4–4.5	55	Integrated with Alternator					13.8–14.8
	1103088	4–4.5	55	Integrated with Alternator					13.8–14.8
	1103100	4–4.5	55	Integrated with Alternator					13.8–14.8
	1103085	4–4.5	55	Integrated with Alternator					13.8–14.8
	1103044	4–4.5	63	Integrated with Alternator					13.8–14.8
	1103091	4–4.5	63	Integrated with Alternator					13.8–14.8
	1103169	4–4.5	63	Integrated with Alternator					13.8–14.8
	1101044	4–4.5	70	Integrated with Alternator					13.8–14.8
	1101066	4–4.5	70	Integrated with Alternator					13.8–14.8
	1101071	4–4.5	70	Integrated with Alternator					13.8–14.8
	1100226	4–4.5	37	Integrated with Alternator					13.8–14.8
	1100246	4–4.5	63	Integrated with Alternator					13.8–14.8
	1100270	4–4.5	78	Integrated with Alternator					13.8–14.8
	1100239	4–4.5	55	Integrated with Alternator					13.8–14.8
	1100247	4–4.5	63	Integrated with Alternator					13.8–14.8
	1100200	4–4.5	78	Integrated with Alternator					13.8–14.8
	1100230	4–4.5	42	Integrated with Alternator					13.8–14.8
	1100260	4–4.5	78	Integrated with Alternator					13.8–14.8
	1100263	4–4.5	78	Integrated with Alternator					13.8–14.8
	1105022	4–4.5	78	Integrated with Alternator					13.8–14.8
	1100237	4–4.5	55	Integrated with Alternator					13.8–14.8
	1100228	4–4.5	37	Integrated with Alternator					13.8–14.8
	1100300	4–4.5	63	Integrated with Alternator					13.8–14.8
	1105041	4–4.5	78	Integrated with Alternator					13.8–14.8

① 13.0–13.6 @ 80°

General Engine Specifications

Year	Engine No. Cyl Displacement (cu in.)	Type Carburetor	Horsepower @ rpm ■	Torque @ rpm (ft. lbs.) ■	Bore and Stroke (in.)	Compression Ratio	Oil Pressure @ 2000 rpm (psi)
1964	6-194	1-bbl	120 @ 4400	177 @ 2400	3.563 x 3.250	8.5:1	35
	6-230	1-bbl	155 @ 4400	215 @ 2000	3.875 x 3.250	8.5:1	35
	6-283	2-bbl	195 @ 4800	285 @ 2800	3.875 x 3.000	9.25:1	35
	8-283	4-bbl	220 @ 4800	295 @ 3200	3.875 x 3.000	9.25:1	35
	8-327	4-bbl	250 @ 4400	350 @ 2800	4.000 x 3.250	10.5:1	35
	8-327	4-bbl	300 @ 5000	360 @ 3200	4.000 x 3.250	10.5:1	35
1965	6-194	1-bbl	120 @ 4400	177 @ 2400	3.563 x 3.250	8.5:1	35
	6-230	1-bbl	140 @ 4400	220 @ 1600	3.875 x 3.250	8.5:1	35
	8-283	2-bbl	195 @ 4800	285 @ 2400	3.875 x 3.000	9.25:1	35
	8-283	4-bbl	220 @ 4800	295 @ 3200	3.875 x 3.000	9.25:1	35
	8-327	4-bbl	250 @ 4400	350 @ 2800	4.001 x 3.250	10.5:1	35
	8-327	4-bbl	300 @ 5000	360 @ 3200	4.001 x 3.250	10.5:1	35
	8-327	4-bbl	350 @ 5800	360 @ 3600	4.001 x 3.250	11.0:1	35
1966	6-194	1-bbl	120 @ 4400	177 @ 2400	3.563 x 3.250	8.5:1	38 ①
	6-230	1-bbl	140 @ 4400	220 @ 1600	3.875 x 3.250	8.5:1	38 ①
	8-283	2-bbl	195 @ 4800	285 @ 2800	3.875 x 3.000	9.25:1	38 ①
	8-283	4-bbl	220 @ 4800	295 @ 3200	3.875 x 3.000	9.25:1	38 ①
	8-327	4-bbl	275 @ 4800	335 @ 2800	4.001 x 3.250	10.5:1	38 ①
	8-327	4-bbl	350 @ 5800	360 @ 3600	4.001 x 3.250	11.0:1	38 ①
	8-396	4-bbl	325 @ 4800	410 @ 3200	4.094 x 3.760	10.25:1	62
	8-396	4-bbl	360 @ 5200	420 @ 3600	4.096 x 3.760	10.25:1	62
	8-396	4-bbl	375 @ 5600	415 @ 3600	4.094 x 3.760	11.0:1	62
1967	6-230	1-bbl	140 @ 4400	220 @ 1600	3.875 x 3.250	8.5:1	38
	6-250	1-bbl	155 @ 4200	235 @ 1600	3.875 x 3.530	8.5:1	38 ①
	8-283	2-bbl	195 @ 4600	285 @ 2400	3.875 x 3.000	9.25:1	38 ①
	8-327	2-bbl	210 @ 4600	320 @ 2400	4.001 x 3.250	8.75:1	38 ①
	8-327	4-bbl	275 @ 4800	355 @ 3200	4.001 x 3.250	10.0:1	38 ①
	8-396	4-bbl	325 @ 4800	410 @ 3200	4.094 x 3.760	10.25:1	57
	8-396	4-bbl	350 @ 5200	415 @ 3400	4.094 x 3.760	10.25:1	57
1968	6-230	1-bbl	145 @ 4400	220 @ 1600	3.875 x 3.250	8.5:1	58
	6-250	1-bbl	155 @ 4200	235 @ 1600	3.875 x 3.530	8.5:1	58
	8-307	2-bbl	200 @ 4600	300 @ 2400	3.875 x 3.250	9.0:1	58
	8-327	2-bbl	210 @ 4600	320 @ 2400	4.001 x 3.250	8.75:1	58
	8-327	4-bbl	275 @ 4800	355 @ 3200	4.001 x 3.250	10.0:1	58
	8-396	4-bbl	325 @ 4800	410 @ 3200	4.094 x 3.760	10.25:1	62
	8-396	4-bbl	350 @ 5200	415 @ 3400	4.094 x 3.760	10.25:1	62
	8-396	4-bbl	375 @ 5600	415 @ 3600	4.094 x 3.760	11.0:1	62
1969	6-230	1-bbl	140 @ 4400	220 @ 1600	3.875 x 3.250	8.5:1	58
	6-250	1-bbl	155 @ 4200	235 @ 1600	3.875 x 3.530	8.5:1	58
	8-307	2-bbl	200 @ 4600	300 @ 2400	3.875 x 3.250	9.0:1	58

General Engine Specifications (cont.)

Year	Engine No. Cyl Displacement (cu in.)	Type Carburetor	Horsepower @ rpm ■	Torque @ rpm (ft. lbs.) ■	Bore and Stroke (in.)	Compression Ratio	Oil Pressure @ 2000 rpm (psi)
1969	8-350	2-bbl	250 @ 4800	345 @ 2800	4.000 x 3.480	9.0:1	62
	8-350	4-bbl	300 @ 4800	380 @ 3200	4.000 x 3.480	10.25:1	62
	8-396	4-bbl	325 @ 4800	410 @ 3200	4.094 x 3.760	10.25:1	62
	8-396	4-bbl	350 @ 5200	415 @ 3400	4.094 x 3.760	10.25:1	62
	8-396	4-bbl	375 @ 5600	415 @ 3600	4.094 x 3.760	11.0:1	62
1970	6-230	1-bbl	140 @ 4400	220 @ 1600	3.875 x 3.250	8.5:1	40
	6-250	1-bbl	155 @ 4200	235 @ 1600	3.875 x 3.530	8.5:1	40
	8-307	2-bbl	200 @ 4600	300 @ 2400	3.875 x 3.250	9.0:1	40
	8-350	2-bbl	250 @ 4800	345 @ 2800	4.000 x 3.480	9.0:1	40
	8-350	4-bbl	300 @ 4800	380 @ 3200	4.000 x 3.480	10.25:1	40
	8-400	2-bbl	265 @ 4400	400 @ 2400	4.125 x 3.760	9.0:1	40
	8-402	4-bbl	330 @ 4800	410 @ 3200	4.126 x 3.760	10.25:1	40
	8-402	4-bbl	350 @ 5200	415 @ 3400	4.126 x 3.760	10.25:1	40
	8-454	4-bbl	360 @ 4400	500 @ 3200	4.251 x 4.000	10.25:1	40
1971	6-250	1-bbl	145 @ 4200	230 @ 1600	3.875 x 3.530	8.5:1	40
	8-307	2-bbl	200 @ 4600	300 @ 2400	3.875 x 3.250	8.5:1	40
	8-350	2-bbl	245 @ 4800	350 @ 2800	4.000 x 3.480	8.5:1	40
	8-350	4-bbl	270 @ 4800	360 @ 3200	4.000 x 3.480	8.5:1	40
	8-350	4-bbl	330 @ 5000	275 @ 5600	4.000 x 3.480	9.0:1	40
	8-402	4-bbl	300 @ 4800	400 @ 3200	4.126 x 3.760	8.5:1	40
	8-454	4-bbl	365 @ 4800	465 @ 3200	4.251 x 4.000	8.5:1	40
	8-454	4-bbl	425 @ 5600	475 @ 4000	4.251 x 4.000	9.0:1	40
1972	6-250	1-bbl	110 @ 3800	185 @ 1600	3.875 x 3.530	8.5:1	40
	8-307	2-bbl	130 @ 4000	230 @ 2400	3.875 x 3.250	8.5:1	40
	8-350	2-bbl	165 @ 4000	280 @ 2400	4.000 x 3.480	8.5:1	40
	8-350	4-bbl	200 @ 4400	300 @ 2800	4.000 x 3.480	8.5:1	40
	8-350	4-bbl	225 @ 5600	280 @ 4000	4.000 x 3.480	9.0:1	40
	8-402	4-bbl	240 @ 4400	345 @ 3200	4.126 x 3.760	8.5:1	40
	8-454	4-bbl	270 @ 4000	390 @ 3200	4.251 x 4.000	8.5:1	40
1973	6-250	1-bbl	100 @ 3800	175 @ 1600	3.875 x 3.530	8.25:1	40
	8-307	2-bbl	115 @ 4000	205 @ 2000	3.875 x 3.250	8.5:1	40
	8-350	2-bbl	145 @ 4000	255 @ 2400	4.000 x 3.480	8.5:1	40
	8-350	4-bbl	175 @ 4400	270 @ 2400	4.000 x 3.480	8.5:1	40
	8-350	4-bbl	245 @ 5200	280 @ 4000	4.000 x 3.480	9.0:1	40
	8-454	4-bbl	245 @ 4000	375 @ 2800	4.251 x 4.000	8.5:1	40
1974	6-250	1-bbl	100 @ 3600	175 @ 1800	3.875 x 3.530	8.25:1	40
	8-350 ②	2-bbl	145 @ 3600	250 @ 2200	4.000 x 3.480	8.5:1	40
	8-350 ③	4-bbl	160 @ 3800	245 @ 2400	4.000 x 3.480	8.5:1	40
	8-350	4-bbl	185 @ 4000	270 @ 2600	4.000 x 3.480	8.5:1	40
	8-400 ②	2-bbl	150 @ 3200	295 @ 2600	4.126 x 3.750	8.5:1	40

General Engine Specifications (cont.)

Year	Engine No. Cyl Displacement (cu in.)	Type Carburetor	Horsepower @ rpm■	Torque @ rpm (ft. lbs.)■	Bore and Stroke (in.)	Compression Ratio	Oil Pressure @ 2000 rpm (psi)
1974	8-400 ③	4-bbl	180 @ 3800	290 @ 2400	4.126 x 3.750	8.5:1	40
	8-454	4-bbl	235 @ 4000	360 @ 2800	4.251 x 4.000	8.25:1	40
1975	6-250	1-bbl	105 @ 3800	185 @ 1200	3.875 x 3.530	8.25:1	40
	8-350 ②	2-bbl	145 @ 3800	250 @ 2200	4.000 x 3.480	8.5:1	40
	8-350 ③	4-bbl	155 @ 3800	250 @ 2400	4.000 x 3.480	8.5:1	40
	8-400	4-bbl	175 @ 3600	305 @ 2000	4.126 x 4.000	8.5:1	40
	8-454 ②	4-bbl	215 @ 4000	350 @ 2400	4.251 x 4.000	8.15:1	40
1976–77	6-250	1-bbl	105 @ 3800	185 @ 1200	3.875 x 3.530	8.25:1	40
	8-305	2-bbl	140 @ 3800	245 @ 2000	3.736 x 3.480	8.5:1	40
	8-350	2-bbl	145 @ 3800	250 @ 2200	4.000 x 3.480	8.5:1	40
	8-350	4-bbl	165 @ 3800	260 @ 2400	4.000 x 3.480	8.5:1	40
	8-400	4-bbl	175 @ 3600	305 @ 2000	4.126 x 4.000	8.5:1	40
1978–79	6-200	2-bbl	95 @ 3800	160 @ 2000	3.500 x 3.480	8.2:1	40
	6-231	2-bbl	105 @ 3400	185 @ 2000	3.800 x 3.400	8.0:1	37
	6-250	1-bbl	110 @ 3800	190 @ 1600	3.875 x 3.530	8.1:1	40
	8-305	4-bbl	155 @ 3800	260 @ 2800	3.736 x 3.480	8.4:1	45
	8-305	2-bbl	145 @ 3800	245 @ 2400	3.736 x 3.480	8.5:1	40
	8-267	2-bbl	125 @ 3800	215 @ 2400	3.500 x 3.480	8.2:1	45
	8-350	4-bbl	170 @ 3800	270 @ 2400	4.000 x 3.480	8.5:1	40
1980	6-229	2-bbl	115 @ 4000	175 @ 2000	3.736 x 3.480	8.6:1	45
	6-231	2-bbl	110 @ 3800	190 @ 1600	3.800 x 3.400	8.0:1	45
	6-231	Turbo	170 @ 4000	265 @ 2400	3.800 x 3.400	8.0:1	37
	8-267	2-bbl	120 @ 3600	215 @ 2000	3.500 x 3.480	8.3:1	45
	8-305	4-bbl	155 @ 4000	240 @ 1600	3.736 x 3.480	8.6:1	45
	8-305 (Calif.)	4-bbl	155 @ 4000	230 @ 2400	3.736 x 3.480	8.6:1	45
1981	6-229	2-bbl	110 @ 4200	170 @ 2000	3.736 x 3.480	8.6:1	45
	6-231	2-bbl	110 @ 3800	190 @ 1600	3.800 x 3.400	8.0:1	45
	6-231	Turbo	170 @ 4000	275 @ 2400	3.800 x 3.400	8.0:1	37
	8-267	2-bbl	115 @ 4000	200 @ 2400	3.500 x 3.480	8.3:1	45
	8-305	4-bbl	150 @ 3800	240 @ 2400	3.736 x 3.480	8.6:1	45
1982–84	6-229	2-bbl	110 @ 4200	170 @ 2000	3.736 x 3.480	8.6:1	45
	6-231	2-bbl	110 @ 3800	190 @ 1600	3.800 x 3.400	8.0:1	45
	6-263	Diesel	85 @ 3600	165 @ 1600	4.057 x 3.385	22.5:1	45 ①
	8-267	2-bbl	115 @ 4000	205 @ 2400	3.50 x 3.48	8.3:1	45
	8-305	4-bbl	145 @ 4000	240 @ 1600	3.736 x 3.480	8.6:1	45
	8-350	Diesel	105 @ 3200	200 @ 1600	4.057 x 3.385	22.5:1	45 ①

■Starting 1972, horsepower and torque are SAE net figures. They are measured at the rear of the transmission with all accessories installed and operating. Since the figures vary when a given engine is installed in different models, some are representative rather than exact.
① Oil pressure at 1500 rpm
② Not available—Calif.
③ Calif. only

Valve Specifications

Year	Engine No. Cyl. Displacement (cu in.)	Seat Angle (deg)	Face Angle (deg)	Spring Test Pressure (lbs @ in.)	Spring Installed Height (in.)	Stem to Guide Clearance (in.)		Stem Diameter (in.)	
						Intake	Exhaust	Intake	Exhaust
1964–65	6-194	46	45	170 @ 1.33	1⅔	0.0010–0.0027	0.0015–0.0033	0.3404–0.3417	0.3410–0.3417
	6-230	46	45	175 @ 1.26	1⅔	0.0010–0.0027	0.0015–0.0033	0.3404–0.3417	0.3410–0.3417
	8-283	46	45	175 @ 1.26	1⅔	0.0010–0.0027	0.0015–0.0033	0.3404–0.3417	0.3410–0.3417
	8-327	46	45	175 @ 1.26	1⅔	0.0010–0.0027	0.0010–0.0027	0.3404–0.3417	0.3410–0.3417
1966	6-194	46	45	60 @ 166	1 21/32	0.0010–0.0037	0.0010–0.0047	0.3414	0.3414
	6-230	46	45	60 @ 166	1 21/32	0.0010–0.0037	0.0010–0.0047	0.3414	0.3414
	8-283	46	45	82 @ 1.66	1 21/32	0.0010–0.0037	0.0010–0.0047	0.3414	0.3414
	8-327	46	45	82 @ 1.66	1 21/32	0.0010–0.0037	0.0010–0.0047	0.3414	0.3414
	8-396 ①	46	45	90 @ 1.88	1⅞	0.0010–0.0037	0.0010–0.0047	0.3414	0.3414
	8-396 ②	46	45	100 @ 1.88	1⅞	0.0010–0.0037	0.0010–0.0047	0.3414	0.3414
1967	6-230	46 ③	45	60 @ 1.66	1 21/32	0.0010–0.0037	0.0015–0.0052	0.3414	0.3414
	6-250	46 ③	45	60 @ 1.66	1 21/32	0.0010–0.0047	0.0015–0.0052	0.3414	0.3414
	8-283	46 ③	45	80 @ 1.70	1 5/32	0.0010–0.0037	0.0010–0.0047	0.3414	0.3414
	8-327	46 ③	45	80 @ 1.70	1 5/32	0.0010–0.0037	0.0010–0.0047	0.3414	0.3414
	8-396 ①	46 ③	45	90 @ 1.88	1⅞	0.0010–0.0035	0.0012–0.0047	0.3717	0.3717
	8-396 ②	46 ③	45	100 @ 1.88	1⅞	0.0010–0.0035	0.0012–0.0047	0.3717	0.3717
1968	6-230	46 ③	45	59 @ 1.66	1 21/32	0.0010–0.0037	0.0015–0.0052	0.3414	0.3414
	6-250	46 ③	45	59 @ 1.66	1 21/32	0.0010–0.0037	0.0015–0.0052	0.3414	0.3414
	8-307	46 ③	45	80 @ 1.70	1 5/32	0.0010–0.0037	0.0010–0.0047	0.3414	0.3414
	8-327	46 ③	45	80 @ 1.70	1 5/32	0.0010–0.0037	0.0010–0.0047	0.3414	0.3414
	8-350	46 ③	45	80 @ 1.70	1 5/32	0.0010–0.0037	0.0010–0.0047	0.3414	0.3414
	8-396	46 ③	45	90 @ 1.88	1⅞	0.0010–0.0035	0.0012–0.0047	0.3719	0.3717
1969	6-230	46 ③	45	59 @ 1.66	1 21/32	0.0010–0.0037	0.0015–0.0052	0.3414	0.3414
	6-250	46 ③	45	59 @ 1.66	1 21/32	0.0010–0.0037	0.0015–0.0052	0.3414	0.3414

	8-307	46③	45	80 @ 1.70	1 23/32	0.0010–0.0037	0.0012–0.0049	0.3414	0.3414
	8-350	46③	45	80 @ 1.70	1 5/32	0.0010–0.0037	0.0010–0.0047	0.3414	0.3414
	8-396 ①	46③	45	90 @ 1.88	1 7/8	0.0010–0.0035	0.0012–0.0047	0.3719	0.3719
	8-396 ④	46③	45	100 @ 1.88	1 7/8	0.0010–0.0035	0.0012–0.0047	0.3719	0.3719
1970	6-230	46③	45	59 @ 1.66	1 21/32	0.0010–0.0037	0.0015–0.0052	0.3414	0.3414
	6-250	46③	45	59 @ 1.66	1 21/32	0.0010–0.0037	0.0015–0.0052	0.3414	0.3414
	8-307	46③	45	80 @ 1.70	1 23/32	0.0010–0.0037	0.0012–0.0049	0.3414	0.3414
	8-350	46③	45	80 @ 1.70	1 23/32	0.0010–0.0037	0.0012–0.0049	0.3414	0.3414
	8-400	46③	45	80 @ 1.70	1 7/8	0.0010–0.0037	0.0012–0.0047	0.3414	0.3414
	8-402	46③	45	75 @ 1.88 ⑤	1 7/8	0.0010–0.0037	0.0012–0.0047	0.3717	0.3719
	8-454	46④	45	75 @ 1.88 ⑤	1 7/8	0.0010–0.0037	0.0012–0.0047	0.3719	0.3717
1971	6-250	46	45	60 @ 1.66	1 21/32	0.0010–0.0037	0.0015–0.0052	0.3414	0.3414
	8-307	46	45	80 @ 1.70	1 23/32	0.0010–0.0037	0.0012–0.0049	0.3414	0.3414
	8-350	46	45	80 @ 1.70	1 23/32	0.0010–0.0037	0.0012–0.0049	0.3414	0.3414
	8-402	46	45	s8175 @ 1.88 ⑤	1 7/8	0.0010–0.0037	0.0012–0.0047	0.3717	0.3719
	8-454	46	45	75 @ 1.88 ⑤	1 7/8	0.0010–0.0037	0.0012–0.0047	0.3717	0.3719
1972	6-250	46	45	60 @ 1.66	1 21/32	0.0010–0.0037	0.0015–0.0052	0.3414	0.3414
	8-307	46	45	80 @ 1.70	1 23/32	0.0010–0.0037	0.0012–0.0049	0.3414	0.3414
	8-350	46	45	80 @ 1.70	1 23/32	0.0010–0.0037	0.0012–0.0049	0.3414	0.3414
	8-402	46	45	75 @ 1.88 ⑤	1 7/8	0.0010–0.0037	0.0012–0.0047	0.3719	0.3719
	8-454	46	45	75 @ 1.88 ⑤	1 7/8	0.0010–0.0037	0.0012–0.0047	0.3717	0.3717
1973	6-250	46	45	60 @ 1.66	1 21/32	0.0010–0.0027	0.0015–0.0032	0.3414	0.3414
	8-307	46	45	80 @ 1.61	1 5/8	0.0010–0.0037	0.0012–0.0047	0.3414	0.3414
	8-350	46	45	80 @ 1.70	1 23/32	0.0012–0.0027	0.0012–0.0029	0.3414	0.3414
	8-454	46	45	80 @ 1.88	1 7/8	0.0010–0.0027	0.0012–0.0027	0.3417	0.3719
1974	6-250	46	45	60 @ 1.66	1 21/32	0.0010–0.0027	0.0012–0.0027	0.3414	0.3414
	8-350	46	45	80 @ 1.70	1 23/32	0.0010–0.0027	0.0010–0.0027	0.3414	0.3414
	8-400	46	45	80 @ 1.70	1 23/32	0.0010–0.0027	0.0010–0.0027	0.3414	0.3414

Valve Specifications (cont.)

Year	Engine No. Cyl. Displacement (cu in.)	Seat Angle (deg)	Face Angle (deg)	Spring Test Pressure (lbs @ in.)	Spring Installed Height (in.)	Stem to Guide Clearance (in.)		Stem Diameter (in.)	
						Intake	Exhaust	Intake	Exhaust
1974	8-454	46	45	80 @ 1.88	1 7/8	0.0010–0.0027	0.0010–0.0027	0.3719	0.3719
1975–77	6-250	46	45	60 @ 1.66	1 21/32	0.0010–0.0027	0.0010–0.0027 ⑥	0.3414	0.3414
	8-305	46	45	80 @ 1.70	1 23/32	0.0010–0.0027	0.0010–0.0027	0.3414	0.3414
	8-350	46	45	80 @ 1.70 ⑦	1 23/32	0.0010–0.0027	0.0010–0.0027	0.3414	0.3414
	8-400	46	45	80 @ 1.70 ⑦	1 23/32	0.0010–0.0027	0.0010–0.0027	0.3414	0.3414
	8-454	46	45	90 @ 1.88	1 7/8	0.0010–0.0027	0.0010–0.0027	0.3719	0.3719
1978–79	6-200	46	45	200 @ 1.25 ⑧	1 23/32 ⑧	0.0010–0.0027	0.0010–0.0027	0.3414	0.3414
	6-231	45	45	168 @ 1.33	1 47/64	0.0015–0.0032	0.0015–0.0032	0.3407	0.3409
	6-250	46	45	175 @ 1.26	1 21/32	0.0010–0.0027	0.0015–0.0032	0.3414	0.3414
	8-267	46	45	200 @ 1.25	1 23/32	0.0010–0.0027	0.0010–0.0027	0.3414	0.3414
	8-305	46	45	200 @ 1.25	1 23/32 ⑧	0.0010–0.0027	0.0010–0.0027	0.3414	0.3414
	8-350	46	45	200 @ 1.25	1 23/32 ⑧	0.0010–0.0027	0.0010–0.0027	0.3414	0.3414
1980–81	6-229	46	45	200 @ 1.25	1 23/32	0.0010–0.0027	0.0010–0.0027	0.3414	0.3414
	6-231	45	45	168 @ 1.33	1 47/64	0.0015–0.0032	0.0015–0.0032	0.3407	0.3409
	8-267	46	45	200 @ 1.25	1 23/32	0.0010–0.0027	0.0010–0.0027	0.3414	0.3414
	8-305	46	45	200 @ 1.25	1 23/32	0.0010–0.0027	0.0010–0.0027	0.3414	0.3414
1982–84	6-229	46	45	200 @ 1.25	1 23/32	0.0010–0.0027	0.0010–0.0027	0.3414	0.3414
	6-231	45	45	168 @ 1.33	1 47/64	0.0015–0.0032	0.0015–0.0032	0.3407	0.3409
	6-263	45	46	189 @ 1.30	1 43/64	0.0010–0.0027	0.0015–0.0032	0.3429	0.3423
	8-267	46	45	200 @ 1.25	1 23/32	0.0010–0.0027	0.0010–0.0027	0.3414	0.3414
	8-305	46	45	200 @ 1.25	1 23/32	0.0010–0.0027	0.0010–0.0027	0.3414	0.3414
	8-350	45	46	189 @ 1.30	1 43/64	0.0010–0.0027	0.0015–0.0032	0.3429	0.3423

① 325 hp
② 360 hp and 375 hp
③ 45° on aluminum heads
④ 350 hp
⑤ Inner spring—30 @ 1.78
⑥ 1976 and later: 0.0015–0.0032
⑦ 80 @ 1.61 for exhaust
⑧ Exhaust valve—1 19/32

Crankshaft and Connecting Rod Specifications
(All measurements are given in in.)

Year	Engine No. Cyl Displacement (cu in.)	Crankshaft				Connecting Rod		
		Main Brg Journal Dia	Main Brg Oil Clearance	Shaft End-Play	Thrust on No.	Journal Diameter	Oil Clearance	Side Clearance
1964	6-194	2.2983–2.2993	0.0008–0.004	0.002–0.006	7	1.999–2.000	0.0007–0.0028	0.008–0.014
	6-230	2.2983–2.2993	0.0008–0.004	0.002–0.006	7	1.999–2.000	0.0007–0.0028	0.008–0.014
	8-283	2.2978–2.2988	0.0008–0.004	0.002–0.006	5	1.999–2.000	0.0007–0.0028	0.008–0.014
1965	6-194	2.2983–2.2993	0.0003–0.0029	0.002–0.006	7	1.999–2.000	0.0007–0.0027	0.009–0.013
	6-230	2.2983–2.2993	0.0003–0.0029	0.002–0.006	7	1.999–2.000	0.0007–0.0027	0.009–0.013
	8-283	2.2978–2.2988	0.0003–0.0029 *	0.002–0.006	5	1.999–2.000	0.0007–0.0027	0.009–0.013
	8-327	2.2978–2.2988	0.0008–0.0034 *	0.002–0.006	5	1.999–2.000	0.0007–0.0027	0.009–0.013
1966	6-194	2.2983–2.2993	0.0003–0.0029	0.002–0.006	7	1.999–2.000	0.0007–0.0027	0.009–0.013
	6-230	2.2983–2.2993	0.0003–0.0029	0.002–0.006	7	1.999–2.000	0.0007–0.0027	0.009–0.013
	8-283	(2)	0.0003–0.0029 (1)	0.003–0.011	5	1.999–2.000	0.0007–0.0028	0.009–0.013
	8-327	(2)	0.0003–0.0034 (1)	0.003–0.011	5	1.999–2.000	0.0007–0.0028	0.009–0.013
	8-396	(3)	(4)	0.006–0.010	5	2.199–2.200	0.0007–0.0028	0.015–0.021
1967	6-230	2.2983–2.2993	0.0003–0.0029	0.002–0.006	7	1.999–2.000	0.0007–0.0027	0.009–0.013
	6-250	2.2983–2.2993	0.0003–0.0029	0.002–0.006	7	1.999–2.000	0.0007–0.0027	0.009–0.013
	8-283	(5)	(7)	0.003–0.011	5	1.999–2.000	0.0007–0.0027	0.009–0.013
	8-327	(5)	(7)	0.003–0.011	5	1.999–2.000	0.0007–0.0028	0.009–0.013
	8-396	(3)	(4)	0.006–0.010	5	2.1999–2.200	0.0007–0.0028	0.015–0.021
1968	6-230	2.2983–2.2993	0.0003–0.0029	0.002–0.006	7	1.999–2.000	0.0007–0.0027	0.009–0.013
	6-250	2.2983–2.2993	0.0003–0.0029	0.002–0.006	7	1.999–2.000	0.0007–0.0027	0.009–0.013
	8-307	2.4484–2.4493 (6)	0.0008–0.002 (8)	0.003–0.011	5	2.099–2.100	0.0007–0.0028	0.009–0.013
	8-327	2.4484–2.4493 (6)	0.0008–0.002 (8)	0.003–0.011	5	2.099–2.100	0.0007–0.0027	0.009–0.013
	8-350	2.4484–2.4493 (6)	0.0008–0.002 (8)	0.003–0.011	5	2.099–2.100	0.0007–0.0028	0.009–0.013
	8-396	(9)	(11)	0.006–0.010	5	2.199–2.200	0.0009–0.0025	0.015–0.021

Crankshaft and Connecting Rod Specifications (cont.)

(All measurements are given in in.)

Year	Engine No. Cyl Displacement (cu in.)	Crankshaft				Connecting Rod		
		Main Brg Journal Dia	Main Brg Oil Clearance	Shaft End-Play	Thrust on No.	Journal Diameter	Oil Clearance	Side Clearance
1968	8-396 (375 HP)	[10]	0.0013–0.0025 [12]	0.006–0.010	5	2.1985–2.1995	0.0014–0.0030	0.019–0.025
1969	6-230	2.2983–2.2993	0.0003–0.0029	0.002–0.006	7	1.999–2.000	0.0007–0.0027	0.009–0.013
	6-250	2.2983–2.2993	0.0003–0.0029	0.002–0.006	7	1.999–2.000	0.0007–0.0027	0.009–0.013
	8-307	2.4479–2.4488	0.0008–0.002 [8]	0.003–0.011	5	2.099–2.100	0.007–0.0027	0.009–0.013
	8-350	2.4479–2.4488	0.0008–0.002 [8]	0.003–0.011	5	2.099–2.100	0.0007–0.0028	0.009–0.013
	8-396	[9]	[11]	0.006–0.010	5	2.199–2.200	0.0009–0.0025	0.015–0.021
	8-396 (375 HP)	[10]	0.0013–0.0025 [12]	0.006–0.010	5	2.1985–2.1995	0.0014–0.0030	0.019–0.025
1970	6-230	2.2983–2.2993	0.0003–0.0029	0.002–0.006	7	1.999–2.000	0.0007–0.0027	0.009–0.013
	6-250	2.2983–2.2993	0.0003–0.0029	0.002–0.006	7	1.999–2.000	0.0007–0.0027	0.009–0.013
	8-307	2.4484–2.4493 [6]	0.0003–0.0015 [13]	0.002–0.006	5	2.099–2.100	0.0007–0.0028	0.008–0.014
	8-350	2.4484–2.4493 [6]	0.0003–0.0015 [13]	0.002–0.006	5	2.099–2.100	0.0007–0.0028	0.008–0.014
	8-400 (Monte Carlo)	2.6584–2.6493 [18]	0.0008–0.0020 [21]	0.002–0.006	5	2.099–2.100	0.0009–0.0025	0.008–0.014
	8-402	2.7487–2.7496 [15]	0.0007–0.0019 [16]	0.006–0.010	5	2.199–2.200	0.0009–0.0025	0.013–0.023
	8-454	2.7485–2.7494 [10]	0.0013–0.0025 [17]	0.006–0.010	5	2.199–2.200	0.0009–0.0025	0.015–0.021
1971	6-250	2.2983–2.2993	0.0003–0.0029	0.002–0.006	7	1.999–2.000	0.0007–0.0027	0.009–0.014
	8-307	2.4484–2.4493 [20]	0.0008–0.0020 [21]	0.002–0.006	5	2.099–2.100	0.0013–0.0035	0.008–0.014
	8-350	2.4484–2.4493 [20]	0.0008–0.0020 [21]	0.002–0.006	5	2.099–2.100	0.0013–0.0035	0.008–0.014
	8-402	2.7487–2.7496 [15]	0.0007–0.0019 [16]	0.006–0.010	5	2.199–2.200	0.0009–0.0025	0.013–0.023
	8-454 (365 HP)	2.7485–2.7494 [10]	0.0013–0.0025 [17]	0.006–0.010	5	2.199–2.200	0.0009–0.0025	0.015–0.021

Year	Engine							
1971	8-454 (425 HP)	2.7481–2.7490 [6]	0.0013–0.0025 [19]	0.006–0.010	5	2.1985–2.1995	0.0009–0.0025	0.019–0.025
1972	6-250	2.2983–2.2993	0.0003–0.0029	0.002–0.006	7	1.999–2.000	0.0007–0.0027	0.009–0.014
	8-307	2.4484–2.4493 [20]	0.0008–0.0020 [21]	0.002–0.006	5	2.099–2.100	0.0013–0.0035	0.008–0.014
	8-350	2.4484–2.4493 [20]	0.0008–0.0020 [21]	0.002–0.006	5	2.099–2.100	0.0013–0.0035	0.008–0.014
	8-402	2.7487–2.7496 [15]	0.0007–0.0019 [16]	0.006–0.010	5	2.199–2.200	0.0009–0.0025	0.013–0.023
	8-454	2.7485–2.7494 [10]	0.0013–0.0025 [17]	0.006–0.010	5	2.199–2.200	0.0009–0.0025	0.015–0.021
1973	6-250	2.3004	0.0003–0.0029	0.002–0.006	7	1.999–2.000	0.0007–0.0027	0.009–0.014
	8-307, 350	2.4502 [22]	0.0008–0.0020 [21]	0.002–0.006	5	2.099–2.100	0.0013–0.0035	0.008–0.014
	8-454	2.7492 [23]	0.0007–0.0019 [24]	0.006–0.010	5	2.199–2.200	0.0009–0.0025	0.015–0.023
1974–77	6-250	2.2988	0.0003–0.0029	0.002–0.006	7	1.9928–2.000	0.0007–0.0027	0.007–0.016
	8-305	2.4489 [26]	[25]	0.002–0.006	5	2.099–2.100	0.0013–0.0035	0.008–0.014
	8-350	2.4489 [26]	[25]	0.002–0.006	5	2.099–2.100	0.0035–0.0035	0.008–0.014
	8-400	2.6489 [27]	0.0008–0.0002 [28]	0.002–0.006	5	2.099–2.100	0.0035–0.0035	0.008–0.014
	8-454	2.7490	0.0013–0.0025 [29]	0.006–0.010	5	2.199–2.200	0.0009–0.0025	0.015–0.021
1978–79	6-200	2.4489	0.0011–0.0023 [30]	0.002–0.006	5	2.0988–2.0998	0.0013–0.0035	0.008–0.014
	6-231	2.4995	0.0004–0.0015	0.004–0.008	2	2.2487–2.2495	0.0005–0.0026	0.006–0.027
	6-250	2.2988	0.0010–0.0024	0.002–0.006	7	1.9980–2.0000	0.0010–0.0026	0.006–0.017
	8-267	2.4489 [31]	0.0020–0.0035 [21]	0.002–0.007	5	2.0978–2.0988	0.0013–0.0035	0.006–0.016
	8-305	2.4489 [31]	0.0011–0.0023 [30]	0.002–0.006	5	2.0988–2.0998	0.0013–0.0035	0.008–0.014
	8-350	2.4489 [31]	0.0011–0.0023 [30]	0.002–0.006	5	2.0988–2.0998	0.0013–0.0035	0.008–0.014
1980–81	6-229	[32]	[33]	0.002–0.006	4	2.0986–2.0998	0.0013–0.0035	0.006–0.014
	6-231	2.4995	0.0004–0.0015	0.004–0.008	2	2.2495–2.2487	0.0005–0.0026	0.006–0.027
	8-267	[32]	[33]	0.002–0.006	5	2.0986–2.0998	0.0013–0.0035	0.006–0.014
	8-305	[32]	[33]	0.002–0.006	5	2.0986–2.0998	0.0013–0.0035	0.006–0.014
1982–84	6-229	[32]	[33]	0.002–0.006	4	2.0986–2.0998	0.0013–0.0035	0.006–0.014
	6-231	2.4995	0.0004–0.0015	0.004–0.008	2	2.2495–2.2487	0.0005–0.0026	0.006–0.027

Crankshaft and Connecting Rod Specifications (cont.)

(All measurements are given in in.)

Year	Engine No. Cyl Displacement (cu in.)	Crankshaft				Journal Diameter	Connecting Rod	
		Main Brg Journal Dia	Main Brg Oil Clearance	Shaft End-Play	Thrust on No.		Oil Clearance	Side Clearance
1982–84	6-263	2.9998	㉞	0.0035–0.0135	3	2.3742–2.375	.0003–.0025	.0082–.0214
	8-267	2.9998 ㉜	㉝	0.002–0.006	5	2.0986–2.0998	0.0013–0.0035	0.006–0.014
	8-305	㉚	㉝	0.002–0.006	5	2.0986–2.0998	0.0013–0.0035	0.006–0.027
	8-350	2.9998	㉟	0.0035–0.0135	3	2.1238–2.1248	0.0005–0.0026	0.006–0.020

* No. 5—0.0010–0.0036
① No. 5—0.0010–0.0036
② No. 1—2.2987–2.29977
  Nos. 2-4—2.2983–2.2993
  No. 5—2.2978–2.2988
③ Nos. 1-2—2.7487–2.7497
  Nos. 3-4—2.7482–2.7492
  No. 5—2.7478–2.7488
④ Nos. 1-2—0.0004–0.002
  Nos. 3-4—0.0009–0.0025
  No. 5—0.0013–0.0029
⑤ No. 1—2.2984–2.2993
  Nos. 2-4—2.2988–2.2993
  No. 5—2.2978–2.2988
⑥ No. 5—2.4478–2.4488
⑦ No. 1—0.0008–0.002
  Nos. 2-4—0.0018–0.002
  No. 5—0.0010–0.0036
⑧ No. 5—0.0018–0.0034
⑨ Nos. 1-2—2.7484–2.7493
  Nos. 3-4—2.7481–2.7490
  No. 5—2.7478–2.7488
⑩ No. 1—2.7484–2.7493
  Nos. 2-4—2.7481–2.7490
  No. 5—2.7478–2.7488

⑪ Nos. 1-2—0.0010–0.0022
  Nos. 3-4—0.0013–0.0025
  No. 5—0.0015–0.0031
⑫ No. 5—0.0015–0.0031
⑬ Nos. 2-4—0.0006–0.0018
  No. 5—0.0008–0.0023
⑭ Nos. 3-4—2.7481–2.7490
  No. 5—2.7473–2.7483
⑮ Nos. 1-2—0.0004–0.002
  Nos. 3-4—0.0013–0.0025
  No. 5—0.0019–0.0025
⑯ Nos. 2-4—0.0013–0.0025
  No. 5—0.0019–0.0025
⑰ Nos. 5—0.0024–0.0040
⑱ No. 5—2.6479–2.6488
⑲ No. 5—0.0029–0.0045
⑳ Nos. 2-4—2.4481–2.4490
  No. 5—2.4479–2.4488
㉑ Nos. 2-4—0.0011–0.0023
  No. 5—0.0017–0.0033
㉒ No. 5—2.4508
㉓ Nos. 2-4—2.7504
  No. 5—2.7499
㉔ Nos. 2-4—0.0013–0.0028
  No. 5—0.0019–0.0035

㉕ w/Auto trans.—No. 1—0.0019–0.0031
  Nos. 2-4—0.0013–0.0025
  No. 5—0.0023–0.0033
㉖ Nos. 2-4—2.4486
  No. 5—2.4485
㉗ No. 5—2.6485
㉘ Nos. 2-4—0.001–0.0023
  No. 5—0.0017–0.0033
㉙ No. 5—0.0024–0.0070
㉚ No. 1—0.0008–0.0020
㉛ Nos. 2-4—2.4486
  No. 5—2.4485
㉜ No. 1—2.4484–2.4493
  Nos. 2,3,4—2.4481–2.4490
  No. 5—2.4479–2.4488
㉝ No. 1—.0008–.0020
  Nos. 2-4—.0011–.0023
  No. 5—.0017–.0032
㉞ Nos. 1,2,3—.0005–.0021
  No. 4—.0020–.0034
㉟ Nos. 1,2,3—.0005–.0021
  No. 4—.0015–.0031

Ring Gap

Year	Engine	Top Compression	Bottom Compression	Year	Engine	Oil Control
1964	All engines	0.010–0.020	0.010–0.020	1964–65	All engines	0.015–0.055
1965	6-194, 230	0.010–0.020	0.010–0.020	1966–77	All engines	0.015–0.055
1965	8-283, 327	0.013–0.023	0.013–0.028	1966–69	8-396	0.010–0.030
1966–75	6-194, 230, 250, 8-283, 307, 396, 400, 402, 454	0.010–0.020	0.010–0.020	1978–84	6-231	0.015–0.035
1966–69	8-327	0.013–0.023 ①	0.013–0.025 ①	1978–79	6-200	0.010–0.030
1968	8-350	0.010–0.020	0.013–0.023	1978–80	8-350	0.015–0.055
1969	8-350	0.013–0.023 ②	0.013–0.025 ②	1978–84	6-229 8-267, 305	0.015–0.055
1970–72	8-350	0.010–0.020 ②	0.013–0.025 ②	1982–84	6-262 8-350	0.015–0.055
1973–75	8-350	0.010–0.020	0.013–0.025			
1976–77	8-305	0.010–0.020	0.010–0.025			
	8-350 2-bbl	0.010–0.020	0.010–0.020			
	8-350 4-bbl	0.010–0.020	0.013–0.025			
1978	6-200 8-305, 350	0.010–0.020	0.010–0.025			
1978–84	6-231	0.010–0.020	0.010–0.020			
1979–84	6-229 8-267	0.010–0.020	0.010–0.025			
1979	6-200	0.010–0.020	0.010–0.020			
1979–84	8-305, 350	0.010–0.020	0.010–0.025			
1982–84	6-263 8-350 ③	0.015–0.025	0.015–0.025			

① 325, 350 hp Top 0.010–0.020 2nd 0.013–0.023   ② 225, 330, 350, 370 hp Top 0.010–0.020 2nd 0.013–0.023   ③ Diesel engines

Ring Side Clearance

Year	Engine	Top Compression	Bottom Compression	Year	Engine	Oil Control
1964–65	All engines	0.0012–0.0027	0.0012–0.0032	1964–65 1965	All engines 8-327, 350 hp	0.0000–0.0050 0.0012–0.0050
1966–72	6-194, 230, 8-283, 307, 327, 400	0.0012–0.0027 ③	0.0012–0.0032 ③	1966–77	6-194, 230, 250 8-283, 305, 307, 327, 350, 400	0.0000–0.0050
1966–67	8-396	0.0012–0.0032	0.0012–0.0032	1966–67	8-396	0.0012–0.0060
1968–69	8-396	0.0017–0.0032	0.0017–0.0032	1968–77	8-396, 402, 454	0.0005–0.0065
1967	6-250	0.0020–0.0035	0.0020–0.0040	1978–84	6-200, 229 8-267, 305, 350	0.002–0.007

Ring Side Clearance (cont.)

Year	Engine	Top Compression	Bottom Compression	Year	Engine	Oil Control
1968–77	6-250	0.0012–0.0027	0.0012–0.0032	1978–84	6-231	0.0035 Max
1967–75	8-305, 350	0.0012–0.0032 ①	0.0012–0.0027 ②	1982–84	6-262 8-350 ④	0.0010–0.0050
1970–77	8-402, 454	0.0017–0.0032	0.0017–0.0032			
1978–79	6-200	0.0012–0.0032	0.0012–0.0032			
1978–84	6-229 8-267, 305, 350	0.0012–0.0032	0.0012–0.0032			
1978–84	6-231	0.0030–0.0050	0.0030–0.0050			
1982–84	6-263 8-350 ④	0.0050–0.0070	0.0030–0.0050 ⑤			

① 0.0012–0.0027 on 1975 2-bbl 350
② 165, 245, 250 hp 350 cu in. engine 0.0012–0.0032
③ 330 hp 400 cu in. engine
Top 0.0017–0.0032

2nd 0.0017–0.0032
④ Diesel engines
⑤ 0.0018–0.0038 on 350 Diesel

Torque Specifications

Year	Model	Cylinder Head Bolts (ft. lbs.)	Rod Bearing Bolts (ft. lbs)	Main Bearing Bolts (ft. lbs.)	Crankshaft Pulley Bolt (ft. lbs.)	Flywheel to Crankshaft Bolts (ft. lbs.)	Manifold (ft. lbs.) Intake	Manifold (ft. lbs.) Exhaust
1964–65	All 6 cyl.	90–95	35–40	60–70	Press Fit	50–65	25–30	15–20
1964–65	All 8 cyl.	60–70	30–35	60–80	Press Fit	55–65	25–35	25–35
1966–75	All 6 cyl.	95	35	65	—	60	30 ⑧	25 ⑦
1966–67	8-283, 327	60–70	35	80	60 ⑥	60	30	20
1968–77	8-305, 307, 327, 350, 500	60–70	45	75 ② ⑨	60 ⑥	60	30	⑤
1966–77	8-396, 402	80 ①	50	105 ③	85 ⑥	65	30	30
	8-427, 454	80 ①	50 ④	105 ③	85	65	30	30
1978–84	6-200, 229 8-267, 305, 350	65	45	70	60	60	30	20 ⑩
1978–84	6-231	80	40	100	175	60	45	25
1982–84	6-263 ⑭	⑪	42	89	⑫	57	41 ⑬	29
1982–84	8-350 ⑭	180 ⑬	57	163	⑮	81	54 ⑬	34

① Aluminum Heads—Short bolts 65, Long bolts 75
② Engines with 4-bolt mains—Outer bolts 65
③ 1966–68 2-bolt mains 95
   1966–67 4-bolt mains 115
④ 7/16 Rod bolts—70
⑤ Center bolts—25–30, end bolts 15–20
⑥ Where applicable
⑦ Exhaust-to-intake
⑧ Manifold-to-head
⑨ 70 starting 1976

⑩ Inside bolts on 350—30 ft lbs
⑪ All bolts except Nos. 5, 6, 11, 12, 13, 14: 142 ft. lbs.
   Nos. 5, 6, 11, 12, 13, 14: 59 ft. lbs.
⑫ Pulley-to-balancer bolts, 30 ft. lbs.
   Balancer-to-crankshaft bolt, 160–350 ft. lbs.
⑬ Dip bolts in engine oil before torquing
⑭ Diesel engine
⑮ Pulley-to-balancer bolts, 27 ft. lbs.
   Balancer-to-crankshaft bolt, 271–420 ft. lbs.

Piston Clearance

Year	Engine No. Cyl Displacement (cu in.)	Piston to Bore Clearance (in.)
1967–68	6-230	0.0005–0.0011
	6-250	0.0005–0.0011
	8-283	0.0024–0.0030
	8-327	0.0005–0.0011
	8-396	0.0007–0.0013
	8-396 ⑤	0.0036–0.0047
1969	6-230	0.005–0.0015
	6-250	0.005–0.0015
	8-307	0.0005–0.0011
	8-327	0.0005–0.0011
	8-350	0.0005–0.0011
	8-350 ⑤	0.0026–0.0030
	8-396	0.0010–0.0018
	8-396 ⑤	0.0036–0.0044
1970	6-230	0.0005–0.0015
	6-250	0.0005–0.0015
	8-307	0.0005–0.0011
	8-350	0.0007–0.0013
	8-350 ⑤	0.0036–0.0042
	8-396	0.0018–0.0026
	8-396 ⑤	0.0036–0.0046
	8-400	0.0034
	8-402	0.0038
	8-454	0.0049
1971–72	6-250	0.0005–0.0015
	8-307	0.0005–0.0011
	8-350	0.0007–0.0013
	8-350 ④	0.0036–0.0042
	8-402	0.0018–0.0026
	8-454	0.0049
	8-454 ⑥	0.0065
1973	6-250	0.0005–0.0015
	8-307	0.0005–0.0011
	8-350	0.0007–0.0013
	8-350 ④	0.0036–0.0042
	8-454	0.0035
1974–75	6-250	0.0005–0.0015
	8-350 ②	0.0005–0.0011
	8-350 ③	0.0007–0.0013

Piston Clearance (cont.)

Year	Engine No. Cyl Displacement (cu in.)	Piston to Bore Clearance (in.)
1974–75	8-400	0.0034
	8-454	0.0035
1976–79	6-200	0.0007–0.0017
	6-231	0.0008–0.0020
	6-250	0.0010–0.0020
	8-267	0.0007–0.0017
	8-305	0.0007–0.0017
	8-305	0.0007–0.0017
	8-400	0.0034
1980–84	6-229	0.0007–0.0017
	6-231	0.0008–0.0020
	6-263 ⑦	0.0035–0.0045
	8-267	0.0007–0.0017
	8-305	0.0007–0.0017
	8-350 ⑦	0.005–0.006

② 2 bbl carb ⑤ 11:1 compression
③ 4 bbl carb ⑥ 425 hp—1971
④ 9:1 compression ⑦ Diesel engine

diesel cylinder heads, intake manifold, ignition and fuel systems are also different from their gasoline engine counterparts. Aircraft-type hydraulic roller valve lifters are used in the diesels.

The Buick-built 231 V6 is the only engine used in the mid-size Chevrolets which is substantially different. This engine follows Buick V8 practice in that its valve gear incorporates rocker shafts instead of the ball-joint style rockers on the other engines.

Engine Removal and Installation

The factory recommended procedure for engine removal is to remove the engine/transmission as a unit and then separate them outside of the car. In the process of removing the engine you will come across a number of steps which call for the removal of a separate component or system, i.e. "Disconnect the exhaust system" or "Remove the radiator." In all of these instances, a detailed removal procedure can be found elsewhere in the chapter, or in some cases, in another chapter which deals with the specific component in question.

1. Remove the hood. Scribe lines around the hinges so that the hood can be installed in its original location.

(59 LB. FT.)

48 LB. FT.

59 LB. FT.

FRONT OF CAR

FRONT OF CAR

29 LB. FT.

(RT SIDE ONLY)

29 LB. FT.

(LT SIDE)

Engine mounting, all models similar

2. Remove the air cleaner.
3. Disconnect the battery cables at the battery.
4. Remove the radiator and shroud.
5. Remove the fan blade and pulley.
6. Disconnect and label wires at:
   a. C.E.C. solenoid
   b. Coil.
   c. Temperature switch.
   d. Alternator.
   e. Starter solenoid.
   f. Oil pressure sending unit.
7. Disconnect:
   a. Accelerator linkage at the pedal.
   b. Oil pressure gauge line, if so equipped.
   c. Exhaust pipes at the manifold flanges.
   d. Engine cooler lines, if so equiped.
   e. Vacuum line to the power brake unit, if so equipped.
   f. Fuel line (front tank) at the fuel pump.

TRANSMISSION

FRONT OF CAR

SHIM

TRANSMISSION MOUNT

WASHER

SPACER

(40 FT. LBS.)

(40 FT. LBS.)

TRANSMISSION SUPPORT

Rear engine mounts on some engines are shimmed

ENGINE OVERHAUL

Most engine overhaul procedures are fairly standard. In addition to specific parts replacement procedures and complete specifications for your individual engine, this chapter also is a guide to accepted rebuilding procedures. Examples of standard rebuilding practice are shown and should be used along with specific details concerning your particular engine.

Competent and accurate machine shop services will ensure maximum performance, reliability and engine life. Procedures marked with the symbol shown above should be performed by a competent machine shop, and are provided so that you will be familiar with the procedures necessary to a successful overhaul.

In most instances it is more profitable for the do-it-yourself mechanic to remove, clean and inspect the component, buy the necessary parts and deliver these to a shop for actual machine work.

On the other hand, much of the rebuilding work (crankshaft, block, bearings, pistons, rods, and other components) is well within the scope of the do-it-yourself mechanic.

Tools

The tools required for an engine overhaul or parts replacement will depend on the depth of your involvement. With a few exceptions, they will be the tools found in a mechanic's tool kit (see Chapter 1). More in-depth work will require any or all of the following:
- a dial indicator (reading in thousandths) mounted on a universal base
- micrometers and telescope gauges
- jaw and screw-type pullers
- scraper
- valve spring compressor
- ring groove cleaner
- piston ring expander and compressor
- ridge reamer
- cylinder hone or glaze breaker
- Plastigage®
- engine stand

Use of most of these tools is illustrated in this chapter. Many can be rented for a one-time use from a local parts jobber or tool supply house specializing in automotive work.

Occasionally, the use of special tools is called for. See the information on Special Tools and the Safety Notice in the front of this book before substituting another tool.

Inspection Techniques

Procedures and specifications are given in this chapter for inspecting, cleaning and assessing the wear limits of most major components. Other procedures such as Magnaflux and Zyglo can be used to locate material flaws and stress cracks. Magnaflux is a magnetic process applicable only to ferrous materials. The Zyglo process coats the material with a flourescent dye penetrant and can be used on any material. Check for suspected surface cracks can be more readily made using spot check dye. The dye is sprayed onto the suspected area, wiped off and the area sprayed with a developer. Cracks will show up brightly.

Overhaul Tips

Aluminum has become extremely popular for use in engines, due to its low weight. Observe the following precautions when handling aluminum parts:
- Never hot tank aluminum parts (the caustic hot-tank solution will eat the aluminum)
- Remove all aluminum parts (identification tag, etc.) from engine parts prior to hot-tanking.
- Always coat threads lightly with engine oil or anti-seize compounds before installation, to prevent seizure.
- Never over-torque bolts or spark plugs, especially in aluminum threads.

Stripped threads in any component can be repaired using any of several commercial repair kits (Heli-Coil, Microdot, Keenserts, etc.)

When assembling the engine, any parts that will be in frictional contact must be pre-lubed to provide lubrication at initial start-up. Any product specifically formulated for this purpose can be used, but engine oil is not recommended as a pre-lube.

When semi-permanent (locked, but removable) installation of bolts or nuts is desired, threads should be cleaned and coated with Loctite® or other similar, commercial non-hardening sealant.

Repairing Damaged Threads

Several methods of repairing damaged threads are available. Heli-Coil® (shown here), Keenserts® and Microdot® are among the most widely used. All involve basically the same principle—drilling out stripped threads, tapping the hole and installing a prewound insert—making welding, plugging and oversize fasteners unnecessary.

Two types of thread repair inserts are usually supplied—a standard type for most Inch Coarse, Inch Fine, Metric Coarse and Metric Fine thread sizes and a spark plug type to fit most spark plug port sizes. Consult the individual manufacturer's catalog to determine exact applications. Typical thread repair kits will contain a selection of prewound threaded inserts, a tap (corresponding to the outside diameter threads of the insert) and an installation tool. Spark plug inserts usually differ because they require a tap equipped with pilot threads and a combined reamer/tap section. Most manufacturers also supply blister-packed thread repair inserts separately in addition to a master kit containing a variety of taps and inserts plus installation tools.

Damaged bolt holes can be repaired with thread repair inserts

Standard thread repair insert (left) and spark plug thread insert (right)

Before effecting a repair to a threaded hole, remove any snapped, broken or damaged bolts or studs. Penetrating oil can be used to free frozen threads; the offending item can be removed with locking pliers or with a screw or stud extractor. After the hole is clear, the thread can be repaired, as follows:

Drill out the damaged threads with specified drill. Drill completely through the hole or to the bottom of a blind hole

With the tap supplied, tap the hole to receive the thread insert. Keep the tap well oiled and back it out frequently to avoid clogging the threads

Screw the threaded insert onto the installation tool until the tang engages the slot. Screw the insert into the tapped hole until it is ¼–½ turn below the top surface, After installation break off the tang with a hammer and punch

Standard Torque Specifications and Fastener Markings

In the absence of specific torques, the following chart can be used as a guide to the maximum safe torque of a particular size/grade of fastener.
- There is no torque difference for fine or coarse threads.
- Torque values are based on clean, dry threads. Reduce the value by 10% if threads are oiled prior to assembly.
- The torque required for aluminum components or fasteners is considerably less.

U.S. Bolts

SAE Grade Number	1 or 2			5			6 or 7		
Number of lines always 2 less than the grade number.									
Bolt Size (Inches)—(Thread)	Maximum Torque			Maximum Torque			Maximum Torque		
	Ft./Lbs.	Kgm	Nm	Ft./Lbs.	Kgm	Nm	Ft./Lbs.	Kgm	Nm
¼ — 20	5	0.7	6.8	8	1.1	10.8	10	1.4	13.5
— 28	6	0.8	8.1	10	1.4	13.6			
⁵⁄₁₆ — 18	11	1.5	14.9	17	2.3	23.0	19	2.6	25.8
— 24	13	1.8	17.6	19	2.6	25.7			
⅜ — 16	18	2.5	24.4	31	4.3	42.0	34	4.7	46.0
— 24	20	2.75	27.1	35	4.8	47.5			
⁷⁄₁₆ — 14	28	3.8	37.0	49	6.8	66.4	55	7.6	74.5
— 20	30	4.2	40.7	55	7.6	74.5			
½ — 13	39	5.4	52.8	75	10.4	101.7	85	11.75	115.2
— 20	41	5.7	55.6	85	11.7	115.2			
⁹⁄₁₆ — 12	51	7.0	69.2	110	15.2	149.1	120	16.6	162.7
— 18	55	7.6	74.5	120	16.6	162.7			
⅝ — 11	83	11.5	112.5	150	20.7	203.3	167	23.0	226.5
— 18	95	13.1	128.8	170	23.5	230.5			
¾ — 10	105	14.5	142.3	270	37.3	366.0	280	38.7	379.6
— 16	115	15.9	155.9	295	40.8	400.0			
⅞ — 9	160	22.1	216.9	395	54.6	535.5	440	60.9	596.5
— 14	175	24.2	237.2	435	60.1	589.7			
1 — 8	236	32.5	318.6	590	81.6	799.9	660	91.3	894.8
— 14	250	34.6	338.9	660	91.3	849.8			

Metric Bolts

Relative Strength Marking	4.6, 4.8			8.8		
Bolt Markings						
Bolt Size Thread Size x Pitch (mm)	Maximum Torque			Maximum Torque		
	Ft./Lbs.	Kgm	Nm	Ft./Lbs.	Kgm	Nm
6 x 1.0	2–3	.2–.4	3–4	3–6	.4–.8	5–8
8 x 1.25	6–8	.8–1	8–12	9–14	1.2–1.9	13–19
10 x 1.25	12–17	1.5–2.3	16–23	20–29	2.7–4.0	27–39
12 x 1.25	21–32	2.9–4.4	29–43	35–53	4.8–7.3	47–72
14 x 1.5	35–52	4.8–7.1	48–70	57–85	7.8–11.7	77–110
16 x 1.5	51–77	7.0–10.6	67–100	90–120	12.4–16.5	130–160
18 x 1.5	74–110	10.2–15.1	100–150	130–170	17.9–23.4	180–230
20 x 1.5	110–140	15.1–19.3	150–190	190–240	26.2–46.9	160–320
22 x 1.5	150–190	22.0–26.2	200–260	250–320	34.5–44.1	340–430
24 x 1.5	190–240	26.2–46.9	260–320	310–410	42.7–56.5	420–550

g. Hoses at the carbon canister.

8. If the car has air conditioning, unbolt the compressor, leaving the hoses attached. Set the compressor out of the way. *Do not disconnect any air conditioning refrigerant lines unless you are familiar with discharge procedures*. Escaping refrigerant can freeze any surface it contacts, including your skin and eyes.

9. Remove the power steering pump, leaving the hoses attached to the pump. Set the pump aside, out of the way.

10. Raise the car on a hoist.

11. Drain the crankcase.

12. Remove the driveshart.

NOTE: *If a plug for the driveshaft opening in the transmission is not available, drain the transmission.*

13. Disconnect:

a. Shift linkage at the transmission.

b. Speedometer cable at the transmission.

c. Transmission cooler lines, if so equipped.

d. TCS switch at the transmission.

14. On vehicles with manual transmissions, disconnect the clutch linkage at the cross-shaft then remove the cross-shaft at the frame bracket.

15. Lower the vehicle, remove the rocker arm covers and install an engine lifting adapter on the cylinder heads.

16. Raise the engine enough to take the weight off the front mounts, then remove the front mount thru-bolts.

17. Remove the rear mount-to-cross member bolts.

NOTE: *Make sure, on 1977 and later models, that the same number of transmission mount shims are reinstalled. These are used to adjust driveshaft angle.*

18. Raise the engine enough to take the weight off the rear mount, then remove the crossmember.

NOTE: *It is necessary to remove the mount from the transmission before the crossmember can be removed.*

19. Remove the engine/tansmission assembly as a unit.

20. To remove the clutch and manual transmission from the engine:

a. Remove the clutch housing cover plate screws.

b. Remove the clutch housing-to-engine attaching bolts, then, remove the transmission and clutch housing as a unit.

CAUTION: *Do not let the weight of the transmission hang on the spline because the clutch disc may be easily damaged.*

c. Remove the starter and clutch housing rear cover plate.

d. Loosen the clutch mounting bolts one turn at a time (to prevent distortion of the clutch cover) until the spring pressure is released. Remove all the bolts, clutch disc and pressure plate assembly.

21. To remove the automatic transmission:

a. Remove the starter and the converter housing underpan.

b. Remove the flywheel-to-converter attaching bolts.

c. Supporting both the engine and transmission, remove the transmission-to-engine mounting bolts.

d. Slowly guide the engine from the transmission.

To install:

1. Attach the engine to the transmission in the reverse order of removal.

2. Bolt the engine lifting tool to the engine and then lower the engine and the transmission into the chassis as a unit. Guide the engine so as to align the front engine mounts with the mounts on the frame.

3. Install one rear transmission crossmember side bolt, swing the crossmember up under the transmission mount and install the bolt in the opposite side rail.

4. Align and install the rear mount bolts.

5. Install the engine front mount bolts and then remove the lifting tool from the engine.

6. Intallation of the remaining components is in the reverse order of removal.

Cylinder Head
REMOVAL AND INSTALLATION
Inline Six Cylinder 1964–79

1. Drain the cooling system and remove the air cleaner. Disconnect the P.C.V. hose.

2. Disconnect the accelerator pedal rod at the bell crank on the manifold, and the fuel and vacuum lines at the carburetor.

3. Disconnect the exhaust pipe at the manifold flange, then remove the manifold bolts and clamps and remove the manifolds and carburetor as an assembly. There is a ring gasket at the exhaust manifold flange, and a gasket for each of the manifolds at the head. These will have to be replaced. On 1977 and later models with an integral intake manifold, remove the carburetor at the intake manifold, and remove the exhaust manifold.

4. Remove the fuel and vacuum line retaining clip from the water outlet. Then disconnect the wire harness from the heat sending unit and coil, leaving the harness clear of the clips on the rocker arm cover.

5. Disconnect the radiator hose at the water outlet housing and the battery ground strap at the cylinder head.

Cylinder head torque sequence—inline six cylinder

6. Number the spark plug wires, then remove the wires and spark plugs. Disconnect the coil-to-distributor primary wire lead at the coil and remove the coil (except integral coil HEI).

7. Remove the rocker arm cover. Back off the rocker arm nuts, pivot the rocker arms to clear the pushrods and remove the pushrods. Be certain to keep the pushrods in the order in which they came out. They must be returned to their original positions.

NOTE: *1977 and later model sixes do not use a rocker arm cover gasket. RTV sealer is used in its place.*

8. Remove the cylinder head bolts, cylinder head and gasket.

To install:

1. Clean the mating surfaces of the cylinder head and block. Check the cylinder head and block for warpage with a straightedge and feeler gauge. Warpage must not exceed 0.006 in. over a six inch span. If this limit is exceeded, the head or block should be milled flat.

2. Clean the head bolts and the threads in the cylinder block, since dirt will affect torque readings.

3. Install a new head gasket over the dowel pins. Do not use sealer on combination steel/asbestos gaskets.

4. Guide and lower the cylinder head into place over dowels and gasket.

5. Oil the cylinder head bolts, install and run them down snug.

6. Tighten the cylinder head bolts a little at a time with a torque wrench in the correct sequence. Final torque should be 90 to 95 ft. lbs. except for the left front head bolt, which should be torqued to 85 ft. lbs.

7. Install the valve pushrods down through the cylinder head openings and seat them in their lifter sockets.

8. Install the rocker arms, balls and nuts and then tighten the rocker arm nuts until all pushrod play is taken up.

9. Install the thermostat, thermostat housing and water outlet using new gaskets. Then connect the radiator hose.

10. Install the heat sending switch and torque to 15–20 ft. lbs.

11. Clean the spark plugs or install new ones.

12. Install the coil, then connect the heat sending unit and the coil primary wires, and

connect the battery ground cable at the cylinder head.

13. Clean the surfaces of the manifold(s) and install a new gasket or gaskets over the manifold studs. Install the manifold(s). Clean and oil the bolts, then install and torque them in sequence to the specified values. Connect the exhaust pipe to the manifold, using a new ring gasket.

14. Install the carburetor if it was removed, and reconnect the carburetor linkage.

15. Connect the P.C.V., fuel and vacuum lines and then secure the lines in the clip at water outlet.

16. Fill the cooling system and check for leaks.

17. Adjust the valve lash.

18. Install the rocker arm cover and position the wiring harness in the clips.

19. Clean and install the air cleaner.

Gasoline V-6 and V-8 (all but 231 V-6)

1. Drain the coolant. Remove the air cleaner.
2. Disconnect:
   a. Battery
   b. Radiator and heater hose from manifold
   c. Throttle linkage
   d. Fuel line
   e. Coil wires
   f. Temperature sending unit
   g. Power brake hose, distributor vacuum hose, and crankcase vent hoses.
3. Remove:
   a. Distributor, marking position
   b. Alternator upper bracket
   c. Coil and its bracket (where so equipped)
4. On 1977 and later engines, remove all of the following with which the engine is equipped:
   a. Air cleaner bracket
   b. Air pump bracket
   c. Accelerator return spring and bracket

Cylinder head torque sequence—229 V6

Cylinder head torque sequence—small block V8

Cylinder head torque sequence—big-block V8

Cylinder head torque sequence—231 V6

    d. Accelerator bellcrank

5. Remove all manifold attaching bolts, and remove the intake manifold.

6. Disconnect the air manifold and tubes, and spark plug wires, remove the air cleaner preheater and spark plug heat shields, loosen and remove the exhaust manifold flange nuts, then lower the exhaust pipe assembly and hang it from the frame with wire.

7. Remove the manifold end bolts, then the center ones and remove the manifold from the engine.

8. Remove rocker cover(s). Loosen rocker nuts and pivot rockers 90° to permit removal of pushrods. Remove pushrods, marking the location of each.

9. Remove the cylinder head bolts, cylinder head, and gasket.

To install:

1. Inspect the gasket surfaces on the head(s). All surfaces must be clean and free of nicks and burrs. The threads on the bolts and inside the boltholes in the block must be clean. Inspect the head for warpage as described in the engine rebuilding section below.

2. Install, reversing the removal procedures, keeping the following important points in mind:

    a. Tighten the head bolts in several stages, going in the pattern specified in the illustration.

    b. Coat new gaskets (both sides) and headbolts with sealer, unless a combination steel-asbestos gasket is used; in that case, put sealer on the head bolts only, let the gasket dry.

    c. Make sure to relocate the pushrods according to their markings. Adjust the valves according to the procedure labeled "Engine Not Running" before running the engine. Then, readjust the valves with the engine hot and running.

    d. Coat *new* rocker cover gaskets with sealer, and tighten cover bolts to specified torque evenly in several stages.

231 V-6

NOTE: *On vehicles equipped with AIR, disconnect the rubber hose at the injection tubing check valve. This way the tubing will not*

have to be removed from the exhaust manifold.

1. Remove the intake manifold as detailed later in this chapter.

2. When removing the right cylinder head:

    a. Loosen and remove all drive belts.

    b. Tag and disconnect the wires leading from the rear of the alternator.

    c. Remove the air conditioning compressor (if so equipped) and position it out of the way with all the hoses still connected.

    d. Remove the alternator and its mounting bracket.

3. When removing the left cylinder head:

    a. Remove the oil gauge rod.

    b. Remove the power steering pump (if so equipped) and its bracket and then position it out of the way with the hoses still attached.

4. Tag and disconnect the spark plug wires and then remove the spark plug wire clips from the cylinder head cover studs.

5. Remove the exhaust manifold mounting bolts from the head which is being removed, and then pull the manifold away from the head.

6. Use an air hose if available, or a bunch of clean rags and clean the dirt off the head and surrounding areas thoroughly. *It is extremely important to avoid getting dirt into the hydraulic valve lifters.*

7. Remove the cylinder head cover from the top of the head that you wish to remove.

8. Remove the rocker arm and shaft assembly from the cylinder head and then remove the pushrods.

NOTE: *If the valve lifters are to be serviced, remove them at this time. Otherwise, protect the lifters and the camshaft from dust and dirt by covering the entire area with a clean cloth. Whenever the lifters or the pushrods are removed from the head it is always a good idea to place them in a wooden block with numbered holes to keep them identified as to their position in the engine.*

9. Loosen and remove all the cylinder head bolts and then lift off the head.

To install:

1. Clean the engine block gasket surface thoroughly. Make sure that no foreign material has fallen into the cylinder bores, the bolt holes or into the valve lifter area. It is always a good

Cylinder head removal, all engines similar

TORQUE ALL BOLTS (EXCEPT 5, 6, 11, 12, 13 & 14) TO 193 N·m (142 FT. LBS.). NUMBERS 5, 6, 11, 12, 13 & 14 TORQUE TO 80 N·m (59 FT. LBS.).

V6 diesel cylinder head torque sequence

idea to clean out the bolt holes with an air hose if one is available.

2. Install a new head gasket with the bead facing down toward the cylinder block. The dowels in the block will hold the gasket in place.

3. Clean the gasket surface of the cylinder head and carefully set it into place on the dowels in the cylinder block.

4. Use a heavy body thread sealer on all of the head bolts since the bolt holes go all the way through into the coolant.

5. Install the head bolts. Tighten the bolts a little at a time about three times around in the sequence shown in the illustration. Tighten the bolts to a final torque equal to that given in the "Torque Specifications" chart.

6. Installation of the remaining components is in the reverse order of removal.

Diesel Engines

1. Remove the intake manifold, using the procedure outlined above.

2. Remove the rocker arm cover(s), after removing any accessory brackets which interfere with cover removal.

3. Disconnect and label the glow plug wiring.

4. If the right cylinder head is being removed, remove the ground strap from the head.

5. Remove the rocker arm bolts, the bridged pivots, the rocker arms, and the pushrods, keeping all the parts in order so that they can be returned to their original positions. It is a good practice to number or mark the parts to avoid interchanging them.

350 V8 diesel cylinder head torque sequence

6. Remove the fuel return lines from the nozzles.

7. Remove the exhaust manifold(s), using the procedure outlined above.

8. Remove the engine block drain plug on the side of the engine from which the cylinder head is being removed.

9. Remove the head bolts. The V6 diesel has Allen-headed pipe plugs screwed in above the head bolts. These must be removed first. Remove the cylinder head.

10. To install, first clean the mating surfaces thoroughly. Install new head gaskets on the engine block. Do NOT coat the gaskets with any sealer. The gaskets have a special coating that eliminates the need for sealer. *The use of sealer will interfere with this coating and cause leaks.* Install the cylinder head onto the block.

11. Clean the head bolts thoroughly. Dip the bolts in clean engine oil and install into the cylinder block until the heads of the bolts lightly contact the cylinder head.

12. Tighten the bolts, in the sequence illustrated, to 100 ft. lbs. When all bolts have been tightened to this figure, begin the tightening sequence again, and torque all bolts to the specifications listed in the "Torque Specifications" chart.

NOTE: *The V6 diesel has a special torque sequence. Refer to the "Torque Specifications" chart for details.*

13. Install the engine block drain plugs, the exhaust manifolds, the fuel return lines, the glow plug wiring, and the ground strap for the right cylinder head.

14. Install the valve train assembly. Refer to the "Diesel Engine Rocker Arm Replacement" in this chapter for the valve lifter bleeding procedures.

15. Install the intake manifold.

16. Install the valve covers. These are sealed with RTV (Room Temperature Vulcanizing) silicone sealer instead of a gasket. Use GM #1052434 or an equivalent. Install the cover to the head within 10 minutes, while the sealer is still wet.

1. Valve cover	8. Exhaust valve	15. Head gasket
2. Screw reinforcements	9. Intake valve	16. Spark plug
3. Gasket	10. Gasket	17. Cylinder head
4. Adjusting nut	11. Exhaust manifold	18. Pushrod
5. Rocker arm	12. Spark plug shield	19. Spring shield
6. Valve spring retainer	13. Bolt	20. Rocker arm stud
7. Valve spring	14. Washer	21. Rocker arm ball

Exploded view of the big-block cylinder head

1. Rocker arm cover
2. Gasket
3. Nut
4. Ball
5. Rocker arms
6. Rocker arm studs
7. Valve keeper locks
8. O-ring seals
9. Valve spring cap
10. Shield
11. Spring
12. Gasket
13. Bolts
14. Cylinder head
15. Head gasket
16. Exhaust manifold
17. Bolts
18. Spark plug and gasket
19. Intake valve
20. Exhaust valve
21. Hydraulic lifters
22. Push rods
23. Intake manifold gaskets
24. Intake manifold
25. Gasket
26. Thermostat
27. Thermostat housing
28. Gasket
29. Distributor
30. Clamp

Exploded view of the small-block cylinder head

Rocker Arms

REMOVAL AND INSTALLATION

All Gasoline V8s and 229 V6

Rocker arms are removed by removing the adjusting nut. Be sure to adjust the valve lash after replacing the rocker arms. Coat the replacement rocker arm and ball with SAE 90° gear oil before installation. Make sure the valves are closed on the cylinder you are working on before installation.

NOTE: *When replacing an exhaust rocker, move an old intake rocker to the exhaust rocker arm stud and install the new rocker arm on the intake stud. This will prevent burning of the new rocker arm on the exhaust position.*

Rocker arms studs that have damaged threads or are loose in the cylinder heads may be replaced by reaming the bore and installing oversize studs. Oversizes available are .003 and .013 in. The bore may also be tapped and screw-in

Inline six cylinder rocker arm components (V8s similar)

Position of rocker arms on shaft—231 V6

Removing nylon retainers, 231 V6 rocker shafts

studs installed. Several aftermarket companies produce complete rocker arm stud kits with installation tools. Mark IV and late high performance smallblock engines use screw-in studs and pushrod guide plates.

231 V6

1. Remove the rocker arm covers.
2. Remove the rocker arm shaft assembly bolts.
3. Remove the rocker arm shaft assembly.
4. To remove the rocker arms from the shaft, the nylon arm retainers must be re-

231 V6 replacement rocker arm identification

moved. They can be removed with a pair of water pump pliers, or they can be broken by hitting them below the head with a chisel.

5. Remove the rocker arms from the shaft. Make sure you keep them in order. Also note that the external rib on each arm points *away* from the rocker arm shaft bolt located between each pair of rocker arms.

6. If you are installing new rocker arms, note that the replacement rocker arms are marked "R" and "L" for right and left side installation. *Do not* interchange them.

7. Install the rocker arms on the shaft and lubricate them with oil.

8. Center each arm on the ¼ in. hole in the shaft. Install new nylon rocker arm retainers in the holes using a ½ in. drift.

9. Locate the push rods in the rocker arms and insert the shaft bolts. Tighten the bolts a little at a time until they are tight.

10. Install the rocker covers using new gaskets.

350 V8 Diesel

NOTE: *When the diesel engine rocker arms are removed or loosened, the lifters must be bled down to prevent oil pressure buildup inside each lifter, which could cause it to raise up higher than normal and bring the valves within striking distance of the pistons.*

1. Remove the valve cover.

2. Remove the rocker arm pivot bolts, the bridged pivot and rocker arms.

3. Remove each rocker set as a unit.

4. To install, lubricate the pivot wear points and position each set of rocker arms in its proper location. Do not tighten the pivot bolts for fear of bending the pushrods when the engine is turned.

5. The lifters can be bled down for six cylinders at once with the crankshaft in either of the following two positions:

　a. For cylinders number 3, 5, 7, 2, 4 and 8, turn the crankshaft so the saw slot on the harmonic balancer is at 0° on the timing indicator.

　b. For cylinders 1, 3, 7, 2, 4 and 6, turn the crankshaft so the saw slot on the harmonic balancer is at 4 o'clock.

6. Tighten the rocker arm pivot bolts to 28 ft. lbs. It will take 45 minutes to completely bleed down the lifters in this position. If additional lifters must be bled, rotate the engine to the other position, tighten the rocker arm pivot bolts, and again wait 45 minutes before rotating the crankshaft.

7. Assemble the remaining components in the reverse of disassembly. The rocker covers do not use gaskets, but are sealed with a bead of RTV (Room Temperature Vulcanizing) silicone sealer.

263 V6 Diesel

1. Follow the "NOTE" and steps 1 through 3 in the 350 V8 procedure above.

2. Before installing any removed rocker arms, rotate the crankshaft so that No. 1 cylinder is 32° BTDC. This is 50mm (2 in.) counter-clockwise from the 0° pointer on the timing indicator on the front of the engine. If only the right valve cover was removed, remove the glow plug from No. 1 cylinder to determine if the piston is in the correct position. If the left valve cover was removed, rotate the crankshaft until the No. 5 cylinder intake valve pushrod ball is 7.0mm (.28 in.) above the No. 5 cylinder exhaust valve pushrod ball.

CAUTION: *Use only hand wrenches to torque the rocker arm pivot bolts to avoid pushrod damage.*

3. If the No. 5 cylinder pivot and rocker arms were removed, install them. Torque the bolts alternately between the intake and exhaust valves until the intake valve begins to open, then stop.

4. Install the remaining rocker arms except

No. 3 exhaust valve, if this rocker was removed.

5. If removed, install but do not torque the No. 3 valve pivots beyond the point that the valve would be fully open. This is indicated by a strong resistance while still turning the pivot retaining bolts. *Going beyond this will bend the pushrod.* Torque the bolts slowly, allowing the lifter to bleed down.

6. Finish torquing the No. 5 cylinder rocker arm pivot bolt slowly. Do not go beyond the point that the valve would be fully open. This is indicated by a strong resistance while still turning the pivot retaining bolts. *Going beyond this will bend the pushrod.*

7. DO NOT turn the engine crankshaft for at least 45 minutes, allowing the lifters to bleed down. *This is important.*

8. Finish reassembling the engine as the lifters are being bled.

Valve Lash Adjustment

Most engines described in this book use hydraulic lifters, which require no periodic adjustment. In the event of cylinder head removal or any operation that requires disturbing the rocker arms, the rocker arms will have to be adjusted.

1964–71

Normalize the engine temperature by running it for several minutes. Shut the engine off and remove the valve cover(s). After valve cover removal, torque the cylinder heads to specification. The use of oil stopper clips, readily available on the market, is recommended to prevent oil splatter when adjusting valve lash. Restart the engine. Valve lash is set with the engine warm and idling.

Turn the rocker arm nut counterclockwise until the rocker arm begins to clatter. Reverse the direction and turn the rocker arm down slowly until the clatter just stops. This is the

Oil splash stopper clips will prevent splatter when adjusting the valves with the engine running

zero lash position. Turn the nut down an additional ¼ turn and wait ten seconds until the engine runs smoothly. Continue with additional ¼ turns, waiting ten seconds each time, until the nut has been turned down one full turn from the zero lash position. This one turn, pre-load adjustment must be performed to allow the lifter to adjust itself and prevents possible interference between the valves and pistons. Noisy lifters should be cleaned or replaced.

1972 and Later

1. Remove the rocker covers and gaskets.
2. Adjust the valves on inline six cylinder engines as follows:

   a. Mark the distributor housing with a piece of chalk at the No. 1 and 6 plug wire positions. Remove the distributor cap with the plug wires attached.

   b. Crank the engine until the distributor rotor points to the No. 1 cylinder and the No. 1 piston is at TDC (both No. 1 cylinder valves closed). At this point, adjust the following valves:

     • No. 1—Exhaust and Intake
     • No. 2—Intake
     • No. 3—Exhaust
     • No. 4—Intake
     • No. 5—Exhaust

   c. Back out the adjusting nut until lash is felt at the pushrod, then turn the adjusting nut in until all lash is removed. This can be determined by checking pushrod end-play while turning the adjusting nut. When all play has been removed, turn the adjusting nut in 1 full turn.

   d. Crank the engine until the distributor rotor points to the No. 6 cylinder and the No. 6 piston is at TDC (both No. 6 cylinder valves closed). The following valves can be adjusted:

     • No. 2—Exhaust
     • No. 3—Intake
     • No. 4—Exhaust
     • No. 5—Intake
     • No. 6—Intake and Exhaust

3. Adjust the valves on V8 and V6 engines as follows:

   a. Crank the engine until the mark on the damper aligns with the TDC or 0° mark on the timing tab and the engine is in the No. 1 firing position. This can be determined by placing the fingers on the No. 1 cylinder valves as the marks align. If the valves do not move, it is in the No. 1 firing position. If the valves move, it is in the No. 6 firing position (No. 4 on V6) and the crankshaft should be rotated one more revolution to the No. 1 firing position.

Inline six cylinder valve adjustment (V6's and V8's similar)

Valve arrangement, Chevrolet small-block V8

Valve arrangement, 263 V6 diesel

   b. The adjustment is made in the same manner as 6 cylinder engines.

   c. With the engine in the No. 1 firing position, the following valves can be adjusted:

     • V8-Exhaust—1,3,4,8
     • V8-Intake—1,2,5,7
     • V6-Exhaust—1,5,6
     • V6-Intake—1,2,3

   d. Crank the engine 1 full revolution until the marks are again in alignment. This is the No. 6 firing position (No. 4 on V6). The following valves can now be adjusted:

Diesel V8 valve arrangement

FRONT | E I I E E I I E E I I E

Inline six cylinder valve arrangement

FRONT

Big-block V8 valve arrangement

- V8-Exhaust—2,5,6,7
- V8-Intake—3,4,6,8
- V6-Exhaust—2,3,4
- V6-Intake—4,5,6

4. Reinstall the rocker arm covers using new gaskets or sealer.

5. Install the distributor cap and wire assembly.

6. Adjust the carburetor idle speed.

Intake Manifold
REMOVAL AND INSTALLATION
Inline Six Cylinder

NOTE: *1975 and later L6 engines are equipped with an intake manifold which is integral with the cylinder head.*

1. Remove the air cleaner.

2. Disconnect the throttle rods at the bellcrank and remove the throttle return spring.

3. Disconnect the fuel and vacuum lines from the carburetor.

4. Disconnect the crankcase ventilation hose from the valve cover and the evaporation control hose from the carbon canister.

5. Disconnect the exhaust pipe from the manifold and throw away the packing.

6. Remove the manifold assembly and scrape off the gaskets.

7. Check the condition of the manifold. If a manifold is cracked or distorted 0.030 in. or more, it should be replaced to prevent exhaust leakage. To detect distortion, lay a straight-

edge along the length of the exhaust port faces. If, at any point, a gap of 0.030 in. or more exists between the straightedge and the manifold, distortion of that amount is present.

8. By removing one bolt and two nuts, the manifold can be separated.

9. To install, reverse the removal procedure using new gaskets. Replace the exhaust pipe packing.

Gasoline V6 and V8 (Except 231 V6)

1. Remove the air cleaner.
2. Drain the radiator.
3. Disconnect:
   a. Battery cables at the battery.
   b. Upper radiator and heater hoses at the manifold.
   c. Crankcase ventilatioin hoses as required.
   d. Fuel line at the carburetor.
   e. Accelerator linkage.
   f. Vacuum hose at the distributor.
   g. Power brake hose at the carburetor base or manifold, if applicable.
   h. Ignition coil and temperature sending switch wires.
   i. Water pump bypass at the water pump (Mark IV only).

4. Remove the distributor cap and scribe the rotor position relative to the distributor body.

5. Remove the distributor.

6. If applicable, remove the alternator upper bracket. As required, remove the oil filler bracket, air cleaner bracket, air conditioning compressor and bracket, and accelerator bellcrank.

7. Remove the manifold-to-head attaching

V8 intake manifold seal location

V6 intake manifold and seal location

bolts, then remove the manifold and carburetor as an assembly.

8. If the manifold is to be replaced, transfer the carburetor (and mounting studs), water outlet and thermostat (use a new gasket) heater hose adapter, EGR valve (use new gasket) and, if applicable, TVS switch and the choke coil. 1975–79 engines use a new carburetor heat choke tube which must be transferred to a new manifold.

9. Before installing the manifold, thoroughly clean the gasket and seal surfaces of the cylinder heads and manifold.

10. Install the manifold end seals, folding the tabs if applicable, and the manifold/head gaskets, using a sealing compound around the water passages.

NOTE: *1974–75 350 V8 engines require a new intake manifold side gasket on 4-bbl en-*

gines. *The new gasket has restricted crossover ports. The 350 2-bbl uses a restricted cross-over gasket on the right-hand side and an open gasket on the left. The 350 4-bbl uses restricted cross-over gaskets on both sides. The correct gaskets are essential.*

11. When installing the manifold, care should be taken not to dislocate the end seals. It is helpful to use a pilot in the distributor opening. Tighten the manifold bolts to 30 ft. lbs. in the sequence illustrated.

12. Install the ignition coil.

13. Install the distributor with the rotor in its original location as indicated by the scribe line. If the engine has been disturbed, refer to "Distributor Removal and Installation" at the beginning of this chapter.

14. If applicable, install the alternator upper bracket and adjust the belt tension.

15. Connect all components disconnected in Steps 3 and 6 above.

16. Fill the cooling system, start the engine, check for leaks and adjust the ignition timing and carburetor idle speed and mixture.

231 V6

NOTE: *A special wrench adapter, available from Snap-On and several other tool manufacturers, is necessary to remove the left front intake manifold bolt.*

1. Disconnect the battery and drain the cooling system. Remove the upper radiator hose, and the coolant bypass hose from the manifold.

2. Remove the air cleaner. Disconnect the throttle linkage from the carburetor. Remove the linkage bracket from the manifold. If the car is equipped with an automatic transmission, remove the downshift linkage.

3. Disconnect the fuel line from the carburetor. If equipped with power brakes, disconnect the power brake line from the manifold. Disconnect the choke pipe and all vacuum lines. Disconnect the anti-dieseling solenoid wire.

4. Remove the manifold bolts. It will be necessary to remove the distributor cap and rotor to gain access to the front left manifold bolt.

Intake manifold torque sequence—V6 (exc. 231) and small-block V8

Intake manifold torque sequence—big-block V8

Intake manifold torque sequence—231 V6

Typical gasoline V6 and V8 intake manifold installation

This is the special bolt, known as a torx bolt. Remove the plug wires from the plugs.

5. Remove the manifold.

6. Installation is in the reverse order of removal. Use a new gasket and seals. Coat the ends of the seals with a non-hardening silicone sealer. The pointed end of the seal should be a snug fit against the block and head. When installing the manifold, start with the center bolts (numbers one and two) and slowly tighten them until *snug*. Continue with the rest of the bolts in sequence, tightening them in several stages to the correct torque.

V6 and V8 Diesel

1. Remove the air cleaner.

2. Drain the radiator. Loosen the upper bypass hose clamp, remove the thermostat housing bolts, and remove the housing and the thermostat from the intake manifold.

3. Remove the breather pipes from the rocker covers and the air crossover. Remove the air crossover.

4. Disconnect the throttle rod and the return spring. If equipped with cruise control, remove the servo.

5. Remove the hairpin clip at the bellcrank and disconnect the cables. Remove the throttle cable from the bracket on the manifold; position the cable away from the engine. Disconnect and label any wiring as necessary.

6. Remove the alternator bracket if necessary. If equipped with air conditioning, re-

Diesel intake manifold and gaskets

V8 diesel intake manifold bolt torque sequence

move the compressor mounting bolts and move the compressor aside, without disconnecting any of the hoses. Remove the compressor mounting bracket from the intake manifold.

7. Disconnect the fuel line from the pump and the fuel filter. Remove the fuel filter and bracket.

8. Remove the fuel injection pump and lines. See Chapter 4, "Fuel System," for procedures.

9. Disconnect and remove the vacuum pump or oil pump drive assembly from the rear of the engine.

10. Remove the intake manifold drain tube.

11. Remove the intake manifold bolts and remove the manifold. Remove the adpter seal. Remove the injection pump adapter.

12. Clean the mating surfaces of the cylinder heads and the intake manifold using a putty knife.

13. On the V8, coat both sides of the gasket surface that seal the intake manifold to the cylinder heads with G.M. sealer #1050026 or the equivalent. On the V6, DO NOT coat the gasket or sealing surfaces with any sealer. Use an RTV sealer only on the end seals. Position the intake manifold gaskets on the cylinder heads. Install the end seals, making sure that the ends are positioned under the cylinder heads.

14. Carefully lower the intake manifold into place on the engine.

15. Clean the intake manifold bolts thoroughly, then dip them in clean engine oil. Install the bolts and tighten to 15 ft. lbs. in the sequence shown. Next, tighten all the bolts to 30 ft. lbs., in sequence, and finally tighten to 40 ft. lbs. in sequence.

16. Install the intake manifold drain tube and clamp.

17. Install injection pump adapter. See

V6 diesel intake manifold bolt torque sequence

Chapter 4. If a new adapter is not being used, skip steps 4 and 9.

18. Install the remaining components in the reverse order of removal.

Exhaust Manifold

REMOVAL AND INSTALLATION

Inline Six—1964–74

Exhaust manifold removal for these model years is covered in the "Intake Manifold Removal and Installation" section earlier in this chapter.

Inline Six With Integral Intake Manifold— 1975–76

1. Remove the air cleaner.

2. Remove the power steering and air pump brackets.

3. Remove the EFE valve bracket.

4. Disconnect the throttle linkage and return spring.

5. Unbolt the exhaust pipe from the flange.

6. Unbolt and remove the manifold.

7. Reverse the procedure for installation. Tighten the four end bolts to specifications last.

Inline six cylinder exhaust manifold torque sequence—1975–79

Inline Six With Integral Intake Manifold— 1977–79

1. Disconnect negative (−) battery cable and remove air cleaner.

2. Remove the power steering and/or AIR pumps and brackets, where they are present. (You need not disconnect powersteering hoses— just support the pump out of the way.)

3. Working from below, with the vehicle safely supported, disconnect the exhaust pipe at the manifold and at the catalytic converter bracket near the transmission mount. If the car uses an exhaust manifold mounted converter, disconnect the pipe at the bottom of the converter, and then remove the converter.

4. Working from above, remove the rear heat shield and accelerator cable bracket.

5. Remove the exhaust manifold bolts, and pull off the manifold.

6. If the manifold is to be replaced, transfer the EFE valve, actuator, and rod assembly to the new part. Otherwise, inspect the manifold as described in Step 7.

7. Clean and then inspect the manifold carefully for cracks, and for free operation of

Typical exhaust manifold and hot air shrouds

Plastic manifold gasket retainers

Exhaust manifold installation—V6, V8 (1980 shown, others similar)

the EFE valve. Repair or replace parts, and free up the EFE valve with solvent, if necessary.

8. Make sure the gasket surface is clean and free of deep scratches. Position a new gasket on the manifold, and then put the manifold in position on the block, and install the bolts hand tight.

9. Torque all bolts *in the proper order* to the specified torque (see illustration).

10. Install the rear heat shield and the accelerator cable bracket.

11. Working from underneath, connect the exhaust pipe at the manifold flange and connect the converter bracket at the transmission mount. If the car has an exhaust manifold converter, first install the converter to the manifold loosely; then attach the exhaust pipe to the converter and align the exhaust system; finally, torque the converter mounting bolts to 15 ft. lbs., in an X pattern, and torquing in several stages.

12. Working from above, install the power steering and A.I.R. pumps as necessary. Then, install the air cleaner and connect the battery ground cable.

V6 and V8

1. If equipped with AIR (Air Injection Reaction), remove the air injector manifold assembly. The ¼ in. pipe threads in the manifold are straight threads. Do not use a ¼ in. tapered pipe tap to clean the threads.

2. Disconnect the battery.

3. If applicable, remove the air cleaner preheater shroud.

4. Remove the spark plug wire heat shields. On Mar IV, remove spark plugs.

5. On the left exhaust manifold, disconnect and remove the alternator.

6. Disconnect the exhaust pipe from the manifold and hang it from the frame out of the way.

7. Bend the locktabs and remove the end bolts, then the center bolts. Remove the manifold.

NOTE: *A 9/16 in. thin wall 6-point socket, sharpened at the leading edge and tapped onto the head of the bolt, simplifies bending the locktabs.*

NOTE: *When installing a new manifold on the right side on 1978 and later V8s you must transfer the heat stove from the old manifold to the new one.*

8. installation is the reverse of removal. Clean all mating surfaces and use new gaskets. Torque all bolts to specifications from the inside working out.

Turbocharger and Actuator—231 V6

REMOVAL AND INSTALLATION

1. Disconnect the exhaust inlet and outlet pipes at the turbocharger.

2. Disconnect the oil feed pipe from the center housing rotating assembly.

3. Remove the nut attaching the air intake elbow to the carburetor and remove the elbow; still attached to the flex tube, from the carburetor.

4. Disconnect the accelerator, cruise and detent linkages at the carb. Remove the linkage bracket from the plenum.

5. Remove the two bolts attaching the plenum to the side bracket.

Turbocharger and plenum assembly

ECS detonation sensor, turbo V6

Turbo V6 exhaust pipe connections

Carburetor-to-plenum installation, turbo V6

6. Disconnect the fuel line and all the vacuum hoses.

7. Drain the cooling system.

8. Disconnect the coolant hoses from the front and rear of the plenum.

9. Disconnect the plenum front bracket by removing one bolt attaching the bracket to the intake manifold. Leave the bracket attached to the manifold.

10. Remove the two bolts attaching the turbine housing to the bracket on the intake manifold.

11. Unscrew the two mounting bolts and then remove the EGR valve manifold.

12. Loosen the clamp attaching the hose from the air by-pass to the pipe to the check valve.

13. Unscrew the three compressor housing-to-intake manifold mounting bolts.

14. Remove the turbocharger and actuator, still attached to the carburetor and plenum assembly from the engine.

15. Unscrew the six bolts and separate the turbocharger assembly from the carburetor.

16. Remove the oil drain from the center housing rotating assembly.

17. Installation is in the reverse order of removal.

Valves and Springs
REMOVAL AND INSTALLATION

1. Remove the head(s), and place on a clean surface.

2. Using a suitable spring compressor (for pushrod-type overhead valve engines), compress the valve spring and remove the valve spring cap key. Release the spring compressor and remove the valve spring and cap (and valve rotator on some engines).

NOTE: *Use care in removing the keys; they are easily lost.*

3. Remove the valve seals from the intake valve guides. Throw these old seals away, as you'll be installing new seals during reassembly.

4. Slide the valves out of the head from the combustion chamber side.

Removing the valve key and cap. A magnet is useful here in removing the keys

Valve train exploded view, all engine similar except 231 V6 (with rocker shafts)

VALVE SPRING COMPRESSOR

Removing the valve springs

5. Make a holder for the valves out of a piece of wood or cardboard, as outlined for the pushrods in "Cylinder Head Removal." Make sure you number each hole in the cardboard to keep the valves in proper order. Slide the valves out of the head from the combustion chamber side; they MUST be installed as they were removed.

INSPECTION

Inspect the valve faces and seats (in the head) for pits, burned spots and other evidence of poor seating. If a valve face is in such bad shape that the head of the valve must be ground in order to true up the face, discard the valve because the sharp edge will run too hot. The correct angle for valve faces is 45 degrees. We recommend the re-facing be done at a reputable machine shop.

Check the valve stem for scoring and burned spots. If not noticeably scored or damaged, clean the valve stem with solvent to remove all gum and varnish. Clean the valve guides using solvent and an expanding wire-type valve guide cleaner. If you have access to a dial indicator for measuring valve stem-to-guide clearance, mount it so that the stem of the indicator is at 90° to the valve stem, and as close to the valve guide as possible. Move the valve off its seat, and measure the valve guide-to-stem clearance by rocking the stem back and forth to actuate the dial indicator. Measure the valve stems using a micrometer, and compare to specifications to determine whether stem or guide wear is responsible for the excess clearance. If a dial indicator and micrometer are not available to you, take your cylinder head and valves to a reputable machine shop for inspection.

Some of the engines covered in this guide are equipped with valve rotators, which double as valve spring caps. In normal operation the rotators put a certain degree of wear on the tip of the valve stem; this ear appears as concentric rings on the stem tip. However, if the rotator is not working properly, the wear may appear as straight notches or "X" patterns across the valve stem tip. Whenever the valves are removed from the cylinder head, the tips should be inspected for improper pattern, which could indicate valve rotator problems. Valve stem tips will have to be ground flat if rotator patterns are severe.

Valve Guides

The engines covered in this guide use integral valve guides; that is, they are a part of the cylinder head and cannot be replaced. The guides can, however, be reamed oversize if they are found to be worn past an acceptable limit. Oc-

Checking the valve stem-to-guide clearance

Valve stem wear

Cutaway of a knurled valve guide

FOR DIMENSIONS, REFER TO SPECIFICATIONS

CHECK FOR BENT STEM

DIAMETER

VALVE FACE ANGLE

1/32" MINIMUM

THIS LINE PARALLEL WITH VALVE HEAD

Critical valve dimensions

Have the valve seat concentricity checked at a machine shop

casionally, a valve guide bore will be oversize as manufactured. These are marked on the inboard side of the cylinder heads on the machined surface just above the intake manifold.

If the guides must be reamed (this service is available at most machine shops), then valves with oversize stems must be fitted. Valves are usually available in 0.001, 0.003 and 0.005 in. stem oversizes. Valve guides which are not excessively worn or distorted may, in some cases, be knurled rather than reamed. Knurling is a process in which the metal on the valve guide bore is displaced and raised, thereby reducing clearance. Knurling also provides excellent oil control. The option of knurling rather than reaming valve guides should be discussed with a reputable machinist or engine specialist.

CYLINDER HEAD CLEANING AND INSPECTION

NOTE: Any diesel cylinder head work should be handled by a reputable machine shop familiar with diesel engines. Disassembly, valve lapping, and assembly can be completed by following the gasoline engine procedures.

Gasoline Engines

Once the complete valve train has been removed from the cylinder head(s), the head itself can be inspected, cleaned and machined (if necessary). Set the head(s) on a clean work space, so the combustion chambers are facing up. Begin cleaning the chambers and ports with a hardwood chisel or other non-metallic tool (to avoid nicking or gouging the chamber, ports, and especially the valve seats). Chip away the major carbon deposits, then remove the remainder of carbon with a wire brush fitted to an electric drill.

NOTE: Be sure that the carbon is actually removed, rather than just burnished.

After decarbonizing is completed, take the head(s) to a machine shop and have the head "hot tanked." In this process, the head is lowered into a hot chemical bath that very effectively cleans all grease, corrosion, and scale from all internal and external head surfaces. Also have the machinist check the valve seats and re-cut them if necessary. When you bring the clean head(s) home, place them on a clean surface. Completely clean the entire valve train with solvent.

WIRE BRUSH

Use a wire brush and electric drill to remove carbon from the combustion chambers and exhaust ports

CHECKING FOR HEAD WARPAGE

Lay the head down with the combustion chambers facing up. Place a straight-edge across the gasket surface of the head, both diagonally and straight across the center. Using a flat feeler

1 & 3 CHECK DIAGONALLY
2 CHECK ACROSS CENTER

Check the cylinder head mating surface for warpage with a precision straight edge

gauge, determine the clearance at the center of the straight-edge. If warpage exceeds .003 in. in a 6 in. span, or .006 in. over the total length, the cylinder head must be resurfaced (which is akin to planing a piece of wood). Resurfacing can be performed at most machine shops.

NOTE: When resurfacing the cylinder head(s) of V6 or V8 engines, the intake manifold mounting position is altered, and must be corrected by machining a proportionate amount from the intake manifold flange.

LAPPING THE VALVES

When valve faces and seats have been re-faced and re-cut, or if they are determined to be in good condition, the valves must be "lapped in" to ensure efficient sealing when the valve closes against the sea.

1. Invert the cylinder head so that the combustion chambers are facing up.

2. Lightly lubricate the valve stems with clean oil, and coat the valve seats with valve grinding compound. Install the valves in the head as numbered.

3. Attach the suction cup of a valve lapping tool to a valve head. *You'll probably have to*

HAND DRILL

ROD

SUCTION CUP

Home-made valve lapping tool

Lapping the valves by hand

moisten the cup to securely attach the tool to the valve.

4. Rotate the tool between the palms, changing position and lifting the tool often to prevent grooving. Lap the valve until a smooth, polished seat is evident (you may have to add a bit more compound after some lapping is done).

5. Remove the valve and tool, and remove ALL traces of grinding compound with solvent-soaked rag, or rinse the head with solvent.

> NOTE: *Valve lapping can also be done by fastening a suction cup to a piece of drill rod in a hand "eggbeater" type drill. Proceed as above, using the drill as a lapping tool. Due to the higher speeds involved when using the hand drill, care must be exercised to avoid grooving the seat. Lift the tool and change direction of rotation often.*

Valve Springs

HEIGHT AND PRESSURE CHECK

1. Place the valve spring on a flat, clean surface next to a square.

2. Measure the height of the spring, and rotate it against the edge of the square to measure distortion (out-of-roundness). If spring

Have the valve spring test pressure checked professionally

height varies between springs by more than $\frac{1}{16}$ in. or if the distortion exceeds $\frac{1}{16}$ in., replace the spring.

A valve spring tester is needed to test spring test pressure, so the valve springs must usually be taken to a professional machine shop for this test. Spring pressure at the installed and compressed heights is checked, and a tolerance of plus or minus 5 lbs. (plus or minus 1 lb. on the 231V6) is permissible on the springs covered in this guide.

VALVE INSTALLATION

New valve seals must be installed when the valve train is put back together. Certain seals slip over the valve stem and guide boss, while others require that the boss be machined. In some applications Teflon guide seals are available. Check with a machinist and/or automotive parts store for a suggestion on the proper seals to use.

> NOTE: *Remember that when installing valve seals, a small amount of oil is able to pass the seal to lubricate the valve guides; otherwise, excessive wear will result.*

To install the valves and rocker assembly:

1. Lubricate the valve stems with clean engine oil.

2. Install the valves in the cylinder head, one at a time, as numbered.

Check the valve spring free length and squareness

Installing valve stem seals

3. Lubricate and position the seals and valve springs, again a valve at a time.

4. Install the spring retainers, and compress the springs.

5. With the valve key groove exposed above the compressed valve spring, wipe some wheel bearing grease around the groove. This will retain the keys as you release the spring compressor.

6. Using needlenose pliers (or your fingers), place the keys in the key grooves. The grease should hold the keys in place. Slowly release the spring compressor; the valve cap or rotator will raise up as the compressor is released, retaining the keys.

7. Install the rocker assembly, and install the cylinder head(s).

Valve Adjustment

In the event of cylinder head removal or any operation that requires disturbing or removing the rocker arms, the rocker arms must be adjusted. See the "Valve Lash" procedure earlier in this chapter.

Valve Lifters

REMOVAL AND INSTALLATION

Gasoline and Diesel

NOTE: *Valve lifters and pushrods should be kept in order so they can be reinstalled in their original position. Some engines will have both standard size .010 in. oversize valve lifters as original equipment. The oversize lifters are etched with an "O" on their sides; the cylinder block will also be marked with an "O" if the oversize lifter is used.*

1. Remove the intake manifold and gasket.

2. Remove the valve covers, rocker arm assemblies and pushrods.

3. If the lifters are coated with varnish, apply carburetor cleaning solvent to the lifter body. The solvent should dissolve the varnish in about 10 minutes.

Diesel valve lifter guide and retainer

4. Remove the lifters. On diesels, remove the lifter retainer guide bolts, and remove the guides. A special tool for removing lifters is available, and is helpful for this procedure.

5. New lifters *must* be primed before installation, *as dry lifters will seize when the engine is started.* On the diesel lifters, submerge the lifters in clean diesel fuel or kerosene and work the lifter plunger up and down to prime. On gasoline engine lifters, submerge the lifters in SAE 10 oil, which is very thin. Carefully insert the end of a ⅛ in. (3mm) drift into the lifter and push down on the plunger. Hold the plunger down while the lifter is still submerged; *do not pump the plunger.* Release the plunger. The lifter is now primed.

6. Coat the bottoms of the gasoline engine lifters, and the rollers of the diesel engine lifters with Molykote® or an equivalent molybdenum-disulfide lubricant before installation. Install the lifters and pushrods into the engine in their original order. On diesels, install the lifter retainer guide.

7. Install the intake manifold gaskets and manifold.

8. Position the rocker arms, pivots and bolts

Hydraulic valve lifter, diesel roller type. Gasoline engine lifters similar but without rollers

Oversize valve lifter bore marking

on the cylinder head. On the 231 V6, position and install the rockers and rocker shafts. Refer to the "Rocker Arm Removal and Installation" procedure in this chapter for lifter bleed-down. New lifters must be bled down; *valve-to-piston contact could occur if this procedure is neglected.*

9. Install the valve covers, connect the spark plug wires and install the air cleaner assembly.
NOTE: *An additive containing EP lube, such as EOS, should always be added to crankcase oil for break-in when new lifters or a new camshaft is installed. This additive is generally available in automotive parts stores.*

Timing Gear Cover
REMOVAL AND INSTALLATION
Inline Six Cylinder

1. Drain the oil and remove the oil pan on models through 1972.
2. Remove the readiator after draining it.
3. Remove the fan, pulley, and belt. Remove any power steering and/or AIR pump drive belts. Remove any braces for the above pumps which will interfere with cover removal and position the pumps out of the way.
4. Remove the crankshaft pulley and damper. Use a puller to remove the damper. Do not attempt to pry or hammer the damper off, or it will be damaged.
5. Remove the retaining bolts, and remove the cover on 1964–72 models.
6. On 1973–79 models, pull the cover forward slightly and cut the oil pan front seal off

Guiding front cover into place, V8 shown

flush with the block. Remove the cover. On installation, cut the tabs off a new oil pan front seal and install it on the cover.

7. On installation, coat the gasket with sealer and use a ⅛ in. bead of silicone sealer at the oil pan-to-cylinder block joint. Replace the damper before tightening the cover bolts down, so that the cover seal will align. The damper must be drawn into place. Hammering it will destroy it.

Typical front cover and timing assembly

Removing harmonic balancer using puller

Cut the oil pan seal flush with the front of the cylinder block (V8 shown, others similar)

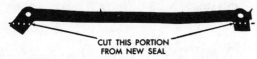

CUT THIS PORTION
FROM NEW SEAL

When the timing gear cover is replaced on most engines, the oil pan front seal must be modified

8. Replace the oil pan if it was removed, and fill the crankcase with oil.

V6 and V8

REMOVAL: ALL SMALL BLOCK V6 (EXCEPT 231) V8 AND 1967–72 MARK IV

1. Drain the oil and remove the oil pan. The pan need not be removed on 1974 and later small block engines.

2. Drain and remove the radiator.

3. Remove the fan, pulley and belt. Remove any power steering and/or AIR pump drive belts. Remove any braces for these pumps which will interfere with cover removal and position the pumps out of the way.

4. Remove the water pump.

5. Remove the crankshaft pulley and damper. Use a puller on the damper. Do not attempt to pry or hammer the damper off.

Use sealer at the timing cover-to-oil pan and the oil pan-to-cylinder block joints

6. Remove the retaining bolts, and remove the timing cover.

INSTALLATION: 1967–74 SMALL BLOCK V8 AND 1967–72 MARK IV

Reverse the preceding steps to install the cover. Use a damper installation tool to pull the damper on. Apply an ⅛ in. bead of silicone rubber sealer to the oil pan and cylinder block joint faces. Lightly coat the bottom of the seal with engine oil.

Refill the engine with oil.

INSTALLATION: 1975–84 V6 (EXC. 231) AND SMALL BLOCK V8

1. Clean the gasket mating surfaces.

2. Remove any oil pan gasket material that may still be adhering to the oil pan-engine block joint face.

3. Apply a ⅛ in. bead of silicone sealant (Part No. 1051435) or the equivalent to the joint formed by the oil pan and cylinder block, as well as to the entire oil pan front lip.

4. Coat the cover gasket with gasket sealer and place it in position on the front cover.

5. Loosely install the front cover on the block. Install the 4 top bolts loosely (about 3 turns). Install two ¼–20 × ½ in. screws in the hole at each side of the front cover and apply a bead of

Installing the drive-on torsional damper

sealant on the bottom of the seal and install it on the cover.

6. Tighten the screws evenly while aligning the dowel pins and holes in the front cover.

7. Remove the ¼–20 × ½ in. screws and install the rest of the cover screws.

8. Further installation is the reverse of removal. Refill the engine with oil.

231 V6

1. Drain the cooling system. Remove the radiator hoses. Remove the radiator.

2. Remove all the drive belts. Remove the fan and fan pulley. Remove the bypass hose.

3. Remove the crank pulley, the fuel pump and the distributor. Note the position of the distributor rotor before you remove the distributor.

4. Remove the alternator and its bracket.

5. Remove the harmonic balancer. You'll need a puller.

6. Remove the two bolts which attach the oil pan to the front cover. Remove the bolts which attach the cover to the block.

7. Remove the cover and remove the gasket material.

8. To install, it is first necessary to remove the oil pump cover and pack the space around the oil pump gears completely full of petroleum jelly. *Do not use gear lube.* There must be no air space left inside the pump. Reinstall the pump cover using a new gasket. This step is very important since the oil pump may lose its prime any time the pump, pump cover or timing cover is disturbed. If the pump is not packed, it may not begin to pump oil as soon as the engine is started.

9. Install the cover, using a sealer and new gaskets. Make sure the dowel pins engage the dowel pin holes before starting the bolts. Apply sealer to the bolt threads.

10. Install the harmonic balancer, bolt and washer. It will be necessary to lock the fly-

Apply sealer to the front pads at the area shown (V8)

wheel in some way to torque the balancer bolt to specifications. Most mechanics remove the flywheel cover and lock the flywheel with suitable locking device.

11. The rest of the installation is in the reverse order of removal.

V8 and V6 Diesel Engines

1. Drain the cooling system and disconnect the radiator hoses.

2. Remove all belts, fan and pulley, crankshaft pulley and balancer, using a balancer puller.

CAUTION: *The use of any other type of puller, such as a universal claw type which pulls on the outside of the hub, can destroy the balancer. The outside ring of the balancer is bonded in rubber to the hub. Pulling on the outside will break the bond. The timing mark is on the outside ring. If it is suspected that the bond is broken, check that the center of the keyway is 16° from the center of the timing slot. In addition, there are chiseled aligning marks between the weight and the hub.*

3. Unbolt and remove the cover, timing indicator, water pump and both dowel pins.

4. It may be necessary to grind a flat on the cover for gripping purposes.

5. Grind a chamfer on one end of each dowel pin.

6. Cut the excess material from the front end of the oil pan gasket on each side of the block.

MAGNETIC PICK-UP TUBE TIMING MARK   ↑ TIMING MARK FOR HAND WELD TIMING LIGHTS

231 V6 harmonic balancer timing marks

CHAMFER

Front cover dowel pin chamfer

Trimming pan seal with razor blade

7. Clean the block, oil pan and front cover mating surfaces with solvent.

8. Trim about ⅛ in. off each end of a new front pan seal.

9. Install a new front cover gasket on the block and a new seal in the front cover.

10. Apply an R.T.V. sealer to the gasket around the coolant holes.

11. Apply an R.T.V. sealer to the block at the junction of the pan and front cover.

12. Place the cover on the block and press down to compress the seal. Rotate the cover left and right and guide the pan seal into the cavity using a small screwdriver. Oil the bolt threads and install two bolts to hold the cover in place. Install both dowel pins (chamfered end first), then install the remaining front cover bolts.

NOTE: *The front cover-to-block bolts on the V6 diesel must be coated with an adhesive, GM part #1052624 or equivalent to avoid coolant leaks and loss of bolt torque.*

13. Apply a lubricant, compatible with rubber, on the balancer seal surface.

14. Install the balancer and bolt. Torque the bolt to 200–300 ft. lbs. (160–350 ft. lbs. on V6).

15. Install the other parts in the reverse order of removal.

TIMING GEAR COVER OIL SEAL REPLACEMENT

All Engines

1. After removing the gear cover, pry the oil seal out of the front of the cover with a small prybar.

2. Install a new lip seal with the lip (open

Oil seal installation with the cover removed

1. CAMSHAFT
2. CRANKSHAFT
3. CAMSHAFT SPROCKET KEY
4. INJECTION PUMP DRIVE GEAR
5. CRANKSHAFT SPROCKET KEY
6. FRONT CAMSHAFT BEARING RETAINER
7. 65 N·m (48 FT. LBS.)
8. CRANKSHAFT SPROCKET
9. TIMING CHAIN
10. CAMSHAFT SPROCKET
11. WASHER
12. 95 N·m (70 FT. LBS.)
13. SLINGER
14. GASKET
15. FRONT COVER
16. 57 N·m (42 FT. LBS.) - APPLY ADHESIVE
17. 28 N·m (21 FT. LBS.) - APPLY ADHESIVE
18. PROBE HOLDER (RPM COUNTER)
19. CRANKSHAFT BALANCER
20. WASHER
21. 217-475 N·m (160 - 350 FT. LBS.)
22. PULLEY ASSEMBLY
23. 40 N·m (30 FT. LBS.)

263 V6 diesel front cover, timing assembly and bolt torque specifics

Oil seal installation with the cover installed

side of seal) inside and drive or press the seal into place.

3. Lightly coat the seal with engine oil before replacing cover on block.

Timing Chain or Gear

REMOVAL AND INSTALLATION

Inline Six Cylinder

The six-cylinder camshaft is gear driven. To remove the camshaft gear, remove the camshaft and press the gear off.

CAUTION: *The thrust plate must be positioned so that the woodruff key in the shaft does not damage it when the shaft is pressed out of the gear. Support the hub of the gear or the gear will be seriously damaged.*

The crankshaft gear may be removed with a gear puller while in place in the block.

The inline six cylinder crankshaft gear is removed with a gear puller

Gasoline V6 and V8 (Except 231 V6)

These engines are equipped with a timing chain. To replace the chain, remove the radiator core, water pump harmonic balancer, and the crankcase front cover. This will allow access to the timing chain. Crank the engine until the zero marks punched on both sprockets are closest to one another and in line between the shaft centers. Then, take out the three bolts that hold the camshaft gear to the camshaft. This gear is

a light press fit on the camshaft and will come off readily. It is located by a dowel.

The chain comes off with the camshaft gear.

A gear puller will be required to remove the crankshaft gear.

V6 and V8 crankshaft sprocket removal using special puller

Timing gear alignment—inline six cylinder

Timing sprocket alignment—1967–78 V8, and V6 diesel 1982 and later

Timing sprocket alignment—1979 and later V6 and V8 including V8 diesel

Timing chain and gears—231 V6

Without disturbing the position of the engine, mount the new crank gear on the shaft, then mount the chain over the camshaft gear. Arrange the camshaft gear in such a way that the timing marks will line up between the shaft centers and the camshaft locating dowel will enter the dowel hole in the cam sprocket.

Place the cam sprocket, with its chain mounted over it, in position on the front of the camshaft and pull up with the three bolts that hold it to the camshaft.

After the gears are in place, turn the engine two full revolutions to make certain that the timing marks are in correct alignment between the shaft centers.

231 V6

1. Remove the timing chain cover.
2. Before removing anything else, make sure the timing marks on the crankshaft and camshaft sprockets are aligned. This will greatly ease reinstallation of parts.
3. It is not necessary to remove the timing chain tensioners unless they are worn or damaged.
4. Remove the front crankshaft oil slinger.
5. Remove the bolt and the special washer that hold the camshaft distributor drive gear and fuel pump eccentric at the forward end of the camshaft. Remove the eccentric and the gear from the camshaft.
6. Using a pair of prybars, alternately pry the camshaft sprocket, then the crankshaft sprocket forward until the camshaft sprocket is free.
7. After the camshaft sprocket and chain are removed, finish pulling the crankshaft sprocket off the crankshaft.
8. To install, if the engine has not been disturbed, proceed to Step Eleven.

9. If the engine has been disturbed, turn the crankshaft so that the number one piston is at top dead center.
10. Temporarily install the sprocket key and the camshaft sprocket on the camshaft. Turn the camshaft so that the index mark of the sprocket is pointing downward. Remove the key and the sprocket from the camshaft.
11. Assemble the timing chain and sprockets. Install the keys, sprockets, and chain assembly on the crankshaft and camshaft so that the index marks of both the sprockets are aligned. It will be necessary to hold the chain tensioners out of the way while installing the timing chain and sprocket assembly.
12. Install the front oil slinger on the crankshaft with the concave side toward the front of the engine.
13. Install the fuel pump eccentric with the oil groove forward.
14. Install the distributor drive gear on the camshaft.
15. Install the front cover.

350 V8 Diesel

1. Remove the front cover.
2. Remove the oil slinger and camshaft bolts, and remove the camshaft and crankshaft sprockets and timing chain as a unit.
3. Remove the fuel pump eccentric from the crankshaft if replacement is necessary.
4. To install, install the key in the crankshaft if removed. Also install the fuel pump eccentric if removed.
5. Install the camshaft and crankshafts sprockets and the timing chain together as a unit and align the timing marks as shown. Torque the camshaft sprocket bolt to 65 ft. lbs.

NOTE: *When the two timing marks are in alignment, number six is at T.D.C. To obtain T.D.C. for number one cylinder, slowly rotate the crankshaft one revolution. This will bring the cam mark to the top; number one will then be in firing position.*

6. Install the oil slinger and front cover.

NOTE: *Any time the timing chain and gears are replaced, it will be necessary to retime the injection system. Refer to the paragraph on Diesel Engine Injection Timing in Chapter 4.*

263 V6 Diesel

1. Remove the front cover.

2. Remove the valve covers and loosen all rocker arm pivot bolts evenly so that lash (looseness) exists between the rocker arms and the valves. See "Rocker Arm Removal" in this chapter. It is not necessary to remove the rockers completely.

3. Remove the crankshaft oil slinger.

4. Remove the camshaft-to-camshaft sprocket bolt and washer, and remove the timing chain, camshaft and crankshaft sprockets as a unit.

NOTE: *If the crank sprocket is a tight fit on the end of the crankshaft, you may have to use a sprocket puller to remove it.*

5. To install, if the camshaft sprocket-to-camshaft key should come out with the camshaft sprocket, perform the following by referring to the exploded drawing of the V6 diesel front cover:

    a. Remove the front camshaft bearing retainer.

    b. Install the key with the injection pump drive gear.

    c. Install the bearing retainer and bolts loose on the block.

    d. Install the camshaft sprocket.

    e. Rotate the camshaft at least 4 turns to center the retainer.

    f. Remove the camshaft sprocket.

    g. Torque the bearing retainer-to-block bolts evenly to 48 ft. lbs.

    h. Rotate the camshaft to make sure it's free. If it is not, repeat steps a through h.

6. Install the key in the crankshaft, if removed.

7. Install the camshaft and crankshaft sprockets and the timing chain together as a unit. Align the timing marks as shown.

8. Torque the camshaft sprocket bolt to 70 ft. lbs.

9. Install the oil slinger.

10. Install the engine front cover. Bleed down the valve lifters as described in the "Rocker Arm" section in this chapter.

11. Install the valve covers and check and reset the injection pump timing.

Camshaft

REMOVAL AND INSTALLATION

Inline Six Cylinder

Due to the length of the inline six cylinder camshaft, a large amount of working room will be required in front of the engine to remove the camshaft. There are two ways to go about this task: either remove the engine from the car, or remove the radiator, grille and all supports which are mounted directly in front of the engine. If the second alternative is chosen, you must also disconnect the motor mounts and raise the front of the engine enough to gain the clearance necessary to remove the cam from the engine.

1. In addition to removing the timing gear cover, remove the grille and radiator.

2. Remove the valve cover and gasket, loosen all the valve rocker arm nuts and pivot the arms clear of the pushrods.

3. Remove the distributor and the fuel pump.

4. Remove the coil, the side cover and its gasket. Remove the pushrods and valve lifters.

5. Remove the two camshaft thrust plate retaining screws by working through the holes in the camshaft gear.

6. Remove the camshaft and gear assembly by pulling it out through the front of the block.

NOTE: *If renewing either the camshaft or the camshaft gear, the gear must be pressed off the camshaft. The replacement parts must be assembled in the same manner (under pressure). In placing the gear on the camshaft, press the gear onto the shaft until it bottoms against the gear spacer ring. The end clearance of the thrust plate should be .001 to .005 in.*

Carefully turn camshaft slightly as you remove it.

Camshaft and oil gallery plugs at rear of block

7. Install the camshaft assembly in the engine.

NOTE: *Pre-lube the cam lobes with E.O.S. or SAE 90 gear lubricant. Do not dislodge the cam bearings when inserting the camshaft.*

8. Turn the crankshaft and the camshaft to align and bring the timing marks together. Push the camshaft into this aligned position. Install the camshaft thrust plate-to-block screws and torque them to 6–7½ lbs.

9. Runout on either the crankshaft or the camshaft gear should not exceed .003 in.

10. Backlash between the two gears should be between .004 and .006 in.

11. Install the timing gear cover and its gasket.

12. Install the oil pan and gaskets.

13. Install the harmonic balancer.

14. Line up the keyway in the balancer with the key on the crankshaft and the drive balancer onto the shaft until it bottoms against the crankshaft gear.

15. Install the valve lifters and pushrods. Install the side cover with new gasket. Attach the coil wires; install the fuel pump.

16. Install the distributor and set the timing as described under "Distributor Installation" at the beginning of this section.

17. Pivot the rocker arms over the pushrods and then adjust the valves.

18. Add oil to the engine. Install and adjust the fan belt.

19. Install the radiator or shroud.

20. Install the grille assembly.

21. Fill the cooling system, start the engine and check for leaks.

22. Check and adjust the timing.

Gasoline V6 and V8 (except 231 V6)

1. Remove the intake manifold, valve lifters and timing chain cover, as described in this section.

2. Remove the grille and radiator.

3. Remove the fuel pump and pump pushrod.

4. Remove the camshaft sprocket bolts, the sprocket and the timing chain. A light blow to the lower edge of a tight sprocket should free it (use a plastic mallet).

5. Install two ⁵⁄₁₆–18 × 4 in. bolts in the cam bolt holes and pull the cam from block.

NOTE: *All camshaft journals are the same diameter and care must be taken while removing the camshaft to avoid damage to the bearings.*

6. To install, reverse removal procedure, aligning the timing marks.

NOTE: *Pre-lube the cam lobes with E.O.S. or SAE 90 gear lubricant. Do not dislodge the cam bearings when installing the camshaft.*

231 V6

1. Drain the engine coolant and remove the radiator and radiator hoses.

2. Remove the water pump and all the drive belts. Remove the alternator.

3. Remove the crankshaft pulley and the vibration damper.

4. Remove the intake manifold. Mark the location of the distributor and remove the distributor.

5. Remove the fuel pump. Remove the timing chain cover and the oil pump.

6. Remove the timing chain and the camshaft sprocket, along with the distributor drive gear and the fuel pump eccentric.

7. Remove the rocker arm covers and the rocker arm assemblies. Mark the pushrods and remove them. Remove the lifters. Mark them so they can be returned to their original position.

8. Carefully remove the camshaft from the engine. Make sure you don't damage the bearings.

9. Installation is in the reverse order of removal. Remember to pack the oil pump with petroleum jelly.

V8 and V6 Diesel Engine

NOTE: *If equipped with air conditioning, the system must be discharged by an air conditioning specialist before the camshaft is removed. The condenser must also be removed from the car.*

Removal of the camshaft also requires removal of the injection pump drive and driven gears, removal of the intake manifold, disassembly of the valve lifters, and re-timing of the injection pump.

1. Disconnect the negative battery cables. Drain the coolant. Remove the radiator.

2. Remove the intake manifold and gasket

Diesel injection pump drive gear

and the front and rear intake manifold seals. Refer to the intake manifold removal and installation procedure.

3. Remove the balancer pulley and the balancer. See "Caution" under Diesel Engine Front Cover Removal and Installation, above. Remove the engine front cover using the appropriate procedure.

4. Remove the valve covers. Remove the rocker arms, pushrods and valve lifters; see the procedure earlier in this section. Be sure to keep the parts in order so that they may be returned to their original positions.

5. Remove the camshaft sprocket retaining bolt, and remove the timing chain and sprockets, using the procedure outlined earlier.

6. Position the camshaft dowel pin at the 3 o'clock position on the V8.

7. On V8s, push the camshaft rearward and hold it there, being careful not to dislodge the oil gallery plug at the rear of the engine. Remove the fuel injection pump drive gear by sliding it from the camshaft while rocking the pump driven gear.

8. To remove the fuel injection pump driven gear, remove the pump adapter, the snap ring, and remove the selective washer. Remove the driven gear and spring.

9. Remove the camshaft by sliding it out the front of the engine. On the V6, install a longer bolt into the front hole on the camshaft, to act as a handle. Be extremely careful not to allow the cam lobes to contact any of the bearings, or the journals to dislodge the bearings during camshaft removal. Do not force the camshaft, or bearing damage will result.

10. If either the injection pump drive or driven gears are to be replaced, replace both gears.

11. Coat the camshaft and the cam bearings with a heavy-weight engine oil, GM lubricant #1052365 or the equivalent.

12. Carefully slide the camshaft into position in the engine.

13. Fit the crankshaft and camshaft sprockets, aligning the timing marks as shown in the timing chain removal and installation procedure, above. Remove the sprockets without disturbing the timing.

14. Install the injection pump driven gear, spring, shim, and snap ring. Check the gear end play. If the end play is not within 0.002–0.006 in. on V8s through 1979 and .002 to .015 in. on 1980 and later, replace the shim to obtain the specified clearance. Shims are available in 0.003 in. increments, from 0.080 to 0.115 in.

15. Position the camshaft dowel pin at the 3 o'clock position. Align the zero marks on the pump drive gear and pump driven gear. Hold the camshaft in the rearward position and slide the pump drive gear onto the camshaft. Install the camshaft bearing retainer.

16. Install the timing chain and sprockets, making sure the timing marks are aligned.

17. Install the lifters, pushrods and rocker arms. See "Rocker Arm Replacement, Diesel Engine" for lifter bleed down procedures. *Failure to bleed down the lifters could bend valves when the engine is turned over.*

18. Install the injection pump adapter and injection pump. See the appropriate sections under "Fuel System" above for procedures.

19. Install the remaining components in the reverse order of removal.

CAMSHAFT INSPECTION

Completely clean the camshaft with solvent, paying special attention to cleaning the oil holes. Visually inspect the cam lobes and bearing journals for excessive wear. If a lobe is questionable, have the cam checked at a reputable machine shop; if a journal or lobe is worn, the camshaft must be reground or replaced. Also have the camshaft checked for straightness on a dial indicator.

NOTE: *If a cam journal is worn, there is a good chance that the bushings are worn.*

CAMSHAFT BEARINGS REMOVAL AND INSTALLATION

If excessive camshaft wear is found, or if the engine is being completely rebuilt, the camshaft bearings should be replaced.

NOTE: *The front and rear bearings should*

Remove camshaft bearings with a puller

CHECKING OIL HOLE ALIGNMENT WITH BRASS ROD. MAKE ROD AS SHOWN USING 3/32" BRASS ROD ABOUT 762 mm (30") LONG

90° BEND

Check cam bearing alignment with this homemade tool

RIDGE CAUSED BY CYLINDER WEAR

CYLINDER WALL

TOP OF PISTON

This ridge must be removed before pistons are removed

be removed last, and installed first. Those bearings act as guides for the other bearings and pilot.

1. Drive the camshaft rear plug from the block.

2. Assemble the removal puller with its shoulder on the bearing to be removed. Gradually tighten the puller nut until the bearing is removed.

3. Remove the remaining bearings, leaving the front and rear for last. To remove these, reverse the position of the puller, so as to pull the bearings towards the center of the block. Leave the tool in this position, pilot the new front and rear bearings on the installer, and pull them into position.

4. Return the puller to its original position and pull the remaining bearings into position.

NOTE: *Ensure that the oil holes align when installing the bearings. This is very important! You can make a simple tool out of a piece of 3/32 in. brass rod to check alignment. See the illustration.*

5. Replace the camshaft rear plug, and stake it into position.

Pistons and Connecting Rods
REMOVAL AND INSTALLATION

Before removing the pistons, the top of the cylinder bore must be examined for a ridge. A ridge at the top of the bore is the result of normal cylinder wear, caused by the piston rings only travelling so far up the bore in the course of the piston stroke. The ridge can be felt by hand; it must be removed before the pistons are removed.

A ridge reamer is necessary for this operation. Place the piston at the bottom of its stroke, and cover it with a rag. Cut the ridge away with the ridge reamer, using extreme care to avoid cutting too deeply. Remove the rag, and remove the cuttings that remain on the piston with a magnet and a rag soaked in clean oil. *Make sure the piston top and cylinder bore are absolutely clean before moving the piston.*

Match connecting rods to their caps with a scribe mark

Match the connecting rods to their cylinders with a number stamp

1. Remove intake manifold and cylinder head or heads.

2. Remove oil pan.

3. Remove oil pump assembly if necessary.

Cut rubber hose for con-rod bolt guides

Carefully tap the piston and rod assembly out with a wooden hammer handle

NOTCHES TOWARD FRONT OF ENGINE

BOSS ON ROD TOWARD REAR OF ENGINE

CHAMFERED CORNERS TOWARD FRONT OF ENGINE

LEFT NO. 1-3-5

Left bank piston and rod assembly, 231 V6

NOTCHES TOWARD FRONT OF ENGINE

BOSS ON ROD TOWARD FRONT OF ENGINE

CHAMFERED CORNERS TOWARD REAR OF ENGINE

RIGHT NO. 2-4-6

Right bank piston and rod assembly, 231 V6

4. Match-mark the connecting rod cap to the connecting rod with a scribe; each cap must be reinstalled on its proper rod in the proper direction. Remove the connecting rod bearing cap and the rod bearing. Number the top of each piston with silver paint or a felt-tip pen for later assembly.

5. Cut lengths of ⅜ in. diameter hose to use as rod bolt guides. Install the hose over the threads of the rod bolts, to prevent the bolt threads from damaging the crankshaft journals and cylinder walls when the piston is removed.

6. Squirt some clean engine oil onto the cylinder wall from above, until the wall is coated. Carefully push the piston and rod assembly up and out of the cylinder by tapping on the bottom of the connecting rod with a wooden hammer handle.

7. Place the rod bearing and cap back on the connecting rod, and install the nuts temporarily. Using a number stamp or punch, stamp the cylinder number on the side of the connecting rod and cap; this will help keep the proper piston and rod assembly on the proper cylinder.

NOTE: *On V6 engines, starting at the front the cylinders are numbered 2-4-6 on the right bank and 1-3-5 on the left. On all V8s, starting at the front the right bank cylinders are 2-4-6-8 and the left bank 1-3-5-7.*

8. Remove remaining pistons in similar manner.

Inline six cylinder piston-to-rod relationship

Small-block V8 and 229 V6 piston-to-rod relationship

Big-block (Mark IV) piston-to-rod relationship

On all engines, the notch on the piston will face the front of the engine for assembly. The chamfered corners of the bearing caps should face toward the front of the left bank and toward the rear of the right bank, and the boss on the connecting rod should face toward the front of the engine for the right bank and to the rear of the engine on the left bank.

On various engines, the piston compression rings are marked with a dimple, a letter "T", a letter "O," "GM" or the word "TOP" to identify the side of the ring which must face toward the top of the piston.

Piston Ring and Wrist Pin
REMOVAL

Some of the engines covered in this guide utilize pistons with pressed-in wrist pins; these must be removed by a special press designed for this purpose. Other pistons have their wrist pins secured by snap rings, which are easily removed with snap ring pliers. Separate the piston from the connecting rod.

A piston ring expander is necessary for removing piston rings without damaging them; any other method (screwdriver blades, pliers, etc.) usually results in the rings being bent, scratched or distorted, or the piston itself being damaged. When the rings are removed, clean the ring grooves using an appropriate ring groove cleaning tool, using care not to cut too deeply. Thoroughly clean all carbon and varnish from the piston with solvent.

CAUTION: *Do not use a wire brush or caustic solvent (acids, etc.) on pistons.*

Inspect the pistons for scuffing, scoring, cracks, pitting, or excessive ring groove wear. If these are evident, the piston must be replaced.

The piston should also be checked in relation to the cylinder diameter. Using a telescoping gauge and micrometer, or a dial gauge, measure the cylinder bore diameter perpendicular (90%) to the piston pin, 2½ in. below

Piston rings and wrist pin

RING EXPANDER

Removing the piston rings

Removing wrist pin clips

RING GROOVE
CLEANER

Clean the piston ring grooves using a ring groove cleaner

90°

Measuring the piston prior to fitting

◄——CENTERLINE OF ENGINE——►

A—AT RIGHT ANGLE TO
CENTERLINE OF ENGINE
B—PARALLEL TO
CENTERLINE OF ENGINE

Cylinder bore measuring points

the cylinder block deck (surface where the block mates with the heads). Then, with the micrometer, measure the piston perpendicular to its wrist pin on the skirt. The difference between the two measurements is the piston clearance. If the clearance is within specifications or slightly below (after the cylinders have been bored or honed), finish honing is all that is necessary. If

Measuring cylinder bore with a dial gauge

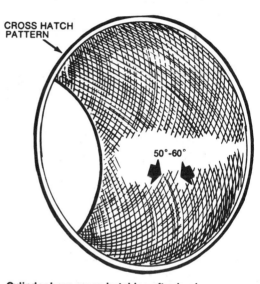

CROSS HATCH
PATTERN

50°-60°

Cylinder bore cross-hatching after honing

the clearance is excessive, try to obtain a slightly larger piston to bring clearance to within specifications. If this is not possible obtain the first oversize piston and hone (or if necessary, bore) the cylinder to size. Generally, if the cylinder bore is tapered .005 in. or more or is out-of-round .003 in. or more, it is advisable to rebore for the smallest possible oversize piston and rings.

After measuring, mark pistons with a felt-tip pen for reference and for assembly.

NOTE: *Cylinder honing and/or boring should be performed by a reputable, professional mechanic with the proper equipment. In some cases, "clean-up" honing can be done with the cylinder block in the car, but most excessive honing and all cylinder boring must be done with the block stripped and removed from the car.*

PISTON RING END GAP

Piston ring end gap should be checked while the rings are removed from the pistons. Incorrect end gap indicates that the wrong size rings are being used; *ring breakage could occur.*

Checking piston ring end gap with a feeler gauge

← **ENGINE LEFT** **ENGINE FRONT** **ENGINE RIGHT** →

2-4-6-8 cyl.

1-3-5-7 cyl.

"SMALL V8"

"A" OIL RING SPACER GAP
(Tang in Hole or Slot within Arc)

"B" OIL RING RAIL GAPS

"C" 2ND COMPRESSION RING CAP

"D" TOP COMPRESSION RING GAP

Ring gap location—all gasoline engines except 231 V6. For diesel ring gap, see diagram furnished with the new rings

Compress the piston rings to be used in a cylinder, one at a time, into that cylinder. Squirt clean oil into the cylinder, so that the rings and the top 2 inches of cylinder wall are coated. Using an inverted piston, press the rings approximately 1 in. below the deck of the block (on diesels, measure ring gap clearance with the ring positioned at the *bottom* of ring travel in the bore). Measure the ring end gap with a feeler gauge, and compare to the "Ring Gap" chart in this chapter. Carefully pull the ring out of the cylinder and file the ends squarely with a fine file to obtain the proper clearance.

PISTON RING SIDE CLEARANCE CHECK AND INSTALLATION

Check the pistons to see that the ring grooves and oil return holes have been properly cleaned.

OIL RING GAP 90° FROM COMPRESSION RING GAPS AND ON CAMSHAFT SIDE OF PISTON

NOTCH TOWARD FRONT OF ENGINE (LEFT BANK PISTON SHOWN)

TOP COMPRESSION RING GAP OPPOSITE NOTCH ON PISTON

2ND COMPRESSION RING GAP BELOW NOTCH ON PISTON

TOP VIEW OF PISTON

TOP COMPRESSION RING GAP | SECOND COMPRESSION RING GAP

180°

90° 90°

PISTON PIN | OIL RING GAP

CAMSHAFT

Piston ring gap location—231 V6

Slide a piston ring into its groove, and check the side clearance with a feeler gauge. On gasoline engines, make sure you insert the gauge between the ring and its lower land (lower edge of the groove), because any wear that occurs forms a step at the inner portion of the lower land. On diesels, insert the gauge between the ring and the *upper* land. If the piston grooves

Checking ring side clearance

have worn to the extent that relatively high steps exist on the lower land, the piston should be replaced, because these will interfere with the operation of the new rings and ring clearances will be excessive. Piston rings are not furnished in oversize widths to compensate for ring groove wear.

Install the rings on the piston, *lowest ring first,* using a piston ring expander. There is a high risk of breaking or distorting the rings, or scratching the piston, if the rings are installed by hand or other means.

Position the rings on the piston as illustrated; *spacing of the various piston ring gaps is crucial to proper oil retention and even cylinder wear.* When installing new rings, refer to the installation diagram furnished with the new parts.

Connecting Rod Bearings

Connecting rod bearings for the engines covered in this guide consist of two halves or shells which are interchangable in the rod and cap. When the shells are placed in position, the ends extend slightly beyond the rod and cap surfaces so that when the rod bolts are torqued the shells will be clamped tightly in place to insure positive seating and to prevent turning. A tang holds the shells in place.

NOTE: *The ends of the bearing shells must never be filed flush with the mating surface of the rod and cap.*

If a rod bearing becomes noisy or is worn so that its clearance on the crank journal is sloppy, a new bearing of the correct undersize must be selected and installed since there is no provision for adjustment.

CAUTION: *Under no circumstances should the rod end or cap be filed to adjust the bearing clearance, nor should shims of any kind be used.*

Inspect the rod bearings while the rod assemblies are out of the engine. If the shells are scored or show flaking, they should be replaced. If they are in good shape check for

proper clearance on the crank journal (see below). Any scoring or ridges on the crank journal means the crankshaft must be replaced, or reground and fitted with undersized bearings.

NOTE: *If turbo V6 crank journals are scored or ridged the crankshaft must be replaced, as regrinding will reduce the durability of the crankshaft.*

CHECKING BEARING CLEARANCE AND REPLACING BEARINGS

NOTE: *Make sure connecting rods and their caps are kept together, and that the caps are installed in the proper direction.*

Replacement bearings are available in standard size, and in undersizes for reground crankshafts. Connecting rod-to-crankshaft bearing clearance is checked using Plastigage® at either the top or bottom of each crank jour-

FLATTENED GAGING PLASTIC

Checking rod bearing clearance with Plastigage® or equivalent

TANG

GM M400

8943

UNDERSIZE STAMP IN THOUSANDS

Undersize marks are stamped on the bearing shells. Tangs fit in the notches in the rod and cap

nal. The Plastigage® has a range of .001 in. to .003 in.

1. Remove the rod cap with the bearing shell. Completely clean the bearing shell and the crank journal, and blow any oil from the oil hole in the crankshaft; Plastigage® is soluble in oil.

2. Place a piece of Plastigage® lengthwise along the bottom center of the lower bearing shell, then install the cap with shell and torque the bolt or nuts to specification. DO NOT turn the crankshaft with Plastigage® in the bearing.

3. Remove the bearing cap with the shell. The flattened Plastigage® will be found sticking to either the bearing shell or crank journal. *Do not remove it yet.*

4. Use the scale printed on the Plastigage® envelope to measure the flattened material at its widest point. The number within the scale which most closely corresponds to the width of the Plastigage® indicates bearing clearance in thousandths of an inch.

5. Check the specifications chart in this chapter for the desired clearance. It is advisable to install a new bearing if clearance exceeds .003 in.; however, if the bearing is in good condition and is not being checked because of bearing noise, bearing replacement is not necessary.

6. If you are installing new bearings, try a standard size, then each undersize in order until one is found that is within the specified limits when checked for clearance with Plastigage®. Each undersize shell has its size stamped on it.

7. When the proper size shell is found, clean off the Plastigage®, oil the bearing thoroughly, reinstall the cap with its shell and torque the rod bolt nuts to specification.

NOTE: *With the proper bearing selected and the nuts torqued, it should be possible to move the connecting rod back and forth freely on the crank journal as allowed by the specified connecting rod end clearance. If the rod cannot be moved, either the rod bearing is too far undersize or the rod is misaligned.*

PISTON AND CONNECTING ROD ASSEMBLY AND INSTALLATION

Install the connecting rod to the piston, making sure piston installation notches and any marks on the rod are in proper relation to one another. Lubricate the wrist pin with clean engine oil, and install the pin into the rod and piston assembly, either by hand or by using a wrist pin press as required. Install snap rings if equipped, and rotate them in their grooves to make sure they are seated. To install the piston and connecting rod assembly:

1. Make sure connecting rod big-end bear-

Piston locations in block, diesel shown

Using a wooden hammer handle, tap the piston down through the ring compressor and into the cylinder

Checking connecting rod side clearance with a feeler gauge. Use a small pry bar to carefully spread the connecting rods

ings (including end cap) are of the correct size and properly installed.

2. Fit rubber hoses over the connecting rod bolts to protect the crankshaft journals, as in the "Piston Removal" procedure. Coat the rod bearings with clean oil.

3. Using the proper ring compressor, insert the piston assembly into the cylinder so that the notch in the top of the piston faces the front of the engine (this assumes that the dimple(s) or other markings on the connecting rods are in correct relation to the piston notch(s)).

4. From beneath the engine, coat each crank journal with clean oil. Pull the connecting rod, with the bearing shell in place, into position against the crank journal.

5. Remove the rubber hoses. Install the bearing cap and cap nuts and torque to specification.

NOTE: *When more than one rod and piston assembly is being installed, the connecting rod cap attaching nuts should only be tightened enough to keep each rod in position until all have been installed. This will ease the installation of the remaining piston assemblies.*

6. Check the clearance between the sides of the connecting rods and the crankshaft using a feeler gauge. Spread the rods slightly with a screwdriver to insert the gage. If clearance is below the minimum tolerance, the rod may be machined to provide adequate clearance. If clearance is excessive, substitute an unworn rod, and recheck. If clearance is still outside specifications, the crankshaft must be welded and reground, or replaced.

7. Replace the oil pump if removed and the oil pan.

8. Install the cylinder head(s) and intake manifold.

Crankshaft and Main Bearings

CRANKSHAFT REMOVAL

1. Drain the engine oil and remove the engine from the car. Mount the engine on a work stand in a suitable working area. Invert the engine, so the oil pan is facing up.

2. Remove the engine front (timing) cover.
3. Remove the timing chain and gears.
4. Remove the oil pan.
5. Remove the oil pump.
6. Stamp the cylinder number on the machined surfaces of the bolt bosses of the connecting rods and caps for identification when reinstalling. If the pistons are to be removed eventually from the connecting rod, mark the cylinder number on the pistons with silver paint or felt-tip pen for proper cylinder identification and cap-to-rod location.

Diesel crankshaft, exploded view. Gasoline engines similar; bearing configuration may differ among engines

1. Rubber hose
2. #4 rod
3. #3 rod
4. Oil pan bolt
5. Note overlap of adjacent rods
6. Rubber bands

Crankshaft removal showing hose lengths on rod bolts

7. Remove the connecting rod caps. Install lengths of rubber hose on each of the connecting rod bolts, to protect the crank journals when the crank is removed.

8. Mark the main bearing caps with a number punch or punch so that they can be reinstalled in their original positions.

9. Remove all main bearing caps.

10. Note the position of the keyway in the crankshaft so it can be installed in the same position.

11. Install rubber bands between a bolt on each connecting rod and oil pan bolts that have been reinstalled in the block (see illustration). This will keep the rods from banging on the block when the crank is removed.

12. Carefully lift the crankshaft out of the block. The rods will pivot to the center of the engine when the crank is removed.

MAIN BEARING INSPECTION AND REPLACEMENT

Like connecting rod big-end bearings, the crankshaft main bearings are shell-type inserts that do not utilize shims and cannot be adjusted. The bearings are available in various standard and undersizes; if main bearing clearance is found to be too sloppy, a new bearing (both upper and lower halves) is required.

NOTE: *Factory-undersized crankshafts are marked, sometimes with a "9" and/or a large spot of light green paint; the bearing caps also will have the paint on each side of the undersized journal.*

Generally, the lower half of the bearing shell (except No. 1 bearing) shows greater wear and fatigue. If the lower half only shows the effects of normal wear (no heavy scoring or discoloration), it can usually be assumed that the upper half is also in good shape; conversely, if the lower half is heavily worn or damaged, both halves should be replaced. *Never replace one bearing half without replacing the other.*

CHECKING CLEARANCE

Main bearing clearance can be checked both with the crankshaft in the car and with the engine out of the car. If the engine block is still in the car, the crankshaft should be supported both front and rear (by the damper and to remove clearance from the upper bearing. Total clearance can then be measured between the lower bearing and journal. If the block has been removed from the car, and is inverted, the crank will rest on the upper bearings and the total clearance can be measured between the lower bearing and journal. Clearance is checked in the same manner as the connecting rod bearings, with Plastigage®.

NOTE: *Crankshaft bearing caps and bearing shells should NEVER be filed flush with the cap-to-block mating surface to adjust for wear in the old bearings. Always install new bearings.*

1. If the crankshaft has been removed, install it (block removed from car). If the block is still in the car, remove the oil pan and oil pump. Starting with the rear bearing cap, remove the cap and wipe all oil from the crank journal and bearing cap.

2. Place a strip of Plastigage® the full width of the bearing, (parallel to the crankshaft), on the journal.

CAUTION: *Do not rotate the crankshaft while the gaging material is between the bearing and the journal.*

3. Install the bearing cap and evenly torque the cap bolts to specification.

4. Remove the bearing cap. The flattened Plastigage® will be sticking to either the bearing shell or the crank journal.

5. Use the graduated scale on the Plastigage® envelope to measure the material at its widest point.

NOTE: *If the flattened Plastigage® tapers towards the middle or ends, there is a difference in clearance indicating the bearing or journal has a taper, low spot or other irregularity. If this is indicated, measure the crank journal with a micrometer.*

6. If bearing clearance is within specifications, the bearing insert is in good shape. Replace the insert if the clearance is not within specifications. *Always replace both upper and lower inserts as a unit.*

7. Standard, .001 in. or .002 in. undersize bearings should produce the proper clearance. If these sizes still produce too sloppy a fit, the crankshaft must be reground for use with the next undersize bearing. Recheck all clearances after installing new bearings.

8. Replace the rest of the bearings in the same manner. After all bearings have been checked, rotate the crankshaft to make sure there is no excessive drag. When checking the No. 1 main bearing, loosen the accessory drive belts (engine in car) to prevent a tapered reading with the Plastigage.®

MAIN BEARING REPLACEMENT
Engine Out of Car

1. Remove and inspect the crankshaft.

2. Remove the main bearings from the bearing saddles in the cylinder block and main bearing caps.

3. Coat the bearing surfaces of the new, correct size main bearings with clean engine oil and install them in the bearing saddles in the block and in the main bearing caps.

Home-made bearing roll-out pin

4. Install the crankshaft. See "Crankshaft Installation."

Engine in Car

1. With the oil pan, oil pump and spark plugs removed, remove the cap from the main bearing needing replacement and remove the bearing from the cap.

2. Make a bearing roll-out pin, using a bent cotter pin as shown in the illustration. Install the end of the pin in the oil hole in the crankshaft journal.

3. Rotate the crankshaft clockwise as viewed from the front of the engine. This will roll the upper bearing out of the block.

4. Lube the new upper bearing with clean engine oil and insert the plain (unnotched) end between the crankshaft and the indented or notched side of the block. Roll the bearing into place, making sure that the oil holes are aligned. Remove the roll pin from the oil hole.

5. Lube the new lower bearing and install the main bearing cap. Install the main bearing cap, making sure it is positioned in proper direction with the matchmarks in alignment.

6. Torque the main bearing cap bolts to specification.

NOTE: *See "Crankshaft Installation" for thrust bearing alignment.*

shaft can be installed. Thoroughly clean the upper and lower bearing surfaces, and lube them with clean engine oil. Install the crankshaft and main bearing caps.

Dip all main bearing cap bolts in clean oil, and torque all main bearing caps, excluding the thrust bearing cap, to specifications (see the "Crankshaft and Connecting Rod" chart in this chapter to determine which bearing is the thrust bearing). Tighten the thrust bearing bolts finger tight. To align the thrust bearing, pry the crankshaft the extent of its axial travel several times, holding the last movement toward the front of the engine. Add thrust washers if required for proper alignment. Torque the thrust bearing cap to specifications.

To check crankshaft end-play, pry the crankshaft to the extreme rear of its axial travel, then to the extreme front of its travel. Using a feeler gauge, measure the end-play at the front of the rear main bearing. End play may also be measured at the thrust bearing. Install a new rear main bearing oil seal in the cylinder block and main bearing cap. Continue to reassemble the engine.

Measuring crankshaft-end-play with a feeler gauge

Roll-out pin installed for removing upper half of main bearing

CRANKSHAFT END PLAY AND INSTALLATION

When main bearing clearance has been checked, bearings examined and/or replaced, the crank-

Oil pan installation. Gaskets and seals differ slightly among engines

PRY FORWARD   THRUST BEARING

PRY BACKWARD   THRUST BEARING

THRUST BEARING

PRY CRANKSHAFT FORWARD   PRY CAP BACKWARD   TIGHTEN CAP

Aligning crankshaft thrust bearing

ENGINE LUBRICATION

Both six-cylinder and V8 engines have pressurized lubrication systems with full-flow oil filters.

Oil Pan

REMOVAL AND INSTALLATION

Inline Six-Cylinder

NOTE: *Pan removal for all engines may be easier if the engine is turned to No. 1 cylinder firing position. This positions the crankshaft in the path of least resistance for pan removal.*

1. Disconnect the battery ground cable.
2. Remove the upper radiator mounting bolts or side mount bolts. Remove the upper and lower hoses from the water pump.
3. Install a piece of heavy cardboard between the fan and the radiator.
4. Disconnect the fuel suction line from the fuel pump.
5. Raise the car and drain the oil.
6. Remove the starter.
7. Remove the flywheel lower pan or converter lower pan and splash shield.
8. Rotate the crankshaft until the timing mark on the damper is at the six o'clock position.
9. Remove the brake line retaining bolts from the crossmember and move the brake line out of the way.
10. Remove the thru-bolts from the front motor mounts.
11. Remove the oil pan bolts.
12. Slowly raise the engine until the motor mounts can be removed from the frame brackets.
13. Remove the mounts and continue to raise the engine until it has been raised three inches.
14. Remove the oil pan by pulling it down from the engine and then twisting it into the opening left by the removal of the left engine mount.
15. When the pan is clear of the engine, tilt the front up and remove it by pulling it down and to the rear.
16. Install the oil pan gaskets to the engine block.
17. Install the oil pan and torque the side bolts to 6–8 ft. lbs. and the end bolts to 9–12 ft. lbs.
18. Install the motor mounts, and then install the remaining components using a reverse procedure of removal.

1964–68 V8

1. Remove the engine from the chassis.
2. Remove the bellhousing or converter underpan.
3. Remove the starter.
4. Remove the oil pan.
5. Reverse the removal procedure to install the pan.

1969 396, 1969 Manual Transmission, and 1970–72, 396 and 402

1. Disconnect the battery ground cable.
2. Remove the air cleaner, dipstick, distributor cap, radiator shroud and upper mounting panel.
3. On big-block models, place a piece of heavy cardboard between the radiator and the fan.
4. Disconnect the engine ground straps. Remove the fuel pump on 307 and 350 engines.
5. Disconnect the accelerator control cable.
6. Drain the oil. Remove the filter on 307 and 350 engines.
7. Remove the driveshaft and plug the rear of transmission.
8. Remove the starter.
9. Disconnect the transmission linkage at the transmission or remove the floorshift lever.
10. Disconnect the speedometer cable and the back-up switch connector.
11. On manual transmission vehicles, disconnect the clutch cross-shaft at the frame. On automatic transmission vehicles, disconnect the

cooler lines, detent cable, rod or switch wire, and the modulator pipe.

12. Remove the crossmember bolts. Jack up the engine and move the crossmember rearward.

13. Remove the crossover or disconnect the dual exhaust pipes.

14. Remove:
   a. Flywheel housing cover;
   b. Transmission;
   c. Flywheel housing and throwout bearing (manual transmission);
   d. Front engine mount through-bolts.

15. Raise the rear of engine approximately 4 in. Support the engine by hoist.

16. Raise the front of the engine approximately 4 in. and insert 2 in. blocks under the front engine mounts.

17. Rotate the crankshaft until the timing mark on the torsional damper is at the six o'clock position.

18. Unbolt and remove the oil pan.

1969–72 Small Block V8s and All 1973 and Later V8s

1. Disconnect the negative battery cable.

2. As a precaution, remove the distributor cap to keep it from getting broken when the engine is raised.

3. Remove the fan shroud retaining bolts.

4. On earlier models it may be necessary to remove the radiator upper mounting panel.

5. Raise the vehicle on a hoist and drain the engine oil.

6. Disconnect the exhaust pipes or crossover pipes.

7. On automatic transmission equipped vehicles, remove the converter housing underpan and splash shield.

8. Rotate the crankshaft until the timing mark on the torsional dampener is at the six o'clock position.

9. The starter can be swung out of the way by disconnecting the brace at the starter, removing the inboard starter bolt and loosening the outboard starter bolt. On 1970 small V8, remove the fuel pump.

10. Remove the front engine mount thrubolts.

11. Raise the engine and insert blocks, at least three in. thick, under the engine mounts.

12. Remove the oil pan bolts and remove the oil pan.

13. To install, clean all gasket and seal surfaces thoroughly, use new gaskets and seals, and reverse the removal procedure.

NOTE: *If the crankshaft was rotated while the pan was off, place the timing mark at the six o'clock position.*

V6

1. Disconnect the negative battery cable.

2. Remove the upper half of the radiator fan shroud.

3. Raise the front of the car and drain the oil.

4. Unscrew the exhaust pipe cross-over tube mounting nuts at the manifold. Lower the crossover tube.

5. On models which are equipped with an automatic transmission, remove the torque converter cover.

6. Remove the upper bolt on the starter brace and then remove the inboard starter bolt and swing the starter assembly aside.

7. Loosen and remove the left-hand motor mount thru-bolt and then loosen the thru-bolt on the right-hand mount.

8. Raise the engine and then reinstall the thru-bolt in the left-hand motor mount. *Do not tighten the bolt.*

9. Unscrew the attaching bolts and remove the oil pan from under the engine.

10. To install, clean all gasket and seal surfaces thoroughly, use new gaskets and seals and reverse the removed procedure.

Diesel Engines

1. Remove the vacuum pump and drive (with A/C) or the oil pump drive (without A/C).

2. Disconnect the batteries and remove the dipstick.

3. Remove the upper raidator support and fan shroud.

4. Raise and support the car. Drain the oil.

5. Remove the flywheel cover.

6. Disconnect the exhaust and crossover pipes.

7. Remove the oil cooler lines at the filter base.

8. Remove the starter assembly. Support the engine with a jack.

9. Remove the engine mounts from the block.

Diesel oil cooler lines, 263 V6 shown

10. Raise the front of the engine and remove the oil pan.

11. Installation is the reverse of removal.

Oil Pump

REMOVAL AND INSTALLATION

In Line Six-Cylinder

1. Remove the oil pan as previously described.

2. Remove the two flange mounting bolts, the pick-up bolt, then remove the pump and screen together.

3. To install, align the oil pump driveshafts to match with the distributor tang and position the flange over the distributor lower bushing. Install the pump mounting bolts.

4. Install the oil pan.

Gasoline and Diesel V6 and V8 (Except 231 V6)

1. Remove the oil pan as previously described.

2. Remove the pump-to-rear main bearing cap bolts and remove the pump and extension shaft.

3. To install align the slot on the top end of the extension shaft with the drive tang on the lower end of the distributor driveshaft (or until the shaft mates into the oil pump drive gear on diesels) and install the rear main bearing cap bolt.

4. Position the pump screen so that the bottom edge is parallel to the oil pan rails.

5. Install the oil pan.

Typical oil pump installation, V6 diesel shown

231 V6

The oil pump is located in the timing chain cover and is connected by a drilled passage to the oil screen housing and pipe assembly in the oil pan. All oil is discharged from the pump to the oil pump cover assembly, on which the oil filter is mounted.

Oil pump, exploded view. All models similar

1. To remove the oil pump cover and gears, first remove the oil filter.

2. Remove the screws which attach the oil pump cover assembly to the timing chain cover.

3. Remove the cover assembly and slide out the oil pump gears. Clean the gears and inspect them for any obvious defects such as chipping or scoring.

4. Remove the oil pressure relief valve cap, spring and valve. Clean them and inspect them for wear or scoring. Check the relief valve spring to see that it is not worn on its side or collapsed. Replace the spring if it seems questionable.

5. Check the relief valve for a correct fit in its bore. It should be an easy slip fit and no more. If any perceptible shake can be felt, the valve and/or the cover should be replaced.

6. To install, lubricate the pressure relief valve and spring and place them in the cover. Install the cap and the gasket. Torque the cap to 35 ft. lbs.

7. Pack the oil pump gear cavity full of petroleum jelly. Do not use gear lube. Reinstall the oil pump gears so that the petroleum jelly is forced into every cavity of the gear pocket, and between the gear teeth. There must be no air spaces. This step is very important. Unless the pump is packed, it may not begin to pump oil as soon as the engine is started.

8. Install the cover assembly using a new gasket and sealer. Tighten the screws to 10 ft. lbs.

9. Install the oil filter.

OVERHAUL

231 V6

The oil pump is located in the timing chain cover and is connected by a drilled passage to the oil screen housing and pipe assembly in the oil pan. All oil is discharged from the pump to the oil

Checking oil pump end clearance

pump cover assembly, on which the oil filter is mounted.

1. To remove the oil pump cover and gears, first remove the oil filter.

2. Remove the screws which attach the oil pump cover assembly to the timing chain cover.

3. Remove the cover assembly and slide out the oil pump gears. Clean the gears and inspect them for any obvious defects such as chipping or scoring.

4. Remove the oil pressure relief valve cap, spring and valve. Clean them and inspect them for wear or scoring. Check the relief valve spring to see that it is not worn on its side or collapsed. Replace the spring if it seems questionable.

5. Check the relief valve for a correct fit in its bore. It should be an easy slip fit and no more. If any perceptible shake can be felt the valve and/or the cover should be replaced.

6. Install the oil pump gears (if removed) and the shaft in the oil pump body section of the timing chain cover to check the gear end clearance and gear side clearance. Check gear end clearance by placing a straight edge over the gears and measure the clearance between the straight edge and the gasket surface. Clearance should be between .002 in. and .006 in. Check gear side clearance by inserting the feeler

Use a feeler gauge to check oil pump side clearance

gauge between the gear teeth and the side wall of the pump body. Clearance should be between .002 in. and .005 in.

7. Check the pump cover flatness by placing a straight edge across the cover face, with a feeler gauge between the straight edge and the cover. If clearance is .001 in. or more, replace the cover.

8. To install, lubricate the pressure relief valve and spring and place them in the cover. Install the cap and the gasket. Torque the cap to 35 ft. lbs.

9. Pack the oil pump gear cavity full of petroleum jelly. *Do not use gear lube.* Reinstall the oil pump gears so that the petroleum jelly is forced into every cavity of the gear pocket, and between the gear teeth. There must be no air spaces. *This step is very important.*

CAUTION: *Unless the pump is primed this way, it won't produce any oil pressure when the engine is started.*

10. Install the cover assembly using a new gasket and sealer. Tighten the screws to 10 ft. lbs.

11. Install the oil filter.

V8 Including V6 and V8 Diesel

1. Remove the oil pump drive shaft extension.

2. Remove the cotter pin, spring and the pressure regulator valve.

NOTE: *Place your thumb over the pressure regulator bore before removing the cotter pin, as the spring is under pressure.*

3. Remove the oil pump cover attaching screws and remove the oil pump cover and gasket. Clean the pump in solvent or kerosene, and wash out the pick-up screen.

4. Remove the drive gear and idler gear from the pump body.

5. Check the gears for scoring and other damage. Install the gears if in good condition, or replace them if damaged. Check gear end clearance by placing a straight edge over the gears and measure the clearance between the straight edge and the gasket surface with a feeler gauge. End clearance for both diesels is .0005 in. to .0075 in., and other V8s is .002 in. to .0065 in. If end clearance is excessive, check for scores in the cover that would bring the total clearance over the specs.

6. Check gear side clearance by inserting the feeler gauge between the gear teeth and the side wall of the pump body. Clearance should be between .002 in. and .005 in.

7. Pack the inside of the pump completely with petroleum jelly. DO NOT use engine oil. The pump MUST be primed this way or it won't produce any oil pressure when the engine is started.

8. Install the cover screws and tighten alternately and evenly to 8 ft. lbs.

9. Position the pressure regulator valve into the pump cover, closed end first, then install the spring and retaining pin.

NOTE: *When assembling the drive shaft extension to the drive shaft, the end of the extension nearest the washers must be inserted into the drive shaft.*

10. Insert the drive shaft extension through the opening in the main bearing cap and block until the shaft mates into the distributor drive gear.

11. Install the pump onto the rear main bearing cap and install the attaching bolts. Torque the bolts to 35 ft. lbs.

12. Install the oil pan.

Rear Main Oil Seal

REPLACEMENT

All Except Diesel and 231 V6

The rear main bearing seal may be replaced without removing the crankshaft. Seals should only be replaced as a pair. Fabrication of a seal installation tool as shown in the figure will prevent damaging the bead on the cylinder block. The seal lips should face the front of the engine when properly installed.

1. Drain the crankcase and remove the oil pan and oil pump.

2. Remove the rear main bearing cap, and pry the seal out from the bottom with a small pry bar.

3. Remove the upper seal with a small hammer and a brass pin punch. Tap on one end of the seal until the opposite end can be gripped with pliers.

4. Clean the bearing cap and the crankshaft.

5. Coat the lips and bead of the seal with a light engine oil. Do not get oil on the seal ends.

6. Insert the tip of the installation tool between the crankshaft and the seal seat of the cylinder block. Place the seal between the tip of the tool and the crankshaft, so that the bead contacts the tip of the tool.

7. Be sure that the seal lip is facing the front of the engine, and work the seal around the

Packing the rear main oil seal

Cutting off the lower seal ends

Removing the lower rear main seal

Dimensions for making an oil seal installation tool

Removing the upper rear main seal

crankshaft, using the installation tool to protect the seal from the corner of the cylinder block.

NOTE: *Do not remove the tool until the opposite end of the seal is flush with the cylinder block surface.*

8. Remove the installation tool, being careful not to pull the seal out at the same time.

9. Using the same procedure, install the lower seal into the bearing cap. Use your finger and thumb to lever the seal into the cap.

10. Apply sealer to the cylinder block only where the cap mates to the surface. Do not apply sealer to the seal ends.

11. Install the rear cap and torque the bolts to specifications. Install the oil pan and pump as previously described.

231 V6

On this engine, the upper half of the rear main bearing oil seal may be repaired, but not replaced, with the crankshaft in place. To completely replace the seal, the crankshaft must be removed. The lower part of the seal may be replaced in the conventional manner when the bearing cap is removed.

NOTE: *Place the new bearing cap neoprene seals in kerosene for two minutes before installing them. The neoprene seals will swell up once exposed to the oil and heat when in the engine. It is normal for the seals to leak for a short time, until they become properly seated. The seals must NOT be cut to fit.*

1. Remove the oil pan and the rear main bearing cap.

2. Using a blunt-edged tool, drive the up-

NEOPRENE COMPOSITION SEAL

APPLY SEALER TO THESE TWO AREAS

231 V6 lower main bearing cap. Sealer application. DO NOT over-apply

per seal into its groove until it is tightly packed. This is usually ¼–¾ in.

3. Cut pieces of a new seal ¹⁄₁₆ in. longer than required to fill the grooves and install them, packing them into place.

4. Carefully trim any protruding edges of the seal.

5. Remove the old seal from the bearing cap, and install a new seal.

NOTE: *To help eliminate oil leakage at the joint where the cap meets the crankcase, apply RTV-type sealer to the rear main bearing cap split line. When applying sealer, use only a thin coat as an overabundance will not allow the cap to seat properly.*

6. Reinstall the cap and the oil pan.

Diesel

The crankshaft need not be removed to replace the rear main bearing upper oil seal. The lower seal is installed in the bearing cap.

Rolling the new lower seal into place

Flywheel installation. Follow torque specifications closely

1. Drain the crankcase oil and remove the oil pan and rear main bearing cap.

2. Using a special main seal tool or a tool that can be made from a dowel (see illustration), drive the upper seal into its groove on each side until it is tightly packed. This is usually ¼–¾ in.

3. Measure the amount the seal was driven up on one side; add ¹⁄₁₆ in., then cut this length from the old seal that was removed from the main bearing cap. Use a single-edge razor blade. Measure the amount the seal was driven up on the other side; add ¹⁄₁₆ in. and cut another length from the old seal. Use the main bearing cap as a holding fixture when cutting the seal as illustrated. Carefully trim the protruding seal.

4. Work these two pieces of seal up into the cylinder block on each side with two nailsets or small screwdrivers. Using the packing tool again, pack these pieces into the block, then trim them flush with a razor blade or hobby knife as shown. *Do not scratch the bearing surface with the razor.*

5. Install a new seal in the rear main bearing cap. Run a ¹⁄₁₆ in. bead of sealer onto the outer mating surface of the bearing cap. Assemble the cap to the block and torque to specifications.

Flywheel and Ring Gear
REMOVAL AND INSTALLATION

The ring gear is an integral part of the flywheel and is not replaceable.

1. Remove the transmission.

2. Remove the six bolts attaching the flywheel to the crankshaft flange. Remove the flywheel.

3. Inspect the flywheel for cracks, and inspect the ring gear for burrs or worn teeth. Replace the flywheel if any damage is apparent. Remove burrs with a mill file.

4. Install the flywheel. The flywheel will only attach to the crankshaft in one position, as the bolt holes are unevenly spaced. Install the bolts and torque to specification.

ENGINE COOLING

The cooling system consists of a radiator, belt-driven fan, thermostat, and a mechanical water pump. Air conditioned and high-performance engines are equipped with a viscous drive fan. This fan restricts operation at 1500 rpm in cold weather and 3500 rpm during warmer temperatures. This fan requires less horsepower to drive during high rpm operation and reduces underhood noise. 1977 and later models are equipped with a special pressure relief radiator cap. Be sure any replacement cap used is the same.

Refer to Chapter 1 for the coolant level checking procedure and to the Appendix for "Antifreeze" charts. The coolant should periodically be drained and the system flushed with clean water, at the intervals specified in Chapter 1. Service stations have reverse flushing equipment available; there also permanently-installed do-it-yourself reverse flushing attachments available.

There is a coolant drain cock at the bottom of most radiators. Six-cylinder engines have a coolant drain plug on the left side of the engine block; V8s have one on each side. Some engines don't have any.

The coolant should always be maintained at a minimum of −20°F freezing protection, regardless of the prevailing temperature. This concentration assures rust protection and the highest possible boiling point. It also prevents the heater core from freezing on air-conditioned models.

Two common causes of corrosion are air-suction and exhaust gas leakage. Air may be drawn into the system due to low coolant level in the radiator, a leaky water pump, loose hose connections, a defective radiator pressure cap, or a leaky overflow hose connection to the radiator on the coolant recovery bottle. Exhaust gas may be blown into the cooling system past the cylinder head gasket or through cracks in the cylinder head and block.

Radiator fan shroud mounting, diesel sedans and wagons. Gasoline-engined cars similar

Some radiator fan shrouds mount like this

Typical coolant recovery tank, mounted on inner fender

Radiator

REMOVAL AND INSTALLATION

1. Drain the cooling system.
2. Disconnect the radiator upper and lower hoses and, if applicable, the transmission cool-

ant lines. Remove the coolant recovery system line, if so equipped.
3. Remove the radiator upper panel if so equipped.
4. If there is a radiator shroud in front of the radiator, the radiator and shroud are removed as an assembly.
5. If there is a fan shroud, remove the shroud attaching screws and let the shroud hang on the fan.
6. Remove the radiator attaching bolts and remove the radiator.
7. Installation is the reverse of the removal procedure.

Thermostat

REMOVAL AND INSTALLATION

1. Drain the radiator until the level is below the thermostat level (below the level of the intake manifold).
2. Remove the water outlet elbow assembly from the engine. Remove the thermostat from inside the elbow.
3. Install new thermostat in the reverse order of removal, making sure the spring side is inserted into the elbow. Clean the gasket surfaces on the water outlet elbow and the intake manifold. Use a new gasket when installing the elbow to the manifold. Refill the radiator to approximately 2½ inches below the filler neck.

Removing thermostat from water outlet elbow

Diesel (left) and gasoline engine thermostat location and outlet elbow mounting

Water Pump

REMOVAL AND INSTALLATION

1. Disconnect the battery.
2. Drain the radiator.
3. Loosen the alternator and other accessories at their adjusting points, and remove the fan belts from the fan pulley.
4. Remove the fan and pulley.
5. Remove any accessory brackets that might interfere with water pump removal.
6. Disconnect the hose from the water pump inlet and the heater hose from the nipple on the pump. Remove the bolts, pump assembly and old gasket from the timing chain cover.
7. Check the pump shaft bearings for end play or roughness in operation. Water pump bearings usually emit a squealing sound with the engine running when the bearings need to be replaced. Replace the pump if the bearings are not in good shape or have been noisy.
8. To install, make sure the gasket surfaces on the pump and timing chain cover are clean. Install the pump assembly with a new gasket. Tighten the bolts uniformly.

WATER PUMP

Typical V8 front cover showing water pump and pump mounting bolts

9. The remainder of installation is the reverse of removal. Fill the cooling system and check for leaks at the pump and hose joints. Make sure all of the accessory belts are properly tensioned.

Emission Controls and Fuel System

4

EMISSION CONTROLS

There are three sources of automotive pollutants: Crankcase fumes, exhaust gases and gasoline evaporation. The pollutants formed from these substances fall into three categories: unburnt hydrocarbons (HC), carbon monoxide (CO) and oxides of nitrogen (NOx). The equipment that is used to limit these pollutants is commonly called emission control equipment.

Positive Crankcase Ventilation

OPERATION

Until 1967, mid-size Chevrolets were available with two types of crankcase ventilation systems: the closed type found on all California cars and some non-California cars, or the open type. The open ventilation system (non-California cars) receives outside air through a vented oil filler cap. This filtered cap permits outside air to enter the valve cover and also allows crankcase vapors to escape from the valve cover into the atmosphere. 1967 California law and later Federal law requires that this filler cap be non-vented to prevent the emission of vapors into the air. To supply this closed system with fresh air, a hose runs from the carburetor air cleaner to an inlet hole in the valve cover. The carburetor end of the hose fits into a cup-shaped flame arrestor and filter in the air cleaner cover. In the event of a carburetor back-fire, this arrestor prevents the spread of fire to the valve cover where it could create an explosion. Included in the system is a PCV (positive crankcase ventilation) valve that fits into an outlet hole in the top of the valve cover. A hose connects this valve to a vacuum outlet at the intake manifold. Contained within the valve housing is a valve (pointed at one end, flat at the other) positioned within a coiled spring. During idle or low speed operation, when manifold vac-

uum is highest, the valve spring tension is overcome by the high vacuum pull and, as a result, the valve is pulled up to very nearly seal off the manifold end of the valve housing. This restricts the flow of crankcase vapors to the intake manifold at a time when crankcase pressures are lowest and least disruptive to engine performance. At times of acceleration or constant speed, intake manifold vacuum is reduced to a point where it can no longer pull against the valve spring and so, spring force pulls the valve away from the housing outlet allowing crankcase vapors to escape through the hose to the intake manifold. Once inside the manifold, the gases enter the combustion chambers to be reburned. At times of engine backfire (at the carburetor) or when the engine is turned off, manifold vacuum ceases permitting the spring to pull the valve against the inlet (crankcase end) end of the valve housing. This seals off the inlet, thereby stopping the entrance of crankcase gases into the valve and preventing the possibility of a backfire spreading through

KEY TO PCV SYSTEM
F = FILTERED AIR
B = BLOW BY GASES
F + B
COMBUSTIBLE MIXTURE

Schematic of PCV system (© Chevrolet Motor Division)

V8 PCV valve location

V6 PCV valve

Closed and positive ventilation systems

the hose and valve to ignite these gases. The carburetor used with this system is set to provide a richer gas mixture to compensate for the additional air and gases going to the intake manifold. A valve that is clogged and stuck closed will not allow this extra air to reach the manifold. Consequently, the engine will run roughly and plugs will foul due to the creation of an overly rich air/fuel mixture. It can be said that the PCV system performs three functions. It reduces air pollution by reburning the crankcase gases rather than releasing them to the atmosphere, and it increases engine life and gas economy. By recirculating crankcase gases, oil contamination that is harmful to engine parts is kept to a minimum. Recirculated gases returned to the intake manifold are combustible and, when combined with the air/fuel mixture from the carburetor, become fuel for operation, slightly increasing gas economy. In 1968, all cars were required to use the closed system and vented filler caps became a thing of the past. For more information on PCV, see Chapter One.

SERVICE

Inspect the PCV system hose and connections at each tune-up and replace any deteriorated hoses. Check the PCV valve at every tune-up and replace it every 24,000 miles on 1967–74 cars, and every 30,000 miles on later cars. See Chapter One for testing procedure.

REMOVAL AND INSTALLATION

The valve is inserted into a rubber grommet in the valve cover at the large end (on 1964–66

V8 engines, the valve is located in, or near the carburetor base). At the narrow end, it is inserted into a hose and clamped. To remove it, gently pull it out of the valve cover, then open the clamp with a pair of pliers. Hold the clamp open while sliding it an inch or two down the hose (away from the valve), and then remove the valve. If the end of the hose is hard or cracked where it holds the valve, it may be feasible to cut the end off if there is plenty of extra hose. Otherwise, replace the hose. Replace the grommet in the valve cover if it is cracked or hard. Replace the clamp if it is broken or weak. In replacing the valve, make sure it is fully inserted in the hose, that the clamp is moved over the ridge on the valve so that the valve will not slip out of the hose, and that the valve is fully inserted into the grommet in the valve cover.

PCV Filter

REMOVAL AND INSTALLATION

1. Slide the rubber coupling that joins the tube coming from the valve cover to the filter off the filter nipple. Then, remove the top of the air cleaner. Slide the spring clamp off the filter, and remove the filter.

2. Inspect the rubber grommet in the valve cover and the rubber coupling for brittleness or cracking. Replace parts as necessary.

3. Insert the new PCV filter through the hole

in the air cleaner with the open portion of the filter upward. Make sure that the square portion of filter behind the nipple fits into the (square) hole in the air cleaner.

4. Install a new spring clamp onto the nipple. Make sure the clamp goes under the ridge on the filter nipple all the way around. Then, reconnect the rubber coupling and install the air cleaner cover.

Evaporative Emission Control
OPERATION

This system which was introduced to California cars in 1970, and other cars in 1971, reduces the amount of escaping gasoline vapors. Float bowl emissions are controlled by internal carburetor modifications. Redesigned bowl vents, reduced bowl capacity, heat shields, and improved intake manifold-to-carburetor insulation reduce vapor loss into the atmosphere. The venting of fuel tank vapors into the air has been stopped by means of the carbon canister storage method. This method transfers fuel vapors to an activated carbon storage device which absorbs and stores the vapor that is emitted from the engine's induction system while the engine

is not running. When the engine is running, the stored vapor is purged from the carbon storage device by the intake air flow and then consumed in the normal combustion process. As the manifold vacuum reaches a certain point, it opens a purge control valve atop the charcoal storage canister. This allows air to be drawn into the canister, thus forcing the existing fuel vapors back into the engine to be burned normally.

In 1981, the purge function on the 231 V6 engine is electronically controlled by a purge solenoid in the line which is itself controlled by the Electronic Control Module (ECM). When the system is in the "Open Loop" mode, the solenoid valve is energized, blocking all vacuum to the purge valve. When the system is in the "Closed Loop" mode, the solenoid is de-energized, thus allowing existing vacuum to operate the purge valve. This releases the trapped fuel vapor and it is forced into the induction system.

Most carbon canisters used are of the 'Open' design, meaning that air is drawn in through the bottom (filter) of the canister. Some 231 V6 canisters are of the 'Closed' design which means that the incoming air is drawn directly from the air cleaner.

Schematic of the evaporative emission system (open)—1972. Most models are similar; open system more common than closed system

Closed canister EECS

SERVICE

The only service required is the periodic replacement of the canister filter (if so equipped).. This procedure is covered in Chapter 1. If the fuel tank cap on your car ever requires replacement, make sure that it is of the same type as the original.

Exhaust Emission Controls

Exhaust emission control systems constitute the largest body of emission control devices installed on your car. Included in this category are: Thermostatic Air Cleaner (THERMAC); Air Injection Reactor System (A.I.R., 1967–80); Air

Typical THERMAC air cleaner

Management System (1981); Anti-Dieseling Solenoid; Transmission Controlled Spark (TCS, 1970–74); Early Fuel Evaporation System (EFE, 1975–and later); Exhaust Gas Recirculation (EGR, 1973–and later); Controlled Combustion System (CCS); Computer Controlled Catalytic Converter System (C-4); Computer Command Control System (CCC); Mixture Control Solenoid (M/C); Throttle Position Sensor (TPS); Idle Speed Control (ISC); Electronic Spark Timing (EST); Electronic Spark Control (ESC); Transmission Converter Clutch (TCC); Catalytic Converter and the Oxygen Sensor System. A brief description of each system and any applicable service procedures follows.

Thermostatic Air Cleaner (THERMAC)

All late model engines utilize the THERMAC system (in 1978 it was called TAC, but was the same). This system is designed to warm the air entering the carburetor when underhood temperatures are low, and to maintain a controlled air temperature into the carburetor at all times. By allowing preheated air to enter the carburetor, the amount of time the choke is on is reduced, resulting in better fuel economy and lower emissions. Engine warm-up time is also reduced.

The Thermac system is composed of the air cleaner body, a filter, sensor unit, vacuum diaphragm, damper door, and associated hoses and connections. Heat radiating from the exhaust manifold is trapped by a heat stove and is ducted to the air cleaner to supply heated air to the carburetor. A movable door in the air cleaner case snorkel allows air to be drawn in from the heat stove (cold operation) or from underhood air (warm operation). The door position is controlled by the vacuum motor, which receives intake manifold vacuum as modulated by the temperature sensor.

SYSTEM CHECKS

1. Check the vacuum hoses for leaks, kinks, breaks, or improper connections and correct any defects.

2. With the engine off, check the position of the damper door within the snorkel. A mirror can be used to make this job easier. The damper door should be open to admit outside air.

3. Apply at least 7 in. Hg of vacuum to the damper diaphragm unit. The door should close. If it doesn't, check the diaphragm linkage for binding and correct hookup.

Schematic of the vacuum motor operation

CHECK VALVE

VIEW A

A

DIVERTER VALVE

AIR PUMP

AIR system—inline six cylinder

CHECK VALVE

CHECK
VALVE

DIVERTER
VALVE

AIR PUMP

AIR system—V8 (229 V6 similar)

4. With vacuum still applied and the door closed, clamp the tube to trap the vacuum. If the door doesn't remain closed, there is a leak in the diaphragm assembly.

Air Injection Reactor System (A.I.R.)—1966–80

This system was first introduced on California cars in 1966. The AIR system injects compressed air into the exhaust system, near enough to the exhaust valves to continue the burning of the normally unburned segment of the exhaust gases. To do this it employs an air injection pump and a system of hoses, valves, tubes, etc., necessary to carry the compressed air from the pump to the exhaust manifolds. Carburetors and distributors for AIR engines have specific modifications to adapt them to the air injection system; those components should not be interchanged with those intended for use on engines that do not have the system.

A diverter valve is used to prevent backfiring. The valve senses sudden increases in manifold vacuum and ceases the injection of air during fuel-rich periods. During coasting, this valve diverts the entire air flow through the pump muffler and during high engine speeds, expels it through a relief valve. Check valves in the system prevent exhaust gases from entering the pump.

NOTE: *The AIR system on the 231 V6 engine is slightly different, but its purpose remains the same.*

SERVICE

The AIR system's effectiveness depends on correct engine idle speed, ignition timing, and dwell. These settings should be strictly adhered to and checked frequently. All hoses and fittings should be inspected for condition and tightness of connections. Check the drive belt for wear and tension every 12 months or 12,000 miles.

COMPONENT REMOVAL

Air Pump

CAUTION: *Do not pry on the pump housing or clamp the pump in a vise: the housing is soft and may become distorted.*

1. Disconnect the air hoses at the pump.
2. Hold the pump pulley from turning and loosen the pulley bolts.
3. Loosen the pump mounting bolt and adjustment bracket bolt. Remove the drive belt.
4. Remove the mounting bolts, and then remove the pump.
5. Install the pump using a reverse of the removal procedure.

Diverter (Anti-afterburn) Valve

1. Detach the vacuum sensing line from the valve.
2. Remove the other hose(s) from the valve.
3. Unfasten the diverter valve from the elbow or the pump body.

Installation is performed in the reverse or-

AIR system—231 V6

der of removal. Always use a new gasket. Tighten the valve securing bolts to 85 in. lbs.

Air Management System—1981 and Later

The Air Management System is used to provide additional oxygen to continue the combustion process after the exhaust gases leave the combustion chamber; much the same as the AIR system described earlier in this chapter. Air is injected into either the exhaust port(s), the exhaust manifold(s) or the catalytic converter by an engine driven air pump. The system is in operation at all times and will bypass air only momentarily during deceleration and at high speeds. The bypass function is performed by the Air Management Valve, while the check valve protects the air pump by preventing any backflow of exhaust gases.

The AIR system helps to reduce HC and CO content in the exhaust gases by injecting air into the exhaust ports during cold engine operation. This air injection also helps the catalytic converter to reach the proper temperature quicker during warm-up. When the engine is warm (closed loop), the AIR system injects air into the beds of a three-way converter to lower the HC and CO content in the exhaust.

The Air Management System utilizes the following components:

1. An engine driven air pump
2. Air management valves (Air Control and Air Switching)
3. Airflow and control hoses
4. Check valves
5. A dual-bed, three-way catalytic converter.

The belt driven, vane-type air pump is located at the front of the engine and supplies clean air to the system for purposes already stated. When the engine is cold, the Electronic Control Module (ECM) energizes an air control solenoid. This allows air to flow to the air switching valve. The air switching valve is then energized to direct air into the exhaust ports.

When the engine is warm, the ECM de-energizes the air switching valve, thus directing the air between the beds of the catalytic converter. This then provides additional oxygen for the oxidizing catalyst in the second bed to decrease HC and CO levels, while at the same time keeping oxygen levels low in the first bed, enabling the reducing catalyst to effectively decrease the levels of NOx.

If the air control valve detects a rapid increase in manifold vacuum (deceleration), certain operating modes (wide open throttle, etc.) or if the ECM self-diagnostic system detects any problems in the system, air is diverted to the air cleaner or directly into the atmosphere.

Removing the air pump; 1981 and later air management system

Check valve and hoses—1981 air management system

The primary purpose of the ECM's divert mode is to prevent backfiring. Throttle closure at the beginning of deceleration will temporarily create air/fuel mixtures which are too rich to burn completely. These mixtures will become burnable when they reach the exhaust if they are combined with injection air. The next firing of the engine will ignite the mixture causing an exhaust backfire. Momentary diverting of the injection air from the exhaust prevents this.

The Air Management System check valves and hoses should be checked periodically for any leaks, cracks or deterioration.

REMOVAL AND INSTALLATION

Air Pump

1. Remove the valves and/or adapter at the air pump.
2. Loosen the air pump adjustment bolt and remove the drive belt.
3. Unscrew the three mounting bolts and then remove the pump pulley.
4. Unscrew the pump mounting bolts and then remove the pump.
5. Installation is in the reverse order of removal. Be sure to adjust the drive belt tension after installing it.

Check Valve

1. Release the clamp and disconnect the air hoses from the valve.
2. Unscrew the check valve from the air injection pipe.

3. Installation is in the reverse order of removal.

Air Management Valve

1. Disconnect the negative battery cable.
2. Remove the air cleaner.
3. Tag and disconnect the vacuum hose from the valve.

Removing the air management valve

4. Tag and disconnect the air outlet hoses from the valve.

5. Bend back the lock tabs and then remove the bolts holding the elbow to the valve.

6. Tag and disconnect any electrical connections at the valve and then remove the valve from the elbow.

7. Installation is in the reverse order of removal.

Pump Filter Removal

1. Remove the drive belt and pump pulley.

2. Using needle-nose pliers, pull the fan from the pump.

NOTE: *Use care to prevent any dirt or fragments from entering the air intake hole. DO NOT insert a screwdriver between the pump and the filter, and do not attempt to remove the metal hub. It is seldom possible to remove the filter without destroying it.*

3. To install a new filter, draw it on with the pulley and pulley bolts. DO NOT hammer or press the filter on the pump.

4. Draw the filter down evenly by torquing the bolts alternately. Make sure the outer edge of the filter slips into the housing. A slight amount of interference with the housing bore is normal.

NOTE: *The new filter may squeal initially until the sealing lip on the pump outer diameter has worn in.*

AIR filter removal

Anti-Dieseling Solenoid

Beginning in 1968 some models may have an idle speed solenoid on the carburetor. All 1972–75 models have idle solenoids. Due to the leaner carburetor settings required for emission control, the engine may have a tendency to "diesel" or "run-on" after the ignition is turned off. The carburetor solenoid, energized when the ignition is on, maintains the normal idle speed. When the ignition is turned off, the so-

Anti-dieseling solenoid

lenoid is de-energized and permits the throttle valves to fully close, thus preventing run-on. For adjustment of carburetors with idle solenoids see the section on carburetor adjustments later in this chapter.

Transmission Controlled Spark (TCS)—1970–74

Introduced in 1970, this system controls exhaust emissions by eliminating vacuum advance in the lower forward gears.

The 1970 system consists of a transmission switch, solenoid vacuum switch, time delay relay, and a thermostatic water temperature switch. The solenoid vacuum switch is energized in the lower gears via the transmission switch and closes off distributor vacuum. The two-way transmission switch is activated by the shifter shaft on manual transmissions, and by oil pressure on automatic transmissions. The switch de-energizes the solenoid in High gear, the plunger extends and uncovers the vacuum port, and the distributor receives full vacuum. The temperature switch overrides the system when engine temperature is below 63° or above 232°. This allows vacuum advance in all gears. A time delay relay opens 15 seconds after the ignition is switched on. Full vacuum advance during this delay eliminates the possibility of stalling.

The 1971 system is similar, except that the vacuum solenoid (now called a Combination Emissions Control or CEC solenoid) serves two functions. One function is to control distributor vacuum; the added function is to act as a deceleration throttle stop in High gear. This cuts down on emissions when the vehicle is coming to a stop in High gear. The CEC solenoid is controlled by a temperature switch, a transmission switch, and a 20 second time delay relay. This system also contains a reversing relay, which energizes the solenoid when the transmission switch, temperature switch or time delay completes the CEC circuit to ground. This

Small V8 TCS system, engine "off" mode shown. Large V8 and inline six basically similar

TCS switch location, Turbo Hydra-Matic 350. Location similar on other transmissions (sides may vary)

system is directly opposite the 1970 system in operation. The 1970 vacuum solenoid was normally open to allow vacuum advance and when energized, closed to block vacuum. The 1971 system is normally closed blocking vacuum advance and when energized, opens to allow vacuum advance. The temperature switch completes the CEC circuit to ground when engine temperature is below 82°. The time delay relay allows vacuum advance (and raised idle speed) for 20 seconds after the ignition key is turned to the "on" position. Models with an automatic transmission and air conditioning also have a solid state timing device which engages the air conditioning compressor for three seconds after the ignition key is turned to the "off" position to prevent the engine from running-on.

The 1972 six-cylinder system is similar to that used in 1971, except that an idle stop solenoid has been added to the system. In the energized position, the solenoid maintains engine speed at a predetermined fast idle. When the solenoid is de-energized by turning off the ignition, the solenoid allows the throttle plates to close beyond the normal idle position; thus cutting off their air supply and preventing engine run-on. The six-cylinder is the only 1972 engine with a C.E.C. valve, which serves the same deceleration function as in 1971. The 1972

time delay relay delays full vacuum 20 seconds after the transmission is shifted into High gear. V8 engines use a vacuum advance solenoid similar to that used in 1970. This relay is normally closed to block vacuum and opens when energized to allow vacuum advance. The solenoid controls distributor vacuum advance and performs no throttle positioning function. The idle stop solenoid used operates in the same manner as the one on six-cylinder engines. All air-conditioned cars have an additional anti-diesel (run-on) solenoid which engages the compressor clutch for three seconds after the ignition is switched off. The 1973 TCS system differs from the 1972 system in three ways. The 23 second upshift delay has been replaced by a 20 second starting relay. This relay closes to complete the TCS circuit and open the TCS solenoid, allowing vacuum advance, for 20 seconds after the key is turned to the "on" position. The operating temperature of the temperature override switch has been raised to 93°, and the switch which was used to engage the A/C compressor when the key was turned "off" has been eliminated. All models are equipped with an electric throttle control solenoid to prevent run-on. The 1973 TCS system is used on all models equipped with a 307 engine and all V8 models equipped with a manual transmission.

The 1974 TCS system is used only on manual transmission models. System components remain unchanged from 1973. The vacuum advance solenoid is located on the coil bracket. The TCS system is not used in 1975 and later cars.

TESTING

If there is a TCS system malfunction, first connect a vacuum gauge in the hose between the solenoid valve and the distributor vacuum unit. Drive the vehicle or raise it on a frame lift and observe the vacuum gauge. If full vacuum is available in all gears, check for the following:

1. Blown fuse.
2. Disconnected wire at the solenoid-operated vacuum valve.
3. Disconnected wire at the transmission switch.
4. Temperature override switch energized due to low engine temperature.
5. Solenoid failure.

If no vacuum is available in any gear, check the following:

1. Solenoid valve vacuum lines switched.
2. Clogged solenoid vacuum valve.
3. Distributor or manifold vacuum lines leaking or disconnected.
4. Transmission switch or wire grounded.

Test for individual components are as follows:

Idle Stop Solenoid

This unit may be checked simply by observing it while an assistant switches the ignition on and off. It should extend further with the current switched on. The unit is not repairable.

Solenoid Vacuum Valve

Check that proper manifold vacuum is available. Connect the vacuum gauge in the line between the solenoid valve and the distributor. Apply 12 volts to the solenoid. If vacuum is still not available, the valve is defective, either mechanically or electrically. The unit is not repairable. If the valve is satisfactory, check the relay next.

Relay

1. With the engine at normal operating temperature and the ignition on, ground the solenoid vacuum valve terminal with the black lead. The solenoid should energize (no vacuum) if the relay is satisfactory.

2. With the solenoid energized as in Step 1, connect a jumper from the relay terminal with the green/white stripe lead to ground. The solenoid should de-energize (vacuum available) if the relay is satisfactory.

3. If the relay worked properly in Steps 1 and 2, check the temperature switch. The relay unit is not repairable.

Temperature Switch

The vacuum valve solenoid should be deenergized (vacuum available) with the engine cold. If it is not, ground the green/white stripe wire from the switch. If the solenoid now de-energizes, replace the switch. If the switch was satisfactory, check the transmission switch.

Transmission Switch

With the engine at normal operating temperature and the transmission in one of the no-vacuum gears, the vacuum valve solenoid should be energized (no vacuum). If not, remove and ground the switch electrical lead. If the solenoid energizes, replace the switch.

Early Fuel Evaporation System (EFE)—1975 and Later

1975 and later models are equipped with this system to reduce engine warm-up time, improve driveability, and reduce emissions. On start-up, a vacuum motor acts to close a heat valve in the exhaust manifold which causes exhaust gases to enter the intake manifold heat riser passages. Incoming fuel mixture is then

EFE system—V8 models

heated and more complete fuel evaporation is provided during warm-up.

The system consists of a Thermal Vacuum Switch, and an Exhaust Heat Valve and actuator. The Thermal Vacuum Switch is located on the coolant outlet housing on V8s, and on the block on in-line six cylinder engines. When the engine is cold, the TVS conducts manifold vacuum to the actuator to close the valve. When engine coolant or, on 6 cylinder engines, oil warms up, vacuum is interrupted and the actuator should open the valve.

NOTE: *On 1981 models with the 231 V6 engine, the EFE system is controlled by the ECM.*

As of 1981, the 231 V6 Turbo utilizes a slightly different system. Although the function of this system remains the same—to reduce engine

Vacuum-servo type EFE

EFE heater on the 231 Turbo

EFE system—231 V6

warm-up time, improve driveability and to reduce emissions—the operation is entirely different. The new system is electric and uses a ceramic heater grid located underneath the primary bore of the carburetor as part of the carburetor insulator/gasket. When the engine coolant is below the specified calibration level, electrical current is supplied to the heater through an ECM controlled relay.

CHECKING THE EFE SYSTEM

1. With the engine overnight cold, have someone start the engine while you observe the Exhaust Heat Valve (on some V8s, the EFE valve actuator arm is covered by a two-piece metal cover, which must be removed for service). The valve should snap to the closed position.

2. Watch the valve as the engine warms up. By the time coolant starts circulating through the radiator (V-type engines) or oil is hot (in-line engines), the valve should snap open.

EFE system—229 V6

3. If the valve does not close, immediately disconnect the hose at the actuator, and check for vacuum by placing your finger over the end of the hose, or with a vacuum gauge. If there is vacuum, replace the actuator. If there is no vacuum, immediately disconnect the hose leading to the TVS from the manifold *at the TVS*. If there is vacuum here, but not at the actuator, replace the TVS. If vacuum does not exist at the hose going to the TVS, check that the vacuum hose is free of cracks or breaks and tightly connected at the manifold, and that the manifold port is clear.

4. If the valve does not open when the engine coolant or oil warms up, disconnect the hose at the actuator, and check for vacuum by placing your finger over the end of the hose or using a vacuum gauge. If there is vacuum, replace the TVS. If there is no vacuum, replace the actuator.

TVS REMOVAL AND INSTALLATION

On V8 engines, drain coolant until the level is below the coolant outlet housing. No oil need be drained on 6 cylinder engines. Apply sealer to threads on V8 engines. Use no sealer on 6 cylinder engines. Note that the valve must be installed until just snug (120 in. lb.) and then turned by hand just far enough to line up the fittings for hose connection.

HEATER GRID REMOVAL AND INSTALLATION (1981 TURBO ONLY)

1. Remove the air cleaner.
2. Tag and disconnect all electrical, vacuum and fuel connections from the carburetor.
3. Disconnect the EFE heater electrical connection.
4. Remove the carburetor as detailed later in this chapter.
5. Lift off the EFE heater.

6. Installation is in the reverse order of removal.

7. Start the engine and check for any leaks.

Exhaust Gas Recirculation (EGR)—1973–81

All 1973 and later engines are equipped with exhaust gas recirculation (EGR). This system consists of a metering valve, a vacuum line to the carburetor, and cast-in exhaust gas passages in the intake manifold. The EGR valve is controlled by carburetor vacuum, and accordingly opens and closes to admit exhaust gases into the fuel/air mixture. The exhaust gases lower the combustion temperature, and reduce the amount of oxides of nitrogen (NO_x) produced. The valve is closed at idle between the two extreme throttle positions.

In most installations, vacuum to the EGR valve is controlled by a thermal vacuum switch (TVS); the switch, which is installed into the engine block, shuts off vacuum to the EGR valve until the engine is hot. This prevents the stalling and lumpy idle which would result if EGR occurred when the engine was cold.

EGR VACUUM CONTROL SOLENOID

To regulate EGR flow on 1981 and later models, a solenoid is used in the vacuum line, and is controlled by the Electronic Control Module (ECM). The ECM uses information from the coolant temperature, throttle position, and manifold pressure sensors to regulate the vacuum solenoid. When the engine is cold, a signal from the ECM energizes the EGR sole-

12. Diaphragm
33. Negative EGR web
34. Positive EGR web

Different EGR valve types

1. EGR control solenoid valve
2. Bolt (tighten to 17 N·m (12 ft. lbs.)

EGR vacuum-controlled solenoid, 229 V6, 305 V8

Negative backpressure EGR valve

DIAPHRAGM IS SEATED WHEN ENGINE IS NOT RUNNING

VACUUM SIGNAL TUBE

DIAPHRAGM PLATE

TRANSDUCER

ORIFICE OPENING .030 (SEE OPTIONAL CONSTRUCTION)

ORIFICE OPENING .020

SEAT

INTAKE MANIFOLD VACUUM

EXHAUST

OPTIONAL CONSTRUCTION

noid, thus blocking vacuum to the EGR valve. (The solenoid is also energized during cranking and wide-open throttle.) When the engine warms up, the EGR solenoid is turned off by the ECM, and the EGR valve operates according to normal ported vacuum and exhaust backpressure signals.

As the car accelerates, the carburetor throttle plate uncovers the vacuum port for the EGR valve. At 3–5 in. Hg, the EGR valve opens and then some of the exhaust gases are allowed to flow into the air/fuel mixture to lower the combustion temperature. At full-throttle the valve closes again.

1. EGR/EFE solenoid valve
2. Harness
3. Rear rocker cover

231 V6 vacuum controlled solenoid locations

Typical EGR valve mounting location

Some California engines are equipped with a dual diaphragm EGR valve. This valve further limits the exhaust gas opening (compared to the single diaphragm EGR valve) during high intake manifold vacuum periods, such as high-speed cruising, and provides more exhaust gas recirculation during acceleration when manifold vacuum is low. In addition to the hose running to the thermal vacuum switch, a second hose is connected directly to the intake manifold.

For 1977, all California models and cars delivered in areas above 4000 ft are equipped with back pressure EGR valves. This valve is also used on all 1978–81 models. The EGR valve receives exhaust back pressure through its hollow shaft. This exerts a force on the bottom of the control valve diaphragm, opposed by a light spring. Under low exhaust pressure (low engine load and partial throttle), the EGR signal is reduced by an air bleed. Under conditions of high exhaust pressure (high engine load and large throttle opening), the air bleed is closed and the EGR valve responds to an unmodified vacuum signal. At wide open throttle, the EGR

Cross section of a positive backpressure EGR valve

EGR System Diagnosis

Condition	Possible Cause	Correction
Engine idles abnormally rough and/or stalls.	EGR valve vacuum hoses misrouted.	Check EGR valve vacuum hose routing. Correct as required.
	Leaking EGR valve.	Check EGR valve for correct operation.
	EGR valve gasket failed or loose EGR attaching bolts.	Check EGR attaching bolts for tightness. Tighten as required. If not loose, remove EGR valve and inspect gasket. Replace as required.
	EGR control solenoid.	Check vacuum into control solenoid from carburetor EGR port with engine at normal operating temperature and at curb idle speed. Then check the vacuum out of the EGR control solenoid to EGR valve. If the two vacuum readings are not equal within ± 1/2 in. Hg. (1.7 kPa), then problem could be within EGR solenoid or ECM unit.
	Improper vacuum to EGR valve at idle.	Check vacuum from carburetor EGR port with engine at stabilized operating temperature and at curb idle speed. Vacuum should not exceed 1.0 in. Hg. If vacuum exceeds this, check carburetor idle.
Engine runs rough on light throttle acceleration and has poor part load performance.	EGR valve vacuum hose misrouted.	Check EGR valve vacuum hose routing. Correct as required.
	Check for loose valve.	Torque valve.
	Failed EGR control solenoid.	Same as listing in "Engine Idles Rough" condition.
	Sticky or binding EGR valve.	Clean EGR passage of all deposits.
		Remove EGR valve and inspect. Replace as required.
	Wrong or no EGR gasket(s) and/or Spacer.	Check and correct as required. Install new gasket(s), install spacer (if used), torque attaching parts.
Engine stalls on decelerations.	Control valve blocked or air flow restricted.	Check internal control valve function per service procedure.
	Restriction in EGR vacuum line or control solenoid signal tube.	Check EGR vacuum lines for kinks, bends, etc. Remove or replace hoses as required. Check EGR control solenoid function.
		Check EGR valve for excessive deposits causing sticky or binding operation. Replace valve.
	Sticking or binding EGR valve.	Remove EGR valve and replace valve.
Part throttle engine detonation.	Control solenoid blocked or air flow restricted.	Check control solenoid function per check chart.
	Insufficient exhaust gas recirculation flow during part throttle accelerations.	Check EGR valve hose routing. Check EGR valve operation. Repair or replace as required. Check EGR control solenoid as listed in "Engine Idles Rough" section. Check EGR passages and valve for excessive deposit. Clean as required.

(NOTICE: Non-Functioning EGR valve could contribute to part throttle detonation.)

		Check EGR per service procedure.

(NOTICE: Detonation can be caused by several other engine variables. Perform ignition and carburetor related diagnosis.)

Engine starts but immediately stalls when cold.	EGR valve hoses misrouted.	Check EGR valve hose routings.
	EGR control solenoid system malfunctioning when engine is cold.	Perform check to determine if the EGR solenoid is operational. Replace as required.

(NOTICE: Stalls after start can also be caused by carburetor problems.)

flow is reduced in proportion to the amount of vacuum signal available.

1979 and later models have a ported signal vacuum EGR valve. The valve opening is controlled by the amount of vacuum obtained from a ported vacuum source on the carburetor and the amount of backpressure in the exhaust system.

FAULTY EGR VALVE SYMPTOMS

An EGR valve that stays open when it should be closed causes weak combustion, resulting in a rough-running engine and/or frequent stalling. Too much EGR flow at idle, cruise, or when cold can cause any of the following:

- Engine stopping after a cold start
- Engine stopping at idle after deceleration
- Surging during cruising
- Rough idle

An EGR valve which is stuck closed and allows little or no EGR flow causes extreme combustion temperatures (too hot) during acceleration. Spark knock (detonation or "pinging"), engine overheating and excess engine emissions can all be a result, as well as engine damage. See the accompanying EGR system diagnosis chart for possible cause and correction procedures.

EGR VALVE REMOVAL AND INSTALLATION

1. Detach the vacuum lines from the EGR valve.

2. Unfasten the two bolts or bolt and clamp which attach the valve to the manifold. Withdraw the valve.

3. Installation is the reverse of removal. Always use a new gasket between the valve and the manifold. On dual diaphragm valves, attach the carburetor vacuum line to the tube at the top of the valve, and the manifold vacuum line to the tube at the center of the valve.

TVS SWITCH REMOVAL AND INSTALLATION

1. Drain the radiator.

2. Disconnect the vacuum lines from the switch noting their locations. Remove the switch.

3. Apply sealer to the threaded portion of the new switch, and install it, torquing to 15 ft. lb.

4. Rotate the head of the switch to a position that will permit easy hookup of vacuum hoses. Then install the vacuum hoses to the proper connectors.

Thermostatic vacuum switch (TVS). Nipple 1 is to distributor; 2 is to TCS solenoid; 4 to intake manifold

EGR VALVE CLEANING

Valves That Protrude from Mounting Face

CAUTION: *Do not wash the valve assembly in solvents or degreasers—permanent damage to the valve diaphragm may result.*

1. Remove the vacuum hose from the EGR valve assembly. Remove the two attaching bolts, remove the EGR valve from the intake manifold and discard the gasket.

2. Holding the valve assembly in hand, tap the valve lightly with a small plastic hammer to remove exhaust deposits from the valve seat. Shake out any loose particles. DO NOT put the valve in a vise.

3. Carefully remove any exhaust deposits from the mounting surface of the valve with a wire wheel or putty knife. Do not damage the mounting surface.

4. Depress the valve diaphragm and inspect the valve seating area through the valve outlet for cleanliness. If the valve and/or seat are not completely clean, repeat step 2.

5. Look for exhaust deposits in the valve outlet, and remove any deposits with an old screwdriver.

6. Clean the mounting surfaces of the intake manifold and valve assembly. Using a new gasket, install the valve assembly to the intake

Cleaning the EGR (valve protruding). Tap lightly with hammer.

manifold. Torque the bolts to 25 ft. lbs. Connect the vacuum hose.

Shielded Valves or Valves That Do Not Protrude

1. Clean the base of the valve with a wire brush or wheel to remove exhaust deposits from the mounting surface.

2. Clean the valve seat and valve in an abrasive-type spark plug cleaning machine or sandblaster. Most machine shops provide this service. Make sure the valve portion is cleaned (blasted) for about 30 seconds, and that the valve is also cleaned with the diaphragm spring fully compressed (valve unseated). The cleaning should be repeated until all deposits are removed.

3. The valve must be blown out with compressed air thoroughly to ensure all abrasive material is removed from the valve.

4. Clean the mounting surface of the intake manifold and valve assembly. Using a new gasket, install the valve assembly to the intake manifold. Torque the bolts to 25 ft. lbs. Connect the vacuum hose.

Controlled Combustion System

The CCS system relies upon leaner air/fuel mixtures and altered ignition timing to improve combustion efficiency. A special air cleaner with a thermostatically controlled opening is used on most CCS equipped models to ensure that air entering the carburetor is kept at 100°F. This allows leaner carburetor settings and improves engine warm-up. A 15°F higher temperature thermostat is employed on CCS cars to further improve emission control.

SERVICE

Since the only extra component added with a CCS system is the thermostatically controlled air cleaner, there is no additional maintenance required; however, tune-up adjustments such as idle speed, ignition timing, and dwell be-

Schematic of the Controlled Combustion System (CCS)

come much more critical. Care must be taken to ensure that these settings are correct, both for trouble-free operation and a low emission level.

Computer Controlled Catalytic Converter System (C-4)

The C-4 System, installed on certain 1979 and all 1980 cars sold in California, is an electronically controlled exhaust emissions system. The purpose of the system is to maintain the ideal air/fuel ratio at which the catalytic converter is most effective.

Major components of the system include an Electronic Control Module (ECM), an oxygen sensor, an electronically controlled carburetor, and a three-way oxidation reduction catalytic converter. The system also includes a maintenance reminder flag connected to the odometer which becomes visible in the instrument cluster at regular intervals, signaling the need for oxygen sensor replacement.

The oxygen sensor, installed in the exhaust manifold, generates a voltage which varies with exhaust gas oxygen content. Lean mixtures (more oxygen) reduce voltage; rich mixtures (less oxygen) increase voltage. Voltage output is sent to the ECM.

An engine temperature sensor installed in the engine coolant outlet monitors engine coolant temperatures. Vacuum control switches and throttle position sensors also monitor engine conditions and supply signals to the ECM.

The Electronic Control Module receives input signals from all sensors. It processes these signals and generates a control signal sent to the carburetor. The control signal cycles between on (lean command) and off (rich command). The amount of on and off time is a function of the input voltage sent to the ECM by the oxygen sensor.

Rochester Dualjet (2-barrel) E2ME and E4ME (4-barrel) carburetors are used with the C-4 System. Basically, an electrically operated mixture control solenoid is installed in the carburetor float bowl. The solenoid controls the air/fuel mixture metered to the idle and main metering systems. Air metering to the idle system is controlled by an idle air bleed valve. It follows the movement of the mixture solenoid to control the amount of air bled into the idle system, enriching or leaning out the mixture as appropriate. Air/fuel mixture enrichment occurs when the fuel valve is open and the air bleed valve is closed. All cycling of this system, which occurs ten times per second, is controlled by the ECM. A throttle position switch informs the ECM of open or closed throttle operation. A number of different switches are used,

C-4 system schematic

varying with application. When the ECM receives a signal from the throttle switch, indicating a change of position, it immediately searches its memory for the last set of operating conditions that resulted in an ideal air/fuel ratio, and shifts to that set of conditions. The memory is continually updated during normal operation.

A "Check-Engine" light is included in the C-4 System installation. When a fault develops, the light comes on, and a trouble code is set into the ECM memory. However, if the fault is intermittent, the light will go out, but the trouble code will remain in the ECM memory as long as the engine is running. The trouble codes are used as a diagnostic aid, and are pre-programmed.

Unless the required tools are available, troubleshooting the C-4 System should be confined to mechancial checks of electrical connectors, vacuum hoses and the like. All diagnosis and repair should be performed by a qualified mechanic.

Computer Command Control System

The Computer Command Control System, installed on all 1981 and later cars, is basically a modified version of the C-4 system. Its main advantage over its predecessor is that it can monitor and control a larger number of interrelated emission control systems.

This new system can monitor up to 15 various engine/vehicle operating conditions and then use this information to control as many as 9 engine related systems. The "System" is

thereby making constant adjustments to maintain good vehicle performance under all normal driving conditions while at the same time allowing the catalytic converter to effectively control the emissions of NOx, HC and CO.

In addition, the "System" has a built in diagnostic system that recognizes and identifies possible operational problems and alerts the driver through a "Check Engine" light in the instrument panel. The light will remain ON until the problem is corrected. The "System" also has built in back-up systems that in most cases of an operational problem will allow for the continued operation of the vehicle in a near normal manner until the repairs can be made.

The CCC system has some components in common with the C-4 system, although they are not interchangeable. These components include the Electronic Control Module (ECM), which, as previously stated, controls many more functions than does its predecessor, an oxygen sensor system, an electronically controlled variable-mixture carburetor, a three-way catalytic converter, throttle position and coolant sensors, a Barometric Pressure Sensor (BARO), a Manifold Absolute Pressure Sensor (MAP) and a "Check Engine" light in the instrument panel.

Components unique to the CCC system include the Air Injection Reaction (AIR) management system, a charcoal canister purge solenoid, EGR valve controls, a vehicle speed sensor (in the instrument panel), a transmission converter clutch solenoid (only on models with automatic transmission), idle speed control and Electronic Spark Timing (EST).

The ECM, in addition to monitoring sensors and sending out a control signal to the carbu-

Computer Command Control (CCC) system schematic

retor, also controls the following components or sub-systems: charcoal canister purge control, the AIR system, idle speed, automatic transmission converter lock-up, distributor ignition timing, the EGR valve, and the air conditioner converter clutch.

The EGR valve control solenoid is activated by the ECM in a fashion similar to that of the charcoal canister purge solenoid described earlier in this chapter. When the engine is cold, the ECM energizes the solenoid, which blocks the vacuum signal to the EGR valve. When the engine is warm, the ECM de-energizes the solenoid and the vacuum signal is allowed to reach and then activate the EGR valve.

The Transmission Converter Clutch (TCC) lock is controlled by the ECM through an electrical solenoid in the automatic transmission. When the vehicle speed sensor in the dash signals the ECM that the car has attained the predetermined speed, the ECM energizes the solenoid which then allows the torque converter to mechanically couple the engine to the transmission. When the brake pedal is pushed, or during deceleration or passing, etc., the ECM returns the transmission to fluid drive.

CCC system schematic

GROUND TO ECM
TIGHTEN TO 7.5 N·m
(66 IN. LBS.)

VIEW A

OXYGEN SENSOR
CONNECTOR

TO EMR VACUUM
SWITCH

EGR SOLENOID

EGR BLEED
SOLENOID

M/C SOLENOID

TPS

OXYGEN
SENSOR

COOLANT
SENSOR

FWD

DWELL METER
CONNECTOR

AIR CONTROL
VALVE

AIR SWITCHING
RELAY

TACH SIGNAL
CONDITIONER

TCC AND EGR
BLEED RELAY

AIR SWITCHING
SOLENOID

TIGHTEN TO 2 N·m
(19 IN. LBS.)

M/C SOLENOID

TO TACH TERMINAL
ON DISTRIBUTOR

TPS

IDLE SPEED CONTROL

TIGHTEN TO 33 N·m
(24 FT. LBS.)

TO TCC SOLENOID

EMR VACUUM
SWITCH

SYSTEM GROUND

AUTOMATIC 200C

TIGHTEN TO 4 N·m
(35 IN. LBS.)

AUTOMATIC
250C

TO TCC
SOLENOID

VIEW C

FWD

VIEW B

CCC component location—229 V6

The idle speed control adjusts the idle speed to all particular engine load conditions and will lower the idle under no-load or low-load conditions in order to conserve fuel.

NOTE: *Not all engines use all systems. Control applications may differ.*

BASIC TROUBLESHOOTING

NOTE: *The following explains how to activate the Trouble Code signal light in the instrument cluster. This is not a full fledged*

C-4 or CCC system troubleshooting and isolation procedure.

Before suspecting the C-4 or CCC system, or any of its components as being faulty, check the ignition system (distributor, timing, spark plugs and wires). Check the engine compression, the air cleaner and any of the emission control components that are not controlled by the ECM. Also check the intake manifold, the vacuum hoses and hose connectors for any leaks. Check the carburetor mounting bolts for tightness.

TO TCC SOLENOID

FWD

TIGHTEN TO
4 N·m (35 IN. LBS.)

VIEW A

OXYGEN SENSOR

EGR, EFE AND
CANISTER PURGE
VALVE

DWELL METER
CONNECTOR

M/C SOLENOID

TPS

IDLE SPEED
CONTROL

COOLANT
SENSOR

ROUTE EST WIRES CLOCKWISE
AROUND DISTRIBUTOR BASE AND
BETWEEN DISTRIBUTOR AND
RADIATOR HOSE.

AIR DIVERT
VALVE

EST CONNECTOR

M/C SOLENOID

FWD

IDLE SPEED
CONTROL

TPS

TIGHTEN TO
(27 N·m
(20 FT. LBS.)

SYSTEM GROUND

A/C COMPRESSOR
CONNECTOR

TO TRANSMISSION

BARO SENSOR
CONNECTOR
(BLUE)

BARO SENSOR

MAP SENSOR

MAP SENSOR
CONNECTOR
(RED)

VIEW B   FWD

GROUND TO ECM

ENGINE GROUND

OXYGEN SENSOR AND
SYSTEM GROUND

TIGHTEN TO
7.5 N·m (66 IN. LBS.)

VIEW C

CCC component location—231 V6

The following symptoms could indicate a possible problem area with the C-4 or CCC systems:

1. Detonation;
2. Stalling or rough idling when the engine is cold;
3. Stalling or rough idling when the engine is hot;
4. Missing;
5. Hesitation;
6. Surging;
7. Poor gasoline mileage;
8. Sluggish or spongy performance;
9. Hard starting when engine is cold;
10. Hard starting when the engine is hot;
11. Objectionable exhaust odors;
12. Engine cuts out;
13. Improper idle speed (CCC only).

As a bulb and system check, the "Check Engine" light will come on when the ignition switch

CCC component location—231 V6 Turbo

is turned to the ON position but the engine is not started.

The "Check Engine" light will also produce the trouble code/codes by a series of flashes which translate as follows: When the diagnostic test lead (C-4) or terminal (CCC) under the instrument panel is grounded, with the ignition in the ON position and the engine not running, the "Check Engine" light will flash once, pause, and then flash twice in rapid succession. This is a Code 12, which indicates that the diagnostic system is working. After a long pause, the Code 12 will repeat itself two more times. This whole cycle will then repeat itself until the engine is started or the ignition switch is turned OFF.

When the engine is started, the "Check Engine" light will remain on for a few seconds and then turn off. If the "Check Engine" light remains on, the self-diagnostic system has de-

CCC component location—V8

tected a problem. If the test lead (C-4) or test terminal (CCC) is then grounded, the trouble code will flash (3) three times. If more than one problem is found to be in existance, each trouble code will flash (3) three times and then change to the next one. Trouble codes will flash in numerical order (lowest code number to highest). The trouble code series will repeat themselves for as long as the test leads or terminal remains grounded.

A trouble code indicates a problem with a given circuit. For example, trouble code 14 indicates a problem in the cooling sensor circuit.

This includes the coolant sensor, its electrical harness and the Electronic Control Module (ECM).

Since the self-diagnostic system cannot diagnose every possible fault in the system, the absence of a trouble code does not necessarily mean that the system is trouble-free. To determine whether or not a problem with the system exists that does not activate a trouble code, a system performance check must be made. This job should be left to a qualified service technician.

In the case of an intermittent fault in the system, the "Check Engine" light will go out when the fault goes away, but the trouble code will remain in the memory of the ECM. Therefore, if a trouble code can be obtained even though the "Check Engine" light is not on, it must still be evaluated. It must be determined if the fault is intermittent or if the engine must be operating under certain conditions (acceleration, deceleration, etc.) before the "Check Engine" light will come on. In some cases, certain trouble codes will not be recorded in the ECM until the engine has been operated at part throttle for at least 5 to 18 minutes.

On the C-4 system, the ECM erases all trouble codes every time that the ignition is turned off. In the case of intermittent faults, a long term memory is desirable. This can be produced by connecting the orange connector/lead from terminal "S" of the ECM directly to the battery (or to a 'hot' fuse panel terminal). This terminal must always be disconnected immediately after diagnosis as it puts an undue strain on the battery.

On the CCC system, a trouble code will be stored until the terminal 'R' at the ECM has been disconnected from the battery for at least 10 seconds.

ACTIVATING THE TROUBLE CODE

On the C-4 system, activate the trouble code by grounding the trouble code test lead. Use the illustrations to help you locate the test lead under the instrument panel (usually a white and black wire with a green connector). Run a jumper wire from the lead to a suitable ground.

On the CCC system, locate the test terminal under the instrument panel (see illustration). Use a jumper wire and ground only the lead.

NOTE: *Ground the test lead/terminal according to the instructions given previously in the "Basic Troubleshooting" section.*

Mixture Control Solenoid (M/C)

The fuel flow through the carburetor idle main metering circuits is controlled by a mixture

C-4 system diagnostic test lead location, above ECM

CCC system diagnostic test terminal located underneath the left side of the instrument panel

control (M/C) solenoid located in the carburetor. The M/C solenoid changes the air/fuel mixture to the engine by controlling the fuel flow through the carburetor. The ECM controls the solenoid by providing a ground. When the solenoid is energized, the fuel flow through the carburetor is reduced, providing a leaner mixture. When the ECM removes the ground, the solenoid is de-energized, increasing the fuel flow and providing a richer mixture. The M/C solenoid is energized and de-energized at a rate of 10 times per second.

Throttle Position Sensor (TPS)— 1980–81

The throttle position sensor is mounted in the carburetor body and is used to supply throttle

FRONT

Electronic Control Module (ECM) location, all models similar

Trouble Code Identification Chart

NOTE: Always ground the test lead/terminal AFTER the engine is running

Trouble Code	Applicable System	Possible Problem Area
12	C-4, CCC	No reference pulses to the ECM. This is not stored in the memory and will only flash when the fault is present (not to be confused with the Code 12 discussed earlier).
13	C-4, CCC	Oxygen sensor circuit. The engine must run for at least 5 min. (18 min. on the C-4 equipped 231 V6) at part throttle before this code will show.
13 & 14 (at same time)	C-4	See code 43.
13 & 14 (at same time)	C-4	See code 43.
14	C-4, CCC	Shorted coolant sensor circuit. The engine must run 2–5 min. before this code will show.
15	C-4, CCC	Open coolant sensor circuit. The engine must run for at least 5 min. (18 min. on the C-4 equipped 231 V6) before this code will show.
21	C-4	Shorted wide open throttle switch and/or open closed-throttle switch circuit (when used).
	C-4, CCC	Throttle position sensor circuit. The engine must run for at least 10 sec. (25 sec.—CCC) below 800 rpm before this code will show.
21 & 22 (at same time)	C-4	Grounded wide open throttle switch circuit (231 V6).
22	C-4	Grounded closed throttle or wide open throttle switch circuit (231 V6).
23	C-4, CCC	Open or grounded carburetor mixture control (M/C) solenoid circuit.
24	CCC	Vehicle speed sensor circuit. The engine must run for at least 5 min, at normal speed before this code will show.
32	C-4, CCC	Barometric pressure sensor (BARO) circuit output is low.
32 & 55 (at same time)	C-4	Grounded +8V terminal or V(REF) terminal for BARO sensor, or a faulty ECM.
34	C-4	Manifold absolute pressure sensor (MAP) output is high. The engine must run for at least 10 sec. below 800 rpm before this code will show.
	CCC	Manifold absolute pressure sensor (MAP) circuit or vacuum sensor circuit. The engine must run for at least 5 min. below 800 rpm before this code will show.
35	CCC	Idle speed control circuit shorted. The engine must run for at least 2 sec. above ½ throttle before this code will show.
42	CCC	Electronic spark timing (EST) bypass circuit grounded.
43	C-4	Throttle position sensor adjustment. The engine must run for at least 10 sec. before this code will show.
44	C-4, CCC	Lean oxygen sensor indication. The engine must run for at least 5 min. in closed loop (oxygen sensor adjusting carburetor mixture) at part throttle under load (drive car) before this code will show.
44 & 45 (at same time)	C-4, CCC	Faulty oxygen sensor circuit.
45	C-4, CCC	Rich oxygen sensor indication. The engine must run for at least 5 min. before this code will show (see 44 for conditions).
51	C-4, CCC	Faulty calibration unit (PROM) or improper PROM installation in the ECM. It will take at least 30 sec. before this code will show.
52 & 53	C-4	"Check Engine" light off: intermittent ECM problem. "Check Engine" light on: faulty ECM—replace.
52	C-4, CCC	Faulty ECM.

Trouble Code Identification Chart (cont.)

NOTE: *Always ground the test lead/terminal AFTER the engine is running*

Trouble Code	Applicable System	Possible Problem Area
53	CCC	Faulty ECM.
54	C-4, CCC	Faulty mixture control solenoid circuit and/or faulty ECM.
55	C-4	Faulty throttle position sensor or ECM (all but 231 V6). Faulty oxygen sensor, open MAP sensor or faulty ECM (231 V6 only).
	CCC	Grounded +8V supply (terminal 19 on ECM connector), grounded 5V reference (terminal 21 on ECM connector), faulty oxygen sensor circuit or faulty ECM.

NOTE: *Not all codes will apply to every model.*

1. Jumper "B" to "A" to display diagnostic codes
2. Test terminal
3. Ground terminal

VIEW A

Under dash test terminal location

Throttle position sensor (TPS)

position information to the ECM. The ECM memory stores an average of operation conditions with the ideal air/fuel ratios for each of those conditions. When the ECM receives a signal that indicates throttle position change, it immediately shifts to the last remembered set of operating conditions that resulted in an ideal air/fuel ratio control. The memory is continually being updated during normal operations.

Idle Speed Control (ISC)
229, 231 V6 (EXCEPT TURBO)

The idle speed control does just what its name implies—it controls the idle. The ISC is used to maintain low engine speeds while at the same time preventing stalling due to engine load changes. The system consists of a motor assembly mounted on the carburetor which moves the throttle lever so as to open or close the throttle blades.

The whole operation is controlled by the ECM. The ECM monitors engine load to determine the proper idle speed. To prevent stalling, it monitors the air conditioning compressor switch, the transmission, the park/neutral switch and the ISC throttle switch. The ECM processes all this information and then uses it to control the ISC motor which in turn will vary the idle speed as necessary.

The Idle Speed Control (ISC) motor is attached to the carburetor

Electronic Spark Timing (EST)

All 1980 models with the 231 V6 engine and all 1981 and later models but those with the 229 V6 engine use EST. The EST distributor, as described in an earlier chapter, contains no vacuum or centrifugal advance mechanism and uses a seven terminal HEI module. It has four wires going to a four terminal connector in addition to the connectors normally found on HEI distributors. A reference pulse, indicating engine rpm is sent to the ECM; terminal "R" on the seven-terminal HEI provides this pulse on all models except the 229 V6. The ECM determines the proper spark advance for the engine operating conditions and then sends an 'EST' pulse back to the distributor.

Under most normal operating conditions, the ECM will control the spark advance. However, under certain operating conditions such as cranking or when setting base timing, the distributor is capable of operating without ECM control. This condition is called BYPASS and is determined by the BYPASS lead which runs from the ECM to the distributor. When the BYPASS lead is at the proper voltage (5), the ECM will control the spark. If the lead is grounded or open circuited, the HEI module itself will control the spark. Disconnecting the 4-terminal EST connector will also cause the engine to operate in the BYPASS mode.

Electronic Spark Control (ESC)
231 V6 TURBO ONLY

The Electronic Spark Control (ESC) system is a closed loop system that controls engine detonation by adjusting the spark timing. There are two basic components in this system, the controller and the sensor.

The controller processes the sensor signal and remodifies the EST signal to the distributor to adjust the spark timing. The process is contin-

V6 turbo detonation sensor, mounted on intake manifold

uous so that the presence of detonation is monitored and controlled. The controller is not capable of memory storage.

The sensor is a magnetorestrictive device, mounted in the engine block that detects the presence, or absence, and intensity of detonation according to the vibration characteristics of the engine. The output is an electrical signal which is sent to the controller.

Transmission Converter Clutch (TCC)

All 1981 models with an automatic transmission use TCC. The ECM controls the converter by means of a solenoid mounted in the transmission. When the vehicle speed reaches a certain level, the ECM energizes the solenoid and allows the torque converter to mechanically couple the transmission to the engine. When the operating conditions indicate that the transmission should operate as a normal fluid coupled transmission, the ECM will de-energize the solenoid. Depressing the brake will also return the transmission to normal automatic operation.

Catalytic Converter

The catalytic converter is a muffler-like container built into the exhaust system to aid in

A schematic view of the EST circuitry

the reduction of exhaust emissions. The catalyst element consists of individual pellets or a honeycomb monolithic substrate coated with a noble metal such as platinum, palladium, rhodium or a combination. When the exhaust gases come into contact with the catalyst, a chemical reaction occurs which will reduce the pollutants into harmless substances like water and carbon dioxide.

There are essentially two types of catalytic converters: an oxidizing type and a three-way type. The oxidizing type is used on all 1975–80 models with the exception of those 1980 models built for California. It requires the addition of oxygen to spur the catalyst into reducing the engine's HC and CO emissions into H_2O and CO_2. Because of this need for oxygen, the AIR system is used with all these models.

The oxidizing catalytic converter, while effectively reducing HC and CO emissions, does little, if anything in the way of reducing NO_x emissions. Thus, the three-way catalytic converter.

The three-way converter, unlike the oxidizing type, is capable of reducing HC, CO and NO_x emissions; all at the same time. In theory, it seems impossible to reduce all three pollu-

Dual-bed type catalytic converter

tants in one system since the reduction of HC and CO requires the addition of oxygen, while the reduction of NO_x calls for the removal of oxygen. In actuality, the three-way system really can reduce all three pollutants, but only if the amount of oxygen in the exhaust system is precisely controlled. Due to this precise oxygen control requirement, the three-way converter system is used only in cars equipped with an oxygen sensor system (1980 Calif. cars and all 1981 models).

There are no service procedures required for the catalytic converter, although the converter body should be inspected occasionally for damage. Some models with the V-6 engine require a catalyst change at 30,000 mile intervals (consult your Owner's Manual).

PRECAUTIONS

1. Use only unleaded fuel.
2. Avoid prolonged idling; the engine should run no longer than 20 min. at curb idle and no longer than 10 min. at fast idle.
3. Do not disconnect any of the spark plug leads while the engine is running.
4. Make engine compression checks as quickly as possible.

CATALYST TESTING

At the present time there is no known way to reliably test catalytic converter operation in the field. The only reliable test is a 12 hour and 40 min. "soak" test (CVS) which must be done in a laboratory.

An infrared HC/CO tester is not sensitive enough to measure the higher tailpipe emissions from a failing converter. Thus, a bad converter may allow enough emissions to escape so that the car is no longer in compliance with Federal or state standards, but will still not cause the needle on a tester to move off zero.

Bead-type catalytic converter

Single-bed monolith catalytic converter

The chemical reactions which occur inside a catalytic converter generate a great deal of heat. Most converter problems can be traced to fuel or ignition system problems which cause unusually high emissions. As a result of the increased intensity of the chemical reactions, the converter literally burns itself up.

A completely failed converter might cause a tester to show a slight reading. As a result, it is occasionally possible to detect one of these.

As long as you avoid severe overheating and the use of leaded fuels it is reasonably safe to assume that the converter is working properly. If you are in doubt, take the car to a diagnostic center that has a tester.

Oxygen Sensor

An oxygen sensor is used on all 1980 models built for Calif. and on all 1981 models. The sensor protrudes into the exhaust stream and monitors the oxygen content of the exhaust gases. The difference between the oxygen content of the exhaust gases and that of the outside air generates a voltage signal to the ECM. The ECM monitors this voltage and, depending upon the value of the signal received, issues a command to adjust for a rich or a lean condition.

No attempt should ever be made to measure the voltage output of the sensor. The current

DO NOT CHECK WITH VOLTMETER. DO NOT SHORT ACROSS TERMINALS.

Oxygen sensor assembly

drain of any conventional voltmeter would be such that it would permanently damage the sensor. No jumpers, test leads or any other electrical connections should ever be made to the sensor. Use these tools ONLY on the ECM side of the wiring harness connector AFTER disconnecting it from the sensor.

REMOVAL AND INSTALLATION

The oxygen sensor must be replaced every 30,000 miles (48,000 km.). The sensor may be difficult to remove when the engine temperature is below 120°F (48°C). Excessive removal force may damage the threads in the exhaust manifold or pipe; follow the removal procedure carefully.

267, 305 V8

229V6

8.0mm (5/16")
MUST BE MAINTAINED
AFTER INSTALLATION

VIEW A

231V6

Oxygen sensor locations on all engines

1. Locate the oxygen sensor. On the V8 engines, it is on the front of the left side exhaust manifold, just above the point where it connects to the exhaust pipe. On the V6 engines, it is on the inside of the exhaust pipe where it bends toward the back of the car.

NOTE: *On the V6 engine you may find it necessary to raise the front of the car and remove the oxygen sensor from underneath.*

2. Trace the wires leading from the oxygen sensor back to the first connector and then disconnect them (the connector on the V6 engine is attached to a bracket mounted on the right, rear of the engine block, while the connector in the V8 engine is attached to a bracket mounted on the top of the left side exhaust manifold).

3. Spray a commercial heat riser solvent onto the sensor threads and allow it to soak in for at least five minutes.

4. Carefully unscrew and remove the sensor.

5. To install, first coat the new sensor's threads with G.M. anti-seize compound no. 5613695 or the equivalent. This is *not* a conventional anti-seize paste. *The use of a regular compound may electrically insulate the sensor, rendering it inoperative. You must coat the threads with an electrically conductive anti-seize compound.*

6. Installation torque is 30 ft. lbs. (42 Nm.). *Do not overtighten.*

7. Reconnect the electrical connector. Be careful not to damage the electrical pigtail.

Check the sensor boot for proper fit and installation. Install the air cleaner, if removed.

DIESEL ENGINE EMISSIONS CONTROLS

Crankcase Ventilation

A Crankcase Depression Regulator Valve (CDRV) is used to regulate (meter) the flow of crankcase gases back into the engine to be burned. The CDRV is designed to limit vacuum in the crankcase as the gases are drawn from the valve covers through the CDRV and into the intake manifold (air crossover).

Fresh air enters the engine through the combination filter, check valve and oil fill cap. The fresh air mixes with blow-by gases and enters both valve covers. The gases pass through a filter installed on the valve covers and are drawn into connecting tubing.

Intake manifold vacuum acts against a spring loaded diaphragm to control the flow of crankcase gases. Higher intake vacuum levels pull the diaphragm closer to the top of the outlet tube. This reduces the amount of gases being drawn from the crankcase and decreases the vacuum level in the crankcase. As the intake vacuum decreases, the spring pushes the diaphragm away from the top of the outlet tube allowing more gases to flow to the intake manifold.

NOTE: *Do not allow any solvent to come in*

1. Crankcase depression regulator (CDR)
2. Ventilation filter
3. Brace clip
4. Ventilation pipes
5. Crankcase depression regulator (CDR)
6. L.H. valve cover
7. Bracket
8. Air crossover
9. Air crossover to regulator valve pipe

V8 diesel crankcase ventilation system

V8 Diesel EGR System Diagnosis

Condition	Possible Causes	Correction
EGR valve will not open. Engine stalls on deceleration Engine runs rough on light throttle	Binding or stuck EGR valve. No vacuum to EGR valve. Control valve blocked or air flow restricted.	Replace EGR valve. Replace EGR valve. Check VRV, RVR, solenoid, T.C.C. Operation, Vacuum Pump and connecting hoses.
EGR valve will not close. (Heavy smoke on acceleration).	Binding or stuck EGR valve. Constant high vacuum to EGR valve.	Replace EGR valve. Check VRV, RVR, solenoid, and connecting hoses.
EGR valve opens partially.	Binding EGR valve. Low vacuum at EGR valve.	Replace EGR valve. Check VRV, RVR, solenoid, vacuum pump, and connecting hoses.

V6 Diesel EGR System Diagnosis

Condition	Possible Cause	Correction
EGR valve will not open.	Binding or stuck EGR valve. No vacuum to EGR valve.	Replace EGR valve. Check VRV, RVR, solenoid TCC Operation (See Section 7A), Vacuum Pump, VMV, and connecting hoses.
EGR valve will not close, or EPR valve will not open. (Heavy smoke on acceleration).	Binding or stuck EGR or EPR valve. Constant high vacuum to EGR and EPR valve.	Replace EGR or EPR valve Check VRV, RVR, solenoid VMV and connecting hoses.
EGR valve opens partially.	Binding EGR valve. Low vacuum at EGR valve.	Replace EGR valve. Check VRV, RVR, solenoid, vacuum pump, VMV and connecting hoses.
Loss of power and heavy smoke on acceleration, EGR valve functions normally.	Binding or stuck EPR valve, constant high vacuum to EPR valve.	Replace EPR valve. Check vacuum hose routing.

contact with the diaphragm of the Crankcase Depression Regulator Valve because the diaphragm will fail.

Exhaust Gas Recirculation (EGR)

To lower the formation of nitrogen oxides (NO_x) in the exhaust, it is necessary to reduce combustion temperatures. This is done in the diesel, as in the gasoline engine, by introducing exhaust gases into the cylinders through the EGR valve.

FUNCTIONAL TESTS OF COMPONENTS

Vacuum Regulator Valve (VRV)

The Vacuum Regulator Valve is attached to the side of the injection pump and regulates vacuum in proportion to throttle angle. Vacuum from the vacuum pump is supplied to port A and vacuum at port B is reduced as the throttle is opened. At closed throttle, the vacuum is 15

V6 diesel crankcase ventilation system

inches; at half throttle—6 inches; at wide open throttle there is zero vacuum.

Exhaust Gas Recirculation (EGR) Valve

Apply vacuum to vacuum port. The valve should be fully open at 10.5″ and closed below 6″.

Vacuum regulator valve, mounted to diesel injection pumps

1. EGR valve
2. Gasket
3. Bolt lock
4. 24 N·m (18 ft.lbs.)

AFTER BOLTS ARE TORQUED TO SPECS BEND LOCK TABS AROUND BOLT HEADS

Diesel EGR valve location on top of intake manifold

TO EGR SOLENOID   TO EGR VALVE

TO VRV
(REGULATED VACUUM)

Diesel vacuum reducer, except California

Response Vacuum Reducer (RVR)

Connect a vacuum gauge to the port marked "To EGR valve or T.C.C. solenoid". Connect a hand operated vacuum pump to the VRV port. Draw a 50.66 kPa (15 inch) vacuum on the pump and the reading on the vacuum gauge should be lower than the vacuum pump reading as follows:

- .75" Except High Altitude
- 2.5" High Altitude

1. Crankcase depression regulator
2. Ventilation filter
3. Breather cap

Diesel crankcase ventilation flow

Torque Converter Clutch Operated Solenoid

When the torque converter clutch is engaged, an electrical signal energizes the solenoid allowing ports 1 and 2 to be interconnected. When the solenoid is not energized, port 1 is closed and ports 2 and 3 are interconnected.

Solenoid Energized

- Ports 1 and 3 are connected.

Solenoid De-Energized

- Ports 2 and 3 are connected.

Engine Temperature Sensor (ETS)
OPERATION

The engine temperature sensor has two terminals. Twelve volts are applied to one terminal and the wire from the other terminal leads to the fast idle solenoid and Housing Pressure Cold Advance solenoid that is part of the injection pump.

The switch contacts are closed below 125°F. At the calibration point, the contacts are open which turns off the solenoids.

Above Calibration

- Open circuit.

Below Calibration

- Closed Circuit.

VACUUM PUMP

EGR VALVE

VACUUM REGULATOR VALVE (VRV) (On Injection Pump)

(Switch Portion of Assy.)

EPR SWITCH ASSY.

EXHAUST PRESSURE REGULATOR PIPE (EPR)

(Solenoid Portion of Assy.)

VENT

12V

TRANSMISSION MODULATOR PIPE

(Vacuum Reducer Portion of Assy.)

(Solenoid Portion of Assy.)

VENT

FROM TRANS. GOVERNOR SPEED SWITCH

12V WHEN TCC ENGAGED

EGR CONTROL ASSY.

Diesel EGR system, except California

AIR CLEANER MOUNTING STUD

GROMMET

EGR VALVE

AIR CLEANER

PIPE TO EXHAUST MANIFOLD

12 VOLTS (AT INJECTION PUMP)

OPEN WHEN ENERGIZED

AIR CROSSOVER

VACUUM PUMP

EGR VACUUM SOLENOID VALVE

N. O. BELOW PRESET VACUUM

INJECTION PUMP

EGR VACUUM SWITCH (EGR-VS)

GROUND

TO TCC VACUUM SWITCH (IF USED)

TO TRANSMISSION VACUUM MODULATOR (IF USED)

VACUUM REGULATOR VALVE (VRV)

California EGR system, V8 Diesel

V6 diesel EGR system

EPR valve, California V6 diesel

Engine Temperature Sensor (ETS), diesels

EPR Valve (California V6)

This valve is found between the right-hand exhaust manifold and the exhaust pipe on California V6 diesel cars. The EPR valve is used in the exhaust flow to increase back pressure in the exhaust system, thus increasing exhaust flow through the EGR system. The valve operates from the same vacuum source as the EGR valve. It should be fully closed at idle, and will open as the throttle is opened until, at full throttle, it will be fully open.

TESTING THE EPR VALVE

To test the EPR valve, apply vacuum to the vacuum port on the valve. The valve should be fully closed at 12 in. Hg of vacuum, and open below 6 in. Hg. of vacuum.

GASOLINE ENGINE FUEL SYSTEM

Fuel Pump

The fuel pump is the single action AC diaphragm type. Two types of fuel pumps are used; serviceable and non-serviceable. The serviceable type is used on all 1964 and 1965 engines, 1966 inline engines without the AIR emission control system, and 1966 283 and 327 V8s. The non-serviceable type is used on all other engines.

The pump is actuated by an eccentric located on the engine camshaft. On inline engines, and the 231 V6 the eccentric actuates the pump rocker arm. On V8 and the 200 V6 engines, a pushrod between the camshaft eccentric and the fuel pump actuates the pump rocker arm.

TESTING THE FUEL PUMP

Fuel pumps should always be tested on the vehicle. The larger line between the pump and tank is the suction side of the system and the smaller line, between the pump and carburetor is the pressure side. A leak in the pressure side would be apparent because of dripping fuel. A leak in the suction side is often only apparent because of a reduced volume of fuel delivered to the pressure side. However, fuel *may* leak out on the suction side when the engine is off.

1. Tighten any loose line connections and look for any kinks or restrictions. Inspect rubber hoses for cracks or leaks and replace if necessary. Inspect the fuel filter for clogging and clean or replace it as necessary.

2. Disconnect the fuel line at the carburetor. Disconnect the distributor-to-coil primary wire or, on HEI systems, the distributor connector. Place a container at the end of the fuel line and crank the engine a few revolutions. If little or no gasoline flows from the line, either the fuel pump is inoperative or the line is plugged. Blow through the lines with compressed air and try to the test again. Reconnect the line.

Fuel pump mounting—229 V6

3. Attach a pressure gauge to the pressure side of the fuel line with a "Tee" fitting.

4. Run the engine and note the reading on the gauge. Stop the engine and compare the reading with the specifications listed in the "Tune-Up Specifications" chart. If the pump is operating properly, the pressure will be as specified and will be constant at idle speed. If pressure varies sporadically or is too high or low, the pump should be replaced.

5. Remove the pressure gauge

REMOVAL AND INSTALLATION

NOTE: *When you connect the fuel pump outlet fitting, always use 2 wrenches to avoid damaging the pump.*

1. Disconnect the fuel intake and outlet lines at the pump and plug the pump intake line.

2. On small-block V6 and V8 engines, remove the upper bolt from the right front mounting boss. Insert a longer bolt (⅜–16 × 2

Fuel pump mounting—inline six cylinder

Fuel pump mounting—231 V6

in.) in this hole to hold the fuel pump pushrod.

3. Remove the two pump mounting bolts and lockwashers; remove the pump and its gasket.

4. If the rocker arm pushrod is to be removed from V6 or V8, remove the two adapter bolts and lockwashers and remove the adapter and its gasket.

5. Install the fuel pump with a new gasket reversing the removal procedure. Coat the mating surfaces with sealer.

6. Connect the fuel lines and check for leaks.

Fuel pump mounting—V8

Carbutetors

Since their introduction in 1964, mid-size Chevrolets have used nineteen different carburetors:

- Carter AFB 4 bbl—1964–65
- Carter WCFB 4 bbl—1964–65
- Carter YF 1 bbl—1966–67
- Carter AVS 4 bbl—1966
- Holley 4150 4 bbl—1965–70
- Holley 4160 4 bbl—1966–71
- Rochester BV 1 bbl—1964–67
- Rochester MV 1 bbl—1968–76
- Rochester ME 1 bbl—1977–79
- Rochester 2GV 2 bbl—1968–74
- Rochester 2GC 2 bbl—1975–79
- Rochester M2ME 2 bbl—1980
- Rochester E2ME 2 bbl—1980 and later
- Rochester 4GC 4 bbl—1964–66
- Rochester 4MV 4 bbl—1967–74
- Rochester M4MC 4 bbl—1975–77
- Rochester 4MC 4 bbl—1977–79
- Rochester M4ME 4 bbl—1980
- Rochester E4ME 4 bbl—1980 and later

MODEL IDENTIFICATION

General Motors Rochester carburetors are identified by their model code. The first number indicates the number of barrels, while one of the last letters indicates the type of choke used. These are V for the manifold mounted choke coil, C for the choke coil mounted in the carburetor body, and E for electric choke, also mounted on the carburetor. Model codes ending in A indicate an altitude-compensating carburetor.

Carburetor I.D. location, all models similar

REMOVAL AND INSTALLATION

All Carburetors

1. Remove the air cleaner and its gasket.

2. Disconnect the fuel and vacuum lines from the carburetor.

3. Disconnect the choke coil rod, heated air line tube, or electrical connector.

4. Disconnect the throttle linkage.

5. On automatic transmission cars, disconnect the throttle valve linkage if so equipped.

6. If CEC equipped remove the CEC valve vacuum hose and electrical connector. Disconnect the EGR line, if so equipped.

7. Remove the idle stop solenoid, if so equipped.

8. Remove the carburetor attaching nuts and/or bolts, gasket or insulator, and remove the carburetor.

9. Install the carburetor using the reverse of the removal procedure. Use a new gasket and fill the float bowl with gasoline to ease starting the engine.

OVERHAUL

All Types

Efficient carburetion depends greatly on careful cleaning and inspection during overhaul, since dirt, gum, water, or varnish in or on the carburetor parts are often responsible for poor performance.

Overhaul your carburetor in a clean, dust-free area. Carefully disassemble the carburetor, referring often to the exploded views and directions packaged with the rebuilding kit. Keep all similar and look-alike parts segregated during disassembly and cleaning to avoid accidental interchange during assembly. Make a note of all jet sizes.

When the carburetor is disassembled, wash all parts (except diaphragms, electric choke units, pump plunger, and any other plastic, leather, fiber, or rubber parts) in clean carburetor solvent. Do not leave parts in the solvent any longer than is necessary to sufficiently loosen the deposits. Excessive cleaning may remove the special finish from the float bowl and choke valve bodies, leaving these parts unfit for service. Rinse all parts in clean solvent and blow them dry with compressed air or allow them to air dry. Wipe clean all cork, plastic, leather, and fiber parts with a clean, lint-free cloth.

Blow out all passages and jets with compressed air and be sure that there are no restrictions or blockages. Never use wire or similar tools to clean jets, fuel passages, or air bleeds. Clean all jets and valves separately to avoid accidental interchange.

Check all parts for wear or damage. If wear or damage is found, replace the defective parts. Especially check the following:

1. Check the float needle and seat for wear. If wear is found, replace the complete assembly.

2. Check the float hinge pin for wear and the float(s) for dents or distortion. Replace the float if fuel has leaked into it.

3. Check the throttle and choke shaft bores for wear or an out-of-round condition. Damage or wear to the throttle arm, shaft, or shaft bore will often require replacement of the throttle body. These parts require a close tolerance of fit; wear may allow air leakage, which could affect starting and idling.

NOTE: *Throttle shafts and bushings are not included in overhaul kits. They can be purchased separately.*

4. Inspect the idle mixture adjusting needles for burrs or grooves. Any such condition requires replacement of the needle, since you will not be able to obtain a satisfactory idle.

5. Test the accelerator pump check valves. They should pass air one way but not the other. Test for proper seating by blowing and sucking on the valve. Replace the valve check ball and spring as necessary. If the valve is satisfactory, wash the valve parts again to remove breath moisture.

6. Check the bowl cover for warped surfaces with a straightedge.

7. Closely inspect the accelerator pump plunger for wear and damage, replacing as necessary.

8. After the carburetor is assembled, check the choke valve for freedom of operation.

Carburetor overhaul kits are recommended for each overhaul. These kits contain all gaskets and new parts to replace those which deteriorate most rapidly. Failure to replace all parts supplied with the kit (especially gaskets) can result in poor performance later.

Some carburetor manufacturers supply overhaul kits of three basic types: minor repair; major repair; and gasket kits. Basically, they contain the following:

Minor Repair Kits:
- All gaskets
- Float needle valve
- All diagrams
- Spring for the pump diaphragm

Major Repair Kits:
- All jets and gaskets
- All diaphragms
- Float needle valve
- Pump ball valve
- Float
- Complete intermediate rod
- Intermediate pump lever
- Some cover hold-down screws and washers

Gasket Kits:
- All gaskets

After cleaning and checking all components, reassemble the carburetor, using new parts and referring to the exploded view. When reassembling, make sure that all screws and jets are tight in their seats, but do not overtighten as the tips will be distorted. Tighten all screws gradually, in rotation. Do not tighten needle valves into their seats; uneven jetting will result. Always use new gaskets. Be sure to adjust the float level when reassembling.

M4MC air horn tightening sequence

M2MC air horn tightening sequence

PRELIMINARY CHECKS (ALL CARBURETORS)

The following should be observed before attempting any adjustments.

1. Thoroughly warm the engine. If the engine is cold, be sure that it reaches operating temperature.

2. Check the torque of all carburetor mounting nuts and assembly screws. Also check the intake manifold-to-cylinder head bolts. If air is leaking at any of these points, any attempts at adjustment will inevitably lead to frustration.

3. Check the manifold heat control valve (if used) to be sure that it is free.

4. Check and adjust the choke as necessary.

5. Adjust the idle speed and mixture. If the mixture screws are capped, don't adjust them unless all other causes of rough idle have been eliminated. If any adjustments are performed that might possibly change the idle speed or mixture, adjust the idle and mixture again when you are finished.

Before you make any carburetor adjustments make sure that the engine is in tune. Many problems which are thought to be carburetor-related can be traced to an engine which is simply out-of-tune. Any trouble in these areas will have symptoms like those of carburetor problems.

Carter AFB—4-BBL Carburetor

AUTOMATIC CHOKE ADJUSTMENT

The automatic choke is correctly adjusted when the scribe mark on the coil housing is aligned with the center notch in the choke housing for automatic transmission cars and one notch lean for manual transmission cars.

FLOAT ADJUSTMENT

Remove the metering rods and the bowl cover. Align the float by sighting down its side to determine if it is parallel with the outer edge of the air horn. Bend the float to adjust. Float level is adjusted with the air horn inverted and the air horn gasket in place. Clearance between each float (at the outer end) and the air horn gasket should be $\frac{5}{16}$ in. Bend to adjust.

FLOAT DROP ADJUSTMENT

Float drop is adjusted by holding the air horn in an upright position and bending the float arm until the vertical distance from the air horn gasket to the outer end of each float measures $\frac{3}{4}$ in.

AFB float adjustment

INTERMEDIATE CHOKE ROD ADJUSTMENT

Remove the choke coil housing assembly, gasket, and baffle plate. Position a .026 in. wire gauge between the bottom of the slot in the piston and the top of the slot in the choke piston housing. Close the choke piston against the gauge and secure it with a rubber band. Bend the intermediate choke rod so that the distance between the top edge of the choke valve and the air horn divider measures .070 in.

ACCELERATOR PUMP ADJUSTMENT

The first step in adjusting the accelerator pump is to push aside the fast-idle cam and firmly seat the throttle valves. Bend the pump rod at the lower angle to obtain a $\frac{1}{2}$ in. clearance between the air horn and the top of the plunger shaft.

UNLOADER, CLOSING SHOE, AND SECONDARY THROTTLE ADJUSTMENT

To adjust the unloader, hold the throttle wide open and bend the unloader tang to obtain a 3/16 in. clearance between the upper edge of the choke valve and the inner wall of the air horn.

The clearance between the positive closing shoes on the primary and secondary throttle valves is checked with the valves closed. Bend the secondary closing shoe as required to obtain a clearance of .020 in.

The secondary throttle opening is governed by the pick-up lever on the primary throttle shaft. It has two points of contact with the loose lever on the primary shaft. If the contact points do not simultaneously engage, bend the pick-up lever to obtain proper engagement. The primary and secondary throttle valve opening must be synchronized.

Carter AVS—4-BBL Carburetor

AIR VALVE ADJUSTMENT

1. Turn the air valve bearing retainer until the air valve freely falls open.
2. Wind the air valve bearing counterclockwise until the air valve just starts to close.
3. Continue to wind the bearing an additional 2⅛ turns, and then tighten the retainer.

AVS air valve adjustment

ACCELERATOR PUMP ADJUSTMENT

1. With the fast idle cam out of the way, back the idle speed screw out until the throttle valves seat in their bores.
2. Hold the throttle valves closed and measure the distance from the air horn to the bottom of the pump S-link.

3. If this distance is not 11/32 in., bend the pump rod to obtain it.

IDLE VENT ADJUSTMENT

Holding the choke valve open and throttle valve closed, the clearance at the idle vent valve should be .030 in. Bend the vent valve lever to adjust.

FAST IDLE CHOKE ROD ADJUSTMENT

Bend the fast idle rod at a lower angle until the fast idle cam index mark lines up with the fast idle adjustment screw. Perform this adjustment while holding the choke valve closed.

FLOAT LEVEL AND DROP ADJUSTMENT

These adjustments are made in the same manner as on the Carter AFB.

CHOKE UNLOADER ADJUSTMENT

1. Hold the throttle wide open and the choke valve toward the closed position with a rubber band.
2. Bend the unloader tang on the throttle shaft lever to obtain a clearance of .170 in. Between the upper edge of the choke valve and the dividing wall of the air horn.

CHOKE VACUUM BREAK ADJUSTMENT

1. Hold the vacuum break in against its stop and the choke valve toward the closed position with a rubber band.
2. Bend the vacuum break link at an offset to obtain .120 in. clearance between the upper edge of the choke valve and the air horn wall.

CLOSING SHOE ADJUSTMENT

1. Hold the primary and secondary throttle valves closed.
2. Bend the secondary closing shoe to obtain .020 in. clearance between the positive closing shoes on the primary and secondary throttle levers.

SECONDARY THROTTLE OPENING

1. Check to see that the pickup lever contacts the loose lever on the primary shaft at both points simultaneously. Bend the pickup lever to obtain proper contact, if necessary.
2. If the primary and secondary throttle valves do not come to the wide open position simultaneously, bend the connecting link until they do.

SECONDARY LOCKOUT ADJUSTMENT

1. When the choke valve is closed, the lockout tang on the secondary throttle lever should engage the lockout dog. When the valve is open, the lockout dog should swing free of the tang.

2. Bend the lockout tang on the secondary throttle lever, if an adjustment is necessary.

Carter YF—1 BBL Carburetor

AUTOMATIC CHOKE ADJUSTMENT

1. Disconnect the choke rod from the choke lever.
2. Hold the choke valve closed and pull the rod up against the stop in the thermostat housing.
3. The top of the rod should be about one rod diameter above the top of the hole in the choke lever. If not, adjust the length of the rod by bending it at the bend.
4. Connect the choke rod at the lever.

HAND CHOKE ADJUSTMENT

1. Push in the hand choke knob until the knob is within ⅛ in. of the dash.
2. Loosen the cable clamp at the carburetor and adjust the cable until the choke is wide open.
3. Tighten the cable clamp and check the operation of the choke.

IDLE VENT ADJUSTMENT

1. With the choke open, back out the idle speed screw until it is free to close the throttle valve.
2. Insert a feeler gauge between the air horn and the vent valve. Adjust to get 0.065 in. clearance.

BEND ROD TO ADJUST

ALIGN MARK AND TANG AS SPECIFIED

Choke rod adjustment (Carter YF) (© Chevrolet Motor Division)

with the upper edge of the tang on the throttle lever. If not, bend the choke rod as necessary.

CHOKE UNLOADER ADJUSTMENT

1. Open the throttle to the wide open position.
2. Using a rubber band, hold the choke valve closed.
3. Bend the unloader tang on the throttle lever to get the proper clearance (0.250 in.) between the lower edge of the choke valve and the air horn wall.

SPECIFIED GAUGE BETWEEN VENT VALVE AND AIR HORN

Adjusting idle vent (Carter YF) (© Chevrolet Motor Division)

SPECIFIED GAUGE BETWEEN CHOKE VALVE AND AIR HORN

BEND TANG

THROTTLE WIDE OPEN

Choke unloader adjustment (Carter YF) (© Chevrolet Motor Division)

FAST IDLE AND CHOKE VALVE ADJUSTMENT

1. Hold the choke valve closed.
2. Close the throttle and mark the position of the throttle lever tang on the fast idle cam.
3. The mark on the fast idle cam should align

Carter Specifications

Year	Model or Type ①	Float Level (in.)		Float Drop (in.)		Pump Travel Setting (in.)	Choke Setting		Secondary Locknut Adj.
		Prim	Sec	Prim	Sec		Unloader (in.)	Housing	
1964–65	AFB-All	$7/32$	$7/32$	$3/4$	$3/4$	$1/2$	$1/4$	1-Lean	0.020
	WCFB-All	$7/32$	$1/4$	$3/4$	$3/4$	$1/2$	$3/16$	Index	—
1966	6 Cyl-YF-4079S, 4080S	$1/2$	—	$1 3/16$	—	—	0.260	—	—
	V8-AVS-4027S, 4028S	$1 15/32$	—	2	—	$11/32$	0.170	—	—
1967	6 Cyl-YF	$7/32$	—	$1 3/16$	—	—	0.250	—	—

① Model number located on the tag or casting

VACUUM BREAK ADJUSTMENT

1. Hold the vacuum break arm against its stop and hold the choke closed with a rubber band.

2. Bend the vacuum break link to establish a clearance of 2.220 in. (automatic transmission) or 0.240 in. (standard transmission) between the lower edge of the choke valve and the air horn wall.

FLOAT LEVEL ADJUSTMENT

1. Turn the bowl cover upside down and measure the float level by measuring the distance between the float (free end) and cover. This distance should be $7/32$ in.; if not, bend the lip of the float, not the float arm.

2. Hold the cover in the proper position (not upside down) and measure the float drop from the cover to the float bottom at the end opposite the hinge. This distance should be $1 3/16$ in.

3. Make any necessary adjustments with the stop tab on the float arm.

ACCELERATOR PUMP ADJUSTMENT

1. Seat the throttle valve by backing off the idle speed screw.

2. Hold the throttle valve closed.

3. Fully depress the diaphragm shaft and check the contact between the lower retainer and the lifter link.

4. This retainer (upper pump spring) should just contact the pump lifter link. Do not compress the spring.

5. Bend the pump connector link at its "U" bend to make corrections.

METERING ROD ADJUSTMENT

1. Insert the metering rod through the metering jet and close the throttle valve. Press down on the upper pump spring until the pump bottoms.

2. The metering rod arm must rest on the pump lifter link; the rod eye should just slide over the arm pin.

3. To adjust, bend the metering rod arm.

SPECIFIED CLEARANCE

BEND ROD TO ADJUST

Accelerator pump adjustment (Carter YF) (© Chevrolet Motor Division)

Rochester BV—1 BBL Carburetor

AUTOMATIC CHOKE ADJUSTMENT

1. Disconnect the choke rod from the choke lever at the carburetor.

2. While holding the choke valve shut, pull the choke rod up against the stop in the thermostat housing.

3. Adjust the length of the choke rod so that the bottom edge of the choke rod is even with the top edge of the hole in the choke lever.

4. Check the linkage for freedom of operation.

IDLE VENT ADJUSTMENT

1. Position the carburetor lever on the low step of the fast idle cam.

2. The distance between the choke valve and the body casting should be 0.050 in.

3. If an adjustment is necessary, turn the valve with a screwdriver.

FAST IDLE AND CHOKE VALVE ADJUSTMENT

1. Position the end of the idle adjusting screw on the next to highest step of the fast idle cam.

Rochester BV Specifications

Year	Carburetor Identifi-cation ①	Float Level (in.)	Float Drop (in.)	Pump Rod (in.)	Idle Vent (in.)	Vacuum Break (in.)	Auto-matic Choke	Choke Rod (in.)	Choke Unloader (in.)	Fast Idle Speed
1964–66	All	1 9/32	1 3/4	—	0.050	—	—	—	0.350	—
1967	7025000	1 9/32	1 3/4	—	0.050	0.140	—	0.090	0.350	—
	7022503	1 9/32	1 3/4	—	0.050	0.160	—	0.100	0.350	—
	7026028	1 9/32	1 3/4	—	0.050	0.140	—	0.090	0.350	—
	7026027	1 9/32	1 3/4	—	0.050	0.160	—	0.100	0.350	—
	7027110	3/4	1 3/4	—	1	0.110	—	0.060	0.215	—
	7027101	3/4	1 3/4	—	1	0.120	—	0.060	0.215	—

① The carburetor identification tag is located at the rear of the carburetor on one of the air horn screws

TURN VALVE TO ADJUST

SPECIFIED GAUGE BETWEEN BOTTOM OF VALVE AND TOP OF AIR HORN

SCREW ON LOW STEP OF CAM

Idle vent adjustment (Rochester BV) (© Chevrolet Motor Division)

2. A 0.050 in. feeler gauge should slide easily between the lower edge of the choke valve and the carburetor bore.

3. If necessary, bend the choke rod until the correct clearance is obtained.

UNLOADER ADJUSTMENT

1. Open the throttle to the wide open position.

2. A 0.230/0.270 in. gauge should slide freely between the lower edge of the choke valve and the bore of the carburetor.

3. If necessary, bend the throttle tang to obtain the proper clearance.

VACUUM BREAK ADJUSTMENT

1. Hold the diaphragm lever against the diaphragm body.

2. The clearance between the lower edge of the choke valve and the air horn wall should be 0.136–0.154 in. on Powerglide cars and 0.154–0.173 in. on manual cars.

3. Bend the diaphragm link, if necessary.

FLOAT LEVEL ADJUSTMENT

1. Remove the air cleaner.

2. Disconnect the fuel line, fast idle rod, cam-to-choke kick lever, vacuum hose at the diaphragm, and the choke rod at the choke lever.

3. Remove the bowl cover screws and carefully lift the cover off the carburetor.

4. Install a new gasket on the cover before making any adjustments.

5. Invert the cover assembly and measure the float level with a float gauge.

NOTE: *Rebuilding kits include a float level gauge.*

6. Check float centering while holding the cover sideways. Use the same gauge as in Step Five. The floats should not touch the gauge.

7. Hold the cover upright and measure the float drop. If the drop is more or less than 1 3/4 in., bend the stop tang until the drop is correct.

BEND FLOAT TANG TO ADJUST

GAUGE FROM GASKET SURFACE TO BOTTOM OF FLOAT

Adjusting float drop (Rochester BV) (© Chevrolet Motor Division)

8. Install the cover and reconnect the lines and linkage in the reverse order of removal.

Rochester MV—1 BBL Carburetor

The model MV carburetor is a single bore, down-drift carburetor with an aluminum throttle body, automatic choke, internally balanced venting, and a hot idle compensating system for cars equipped with automatic transmissions. Newer models are also equipped with Combination Emission Control valves (C.E.C.) and an Exhaust Gas Recirculation (EGR) system. An electrically operated idle stop solenoid replaces the idle stop screw of older models.

The MV carburetor is used on six cylinder cars from 1968 and service procedures apply to all MV carburetors.

FAST IDLE ADJUSTMENT

NOTE: *The fast idle adjustment must be made with the transmission in Neutral.*
1. Position the fast idle lever on the high step of the fast idle cam.
2. Be sure that the choke is properly adjusted and in the wide open position with the engine warm.
3. Bend the fast idle lever until the specified speed is obtained.

CHOKE ROD (FAST IDLE CAM) AJUSTMENT

NOTE: *Adjust the fast idle before making choke rod adjustments.*
1. Place the fast idle cam follower on the second step of the fast idle cam and hold it firmly against the rise to the high step.
2. Rotate the choke valve in the direction of a closed choke by applying force to the choke coil lever.
3. Bend the choke rod, at the point shown in the illustration, to give the specified opening between the lower edge (upper edge—1976), of the choke valve and the inside air horn wall.
NOTE: *Measurement must be made at the center of the choke valve.*

CHOKE VACUUM BREAK ADJUSTMENT

The adjustment of the vacuum break diaphragm unit insures correct choke valve opening after engine starting.
1. Remove the air cleaner. On vehicles with the THERMAC air cleaner, plug the sensor's vacuum take off port.
2. Using an external vacuum source, apply vacuum to the vacuum break diaphragm until the plunger is fully seated.
3. When the plunger is seated, push the choke valve toward the closed position.

BEND TANG TO ADJUST GAUGE BETWEEN LOWER EDGE OF CHOKE VALVE AND AIR HORN WALL

RUBBER BAND OR SPRING KEEPING CHOKE VALVE TOWARDS CLOSED POSITION

SEAT DIAPHRAGM BY PUSHING PLUNGER IN WITH NEEDLE NOSED PLIERS

Vacuum break adjustment (MV) (© Chevrolet Motor Division)

CHOKE UNLOADER ADJUSTMENT

1. While holding the choke valve closed, apply pressure to the choke operating lever.
2. Turn the throttle lever to the wide open position.
3. Measure the distance between the lower edge of the choke plate and the air horn wall.
4. If an adjustment is necessary, bend the unloader tang on the throttle lever.

FLOAT LEVEL ADJUSTMENT

1. While holding the float retainer in place, push down on the outer end of the float arm.
2. Measure the distance from the top of the float bowl casting (no gasket) and the toe of the float.
3. Bend the float as necessary to obtain the specified measurement.

METERING ROD ADJUSTMENT

1. Back out the idle adjusting screw or idle stop solenoid to close the throttle valve.
2. Apply pressure to the power piston hanger and hold the piston against its stop.
3. While holding the power piston down, turn the metering rod holder over to the flat surface of the bowl casting until the metering rod lightly touches the inside edge of the bowl.
4. Measure the space between the bowl and the bottom of the metering rod holder. This dimension should be between 0.070 and 0.078 in.
5. Bend the metering rod holder if an adjustment is necessary.

CHOKE ROD ADJUSTMENT

1. Disconnect the choke rod from the upper choke lever and hold the choke valve closed.
2. Push the choke rod down to the bottom of its travel.
3. The top of the rod should be even with the bottom of the hole in the choke lever; bend the rod if necessary.

1. Air horn assembly
2. Screw—air horn—long
3. Screw—air horn—short
4. Bracket—air cleaner stud
5. Screw—bracket attaching
7. Gasket—air horn
8. Choke shaft and lever assembly
9. Choke valve
10. Screw—choke valve
11. Lever—vacuum break link
12. Vacuum break link assy.
13. Diaphragm—vacuum break
14. Cover—vacuum break
15. Screw—cover
16. Choke rod
17. Choke lever
18. Screw—choke lever
19. Cam—fast idle
20. Screw—cam attaching
21. Float bowl assembly
22. Idle tube assembly
23. Jet—main metering
24. Ball—pump discharge
25. Spring—pump discharge
26. Guide—pump discharge
27. Needle and seat assy.
28. Gasket—needle seat
29. Idle compensator assembly
30. Gasket—idle compensator
31. Cover—idle compensator
32. Screw—cover
33. Float assembly
34. Hinge pin—float
35. Power piston assembly
36. Spring—power piston
37. Rod—power piston
38. Metering rod and spring assembly
39. Filter nut—fuel inlet
40. Gasket—filter nut
41. Filter—fuel inlet
42. Spring—fuel filter
43. Screw—slow idle
44. Pump assembly
45. Lever—pump actuating
46. Spring—pump return
47. Throttle body assembly
48. Gasket—throttle body
49. Idle needle
50. Spring—idle needle
51. Screw—throttle body
52. Lever—pump and power rods—new
53. Screw—lever attaching
54. Link—power piston rod
55. Link—pump lever

Exploded view of an MV carburetor (© Chevrolet Motor Division)

Rochester MV Specifications

Year	Carburetor Identification ①	Float Level (in.)	Metering Rod (in.)	Pump Rod	Idle Vent (in.)	Vacuum Break (in.)	Auxiliary Vacuum Break (in.)	Fast Idle Off Car (in.)	Choke Rod (in.)	Choke Unloader (in.)	Fast Idle Speed (rpm)
1968	7028014	9/32	0.120	—	0.050	0.245	—	1½	0.150	0.350	2400 ②
	7028015	9/32	0.130	—	0.050	0.275	—	1½	0.150	0.350	2400 ②
	7028017	9/32	0.130	—	0.050	0.275	—	1½	0.150	0.350	2400 ②
1969	7029014	¼	0.070	—	0.050	0.245	—	0.100	0.170	0.350	2400 ②
	7029015	¼	0.090	—	0.050	0.275	—	0.100	0.200	0.350	2400 ②
	7029017	¼	0.090	—	0.050	0.275	—	0.100	0.200	0.350	2400 ②
1970	7040014	¼	0.070	—	—	0.200	—	0.110	0.170	0.350	2400 ②
	7040017	¼	0.090	—	—	0.160	—	0.100	0.190	0.350	2400 ②
1971	7041014	¼	0.080	—	—	0.200	—	0.100	0.160	0.350	—
	7041017	¼	0.080	—	—	0.230	—	0.100	0.180	0.350	—
	7041023	1/16	—	—	—	0.200	—	0.110	0.120	0.350	—
1972	7042014	¼	0.080	—	—	0.190	—	—	0.125	0.500	2400 ②
	7042017	¼	0.078	—	—	0.225	—	—	0.150	0.500	2400 ②
	7042984	¼	0.078	—	—	0.190	—	—	0.125	0.500	2400 ②
	7042987	¼	0.076	—	—	0.225	—	—	0.150	0.500	2400 ②
1973	7043014	¼	0.080	—	—	0.300	—	—	0.245	0.500	1800 ②
	7043017	¼	0.080	—	—	0.350	—	—	0.275	0.500	1800 ②
1974	7044014	3/10	0.079	—	—	0.275	—	—	0.230	0.500	1800 ② ③
	7044017	3/10	0.072	—	—	0.350	—	—	0.275	0.500	1800 ② ③
	7044314	3/10	0.073	—	—	0.300	—	—	0.245	0.500	1800 ② ③
1975	7045013	11/32	0.080	—	—	0.200	0.215	—	0.160	0.215	1800 ④
	7045012	11/32	0.080	—	—	0.350	0.312	—	0.275	0.275	1800 ④
	7045314	11/32	0.080	—	—	0.275	0.312	—	0.230	0.275	1800 ④
1976	17056012	11/32	0.084	—	—	0.140	0.265	—	0.100	0.260	⑤
	17056013	11/32	0.082	—	—	0.140	0.325	—	0.140	0.260	⑤
	17056014	—	—	—	—	—	—	—	—	—	—

① The carburetor identification tag is located at the rear of the carburetor on one of the air horn screws
② High step of cam
③ Without vacuum advance
④ 1700 rpm with automatic transmission in Neutral
⑤ 2100 rpm—49 states with transmission in Neutral; 2200 rpm—49 states with non-integral head; 1700 rpm—California

Rochester 1ME—1 BBL Carburetors

FLOAT LEVEL ADJUSTMENT

1. Push down on the end of the float arm and against the top of the float needle to hold the retaining pin firmly in place.

2. While holding the position of the retaining pin, gauge from the top of the casting to the top of the index point at the toe of the float.

3. If float level needs to be changed do it by bending the float arm just on the float side of the float needle.

FAST IDLE ADJUSTMENT

1. If the carburetor has a stepped fast idle cam, put the cam follower on the high step of the cam. If the cam has a smooth contour, open the throttle slightly and rotate the cam to its highest position, then release throttle.

2. Support the lever with a pair of pliers, and bend the tang in or out to achieve specified

Float level adjustment (MV) (© Chevrolet Motor Division)

rpm. Perform the adjustment with the engine hot and the choke open.

CHOKE COIL LEVER ADJUSTMENT

NOTE: *This adjustment requires a plug gauge or other metal rod of .120″ diameter.*

1. Place the fast idle cam follower on the highest step of the cam or rotate the cam to its highest possible position. Close the choke all the way and hold.
2. Insert the plug gauge through the small hole in the outer end of the choke lever. Bend the link at the lowest point of the curved portion until the gauge will enter the hole in the carburetor casting.

CHOKE ADJUSTMENT

1. Place the fast idle cam follower on the high step of the cam or rotate the cam until it is at the highest position.
2. Slightly loosen the three screws which retain the choke cover just enough to turn the cover—don't loosen them more than neces-

Choke rod adjustment (MV) (© Chevrolet Motor Division)

sary, or the lever may slip out of the tang inside.

3. Turn the cover until the mark on the cover lines up with the appropriate mark on the choke housing—see specifications.

METERING ROD ADJUSTMENT

1. Hold the throttle wide open. Push downward on the metering rod until it can be slid out of the slot in the holder. Slide the rod out of the holder and remove it from the main metering jet.
2. Back out the solenoid hex screw until the throttle can be closed all the way.
3. Remove the float bowl gasket.
4. Holding power piston down and throttle

Rochester ME Specifications

Year	Carburetor Identifi- cation	Float Level (in.)	Metering Rod (in.)	Pump Rod	Idle Vent (in.)	Vacuum Break (in.)	Auxiliary Vacuum Break (in.)	Fast Idle Break (in.)	Choke ① Rod (in.)	Choke Unloader (in.)	Fast Idle Speed (rpm) ②
1977	17057013	3/8	.070	—	—	.125	—	—	1 CCW	.375	2000
	17057014	3/8	.070	—	—	.120	—	—	2 CCW	.325	2000
	17057310	3/8	.070	—	—	—	—	—	Index	—	1800
1978	17058013	3/8	.080	—	—	.200	—	—	Index	.200	2000
	17058014	5/16	.160	—	—	.200	—	—	Index	.200	2100
	17058314	3/8	.160	—	—	.243	—	—	Index	.245	2000
1979	17059013	—	—	Information not available							
	17059014	—	—	Information not available							
	17059314	—	—	Information not available							

① Choke adjustment—Index, CCW—counterclockwise in notches, or CW—clockwise in notches
② Transmission in Neutral

closed, swing the metering rod holder over the flat surface of the bowl casting next to the throttle bore. Measure the distance from the flat surface to the outer end of the rod holder with the specified gauge (see specifications), or a metal rod of equivalent diameter.

5. Bend the horizontal portion of the rod holder where it joins the vertical portion until the gauge just passes between the holder and surface of the bowl casting with power piston bottomed.

Rochester 2GC, 2GV—2 BBL Carburetors

These procedures are for both the 1¼ and 1½ models; where there are differences these are noted. The 1½ model has larger throttle bores and an additional fuel feed circuit to make it suitable for use on the 350 V8s.

FAST IDLE ADJUSTMENT

On 2GC and 2GV models the fast idle is set automatically when the curb idle and mixture is set.

FAST IDLE CAM ADJUSTMENT

1. Turn the idle screw onto the second step of the fast idle cam, abutting against the top step.
2. Hold the choke valve toward the closed position and check the clearance between the upper edge of the choke valve and the air horn wall.
3. If this measurement varies from specifications, bend the tang on the choke lever.

CHOKE UNLOADER ADJUSTMENT

1. Hold the throttle valves wide open and use a rubber band to hold the choke valve toward the closed position.
2. Measure the distance between the upper edge of the choke valve and the air horn wall.
3. If this measurement is not within specifications, bend the unloader tang on the throttle lever to correct it.

ACCELERATOR PUMP ROD ADJUSTMENT

1. Back out the idle stop screw and close the throttle valves in their bores.
2. Measure the distance from the top of the air horn to the top of the pump rod.
3. Bend the pump rod at angle to correct this dimension.

FLOAT LEVEL ADJUSTMENT

Invert the air horn and, with the gasket in place and the needle seated, measure the level as follows:

Fast idle cam adjustment (2GV) (© Chevrolet Motor Division)

Accelerator pump rod adjustment (2GV) (© Chevrolet Motor Division)

Float level adjustment—nitrophyl (2GV) (© Chevrolet Motor Division)

1. Pump rod	7. Power piston
2. Pump outlet lever	8. Air horn-to-bowl
3. Accelerator pump	gasket
4. Washer	9. Choke valve
5. Pump inner lever	10. Choke rod
6. Pump inner lever	11. Choke shaft
retainer	12. Choke kick lever

13. Air horn	20. Fuel filter
14. Vent valve and shield	21. Filter spring
15. Vacuum diaphragm	22. Float needle and
16. Choke lever	seat
17. Diaphragm link	23. Float hinge pin
18. Fuel inlet nut	24. Splash shield
19. Gaskets	25. Float

Exploded view of 2GV (1¼) air horn (© Chevrolet Motor Division)

1. Cluster assembly	9. Throttle body assembly
2. Gasket	10. Pump discharge check
3. Splash shield—main	assembly
well	11. Accelerator pump spring
4. Power valve assembly	12. Fast idle cam
5. Main jets	13. Idle mixture
6. Air horn gasket	screws
7. Bowl assembly	14. Choke rod
8. Throttle body-to-	
bowl gasket	

Exploded view of 2GV (1¼) float bowl (© Chevrolet Motor Division)

1. Cluster assembly
2. Cluster gasket
3. Hot idle compensator
4. Power valve assembly
5. Main jets
6. Bowl assembly
7. Throttle body-to-bowl gasket
8. Throttle body assembly
9. Idle speed screw
10. Choke rod
11. Idle mixture screws
12. Fast idle cam
13. Accelerator pump spring
14. Pump discharge check assembly

Exploded view of 2GV (1½) float bowl (© Chevrolet Motor Division)

1. Pump rod
2. Pump outer lever
3. Washer
4. Accelerator pump
5. Pump inner lever
6. Pump inner lever retainer
7. Power piston
8. Air horn-to-bowl gasket
9. Choke valve
10. Choke shaft
11. Choke rod
12. Choke kick lever
13. Air horn
14. Vent valve and shield
15. Vacuum diaphragm
16. Choke lever
17. Fuel inlet nut
18. Gaskets
19. Fuel filter
20. Filter spring
21. Diaphragm link
22. Float needle and seat
23. Float hinge pin
24. Splash shields
25. Float

Exploded view of 2GV (1½) air horn (© Chevrolet Motor Division)

Rochester 2GC, 2GV Specifications

Year	Carburetor Identifi- cation ①	Float Level (in.)	Float Drop (in.)	Pump Rod (in.)	Idle Vent (in.)	Vacuum Break (in.)	Auto- matic ② Choke	Choke Rod (in.)	Choke Unloader (in.)	Fast Idle Speed
1967	7027101	¾	1¾	1⅛	1.000	0.120	—	0.060	0.215	—
	7027103	¾	1¾	1⅛	1.000	0.120	—	0.060	0.215	—
	7027110	¾	1¾	1⅛	1.000	0.110	—	0.060	0.215	—
	7027112	¾	1¾	1⅛	1.000	0.110	—	0.060	0.215	—
	7037103	¾	1¾	1⅛	1.000	0.130	—	0.060	0.215	—
	7037110	¾	1¾	1⅛	1.000	0.110	—	0.060	0.215	—
	7037112	¾	1¾	1⅛	1.000	0.110	—	0.060	0.215	—
1968	7028110	¾	1¾	1⅛	1.000	0.100	—	0.060	0.200	—
	7028101	¾	1¾	1⅛	1.000	0.100	—	0.060	0.200	—
	7028112	¾	1¾	1⅛	1.000	0.100	—	0.060	0.200	—
	7028103	¾	1¾	1⅛	1.000	0.100	—	0.060	0.200	—
1969	7029101	27/32	1¾	1⅛	0.020	0.100	—	0.060	0.215	—
	7029103	27/32	1¾	1⅛	0.020	0.100	—	0.060	0.215	—
	7029110	27/32	1¾	1⅛	0.020	0.100	—	0.060	0.215	—
	7029112	27/32	1¾	1⅛	0.020	0.100	—	0.060	0.215	—
	7029102	¾	1¾	1 13/32	0.020	0.215	—	0.085	0.275	—
	7029104	¾	1¾	1 13/32	0.020	0.215	—	0.085	0.275	—
	7029127	¾	1¾	1 13/32	0.020	0.215	—	0.085	0.275	—
	7029129	¾	1¾	1 13/32	0.020	0.215	—	0.085	0.275	—
	7029117	¾	1¾	1 13/32	0.020	0.215	—	0.085	0.275	—
	7029118	¾	1¾	1 13/32	0.020	0.215	—	0.085	0.275	—
	7029119	⅝	1¾	1 13/32	0.020	0.215	—	0.085	0.275	—
	7029120	⅝	1¾	1 13/32	0.020	0.215	—	0.085	0.275	—
1970	7040110	27/32	1¾	1⅛	0.020	0.100	—	0.060	0.215	—
	7040112	27/32	1¾	1⅛	0.020	0.100	—	0.060	0.215	—
	7040101	27/32	1¾	1⅛	0.020	0.125	—	0.060	0.160	—
	7040103	27/32	1¾	1⅛	0.020	0.125	—	0.060	0.225	—
	7040114	23/32	1⅜	1 17/32	0.020	0.200	—	0.085	0.325	—
	7040116	23/32	1⅜	1 17/32	0.020	0.200	—	0.085	0.325	—
	7040113	23/32	1⅜	1 17/32	0.020	0.215	—	0.085	0.275	—
	7040115	23/32	1⅜	1 17/32	0.020	0.215	—	0.085	0.275	—
	7040118	23/32	1⅜	1 17/32	0.020	0.215	—	0.085	0.325	—
	7040120	23/32	1⅜	1 17/32	0.020	0.215	—	0.085	0.325	—
	7040117	23/32	1⅜	1 17/32	0.020	0.215	—	0.085	0.325	—
	7040119	23/32	1⅜	1 17/32	0.020	0.215	—	0.085	0.325	—
1971	7041024	1/16	—	—	—	0.140	—	0.080	0.350	—
	7041101	13/16	1¾	1 3/64	—	0.110	—	0.075	0.215	—
	7041110	13/16	1¾	1 3/64	—	0.080	—	0.040	0.215	—
	7041102	25/32	1⅜	1 5/32	—	0.170	—	0.100	0.325	—
	7041114	25/32	1⅜	1 5/32	—	0.170	—	0.100	0.325	—

Rochester 2GC, 2GV Specifications (cont.)

Year	Carburetor Identification ①	Float Level (in.)	Float Drop (in.)	Pump Rod (in.)	Idle Vent (in.)	Vacuum Break (in.)	Automatic ② Choke	Choke Rod (in.)	Choke Unloader (in.)	Fast Idle Speed
1971	7041113	23/32	1 3/8	1 5/32	—	0.180	—	0.100	0.325	—
	7041127	23/32	1 3/8	1 5/32	—	0.180	—	0.100	0.325	—
	7041118	23/32	1 3/8	1 5/32	—	0.170	—	0.100	0.325	—
	7041181	5/8	1 3/4	1 3/8	—	0.120	—	0.080	0.180	—
	7041182	5/8	1 3/4	1 3/8	—	0.120	—	0.080	0.180	—
1972	7042111	23/32	1 9/32	1 1/2	—	0.180	—	0.100	0.325	—
	7042831	23/32	1 9/32	1 1/2	—	0.180	—	0.100	0.325	—
	7042112	23/32	1 9/32	1 1/2	—	0.170	—	0.100	0.325	—
	7042832	23/32	1 9/32	1 1/2	—	0.170	—	0.100	0.325	—
	7042100	25/32	1 31/32	1 5/16	—	0.080	—	0.040	0.215	—
	7042820	25/32	1 31/32	1 5/16	—	0.080	—	0.040	0.215	—
	7042101	25/32	1 31/32	1 5/16	—	0.110	—	0.075	0.215	—
	7042821	25/32	1 31/32	1 5/16	—	0.110	—	0.075	0.215	—
1973	7043100	21/32	1 9/32	1 5/16	—	0.080	—	0.150	0.215	—
	7043101	21/32	1 9/32	1 5/16	—	0.080	—	0.150	0.215	—
	7043120	21/32	1 9/32	1 5/16	—	0.080	—	0.150	0.215	—
	7043105	21/32	1 9/32	1 5/16	—	0.080	—	0.150	0.215	—
	7043112	19/32	1 9/32	1 7/16	—	0.130	—	0.245	0.325	—
	7043111	19/32	1 9/32	1 7/16	—	0.140	—	0.200	0.250	—
1974	7043100	21/32	1 9/32	1 5/16	—	0.080	—	0.150	0.215	—
	7043101	21/32	1 9/32	1 5/16	—	0.080	—	0.150	0.215	—
	7043120	21/32	1 9/32	1 5/16	—	0.080	—	0.150	0.215	—
	7043105	21/32	1 9/32	1 5/16	—	0.080	—	0.150	0.215	—
	7043112	19/32	1 9/32	1 7/16	—	0.130	—	0.245	0.325	—
	7043111	19/32	1 9/32	1 7/16	—	0.140	—	0.200	0.250	—
1975	7045111	21/32	31/32	1 5/8	—	0.130	—	—	0.350	—
	7045112	21/32	31/32	1 5/8	—	0.130	—	—	0.350	—
1976	17056111	9/16	1 9/32	1 21/32	—	0.140	—	—	0.325	—
	17056112	9/16	1 9/32	1 21/32	—	0.140	—	—	0.325	—
	17056412	9/16	1 9/32	1 11/16	—	0.140	—	—	0.325	—
1977	17057111	19/32	1 9/32	1 21/32	—	0.130 ③	Index	—	0.325	—
	17057108	19/32	1 9/32	1 21/32	—	0.130 ③	Index	—	0.325	—
	17057412	21/32	1 9/32	1 21/32	—	0.140 ③	1/2 CCW	—	0.325	—
1978	17058102	15/32	1 9/32	1 17/32	0	0.130 ④	Index	—	0.325	—
	17058103	15/32	1 9/32	1 17/32	0	0.130 ④	Index	—	0.325	—
	17058104	15/32	1 9/32	1 21/32	0	0.130 ③	Index	—	0.325	—
	17058105	15/32	1 9/32	1 21/32	0	0.130 ③	Index	—	0.325	—
	17058107	15/32	1 9/32	1 17/32	0	0.130 ③	Index	—	0.325	—
	17058109	15/32	1 9/32	1 17/32	0	0.130 ③	Index	—	0.325	—
	17058404	1/2	1 9/32	1 21/32	0	0.140 ③	1/2 CCW	—	0.325	—

Rochester 2GC, 2GV Specifications (cont.)

Year	Carburetor Identifi- cation ①	Float Level (in.)	Float Drop (in.)	Pump Rod (in.)	Idle Vent (in.)	Vacuum Break (in.)	Auto- matic ② Choke	Choke Rod (in.)	Choke Unloader (in.)	Fast Idle Speed
1978	17058405	½	1⁹/₃₂	1²¹/₃₂	0	0.140 ③	½ CCW	—	0.325	—
1979	17059135	—	—	Information not available						
	17059134	—	—	Information not available						
	17059434	—	—	Information not available						

① The carburetor identification tag is located at the rear of the carburetor on one of the air horn screws
② Index or notches clockwise (CW) or counterclockwise (CCW)
③ .160 after 22,500 miles or first tune-up
④ .150 after 22,500 miles or first tune-up

On nitrophyl floats, measure from the air horn gasket to the lip on the toe of the float.

On brass floats, measure the air horn gasket to the lower edge of the float seam.

Bend the float tang to adjust the level.

FLOAT DROP ADJUSTMENT

Holding the air horn right side up, measure float drop as follows:

On nitrophyl floats, measure from the air horn gasket to the lip at the toe of the float.

On brass floats, measure from the air horn gasket to the bottom of the float.

Bend the float tang to adjust either type of float.

BEND FLOAT TANG TO ADJUST FOR PROPER SETTING

MEASURE SPECIFIED DISTANCE FROM GASKET SURFACE TO NOTCH AT TOE OF FLOAT

Float drop adjustment—nitrophyl (2GV) (© Chevrolet Motor Division)

Rochester 4GC—4-BBL CARBURETOR

AUTOMATIC CHOKE ADJUSTMENT

Set the cover index mark on the one notch lean mark on the housing.

INTERMEDIATE CHOKE ROD

The intermediate choke rod is adjusted with the choke cover and baffle removed.

1. Hold the choke valve closed, exert a light pressure on the choke piston to take up any lash, and then note if the choke piston is at the end of its sleeve.

2. If necessary, bend the intermediate choke rod for correct piston positioning.

3. Install the choke baffle and cover.

CHOKE ROD ADJUSTMENT

1. Turn the idle speed screw in until it just touches the second step of the fast idle cam.

2. Ensure that the choke trip lever is touching the choke counterweight lever.

3. While holding the idle speed screw on the second cam step and against the shoulder of the high step, there should be .043 in. clearance between the choke valve edge and the air horn dividing wall.

Rochester 4GC Specifications

Year	Model or Type	Float Level (in.)		Float Drop (in.)		Pump Travel Setting (in.)	Choke Setting	
		Prim	Sec	Prim	Sec		Unloader (in.)	Housing
1964	All	1³³/₆₄	1³³/₆₄	2¼	2¼	1¹/₁₆	0.235	Index
1965	All	1³³/₆₄	1³⁷/₆₄	2¼	2¼	1¹/₁₆	0.250	Index
1966	All	1¹⁷/₃₂	1¹⁹/₃₈ ¼	2¼	2¼	1¹/₁₆	0.250	Index

1. Secondary cluster
2. Secondary cluster gasket
3. Primary cluster
4. Primary cluster gasket
5. Pump return spring
6. Retaining ring
7. Screen
8. Check ball
9. Discharge spring guide
10. Discharge spring
11. Discharge ball
12. Power valve
13. Idle compensator
14. Power valve gasket
15. Primary main metering jets
16. Secondary main metering jets
17. Float bowl
18. Auxiliary throttle valves
19. Throttle flange gasket
20. Choke coil cover retainer
21. Choke coil cover
22. Choke coil spring
23. Choke cover gasket
24. Baffle plate
25. Choke piston and pin
26. Choke piston lever
27. Choke housing screw
28. Choke housing
29. Choke housing O-ring
30. Choke shaft

Exploded view of 4GC carburetor body

4. Bend the choke rod at a lower angle, if necessary.

CHOKE UNLOADER ADJUSTMENT

1. Hold the throttle valve wide open, while the choke trip lever touches the choke counterweight.
2. Clearance between the top of the choke valve and the dividing wall of the air horn should now be .235 in. Bend the fast idle cam tang, if necessary.

SECONDARY THROTTLE LOCKOUT ADJUSTMENT

1. Close the choke valve so that the secondary lockout tang is in the fast idle cam slot. Clearance between the fast idle cam and the tang should be .015 in.
2. Bend the tang horizontally as necessary to obtain the correct clearance.

FLOAT LEVEL AND DROP ADJUSTMENT

1. Remove the bowl cover.
2. Install a new gasket on the bowl cover surface.

4GC float level adjustment

4GC float level adjustment

CHILTON'S
FUEL ECONOMY
& TUNE-UP TIPS

Tune-up • Spark Plug Diagnosis • Emission Controls

Fuel System • Cooling System • Tires and Wheels

General Maintenance

55 WAYS TO IMPROVE FUEL ECONOMY

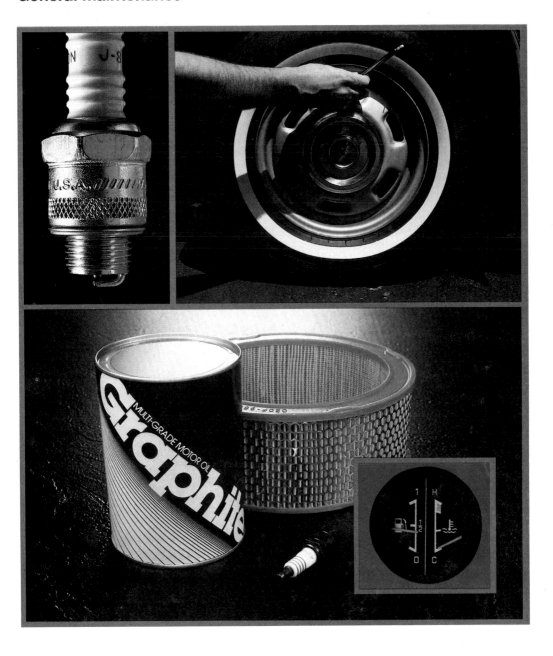

CHILTON'S FUEL ECONOMY & TUNE-UP TIPS

Fuel economy is important to everyone, no matter what kind of vehicle you drive. The maintenance-minded motorist can save both money and fuel using these tips and the periodic maintenance and tune-up procedures in this Repair and Tune-Up Guide.

There are more than 130,000,000 cars and trucks registered for private use in the United States. Each travels an average of 10-12,000 miles per year, and, and in total they consume close to 70 billion gallons of fuel each year. This represents nearly ⅔ of the oil imported by the United States each year. The Federal government's goal is to reduce consumption 10% by 1985. A variety of methods are either already in use or under serious consideration, and they all affect you driving and the cars you will drive. In addition to "down-sizing", the auto industry is using or investigating the use of electronic fuel delivery, electronic engine controls and alternative engines for use in smaller and lighter vehicles, among other alternatives to meet the federally mandated Corporate Average Fuel Economy (CAFE) of 27.5 mpg by 1985. The government, for its part, is considering rationing, mandatory driving curtailments and tax increases on motor vehicle fuel in an effort to reduce consumption. The government's goal of a 10% reduction could be realized — and further government regulation avoided — if every private vehicle could use just 1 less gallon of fuel per week.

How Much Can You Save?

Tests have proven that almost anyone can make at least a 10% reduction in fuel consumption through regular maintenance and tune-ups. When a major manufacturer of spark plugs sur-

TUNE-UP

1. Check the cylinder compression to be sure the engine will really benefit from a tune-up and that it is capable of producing good fuel economy. A tune-up will be wasted on an engine in poor mechanical condition.

2. Replace spark plugs regularly. New spark plugs alone can increase fuel economy 3%.

3. Be sure the spark plugs are the correct type (heat range) for your vehicle. See the Tune-Up Specifications.

Heat range refers to the spark plug's ability to conduct heat away from the firing end. It must conduct the heat away in an even pattern to avoid becoming a source of pre-ignition, yet it must also operate hot enough to burn off conductive deposits that could cause misfiring.

The heat range is usually indicated by a number on the spark plug, part of the manufacturer's designation for each individual spark plug. The numbers in bold-face indicate the heat range in each manufacturer's identification system.

Periodically, check the spark plugs to be sure they are firing efficiently. They are excellent indicators of the internal condition of your engine.

Manufacturer	Typical Designation
AC	R **45** TS
Bosch (old)	WA **145** T30
Bosch (new)	HR **8** Y
Champion	RBL **15** Y
Fram/Autolite	4**15**
Mopar	P-**62** PR
Motorcraft	BRF-**42**
NGK	BP **5** ES-15
Nippondenso	W **16** EP
Prestolite	14GR **5** 2A

On AC, Bosch (new), Champion, Fram/Autolite, Mopar, Motorcraft and Prestolite, a higher number indicates a hotter plug. On Bosch (old), NGK and Nippondenso, a higher number indicates a colder plug.

4. Make sure the spark plugs are properly gapped. See the Tune-Up Specifications in this book.

5. Be sure the spark plugs are firing efficiently. The illustrations on the next 2 pages show you how to "read" the firing end of the spark plug.

6. Check the ignition timing and set it to specifications. Tests show that almost all cars have incorrect ignition timing by more than 2°.

veyed over 6,000 cars nationwide, they found that a tune-up, on cars that needed one, increased fuel economy over 11%. Replacing worn plugs alone, accounted for a 3% increase. The same test also revealed that 8 out of every 10 vehicles will have some maintenance deficiency that will directly affect fuel economy, emissions or performance. Most of this mileage-robbing neglect could be prevented with regular maintenance.

Modern engines require that all of the functioning systems operate properly for maximum efficiency. A malfunction anywhere wastes fuel. You can keep your vehicle running as efficiently and economically as possible, by being aware of your vehicle's operating and performance characteristics. If your vehicle suddenly develops performance or fuel economy problems it could be due to one or more of the following:

PROBLEM	POSSIBLE CAUSE
Engine Idles Rough	Ignition timing, idle mixture, vacuum leak or something amiss in the emission control system.
Hesitates on Acceleration	Dirty carburetor or fuel filter, improper accelerator pump setting, ignition timing or fouled spark plugs.
Starts Hard or Fails to Start	Worn spark plugs, improperly set automatic choke, ice (or water) in fuel system.
Stalls Frequently	Automatic choke improperly adjusted and possible dirty air filter or fuel filter.
Performs Sluggishly	Worn spark plugs, dirty fuel or air filter, ignition timing or automatic choke out of adjustment.

Check spark plug wires on conventional point type ignition for cracks by bending them in a loop around your finger.

Be sure that spark plug wires leading to adjacent cylinders do not run too close together. (Photo courtesy Champion Spark Plug Co.)

7. If your vehicle does not have electronic ignition, check the points, rotor and cap as specified.

8. Check the spark plug wires (used with conventional point-type ignitions) for cracks and burned or broken insulation by bending them in a loop around your finger. Cracked wires decrease fuel efficiency by failing to deliver full voltage to the spark plugs. One misfiring spark plug can cost you as much as 2 mpg.

9. Check the routing of the plug wires. Misfiring can be the result of spark plug leads to adjacent cylinders running parallel to each other and too close together. One wire tends to pick up voltage from the other causing it to fire "out of time".

10. Check all electrical and ignition circuits for voltage drop and resistance.

11. Check the distributor mechanical and/or vacuum advance mechanisms for proper functioning. The vacuum advance can be checked by twisting the distributor plate in the opposite direction of rotation. It should spring back when released.

12. Check and adjust the valve clearance on engines with mechanical lifters. The clearance should be slightly loose rather than too tight.

SPARK PLUG DIAGNOSIS

Normal

APPEARANCE: This plug is typical of one operating normally. The insulator nose varies from a light tan to grayish color with slight electrode wear. The presence of slight deposits is normal on used plugs and will have no adverse effect on engine performance. The spark plug heat range is correct for the engine and the engine is running normally.

CAUSE: Properly running engine.

RECOMMENDATION: Before reinstalling this plug, the electrodes should be cleaned and filed square. Set the gap to specifications. If the plug has been in service for more than 10-12,000 miles, the entire set should probably be replaced with a fresh set of the same heat range.

Oil Deposits

APPEARANCE: The firing end of the plug is covered with a wet, oily coating.

CAUSE: The problem is poor oil control. On high mileage engines, oil is leaking past the rings or valve guides into the combustion chamber. A common cause is also a plugged PCV valve, and a ruptured fuel pump diaphragm can also cause this condition. Oil fouled plugs such as these are often found in new or recently overhauled engines, before normal oil control is achieved, and can be cleaned and reinstalled.

RECOMMENDATION: A hotter spark plug may temporarily relieve the problem, but the engine is probably in need of work.

Incorrect Heat Range

APPEARANCE: The effects of high temperature on a spark plug are indicated by clean white, often blistered insulator. This can also be accompanied by excessive wear of the electrode, and the absence of deposits.

CAUSE: Check for the correct spark plug heat range. A plug which is too hot for the engine can result in overheating. A car operated mostly at high speeds can require a colder plug. Also check ignition timing, cooling system level, fuel mixture and leaking intake manifold.

RECOMMENDATION: If all ignition and engine adjustments are known to be correct, and no other malfunction exists, install spark plugs one heat range colder.

Photos Courtesy Fram Corporation

Carbon Deposits

APPEARANCE: Carbon fouling is easily identified by the presence of dry, soft, black, sooty deposits.

CAUSE: Changing the heat range can often lead to carbon fouling, as can prolonged slow, stop-and-start driving. If the heat range is correct, carbon fouling can be attributed to a rich fuel mixture, sticking choke, clogged air cleaner, worn breaker points, retarded timing or low compression. If only one or two plugs are carbon fouled, check for corroded or cracked wires on the affected plugs. Also look for cracks in the distributor cap between the towers of affected cylinders.

RECOMMENDATION: After the problem is corrected, these plugs can be cleaned and reinstalled if not worn severely.

MMT Fouled

APPEARANCE: Spark plugs fouled by MMT (Methycyclopentadienyl Maganese Tricarbonyl) have reddish, rusty appearance on the insulator and side electrode.

CAUSE: MMT is an anti-knock additive in gasoline used to replace lead. During the combustion process, the MMT leaves a reddish deposit on the insulator and side electrode.

RECOMMENDATION: No engine malfunction is indicated and the deposits will not affect plug performance any more than lead deposits (see Ash Deposits). MMT fouled plugs can be cleaned, regapped and reinstalled.

High Speed Glazing

APPEARANCE: Glazing appears as shiny coating on the plug, either yellow or tan in color.

CAUSE: During hard, fast acceleration, plug temperatures rise suddenly. Deposits from normal combustion have no chance to fluff-off; instead, they melt on the insulator forming an electrically conductive coating which causes misfiring.

RECOMMENDATION: Glazed plugs are not easily cleaned. They should be replaced with a fresh set of plugs of the correct heat range. If the condition recurs, using plugs with a heat range one step colder may cure the problem.

Ash (Lead) Deposits

APPEARANCE: Ash deposits are characterized by light brown or white colored deposits crusted on the side or center electrodes. In some cases it may give the plug a rusty appearance.

CAUSE: Ash deposits are normally derived from oil or fuel additives burned during normal combustion. Normally they are harmless, though excessive amounts can cause misfiring. If deposits are excessive in short mileage, the valve guides may be worn.

RECOMMENDATION: Ash-fouled plugs can be cleaned, gapped and reinstalled.

Detonation

APPEARANCE: Detonation is usually characterized by a broken plug insulator.

CAUSE: A portion of the fuel charge will begin to burn spontaneously, from the increased heat following ignition. The explosion that results applies extreme pressure to engine components, frequently damaging spark plugs and pistons.

Detonation can result by over-advanced ignition timing, inferior gasoline (low octane) lean air/fuel mixture, poor carburetion, engine lugging or an increase in compression ratio due to combustion chamber deposits or engine modification.

RECOMMENDATION: Replace the plugs after correcting the problem.

Photos Courtesy Champion Spark Plug Co.

EMISSION CONTROLS

13. Be aware of the general condition of the emission control system. It contributes to reduced pollution and should be serviced regularly to maintain efficient engine operation.

14. Check all vacuum lines for dried, cracked or brittle conditions. Something as simple as a leaking vacuum hose can cause poor performance and loss of economy.

15. Avoid tampering with the emission control system. Attempting to improve fuel econ-

FUEL SYSTEM

Check the air filter with a light behind it. If you can see light through the filter it can be reused.

Extremely clogged filters should be discarded and replaced with a new one.

18. Replace the air filter regularly. A dirty air filter richens the air/fuel mixture and can increase fuel consumption as much as 10%. Tests show that ⅓ of all vehicles have air filters in need of replacement.

19. Replace the fuel filter at least as often as recommended.

20. Set the idle speed and carburetor mixture to specifications.

21. Check the automatic choke. A sticking or malfunctioning choke wastes gas.

22. During the summer months, adjust the automatic choke for a leaner mixture which will produce faster engine warm-ups.

COOLING SYSTEM

29. Be sure all accessory drive belts are in good condition. Check for cracks or wear.

30. Adjust all accessory drive belts to proper tension.

31. Check all hoses for swollen areas, worn spots, or loose clamps.

32. Check coolant level in the radiator or expansion tank.

33. Be sure the thermostat is operating properly. A stuck thermostat delays engine warm-up and a cold engine uses nearly twice as much fuel as a warm engine.

34. Drain and replace the engine coolant at least as often as recommended. Rust and scale

TIRES & WHEELS

38. Check the tire pressure often with a pencil type gauge. Tests by a major tire manufacturer show that 90% of all vehicles have at least 1 tire improperly inflated. Better mileage can be achieved by over-inflating tires, but never exceed the maximum inflation pressure on the side of the tire.

39. If possible, install radial tires. Radial tires deliver as much as ½ mpg more than bias belted tires.

40. Avoid installing super-wide tires. They only create extra rolling resistance and decrease fuel mileage. Stick to the manufacturer's recommendations.

41. Have the wheels properly balanced.

omy by tampering with emission controls is more likely to worsen fuel economy than improve it. Emission control changes on modern engines are not readily reversible.

16. Clean (or replace) the EGR valve and lines as recommended.

17. Be sure that all vacuum lines and hoses are reconnected properly after working under the hood. An unconnected or misrouted vacuum line can wreak havoc with engine performance.

23. Check for fuel leaks at the carburetor, fuel pump, fuel lines and fuel tank. Be sure all lines and connections are tight.

24. Periodically check the tightness of the carburetor and intake manifold attaching nuts and bolts. These are a common place for vacuum leaks to occur.

25. Clean the carburetor periodically and lubricate the linkage.

26. The condition of the tailpipe can be an excellent indicator of proper engine combustion. After a long drive at highway speeds, the inside of the tailpipe should be a light grey in color. Black or soot on the insides indicates an overly rich mixture.

27. Check the fuel pump pressure. The fuel pump may be supplying more fuel than the engine needs.

28. Use the proper grade of gasoline for your engine. Don't try to compensate for knocking or "pinging" by advancing the ignition timing. This practice will only increase plug temperature and the chances of detonation or pre-ignition with relatively little performance gain.

Increasing ignition timing past the specified setting results in a drastic increase in spark plug temperature with increased chance of detonation or preignition. Performance increase is considerably less. (Photo courtesy Champion Spark Plug Co.)

that form in the engine should be flushed out to allow the engine to operate at peak efficiency.

35. Clean the radiator of debris that can decrease cooling efficiency.

36. Install a flex-type or electric cooling fan, if you don't have a clutch type fan. Flex fans use curved plastic blades to push more air at low speeds when more cooling is needed; at high speeds the blades flatten out for less resistance. Electric fans only run when the engine temperature reaches a predetermined level.

37. Check the radiator cap for a worn or cracked gasket. If the cap does not seal properly, the cooling system will not function properly.

42. Be sure the front end is correctly aligned. A misaligned front end actually has wheels going in differed directions. The increased drag can reduce fuel economy by .3 mpg.

43. Correctly adjust the wheel bearings. Wheel bearings that are adjusted too tight increase rolling resistance.

Check tire pressures regularly with a reliable pocket type gauge. Be sure to check the pressure on a cold tire.

GENERAL MAINTENANCE

Check the fluid levels (particularly engine oil) on a regular basis. Be sure to check the oil for grit, water or other contamination.

A vacuum gauge is another excellent indicator of internal engine condition and can also be installed in the dash as a mileage indicator.

44. Periodically check the fluid levels in the engine, power steering pump, master cylinder, automatic transmission and drive axle.

45. Change the oil at the recommended interval and change the filter at every oil change. Dirty oil is thick and causes extra friction between moving parts, cutting efficiency and increasing wear. A worn engine requires more frequent tune-ups and gets progressively worse fuel economy. In general, use the lightest viscosity oil for the driving conditions you will encounter.

46. Use the recommended viscosity fluids in the transmission and axle.

47. Be sure the battery is fully charged for fast starts. A slow starting engine wastes fuel.

48. Be sure battery terminals are clean and tight.

49. Check the battery electrolyte level and add distilled water if necessary.

50. Check the exhaust system for crushed pipes, blockages and leaks.

51. Adjust the brakes. Dragging brakes or brakes that are not releasing create increased drag on the engine.

52. Install a vacuum gauge or miles-per-gallon gauge. These gauges visually indicate engine vacuum in the intake manifold. High vacuum = good mileage and low vacuum = poorer mileage. The gauge can also be an excellent indicator of internal engine conditions.

53. Be sure the clutch is properly adjusted. A slipping clutch wastes fuel.

54. Check and periodically lubricate the heat control valve in the exhaust manifold. A sticking or inoperative valve prevents engine warm-up and wastes gas.

55. Keep accurate records to check fuel economy over a period of time. A sudden drop in fuel economy may signal a need for tune-up or other maintenance.

1. Bowl cover
2. Choke valve
3. Pump plunger rubber seal
4. Pump shaft and lever
5. Choke trip lever
6. Choke counterweight
7. Inlet filter spring
8. Inlet filter
9. Inlet gaskets
10. Inlet fitting
11. Bowl cover gasket
12. Float valve gasket
13. Float valve
14. Float valve needle
15. Power valve piston
16. Pump spring clip
17. Pump spring washer
18. Pump duration spring
19. Pump plunger
20. Float tension spring
21. Float hinge pin
22. Primary float
23. Secondary float
24. Choke valve shaft

Exploded view of 4GC air horn

3. Invert the cover and install the float level gauges supplied with a carburetor rebuilding kit over the primary and secondary floats. The floats should just touch the gauges. The height from the bottom of the float to the bowl cover gasket is $1^{33}/_{64}$ in. for the primaries and $1^{37}/_{64}$ in. for the secondaries. Bend the float arms as necessary to obtain the correct level.

4. Center the floats in the level gauge,

bending them to the left or right as necessary.

5. While holding the bowl cover in an upright position, measure the distance from the bowl cover gasket to the bottom of the float. This distance, float drop, should be $2^{1}/_{4}$ in. Bend the float tang on the end of the hinge arm to correct the drop.

6. Install the bowl cover as outlined under overhaul.

Rochester 4MC, 4MV, M4MC—4 BBL Carburetors

The Rochester Quadrajet carburetor is a two stage, four-barrel downdraft carburetor. The designation MC or MV refers to the type of choke system the carburetor is designed for. The MV model is equipped with a manifold thermostatic choke coil. The MC model has a choke housing and coil mounted on the side of the float bowl.

The primary side of the carburetor is equipped with $1^{3}/_{8}$ diameter bores and a triple venturi with plain tube nozzles. During off idle and part throttle operation, the fuel is metered through tapered metering rods operating in specially designed jets positioned by a manifold vacuum responsive piston.

The secondary side of the carburetor contains two $2^{1}/_{4}$ in. bores. An air valve is used on the secondary side for metering control and supplements the primary bores.

The secondary air valve operates tapered metering rods which regulate the fuel in constant proportion to the air being supplied.

ACCELERATOR PUMP

1. Close the primary throttle valves by backing out the slow idle screw and making sure that the fast idle cam follower is off the steps of the fast idle cam.

2. Bend the secondary throttle closing tang away from the primary throttle lever.

3. With the pump in the appropriate hole in the pump lever, measure from the top of the choke valve wall to the top of the pump stem.

4. To adjust, bend the pump lever while supporting it with a screwdriver.

5. After adjusting, readjust the secondary throttle tang and the slow idle screw.

IDLE VENT ADJUSTMENT

NOTE: *This adjustment is not required on 1977–79 carburetors.*

After adjusting the accelerator pump rod as specified above, open the primary throttle valve enough to just close the idle vent. Measure from the top of the choke valve wall to the top of the pump plunger stem. If adjustment is necessary, bend the wire tang on the pump lever.

FLOAT LEVEL

With the air horn assembly upside down, measure the distance from the air horn gasket surface (gasket removed) to the top of the float at the toe. Measure at a point 3/16″ back from the top of the float on 1977–79 carburetors.

NOTE: *Make sure the retaining pin is firmly held in place and that the tang of the float is firmly against the needle and seat assembly.*

FAST IDLE

1. Position the fast idle lever on the high step of the fast idle cam. Disconnect and plug the vacuum hose at the EGR valve.

2. Be sure that the choke is wide open and the engine warm.

3. Turn the fast idle screw to gain the proper fast idle rpm.

CHOKE ROD ADJUSTMENT

Position the cam follower on the second step of the fast idle cam, touching the high step. Close the choke valve directly on models up to 1976. On 1977 models, remove the choke thermostatic cover, and then hold the choke closed by pushing upward on the choke coil lever. Gauge the clearance between the lower edge of the choke valve and the carburetor body on models to 1975, and between the upper edge of the choke valve and the carburetor body on 1976 and 1977 models. Bend the choke rod to obtain the specified clearance. On 1977 models, install the choke thermostatic cover and adjust it to specification when the adjustment is complete. This adjustment requires sophisticated special tools on 1978 and later models, and so is not included here.

AIR VALVE DASHPOT ADJUSTMENT

Set the vacuum break diaphragm. On 1977–79 models, this requires plugging the bleed purge hole on the back of the diaphragm with tape, and the use of an external vacuum source. Hold the air valve tightly closed on all models. Gauge

AIR VALVE COMPLETELY CLOSED

DIAPHRAGM SEATED

BEND HERE FOR SPECIFIED CLEARANCE BETWEEN ROD AND END OF SLOT

Air valve dashpot adjustment (4MV) (© Chevrolet Motor Division)

the clearance between the dashpot rod and the end of the slot in the air valve lever. Bend the rod to adjust. Remove the tape from the bleed purge hole.

CHOKE COIL ROD

1967–76

1. Close the choke valve by rotating the choke coil lever counterclockwise.

2. Disconnect the thermostatic coil rod from the upper lever.

3. Push down on the rod until it contacts the bracket of the coil.

4. The rod must fit in the notch of the upper lever.

5. If it does not, it must be bent on the curved portion just below the upper lever.

CHOKE COIL LEVER AND CHOKE THERMOSTATIC COIL

1977–79

1. Remove the three mounting screws and retainers, and pull the thermostatic coil cover assembly off the choke housing and set it aside.

2. Place the fast idle cam follower on the high step of the cam and then push up on the thermostatic coil tang in the choke housing until the choke is closed.

3. Insert a .120″ plug gauge or rod of that diameter into the hole in the housing located just below the lever. With the choke closed, the lever should just touch the gauge.

4. Adjust the choke rod by changing the angle of the bend it makes just below the choke itself, if necessary.

5. Then, install the coil cover back on the choke housing, making sure that the thermostatic coil engages the tang. Install the three retainers and screws, but do not tighten. With the fast idle cam follower still on the high step of the cam, rotate the cover assembly counterclockwise until the choke closes. Set all models 2 notches lean except 1977 models with manual transmission; set these three notches lean. Hold the position of the housing while tightening screws evenly.

VACUUM BREAK

1967–76

1. Fully seat the vacuum break diaphragm using an outside vacuum source.

2. Open the throttle valve enough to allow the fast idle cam follower to clear the fast idle cam.

3. The end of the vacuum break rod should be at the outer end of the slot in the vacuum break diaphragm plunger.

1. Fuel inlet nut
2. Gasket
3. Fuel filter
4. Fuel filter spring
5. Vacuum break hose
6. Vacuum diaphragm
7. Air valve dashpot
8. Choke control bracket
9. Fast idle cam
10. Secondary throttle lockout
11. Throttle body-to-bowl gasket

12. Float bowl assembly
13. Idle speed screw
14. Primary jets
15. Pump discharge ball
16. Pump return spring
17. Accelerator pump
18. Power piston spring
19. Primary metering rods
20. Power piston
21. Metering rod retainer
22. Float

23. Secondary air baffle
24. Float bowl insert
25. Float hinge pin
26. Float needle pull clip
27. Float needle
28. Float needle seat
29. Needle seat gasket
30. Discharge ball retainer
31. Choke rod
32. Choke lever

Exploded view of float bowl (4MV) (© Chevrolet Motor Division)

1. Air horn-to-bowl gasket
2. Air horn assembly
3. Air horn-to-bowl retaining screws
4. Idle vent valve lever
5. Idle vent valve
   a. Bimetal
   b. Spring
6. Choke shaft and lever
7. Choke valve
8. Idle vent shield
9. Countersunk air horn retaining screws
10. Secondary metering rods
11. Metering rod hanger

Exploded view of 4MV air horn (© Chevrolet Motor Division)

4. The specified clearance should register from the lower end of the choke valve to the inside air horn wall.

5. If the clearance is not correct, bend the vacuum break link.

1977

NOTE: *Adjustment procedures for 1978 and later models require the use of an expensive and sophisticated special tool, so procedures are not included here.*

1. Remove the choke thermostatic cover. Place the fast idle cam follower on the high step of the cam.

2. Where there is a purge bleed hole on the back of the choke vacuum break, put tape over the hole. Then, seat the diaphragm using an outside vacuum source.

3. Push the inside choke coil lever counterclockwise until the tang on the vacuum break lever touches the tang on the vacuum break plunger stem.

4. Place a gauge of the following diameter between the upper edge of the choke butterfly and the inside wall of the air horn:
• California Engines: .165″
• All Other Engines: .160″

5. If the dimension is incorrect, adjust the screw on the vacuum break plunger stem until all play is taken up and choke butterfly just touches the gauge when it's held vertically.

6. Reconnect the vacuum line to vacuum break port of carburetor, remove tape from purge hole (if applied) and reinstall and adjust choke thermostat (see above).

CHOKE UNLOADER ADJUSTMENT

NOTE: *Performing this adjustment on 1978 and later models requires sophisticated special tools, so the procedure is not included here.*

On 1977 models, make sure the choke thermostatic spring is properly adjusted (see above).

Close the choke valve and secure it with a rubber band hooked to the vacuum break lever. Open the primary throttles all the way. Then measure the distance between the air horn and edge of the choke butterfly. On models up to and including 1976, use the bottom side of the butterfly for this measurement; on 1977 models, use the top side. Bend the fast idle lever tang to achieve the proper opening of the choke.

SECONDARY LOCKOUT ADJUSTMENT

1967–76

Completely open the choke valve and rotate the vecuum break lever clockwise. Bend the lever if the measurement between the lever and the secondary throttle exceeds specifications. Close the choke and gauge the distance between the lever and the secondary throttle shaft pin. Bend the lever to adjust.

1977–79

1. See illustration below.

Secondary Lockout adjustment procedure (1977–79) (© Chevrolet Motor Division)

Rochester 4MV, 4MC, M4MC Specifications

Year	Carburetor Identification ①	Float Level (in.)	Air Valve Spring	Pump Rod (in.)	Idle Vent (in.)	Vacuum Break (in.)	Secondary Opening (in.)	Choke Rod (in.)	Choke Unloader (rpm)	Fast Idle Speed
1967	7027202	9/32	7/8 turn	13/32	3/8	0.160	0.015	0.100	0.260	—
	7027203	9/32	7/8 turn	13/32	3/8	0.200	0.015	0.100	0.300	—
	7027200	9/32	7/8 turn	13/32	3/8	0.160	0.015	0.100	0.300	—
	7027201	9/32	7/8 turn	13/32	3/8	0.240	0.015	0.100	0.300	—
	7027202	9/32	7/8 turn	13/32	3/8	0.160	0.015	0.100	0.260	—
	7027203	9/32	7/8 turn	13/32	3/8	0.200	0.015	0.100	0.300	—

Rochester 4MV, 4MC, M4MC Specifications (cont.)

Year	Carburetor Identifi- cation ①	Float Level (in.)	Air Valve Spring	Pump Rod (in.)	Idle Vent (in.)	Vacuum Break (in.)	Secondary Opening (in.)	Choke Rod (in.)	Choke Unloader (rpm)	Fast Idle Speed
1968	7028212	9/32	3/8 turn	9/32	3/8	0.160	0.010	0.100	0.260	—
	7028213	9/32	3/8 turn	9/32	3/8	0.245	0.010	0.100	0.300	—
	7028229	9/32	7/8 turn	9/32	3/8	0.245	0.010	0.100	0.300	—
	7028208	9/32	3/8 turn	9/32	3/8	0.160	0.010	0.100	0.260	—
	7028207	9/32	3/8 turn	9/32	3/8	0.245	0.010	0.100	0.300	—
	7028219	9/32	7/8 turn	9/32	3/8	0.245	0.010	0.100	0.300	—
	7028218	3/16	7/8 turn	9/32	3/8	0.160	0.010	0.100	0.300	—
	7028217	3/16	7/8 turn	9/32	3/8	0.245	0.010	0.100	0.300	—
	7028210	3/16	7/8 turn	9/32	3/8	0.160	0.010	0.100	0.300	—
	7028211	3/16	7/8 turn	9/32	3/8	0.245	0.010	0.100	0.300	—
	7028216	3/16	7/8 turn	9/32	3/8	0.160	0.010	0.100	0.300	—
	7028209	3/16	7/8 turn	9/32	3/8	0.245	0.010	0.100	0.300	—
1969	7029203	7/32	7/16 turn	5/16	3/8	0.245	0.015	0.100	0.450	—
	7029202	7/32	7/16 turn	5/16	3/8	0.180	0.015	0.100	0.450	—
	7029207	3/16	13/16 turn	5/16	3/8	0.245	0.015	0.100	0.450	—
	7029215	1/4	13/16 turn	5/16	3/8	0.245	0.015	0.100	0.450	—
	7029204	1/4	13/16 turn	5/16	3/8	0.180	0.015	0.100	0.450	—
1970	7040202	1/4	7/16 turn	5/16	—	0.245	—	0.100	0.450	—
	7040203	1/4	7/16 turn	5/16	—	0.275	—	0.100	0.450	—
	7040207	1/4	13/16 turn	5/16	—	0.275	—	0.100	0.450	—
	7040200	1/4	13/16 turn	5/16	—	0.245	—	0.100	0.450	—
	7040201	1/4	13/16 turn	5/16	—	0.275	—	0.100	0.450	—
	7040204	1/4	13/16 turn	5/16	—	0.245	—	0.100	0.450	—
	7040205	1/4	13/16 turn	5/16	—	0.275	—	0.100	0.450	
1971	7041200	1/4	7/16 turn	—	—	0.260	—	0.100	—	—
	7041202	1/4	7/16 turn	—	—	0.260	—	0.100	—	—
	7041204	1/4	7/16 turn	—	—	0.260	—	0.100	—	—
	7041212	1/4	7/16 turn	—	—	0.260	—	0.100	—	—
	7041201	1/4	7/16 turn	—	—	0.275	—	0.100	—	—
	7041203	1/4	7/16 turn	—	—	0.275	—	0.100	—	—
	7041205	1/4	7/16 turn	—	—	0.275	—	0.100	—	—
	7041213	1/4	7/16 turn	—	—	0.275	—	0.100	—	—
1972	7042202	1/4	1/2 turn	3/8	—	0.215	—	0.100	0.450	—
	7042203	1/4	1/2 turn	3/8	—	0.215	—	0.100	0.450	—
	7042902	1/4	1/2 turn	3/8	—	0.215	—	0.100	0.450	—
	7042903	1/4	1/2 turn	3/8	—	0.215	—	0.100	0.450	—
1973	7043212	7/32	1 turn	13/32	—	0.250	—	0.430	0.450	—
	7043213	7/32	1 turn	13/32	—	0.250	—	0.430	0.450	—
1974	7044202	1/4	7/8 turn	13/32 ②	—	0.230	—	0.430	0.450	1600 ③– 1300 ④

Rochester 4MV, 4MC, M4MC Specifications (cont.)

Year	Carburetor Identification ①	Float Level (in.)	Air Valve Spring	Pump Rod (in.)	Idle Vent (in.)	Vacuum Break (in.)	Secondary Opening (in.)	Choke Rod (in.)	Choke Unloader (rpm)	Fast Idle Speed
1974	7044203	¼	⅞ turn	¹³⁄₃₂ ②	—	0.230	—	0.430	0.450	1600 ③– 1300 ④
	7044208	¼	1 turn	¹³⁄₃₂ ②	—	0.230	—	0.430	0.450	1600 ③– 1300 ④
	7044209	¼	1 turn	¹³⁄₃₂ ②	—	0.230	—	0.430	0.450	1600 ③– 1300 ④
	7044502	¼	⅞ turn	¹³⁄₃₂ ②	—	0.230	—	0.430	0.450	1600 ③– 1300 ④
	7044503	¼	⅞ turn	¹³⁄₃₂ ②	—	0.230	—	0.430	0.450	1600 ③– 1300 ④
1975	7045202	¹⁵⁄₃₂	⅞ turn	0.275 ⑤	—	0.180 ⑥	—	0.300	0.325	—
	7045203	¹⁵⁄₃₂	⅞ turn	0.275 ⑤	—	0.180 ⑥	—	0.300	0.325	—
	7045208	¹⁵⁄₃₂	⅞ turn	0.275 ⑤	—	0.180 ⑥	—	0.300	0.325	—
	7045209	¹⁵⁄₃₂	⅞ turn	0.275 ⑤	—	0.180 ⑥	—	0.300	0.325	—
1976	17056202	¹³⁄₃₂	⅞ turn	⁹⁄₃₂	—	0.185	—	0.325	0.325	—
	17056203	¹³⁄₃₂	⅞ turn	⁹⁄₃₂	—	0.170	—	0.325	0.325	—
	17056528	¹³⁄₃₂	⅞ turn	⁹⁄₃₂	—	0.185	—	0.325	0.325	—
1977	17057203	¹⁵⁄₃₂	⅞	⁹⁄₃₂ ⑤	—	0.160	—	0.325	0.280	1300
	17057202	¹⁵⁄₃₂	—	⁹⁄₃₂ ⑤	—	0.160	—	0.325	—	1600 ⑤
	17057502	¹⁵⁄₃₂	⅞	⁹⁄₃₂ ⑤	—	0.165	—	0.325	0.280	1600 ⑤
1978	17058203	¹⁵⁄₃₂	⅞	⁹⁄₃₂	—	0.179	—	0.314	0.277	⑦
	17058202	¹⁵⁄₃₂	⅞	⁹⁄₃₂	—	0.179	—	0.314	0.277	⑦
	17058502	¹⁵⁄₃₂	⅞	⁹⁄₃₂	—	0.187	—	0.314	0.277	⑦
1979	17059203	¹⁵⁄₃₂	⅞	¼	—	0.157	—	0.243	0.243	⑦
	17059207	¹⁵⁄₃₂	⅞	¼	—	0.157	—	0.243	0.243	⑦
	17059216	¹⁵⁄₃₂	⅞	¼	—	0.157	—	0.243	0.243	⑦
	17059217	¹⁵⁄₃₂	⅞	¼	—	0.157	—	0.243	0.243	⑦
	17059218	¹⁵⁄₃₂	⅞	¼	—	0.164	—	0.243	0.243	⑦
	17059222	¹⁵⁄₃₂	⅞	¼	—	0.164	—	0.243	0.243	⑦
	17059502	¹⁵⁄₃₂	⅞	¼	—	0.164	—	0.243	0.243	⑦
	17059504	¹⁵⁄₃₂	⅞	¼	—	0.164	—	0.243	0.243	⑦
	17059582	¹⁵⁄₃₂	⅞	¹¹⁄₃₂	—	0.203	—	0.243	0.314	⑦
	17059584	¹⁵⁄₃₂	⅞	¹¹⁄₃₂	—	0.203	—	0.243	0.314	⑦
	17059210	¹⁵⁄₃₂	1	⁹⁄₃₂	—	0.157	—	0.243	0.243	⑦
	17059211	¹⁵⁄₃₂	1	⁹⁄₃₂	—	0.157	—	0.243	0.243	⑦
	17029228	¹⁵⁄₃₂	1	⁹⁄₃₂	—	0.157	—	0.243	0.243	⑦

① The carburetor identification tag is located at the rear of the carburetor on one of the air horn screws
② Without vacuum advance
③ With automatic transmission; vacuum advance connected and EGR disconnected and the throttle positioned on the high step of cam
④ With manual transmission; without vacuum advance and the throttle positioned on the high step of cam
⑤ Inner pump rod location
⑥ Front vacuum break given; rear—0.170 in.
⑦ See engine compartment sticker

AIR VALVE SPRING ADJUSTMENT

NOTE: *Loosening and tightening the locking screw to adjust the air valve spring requires a hex wrench on 1977 and later model carburetors.*

Remove all spring tension by loosening the locking screw and backing out the adjusting screw. Close the air valve and turn the adjusting screw in until the torsion spring touches the pin on the shaft, and then turn it the additional number of turns specified. Secure the locking screw.

SECONDARY CLOSING ADJUSTMENT

This adjustment assures proper closing of the secondary throttle plates.

1. Set the idle as per instructions in the appropriate section. Make sure that the fast idle cam follower is not resting on the fast idle cam.
2. There should be 0.020 in. clearance between the secondary throttle actuating rod and the front of the slot on the secondary throttle lever with the closing tang on the throttle lever resting against the actuating lever.
3. Bend the tang on the primary throttle actuating rod to adjust.

SECONDARY OPENING ADJUSTMENT

1. Open the primary throttle valves until the actuating link contacts the upper tang on the secondary lever.
2. With two point-linkage, the bottom of the link should be in the center of the secondary lever slot.
3. With three point linkage, there should be 0.070 in. clearance between the link and the middle tang.
4. Bend the upper tang on the secondary lever to adjust as necessary.

Holly 4150, 4160—4 BBL Carburetors

These carburetors are basically similar in design. The 4160 is an end-inlet carburetor, while the 4150 carburetor has been both an end and center inlet design.

CHOKE ADJUSTMENT

The 1965 model 4150 uses a bimetallic choke mounted on the carburetor. It is correctly set when the cover scribe mark aligns with the specified notch mark. The later model 4150 and 4160 employ a remotely located choke. To adjust, disconnect the choke rod at the choke lever and secure the choke lever shut. Bend the rod so that when the rod is depressed to the contact stop, the top is even with the bottom of the hole in the choke lever.

FLOAT LEVEL ADJUSTMENT

Position the car on a flat, level surface and start the engine. Remove the sight plugs and check to see that the fuel level reaches the bottom threads of the sight plug port. A plus or minus tolerance of $\frac{1}{32}$ in. is acceptable. To change the level, loosen the fuel inlet needle locking screw and adjust the nut. Turning it clockwise lowers the fuel level and counterclockwise raises it. Turn the nut $\frac{1}{6}$ of a turn for each $\frac{1}{16}$ in. desired change. Open the primary throttle slightly to assure a stabilized adjusting condition on the secondaries. There is no required float drop adjustment.

FAST IDLE ADJUSTMENT

1965 4150

Bring the engine to the normal operating temperature with the air cleaner off. Open the throttle. Place the fast idle cam on its high step and close the throttle. Adjust the fast idle screw to reach the specified idle speed.

Float level adjustment (Holley) (© Chevrolet Motor Division)

1966 and Later 4150 and 4160

Open the throttle and place the choke plate fast idle lever against the top step of the fast idle cam. Bend the fast idle lever to obtain the specified throttle plate opening.

CHOKE UNLOADER ADJUSTMENT

Adjustment should be made with the engine not running. Fully open and secure the throttle plate. Force the choke valve toward a closed position, so that contact is made with the unloader tang. Bend the choke rod to gain the specified clearance between the main body and the lower edge of the choke valve.

1. Main body assembly
2. Pump discharge needle
3. Pump discharge nozzle gasket
4. Pump discharge nozzle
5. Pump discharge nozzle screw gasket
6. Pump discharge nozzle screw
7. Choke valve
8. Choke valve screw
9. Choke rod
10. Choke shaft and lever
11. Choke rod seal
12. Vacuum break
13. Vacuum break link
14. Choke lever
15. Fast idle cam
16. Choke lever retainer
17. Vacuum break screw

**Exploded view of main body assembly (Holley)
(© Chevrolet Motor Division)**

1. Fuel inlet nut
2. Inlet nut gasket
3. Fuel filter gasket
4. Fuel filter
5. Fuel filter spring
6. Fuel bowl
7. Inlet needle and seat assembly
8. Adjusting nut gasket
9. Fuel inlet adjusting nut
10. Inlet nut lock screw gasket
11. Inlet nut lock screw
12. Vent valve lever
13. Float
14. Float hinge pin
15. Fuel displacement block
16. Pump diaphragm spring
17. Pump diaphragm (primary only)
18. Pump cover
19. Vent valve cover
20. Vent valve
21. Vent valve spring

**Exploded view of fuel bowl assembly (Holley)
(© Chevrolet Motor Division)**

ACCELERATOR PUMP ADJUSTMENT

With the engine off, block the throttle open and push the pump lever down. Clearance between the pump lever arm and the spring adjusting nut should be 0.015 in. minimum. Turn the screw or nut to adjust this clearance.

Holley 4150, 4160 Specifications

Year	Model or Type	Float Level (in.) Prim	Float Level (in.) Sec	Float Drop (in.) Prim	Float Drop (in.) Sec	Pump Travel Setting (in.)	Choke Setting Unloader (in.)	Choke Setting Housing	Secondary Locknut Adj.
1965	327 (4150)	①	①	—	0.015		0.375	—	—
1966	327-350 hp (4150)	①	①	0.065	0.015		0.260	—	—
	327 (4160)	①	①	0.065	0.015		0.260	—	—
	396 (4160)	①	①	0.065	0.015		0.260	—	—
1967–68	327-325 hp-4 bbl (4150)	A①	A①	0.065	0.015		0.265	—	—
1967	327,396, 427-4 bbl (4160)	A①	A①	0.065	0.015		0.265	—	—
1968–69	V8-396 (4150)	B①	B①	0.065	0.015		0.350	—	—
1970	454 (4150)		0.350	—	—	0.015	0.350	—	—
1971	454 (4160)		②	①	—	0.015	0.350	—	—

A—Primary 0.170, Secondary 0.300
B—Primary 0.350, Secondary 0.500
① Float adjustment: Fuel level should be plus or minus 1/32 in. with threads at bottom of sight holes. To adjust turn adjusting nut on top of bowl clockwise, to lower, counterclockwise to raise.
② Float centered in bowl

Accelerator pump adjustment (Holley) (© Chevolet Motor Division)

SECONDARY THROTTLE VALVE ADJUSTMENT

Close the throttle plates, and then turn the adjustment screw until it contacts the throttle lever. Advance the screw ½ turn more.

AIR VENT VALVE ADJUSTMENT

Close the throttle valves and open the choke valve so that the throttle arm is free of the idle screw. Bend the air vent valve rod to obtain the specified clearance between the choke valve and seat. Advance the idle speed screw until it touches the throttle lever, and then advance it 1½ turns.

VACUUM BREAK ADJUSTMENT

Secure the choke valve closed and the vacuum break against the stop. Bend the vacuum break link to gain the specified clearance between the

Secondary throttle valve adjustment (Holley) (© Chevrolet Motor Division)

main body and the lower edge of the choke valve.

Rochester M2ME and E2ME—2 BBL Carburetors

FLOAT ADJUSTMENT

1. Remove the air horn from the throttle body.
2. Using your fingers, hold the retainer in place and then push the float down into light contact with the needle.
3. Measure the distance from the toe of the float (furthest from the hinge) to the top of the carburetor (gasket removed).
4. To adjust, remove the float and gently

Adjusting the float—M2ME, E2ME

bend the arm to specifications. After adjustment, check the float alignment in the chamber. On engines equipped with the C-4 or the CCC system, where the float level varies more than ¹⁄₁₆ in. from specifications, adjust the float as follows.

Float too high:

1. Hold the retainer firmly in place and then push down the center of the float pontoon until the correct setting is obtained.

Float too low:

1. Lift out the meter rods and remove the solenoid connector screw.

2. Turn the lean mixture solenoid screw clockwise until the screw is bottomed lightly in the float bowl. *Count and record the number of turns before the screw is bottomed.*

3. Turn the screw counterclockwise and remove it. Lift the solenoid and the connector from the float bowl.

4. Remove the float and bend the arm up to adjust it. Put the float back in and check its alignment.

5. Installation is in the reverse order of removal. Make sure that the solenoid lean mixture screw is backed out of the float bowl EX-ACTLY the same number of turns as were recorded in Step 2.

PUMP ADJUSTMENT

NOTE: *All 1980 and later engines equipped with the C-4 or the CCC system have a non-*

Pump adjustment—M2ME, E2ME (all but C-4 or CCC)

adjustable pump lever. No adjustments are either necessary or possible.

1. With the throttle closed and the fast idle screw off the steps of the fast idle cam, measure the distance from the air horn casting to the top of the pump stem.

2. To adjust the lever, support it firmly with a screwdriver and then bend it to obtain the proper specifications.

3. When the adjustment is correct, open and close the throttle a few times to check the linkage movement and alignment.

CHOKE COIL LEVER ADJUSTMENT

NOTE: *To complete this procedure you will need a Stat Cover Retainer kit; available at most auto parts suppliers.*

Adjusting the choke coil lever—M2ME, E2ME

NOTE: RECHECK FAST
IDLE ADJUSTMENT ON
THE VEHICLE SETTING
TO SPECIFICATIONS.

(1) HOLD CAM
FOLLOWER ON
HIGHEST STEP
OF FAST IDLE CAM

(3) TURN SCREW IN TO
CONTACT LEVER THEN
TURN SCREW IN 4½
TURNS (NOTE)

(2) TURN FAST IDLE SCREW
OUT UNTIL PRIMARY
THROTTLE VALVES ARE
CLOSED.

Adjusting the fast idle with the carburetor off the car—M2ME, E2ME

1. Drill out and remove the rivets which retain the choke housing cover and then remove the thermostatic cover and coil assembly from the choke housing.

2. Place the fast idle cam follower on the high step of the fast idle cam.

3. Close the choke valve by pushing up on the thermostatic coil tang (counterclockwise).

4. Insert a drill or gauge of the specified size into the hole in the choke housing. The lower edge of the choke lever should be just touching the side of the gauge.

5. If the choke lever is not touching the side of the gauge, bend the choke rod until you see that it does.

FAST IDLE ADJUSTMENT

1. Set the ignition timing and curb idle speed. Disconnect and plug any hoses as directed on the emission control sticker.

(5) LEVELING
BUBBLE
(CENTERED)

(2) DEGREE
SCALE

(3) POINTER
MAGNET

(4) CHOKE
VALVE
CLOSED

FIGURE 1

(8) CLOSE CHOKE BY
PUSHING UPWARD
ON CHOKE COIL
LEVER OR
VACUUM BREAK
LEVER TANG (HOLD
IN POSITION WITH
RUBBER BAND).

(10) REMOVE GAUGE.

(1) MAKE CHOKE COIL LEVER
AND FAST IDLE ADJUSTMENT
(BENCH OR ON-THE-CAR SETTING).

(6) SPECIFIED
ANGLE (SEE SPECS.)

(9) TO ADJUST, BEND TANG
ON FAST IDLE CAM
UNTIL BUBBLE IS
CENTERED.

FAST IDLE CAM

FIGURE 2

(7) PLACE CAM FOLLOWER
ON SECOND STEP OF
CAM AGAINST RISE OF
HIGH STEP.

Fast idle cam (choke rod) adjustment—M2ME, E2ME

Rochester M2ME, E2ME Specifications

Year	Carburetor Identification ①	Float Level (in.)	Choke Rod (deg./in.)	Choke Unloader (deg./in.)	Vacuum Break Lean or Front (deg./in.)	Vacuum Break Rich or Rear (deg./in.)	Pump Rod (in.)	Choke Coil Lever (in.)	Automatic Choke (notches)
1980	17080108	3/8	38/0.243	38/0.243	25/0.142	—	5/16 ②	0.120	Fixed
	17080110	3/8	38/0.243	38/0.243	25/0.142	—	5/16 ②	0.120	Fixed
	17080130	5/16	38/0.243	38/0.243	25/0.142	—	5/16 ②	0.120	Fixed
	17080131	5/16	38/0.243	38/0.243	25/0.142	—	5/16 ②	0.120	Fixed
	17080132	5/16	38/0.243	38/0.243	25/0.142	—	5/16 ②	0.120	Fixed
	17080133	5/16	38/0.243	38/0.243	25/0.142	—	5/16 ②	0.120	Fixed
	17080138	3/8	38/0.243	38/0.243	25/0.142	—	5/16 ②	0.120	Fixed
	17080140	3/8	38/0.243	38/0.243	25/0.142	—	5/16 ②	0.120	Fixed
	17080493	5/16	38/0.139	38/0.243	25/0.117	–/0.179	Fixed	0.120	Fixed
	17080495	5/16	38/0.139	38/0.243	25/0.117	–/0.179	Fixed	0.120	Fixed
	17080496	5/16	38/0.139	38/0.243	25/0.117	–/0.203	Fixed	0.120	Fixed
	17080498	5/16	38/0.139	38/0.243	25/0.117	–/0.203	Fixed	0.120	Fixed
1981	17080185	9/32	24.5/0.139	38/0.243	19/0.103	14/0.071	1/4 ②	0.120	Fixed
	17080187	9/32	24.5/0.139	38/0.243	19/0.103	14/0.071	1/4 ②	0.120	Fixed
	17080191	9/32	24.5/0.139	38/0.243	18/0.096	18/0.096	1/4 ②	0.120	Fixed
	17080491	5/16	24.5/0.139	38/0.243	21/0.117	35/0.220	Fixed	0.120	Fixed
	17080496	5/16	24.5/0.139	38/0.243	21/0.117	33/0.203	Fixed	0.120	Fixed
	17080498	5/16	24.5/0.139	38/0.243	21/0.117	33/0.203	Fixed	0.120	Fixed
	17081130	3/8	20/0.110	38/0.243	25/0.142	—	Fixed	0.120	Fixed
	17081131	3/8	20/0.110	38/0.243	25/0.142	—	Fixed	0.120	Fixed
	17081132	3/8	20/0.110	38/0.243	25/0.142	—	Fixed	0.120	Fixed
	17081133	3/8	20/0.110	38/0.243	25/0.142	—	Fixed	0.120	Fixed
	17081138	3/8	20/0.110	40/0.260	25/0.142	—	Fixed	0.120	Fixed
	17081140	3/8	20/0.110	40/0.260	25/0.142	—	Fixed	0.120	Fixed
	17081191	5/16	24.5/0.139	38/0.243	28/0.139	24/0.136	Fixed	0.120	Fixed
	17081192	5/16	24.5/0.139	38/0.243	28/0.139	24/0.136	Fixed	0.120	Fixed
	17081194	5/16	24.5/0.139	38/0.243	21/0.117	24/0.136	Fixed	0.120	Fixed
	17081196	5/16	24.5/0.139	38/0.243	28/0.139	24/0.136	Fixed	0.120	Fixed
	17081197	5/16	18/0.096	38/0.243	28/0.139	24/0.136	Fixed	0.120	Fixed
	17081198	3/8	24.5/0.139	38/0.243	28/0.139	24/0.136	Fixed	0.120	Fixed
	17081199	3/8	18/0.096	38/0.243	28/0.139	24/0.136	Fixed	0.120	Fixed
1982	17082130	3/8	20/–	38/0.243	27	—	Fixed	0.120	Fixed
	17082132	3/8	20/–	38/0.243	27	—	Fixed	0.120	Fixed
	17082138	3/8	20/–	38/0.243	27	—	Fixed	0.120	Fixed
	12082140	3/8	20/–	38/0.243	27	—	Fixed	0.120	Fixed
	17082497	5/16	24.5/0.139	32/–	28	24	Fixed	0.120	Fixed
1983	17082130	3/8	20/–	38/–	27	—	Fixed	0.120	Fixed
	17082132	3/8	20/–	38/–	27	—	Fixed	0.120	Fixed
	17083130	3/8	20/–	38/–	27	—	Fixed	0.120	Fixed

Rochester M2ME, E2ME Specifications (cont.)

Year	Carburetor Identification ①	Float Level (in.)	Choke Rod (deg./in.)	Choke Unloader (deg./in.)	Vacuum Break Lean or Front (deg./in.)	Vacuum Break Rich or Rear (deg./in.)	Pump Rod (in.)	Choke Coil Lever (in.)	Automatic Choke (notches)
1983	17083132	⅜	20/—	38/—	27	—	Fixed	0.120	Fixed
	17083190	5⁄16	18/—	32/—	28	24	Fixed	0.120	Fixed
	17083192	5⁄16	18/—	32/—	28	24	Fixed	0.120	Fixed
	17083193	5⁄16	17/—	27/—	23	28	Fixed	0.120	Fixed

① The carburetor identification number is stamped on the float bowl, next to the fuel inlet nut.
② Inner hole

2. Place the fast idle screw on the highest step of the fast idle cam.

3. Start the engine and adjust the engine speed to specifications with the fast idle screw.

FAST IDLE CAM (CHOKE ROD) ADJUSTMENT

NOTE: *A special angle gauge should be used. If it is not available, an inch measurement can be used.*

1. Adjust the choke coil lever and the fast idle as previously detailed.

2. Rotate the degree scale until it is zeroed.

3. Close the choke valve completely and place the magnet on top of it.

4. Center the bubble.

5. Rotate the scale so that the specified degree is opposite the pointer.

6. Place the fast idle screw on the second step of the cam, against the rise of the high step.

7. Close the choke by pushing up on the choke coil lever or the vacuum break lever tang. You may hold it in position with a rubber band.

8. To adjust, bend the tang on the fast idle cam until the bubble is centered.

FRONT VACUUM BREAK ADJUSTMENT

1. Follow Steps 1–5 of the "Fast Idle Cam Adjustment" procedure.

2. Set the choke vacuum diaphragm using an outside vacuum source.

3. Close the choke valve by pushing up on the choke coil lever or the vacuum break lever. You may hold it in position with a rubber band.

4. To adjust, turn the screw in or out until the bubble in the gauge is centered.

REAR VACUUM BREAK ADJUSTMENT

1. Follow Steps 1–3 of the "Front Vacuum Break Adjustment" procedure.

2. To adjust, use a ⅛ in. Allen wrench to turn the screw in the rear cover until the bubble is centered. After adjusting, apply silicone

Front vacuum break adjustment—M2ME, E2ME

① REMOVE VACUUM BREAK FROM CARBURETOR. PLACE BRACKET IN A VISE AND, USING SAFETY PRECAUTIONS, GRIND OFF ADJUSTMENT SCREW CAP. RE-INSTALL VACUUM BREAK.

⑨ TO ADJUST, USING 1/8" HEX WRENCH TURN SCREW IN REAR COVER UNTIL BUBBLE IS CENTERED. APPLY SEALER (SUCH AS SILICONE SEALANT RTV RUBBER OR EQUIVALENT) OVER SCREW HEAD TO SEAL SETTING.

RUBBER BAND

PLUNGER BUCKING SPRING

⑦ SEAT DIAPHRAGM USING VACUUM SOURCE (SEE NOTE 2)

FIGURE 2

⑥ SPECIFIED ANGLE (SEE SPECS.)

⑤ LEVELING BUBBLE (CENTERED)

② DEGREE SCALE
③ POINTER MAGNET

④ CHOKE VALVE CLOSED

FIGURE 1

PUMP PLUNGER CUP   FIGURE 3

⑧ LIGHTLY CLOSE CHOKE BY PUSHING UPWARD ON CHOKE COIL LEVER OR VACUUM BREAK LEVER TANG (HOLD IN POSITION WITH RUBBER BAND). MAKE SURE PLUNGER BUCKING SPRING (IF USED) IS COMPRESSED AND SEATED.

Rear vacuum break adjustment—M2ME, E2ME

sealant RTV over the screw head to seal the setting.

UNLOADER ADJUSTMENT

1. Follow Steps 1–5 of the "Fast Idle Cam Adjustment" procedure.
2. If they have been previously removed, install the choke thermostatic cover and the coil assembly into the choke housing.
3. Close the choke valve by pushing up on the tang on the vacuum break lever (you may hold it with a rubber band).
4. Hold the primary throttle valves wide open.
5. To adjust, bend the tang on the fast idle

lever until the bubble on the gauge is centered.

Rochester M4ME and E4ME—4 BBL Carburetors

NOTE: *Float, pump, choke coil lever, fast idle, fast idle cam (choke rod), front and rear vacuum break and unloader adjustments on these two carburetors are identical to those detailed in the preceding "M2ME and E2ME" section. Please refer to them. There are, however, a number of procedures that apply only to these 4 bbl carburetors.*

④ LEVELING BUBBLE (CENTERED)
① DEGREE SCALE
② POINTER MAGNET
③ CHOKE VALVE CLOSED
RUBBER BAND
⑦ HOLD THROTTLE VALVES WIDE OPEN.
⑤ SPECIFIED ANGLE (SEE SPECS.)
FIGURE 1
⑥ INSTALL CHOKE THERMOSTATIC COVER AND COIL ASSEMBLY IN HOUSING. ALIGN INDEX MARK WITH SPECIFIED POINT ON HOUSING.
FIGURE 2
⑨ BEND TANG TO ADJUST UNTIL BUBBLE IS CENTERED.
⑧ ON WARM ENGINE, CLOSE CHOKE VALVE BY PUSHING UP ON TANG ON VACUUM BREAK LEVER (HOLD IN POSITION WITH RUBBER BAND).

Unloader adjustment—M2ME, E2ME

Adjusting the air valve rod—M4ME, E4ME

AIR VALVE ROD ADJUSTMENT

1. Using an outside vacuum source, seat the choke vacuum diaphragm. Put a piece of tape over the purge bleed hole if so equipped.
2. Close the air valve completely.
3. Insert the gauge between the rod and the end of the slot in the lever.
4. Bend the rod to adjust the clearance.

SECONDARY LOCKOUT ADJUSTMENT

1. Pull the choke wide open by pushing out on the choke lever.
2. Open the throttle until the end of the secondary actuating lever is opposite the toe of the lockout lever.
3. Measure the clearance between the lockout lever and the secondary lever.
4. Bend the lockout pin until the clearance is in accordance with the proper specifications.

SECONDARY CLOSING ADJUSTMENT

1. Make sure that the idle speed is set to the proper specifications.
2. The choke valve should be wide open with the cam follower off of the steps of the fast idle cam.
3. There should be 0.020 in. clearance between the secondary throttle actuating rod and the front of the slot on the secondary throttle lever with the closing tang on the throttle lever resting against the actuating lever.
4. To adjust, bend the secondary closing tang on the primary throttle actuating rod.

SECONDARY OPENING ADJUSTMENT

1. Open the primary throttle valves until the actuating link contacts the upper tang on the secondary lever.
2. With the two point linkage, the bottom

Secondary lockout adjustment—M4ME, E4ME

Secondary closing adjustment—M4ME, E4ME

of the link should be in the center of the secondary lever slot.

3. With the three point linkage, there should be 0.070 in. clearance between the link and the middle tang.

4. To adjust, bend the upper tang on the secondary lever.

Secondary opening adjustment—M4ME, E4ME

AIR VALVE SPRING ADJUSTMENT

To adjust the air valve spring windup, loosen the Allen head lockscrew and then turn the adjusting screw counterclockwise so as to remove all spring tension. With the air valve closed, turn the adjusting screw clockwise the specified number of turns after the torsion spring contacts the pin on the shaft. Hold the adjusting screw in this position and tighten the lockscrew.

DIESEL ENGINE FUEL SYSTEM

Fuel Supply Pump

REMOVAL AND INSTALLATION

The V8 diesel fuel supply pump is serviced in the same manner as the fuel pump on the gasoline engines. The V6 diesel fuel supply pump is electric and is mounted on the intake manifold adjacent to a valve cover. It is important

Adjusting the air valve spring—M4ME, E4ME

Rochester M4ME, E4ME Specifications

Year	Carburetor Identification ①	Float Level (in.)	Air Valve Spring (turn)	Pump Rod (in.)	Primary Vacuum Break (deg./in.)	Secondary Vacuum Break (deg./in.)	Secondary Opening (in.)	Choke Rod (deg./in.)	Choke Unloader (deg./in.)	Fast Idle Speed ② (rpm)
1980	17080202	7/16	7/8	1/4 ③	27/0.157	—	⑤	20/0.110	38/0.243	⑥
	17080204	7/16	7/8	1/4 ③	27/0.157	—	⑤	20/0.110	38/0.243	⑥
	17080207	7/16	7/8	1/4 ③	27/0.157	—	⑤	20/0.110	38/0.243	⑥
	17080228	7/16	7/8	9/32 ③	30/0.179	—	⑤	20/0.110	38/0.243	⑥
	17080243	3/16	9/16	9/32 ③	16/0.016	−/0.083	⑤	14.5/0.074	30/0.179	⑥
	17080274	15/32	5/8	5/16 ④	20/0.110	−/0.164	⑤	16/0.083	33/0.203	⑥
	17080282	7/16	7/8	11/32 ④	25/0.142	—	⑤	20/0.110	38/0.243	⑥
	17080284	7/16	7/8	11/32 ④	25/0.142	—	⑤	20/0.110	38/0.243	⑥
	17080502	1/2	7/8	Fixed	−/0.136	−/0.179	⑤	20/0.110	38/0.243	⑥
	17080504	1/2	7/8	Fixed	−/0.136	−/0.179	⑤	20/0.110	38/0.243	⑥
	17080542	3/8	9/16	Fixed	−/0.103	−/0.066	⑤	14.5/0.074	38/0.243	⑥
	17080543	3/8	9/16	Fixed	−/0.103	−/0.129	⑤	14.5/0.074	38/0.243	⑥
1981	17081202	11/32	7/8	Fixed	26/0.149	—	⑤	20/0.110	38/0.243	⑦
	17081203	11/32	7/8	Fixed	26/0.149	—	⑤	20/0.110	38/0.243	⑦
	17081204	11/32	7/8	Fixed	26/0.149	—	⑤	20/0.110	38/0.243	⑦
	17081207	11/32	7/8	Fixed	26/0.149	—	⑤	20/0.110	38/0.243	⑦
	17081216	11/32	7/8	Fixed	26/0.149	—	⑤	20/0.110	38/0.243	⑦
	17081217	11/32	7/8	Fixed	26/0.149	—	⑤	20/0.110	38/0.243	⑦
	17081218	11/32	7/8	Fixed	26/0.149	—	⑤	20/0.110	38/0.243	⑦
	17081242	5/16	7/8	Fixed	17/0.090	−/0.077	⑤	24.5/0.139	38/0.243	⑦
	17081243	1/4	7/8	Fixed	19/0.103	−/0.090	⑤	24.5/0.139	38/0.243	⑦
1982	17082202	11/32	7/8	Fixed	27	—	⑤	20/−	38/−	⑦
	17082204	11/32	7/8	Fixed	27	—	⑤	20/−	38/−	⑦
1983	17083202	11/32	7/8	Fixed	—	27/−	⑤	20/−	38/−	⑦
	17083203	11/32	7/8	Fixed	—	27/−	⑤	38/−	38/−	⑦
	17083204	11/32	7/8	Fixed	—	27/−	⑤	20/−	38/−	⑦
	17083207	11/32	7/8	Fixed	—	27/−	⑤	38/−	38/−	⑦
	17083216	11/32	7/8	Fixed	—	27/−	⑤	20/−	38/−	⑦
	17083218	11/32	7/8	Fixed	—	27/−	⑤	20/−	38/−	⑦
	17083236	11/32	7/8	Fixed	—	27/−	⑤	20/−	38/−	⑦
	17083506	7/16	7/8	Fixed	27/−	36/−	⑤	20/−	36/−	⑦
	17083508	7/16	7/8	Fixed	27/−	36/−	⑤	20/−	36/−	⑦
	17083524	7/16	7/8	Fixed	25/−	36/−	⑤	20/−	36/−	⑦
	17083526	7/16	7/8	Fixed	25/−	36/−	⑤	20/−	36/−	⑦

① The carburetor identification number is stamped on the float bowl, near the secondary throttle lever.
② With manual transmission; w/o vacuum advance and the throttle positioned on the high step of the cam
③ Inner hole
④ Outer hole
⑤ No measurement necessary on two point linkage; see text
⑥ 4 turns after contacting lever for preliminary setting
⑦ 4½ turns after contacting lever for preliminary setting

VIEW A

(11 FT. LBS.)

V6 diesel fuel pump and fuel filter locations; fuel filter shown below

V6 diesel fuel supply pump mounted on intake manifold

that the mounting surfaces be clean and tight for proper pump operation. Disconnect the fuel lines and electric leads, and disconnect the pump. Make sure no dirt enters the fuel lines when the pump is removed.

Fuel Filter

REMOVAL AND INSTALLATION

See "Fuel Filter" service procedures in Chapter 2.

WATER IN FUEL (DIESEL)

Water is the worst enemy of the diesel fuel injection system. The injection pump, which is designed and constructed to extremely close tolerances, and the injectors can be easily damaged if enough water is forced through them in

the fuel. Engine performance will also be drastically affected, and engine damage can occur.

Diesel fuel is much more susceptible than gasoline to water contamination. Diesel-engined cars are equipped with an indicator lamp system that turns on an instrument panel lamp if water (1 to 2½ gallons) is detected in the fuel tank. The lamp will come on for 2 to 5 seconds each time the ignition is turned on, assuring the driver the lamp is working. If there is water in the fuel, the light will come back on after a 15 to 20 second off delay, and then remain on.

PURGING THE FUEL TANK

Cars which have a "Water in Fuel" light may have the water removed from the tank with a siphon pump. The pump hose should be hooked up to the ¼ in. fuel return hose (the smaller of the two hoses) above the rear axle or under the hood near the fuel pump. Siphoning should continue until all water is removed from the tank. Use a clear plastic hose or observe the filter bowl on the siphon pump (if equipped) to determine when clear fuel begins to flow. Be sure to remove the cap on the fuel tank while purging. Replace the cap when finished. Discard the fuel filter and replace with a new filter.

Fuel Injection

PUMP REMOVAL AND INSTALLATION

NOTE: *The V6 and V8 diesel injection systems may use either a CAV injection pump, or a Roosa-Master/Stanodyne pump.*

1. Remove the air cleaner.
2. Remove the filters and pipes from the valve covers and air crossover.
3. Remove the air crossover and cap and intake manifold with screen covers (tool J-26996-1).
4. Disconnect the throttle rod and return spring.
5. Remove the bellcrank.
6. Remove the throttle and transmission cables from the intake manifold brackets.

Diesel fuel injection system circuit, V8 shown

Offset on diesel injection pump driven gear

Diesel timing marks and injection pump lines, V8

7. Disconnect the fuel lines from the filter and remove the filter.

8. Disconnect the fuel inlet line at the pump.

9. Remove the rear A/C compressor brace and remove the fuel line.

10. Disconnect the fuel return line from the injection pump.

11. Remove the clamps and pull the fuel return lines from each injection nozzle.

12. Using two wrenches, disconnect the high pressure lines at the nozzles.

13. Remove the three injection pump retaining nuts with tool J-26987 or its equivalent.

14. Remove the pump and cap all lines and nozzles.

To install:

15. Remove the protective caps.

16. Line up the offset tang on the pump driveshaft with the pump driven gear and install the pump.

17. Install, but do not tighten the pump retaining nuts.

18. Connect the high pressure lines at the nozzles.

19. Using two wrenches, torque the high pressure line nuts to 25 ft. lbs.

20. Connect the fuel return lines to the nozzles and pump.

21. Align the timing mark on the injection pump with the line on the timing mark adaptor and torque the mounting nuts to 35 ft. lbs.

NOTE: *A ¾ in. open end wrench on the boss at the front of the injection pump will aid in rotating the pump to align the marks.*

22. Adjust the throttle rod:

   a. remove the clip from the cruise control rod and remove the rod from the bellcrank.

   b. loosen the locknut on the throttle rod a few turns, then shorten the rod several turns.

   c. rotate the bellcrank to the full throttle stop, then lengthen the throttle rod until the injection pump lever contacts the injection pump full throttle stop, then release the bellcrank.

   d. tighten the throttle rod locknut.

23. Install the fuel inlet line between the transfer pump and the filter.

24. Install the rear A/C compressor brace.

25. Install the bellcrank and clip.

26. Connect the throttle rod and return spring.

27. Adjust the transmission cable:

   a. push the snap-lock to the disengaged position.

   b. rotate the injection pump lever to the full throttle stop and hold it there.

   c. push in the snap-lock until it is flush.

   d. release the injection pump lever.

28. Start the engine and check for fuel leaks.

29. Remove the screened covers and install the air crossover.

30. Install the tubes in the air flow control valve in the air crossover and install the ventilation filters in the valve covers.

31. Install the air cleaner.

32. Start the engine and allow it to run for two minutes. Stop the engine, let it stand for two minutes, then restart. This permits the air to bleed off within the pump.

Slow Idle Speed Adjustment

1. Run the engine to normal operating temperature.

2. Insert the probe of a magnetic pickup tachometer into the timing indicator hole.

Diesel injection pump slow idle screw, Roosa Master/Stanodyne pump

CAV injection pump slow idle screw

3. Set the parking brake and block the drive wheels.

4. Place the transmission in Drive and turn the A/C Off.

5. Turn the slow idle screw on the injection pump to obtain the idle specification on the emission control label.

Fast Idle Solenoid Adjustment

1. Set the parking brake and block the drive wheels.

2. Run the engine to normal operating temperature.

(6 FT. LBS.)

Fast idle solenoid adjustment. Solenoid mounted on side of injection pump

3. Place the transmission in Drive, disconnect the compressor clutch wire and turn the A/C On. On cars without A/C, disconnect the solenoid wire, and connect jumper wires to the solenoid terminals. Ground one of the wires and connect the other to a 12 volt power source to activate the solenoid.

4. Adjust the fast idle solenoid plunger to obtain 650 rpm.

Cruise Control Servo Relay Rod Adjustment

1. Turn the engine Off.

2. Adjust the rod to minimum slack then put the clip in the first free hole closest to the bellcrank, but within the servo bail.

Injection Timing
CHECKING

NOTE: *A special diesel timing meter is needed to check injection timing. There are a few variations of this meter, but the type desirable here uses a signal through a glow plug probe to determine combustion timing. The meter picks up the engine speed in RPM and the crankshaft position from the crankshaft balancer. This tool is available at automotive supply houses and from tool jobbers, and is the counterpart to a gasoline engine timing light, coupled with a tachometer. An intake manifold cover is also needed.*

NOTE: *The marks on the pump and adapter flange will normally be aligned within .030 in. on the V8 and .050 in. on the V6.*

1. Place the transmission shift lever in "Park", apply the parking brake and block the rear wheels.

2. Start the engine and let it run at idle until fully warm. Shut off the engine.

NOTE: *If the engine is not allowed to completely warm up, the probe may soot up, causing incorrect timing readings.*

3. Remove the air cleaner assembly and carefully install cover J-26996-1. *This cover over the intake is important.* Disconnect the EGR valve hose.

4. Clean away all dirt from the engine probe holder (RPM counter) and the crankshaft balancer rim.

5. Clean the lens on both ends of the glow plug probe and clean the lens in the photoelectric pick-up. Use a tooth pick to scrape the carbon from the combustion chamber side of the glow plug probe, then look through the probe to make sure it's clean. *Cleanliness is crucial for accurate readings.*

6. Install the probe into the crankshaft RPM counter (probe holder) on the engine front cover.

7. Remove the glow plug from N. 3 cylinder on the V8 and from No. 1 on the V6. Install the glow plug probe in the glow plug opening, and torque to 8 ft. lbs.

8. Set the timing meter offset selector to "B" (99.5) on the V8, and to "A" (20) on the V6.

9. Connect the battery leads, red to positive, black to negative.

10. Disconnect the two-lead connector at the generator.

11. Start the engine. Adjust the engine RPM to the speed specified on the emissions control decal.

12. Observe the timing reading, then observe it again in 2 minutes. When the readings stabilize over the 2 minutes intervals, compare that final stabilized reading to the one specified on the emissions control decal. The timing reading will be an ATDC (After Top Dead Center) reading when set to specifications.

13. Disconnect the timing meter and install the removed glow plug, torquing it to 12 ft. lbs. on the V8 and 15 ft. lbs. on the V6.

14. Connect the generator two-lead connection.

15. Install the air cleaner assembly and connect the EGR valve hose.

Adjustment

1. Shut off the engine.

2. Note the relative position of the marks on the pump flange and either the pump intermediate adapter (V6) or pump adaptor (V8).

3. Loosen the nuts or bolts holding the pump to a point where the pump can just be rotated. Use a ¾ in. open-end wrench on the boss at the front of the injection pump on the V8 and a 1 in. open-end wrench on the V6. You may need a wrench with a slight offset to clear the fuel return line on the V6.

4. Rotate the pump to the left to advance the timing and to the right to retard the timing. On the V8 the width of the mark on the adaptor is equal to about one degree of timing. On the V6 the width of the mark on the intermediate adaptor is about ⅔ of a degree. Move the pump the amount that is needed and tighten the pump retaining nuts to 18 ft. lbs. on the V8 and 35 ft. lbs. on the V6.

5. Start the engine and recheck the timing as described earlier. Reset the timing if necessary.

6. Adjust the injection pump rod on the V8. On both engines, reset the fast and curb idle speeds.

NOTE: *Wild needle fluctuations on the timing meter indicate a cylinder not firing properly. Correction of this condition must be made prior to adjusting the timing.*

7. If after reseting the timing, the timing marks are far apart and the engine still runs poorly, the dynamic timing could still be off. It is possible that a malfunctioning cylinder will cause incorrect timing. If this occurs, it is essential that timing be checked in cylinders 2 or 3 on the V8 and 1 or 4 on the V6. If different timing exists between cylinders, try both positions to determine which timing works best.

Injection Nozzle
REMOVAL AND INSTALLATION
Lines Removed

1. Remove the fuel return line from the nozzle.

2. Remove the nozzle hold-down clamp and spacer using tool J-26952.

3. Cap the high pressure line and nozzle tip. NOTE: *The nozzle tip is highly susceptible to damage and must be protected at all times.*

4. If an old nozzle is to be reinstalled, a new compression seal and carbon stop seal must be installed after removal of the used seals.

5. Remove the caps and install the nozzle, spacer and clamp. Torque to 25 ft. lbs.

6. Replace return line, start the engine and check for leaks.

Checking injection nozzle seat tightness

INLET FITTING TO BODY TORQUE
DIESEL EQUIPMENT — 45 FT. LBS.
C.A.V. LUCAS — 25 FT. LBS.

DIESEL EQUIPMENT   **C.A.V. LUCAS**

Injection nozzles, two types

Injection nozzle and glow plug installation

Marking injection pump adapter

Installing adapter seal

Injection pump adapter bolts

Injection Pump Adapter, Adapter Seal, and New Adapter Timing Mark

REMOVAL AND INSTALLATION

1. Remove injection pump and lines as described earlier.

2. Remove the injection pump adapter.

3. Remove the seal from the adapter.

4. File the timing mark from the adapter. Do not file the mark off the pump.

5. Position the engine at TDC of No. 1 cylinder. Align the mark on the balancer with the zero mark on the indicator. The index is offset to the right when No. 1 is at TDC.

6. Apply a chassis lube to the seal areas. Install, but do not tighten the injection pump.

7. Install the new seal on the adapter using tool J-28425, or its equivalent.

8. Torque the adapter bolts to 25 ft. lbs.

9. Install timing tool J-26896 into the injection pump adapter. Torque the tool, toward No.

1 cylinder to 50 ft. lbs. Mark the injection pump adapter. Remove the tool.

10. Install the injection pump.

Fuel Tank

DRAINING

1. Remove the fuel tank cap.

2. Connect a siphon pump to the ¼ in. fuel return hose (the smaller of the two hoses) above the rear axle, or under the hood near the fuel pump on the passenger's side of the engine, near the front.

3. Operate the siphon pump until all fuel is removed from the fuel tank. Be sure to reinstall the fuel return hose and the fuel cap.

REMOVAL AND INSTALLATION

1964–Sedan, 1964 Station Wagon and El Camino

1. Siphon the fuel from the tank, as there is no drain plug.

2. Disconnect the fuel line and the gauge sending unit wire from the tank.

3. Disconnect the vent hose from the tank.

4. Remove the retaining bolts from the tank straps, lower the support straps, and then carefully lower the tank from the car.

5. Reverse the removal procedure to install the fuel tank.

1965–67 Station Wagon and El Camino

1. Follow Steps 1 through 3 of the preceding procedure.

2. Remove the tank support straps.

3. Remove the frame attaching screws from the front support.

4. Slide the tank forward, and then carefully lower it from the car.

5. Reverse the removal procedure to install the fuel tank.

1968 and Later Sedan and El Camino

1. Siphon the fuel from the tank, as there is no drain plug.

Fuel meter and wiring—Chevelle station wagon

Typical fuel tank mounting

Installing fuel gauge in unit into fuel tank—typical

2. Disconnect the fuel gauge sending unit wire from the rear wiring harness connector. On sedans, push the grommet out and work the gauge wire through the trunk floor hole.

3. Raise the car to a convenient working height.

4. Remove the fuel gauge ground wire screw from the underbody.

5. Disconnect the fuel line at the sending unit pickup line.

6. Remove the vent hose (hoses for evaporative control on 1970 and later models).

7. Remove the tank filler neck bolt on the El Camino.

8. Remove the strap retaining bolts, lower the support straps, and carefully drop the tank out of the car.

9. Reverse the removal steps to install the fuel tank.

1968 and Later Station Wagon

1. Siphon the fuel from the tank.

2. Jack the car up, and place the rear on stands.

3. Lower the rear axle into the full rebound position, and remove the left rear wheel assembly.

4. Disconnect the fuel gauge sending unit wire at the rear wiring harness.

5. Remove the fuel tank front shield.

6. Remove the fuel gauge ground wire from the rear quarter panel.

7. Remove the fuel line and wires from the gauge sending unit.

8. On 1974 and later models, remove the left rear shock absorber and lift the right rear wheel slightly to allow movement of the left wheel down and out of the way.

9. Remove the strap retaining bolts and lower the tank carefully.

10. Reverse the removal procedure to install the tank.

Chassis Electrical

5

UNDERSTANDING AND TROUBLESHOOTING ELECTRICAL SYSTEMS

For any electrical system to operate, it must make a complete circuit. This simply means that the power flow from the battery must make a complete circle. When an electrical component is operating, power flows from the battery to the component, passes through the component causing it to perform its function (lighting a light bulb, for example) and then returns to the battery through the component causing it to perform its function (lighting a light bulb, for example) and then returns to the battery through the ground of the circuit. This ground is usually (but not always) the metal part of the car on which the electrical component is mounted.

Perhaps the easiest way to visualize this is to think of connecting a light bulb with two wires attached to it to your car battery. The battery in your car has two posts (negative and positive). If one of the two wires attached to the light bulb was attached to the negative post of the battery and the other wire was attached to the positive post of the battery, you would have a complete circuit. Current from the battery would flow out one post, through the wire attached to it and then to the light bulb, causing it to light. It would then leave the light bulb, travel through the other wire, and return to the other post of the battery.

The normal automotive circuit differs from this simple example in two ways. First, instead of having a return wire from the bulb to the battery, the light bulb returns the current to the battery through the chassis of the vehicle. Since the negative battery cable is attached to the chassis and the chassis is made of electrically conductive metal, the chassis of the vehicle can serve as a ground wire to complete the circuit. Secondly, most automotive circuits

contain switches to turn components on and off as required.

There are many types of switches, but the most common simply serves to prevent the passage of current when it is turned off. Since the switch is a part of the circle necessary for a complete circuit, it operates to leave an opening in the circuit, and thus an incomplete or open circuit, when it is turned off.

Some electrical components which require a large amount of current to operate also have a relay in their circuit. Since these circuits carry a large amount of current, the thickness of the wire (gauge size) in the circuit is also greater. If this large wire were connected from the component to the control switch on the instrument panel, and then back to the component, a voltage drop would occur in the circuit. To prevent this potential drop in voltage, an electromagnetic switch (relay) is used. The large wires in the circuit are connected from the car battery to one side of the relay, and from the opposite side of the relay to the component. The relay is normally open, preventing current from passing through the circuit. An additional, smaller, wire is connected from the relay to the control switch for the circuit. When the control switch is turned on, it completes the circuit. This closes the relay and allows current to flow from the battery to the component. The horn, headlight, and starter circuits are three which use relays.

You have probably noticed how the car's instrument panel lights get brighter the faster you rev the engine. This happens because your alternator (which supplies the battery) puts out more current at speeds above idle. This is normal. However, it is possible for larger surges of current to pass through the electrical system of your car. If this surge of current were to reach an electrical component, it could burn the component out. To prevent this from happening, fuses are connected into the current supply wires of most of the major electrical systems of your car. The fuse serves to head off the surge at the pass. When an electrical current of excessive power passes through the component's fuse, the fuse blows out and breaks the circuit, saving it from destruction.

The fuse also protects the component from damage if the power supply wire to the component is grounded before the current reaches the component.

There is another important rule to the complete circle circuit. *Every complete circuit from a power source must include a component which is using the power from the power source.* If you were to disconnect the light bulb (from the previous example of a light bulb being connected to the battery by two wires together (take our word for it—don't try it) the result would literally be shocking. A similar thing happens (on a smaller scale) when the power supply wire to a component or the electrical component itself becomes grounded before the normal ground connection for the circuit. To prevent damage to the system, the fuse for the circuit blows to interrupt the circuit—protecting the components from damage. Because grounding a wire from a power source makes a complete circuit—less the required component to use the power—this phenomenon is called a short circuit. The most common causes of short circuits are: the rubber insulation on a wire breaking or rubbing through to expose the current carrying core of the wire to a metal part of the car, or a short switch.

Some electrical systems on the car are protected by a circuit breaker which is, basically, a self-repairing fuse. When either of the above-described events takes place in a system which is protected by a circuit breaker, the circuit breaker opens the circuit the same way a fuse does. However, when either the short is removed from the circuit or the surge subsides, the circuit breaker resets itself and does not have to be replaced as a fuse does.

The final protective device in the chassis electrical system is a fuse link. A fuse link is a wire that acts as a fuse. It is connected between the starter relay and the main wiring harness for the car. This connection is under the hood, very near a similar fuse link which protects all the chassis electrical components. It is the probable cause of trouble when none of the electrical components function, unless the battery is disconnected or dead.

Electrical problems generally fall into one of three areas:

1. The component that is not functioning is not receiving current.

2. The component itself is not functioning.

3. The component is not properly grounded.

Problems that fall into the first category are by far the most complicated. It is the current supply system to the component which contains all the switches, relays, fuses, etc.

The electrical system can be checked with a test light and a jumper wire. A test light is a device that looks like a pointed screwdriver with a wire attached to it. It has a light bulb in its handle. A jumper wire is a piece of insulated wire with an alligator clip attached to each end.

If a light bulb is not working, you must follow a systematic plan to determine which of the three causes is the villain.

1. Turn on the switch that controls the inoperable bulb.

2. Disconnect the power supply wire from the bulb.

3. Attach the ground wire on the test light to a good metal ground.

4. Touch the probe end of the test light to the end of the power supply wire that was disconnected from the bulb. If the bulb is receiving current, the test light will go on.

NOTE: *If the bulb is one which works only when the ignition key is turned on (turn signal), make sure the key is turned on.*

If the test light does not go on, then the problem is in the circuit between the battery and the bulb. As mentioned before, this includes all the switches, fuses, and relays in the system. The problem is an open circuit between the battery and the bulb. If the fuse is blown and, when replaced, immediately blows again, there is a short circuit in the system which must be located and repaired. If there is a switch in the system, bypass it with a jumper wire. This is done by connecting one end of the jumper wire to the power supply wire into the switch, and the other end of the jumper wire to the wire coming out of the switch. If the test light lights with the jumper wire installed, the switch or whatever was bypassed is defective.

NOTE: *Never substitute the jumper wire for the bulb, as the bulb is the component required to use the power from the power source.*

5. If the bulb in the test light goes on, then the current is getting to the bulb that is not working in the car. This eliminates the first of the three possible causes. Connect the power supply wire and connect a jumper wire from the bulb to a good metal ground. Do this with the switch which controls the bulb turned on, and also the ignition switch turned on if it is required for the light to work. If the bulb works with the jumper wire installed, then it has a bad ground. This is usually caused by the metal area on which the bulb mounts to the car being coated with some type of foreign matter or rust.

6. If neither test located the source of the

trouble, then the light bulb itself is defective.

The above test procedure can be applied to any of the components of the chassis electrical system by substituting the component that is not working for the light bulb. *Remember that for any electrical system to work, all connections must be clean and tight.*

HEATER

Heater Blower

REMOVAL AND INSTALLATION

1964–67

1. Disconnect the battery.
2. Unclip the hoses from the fender skirt.
3. Disconnect the electrical feed from the motor.
4. Turn the front wheels to the extreme right.
5. Remove the right front fender skirt bolts and allow the skirt to drop, resting it on top of tire. It may be wedged away from the fender lower flange with a block of wood to provide better access to the bolts.
6. Remove the screws attaching the motor mounting plate to the air inlet housing.
7. Remove the screws attaching the motor to the mounting plate.
8. Remove the clip attaching the cage to the shaft and remove the blower motor.
9. Install in the reverse of above.

1968–72

1. Disconnect the battery ground cable.
2. Disconnect the hoses and wiring from the fender skirt.
3. Remove all fender skirt attaching bolts except those attaching the skirt to the radiator support.
4. Pull out, then down, on the skirt. Place a block between the skirt and the fender.
5. Remove the blower-to-case attaching screws. Remove the blower assembly.
6. Remove the blower wheel retaining nut and separate the motor and the wheel.
7. Reverse the procedure to install. The open end of blower should be away from the motor.

1973–77

1. Disconnect the battery ground cable.
2. Disconnect the motor lead wire.
3. Remove the blower-to-case screws and the blower.
4. Remove the retaining nut to separate the motor and wheel.
5. Reverse the procedure for installation. The open end of the blower wheel should be away from the motor.

1978 and later

1. Disconnect the battery ground cable.
2. Disconnect the hoses and wiring from the right side inner fender panel.

1978 heater control cable assembly

HEATER MODULE

A

I/P MOUNTING BRACKET

B

RESISTOR

RADIO GROUND STRAP

EXISTING DIMPLE

NOTE:
GROUND CLIPS MUST
BE INSTALLED SO THEY
WILL NOT INTERFERE WITH
THE OPERATION OF THE DOOR
OR OBSTRUCT THE BOWDEN
CABLE.

VIEW A

VIEW B

Heater module service, 1978 Malibu shown

HEATER MODULE

SEAL
PULL OFF

MODULE LEAF SCREEN
R&R SCREWS

①

②

BLOWER MOTOR
D&C ELECTRICAL CONNECTORS
R&R MOTOR SCREWS

APPLY TO TOP AND SIDES ONLY
EXTEND COVERAGE BELOW LOWER
SCREW ON BOTH VERTICAL FLANGES.
*SCREW ATTACHING SEQUENCE
AS FOLLOWS: ①,②. THEN CLOCKWISE
AROUND MODULE.

HEATER CORE
R&R HEATER HOSES
D&C ELECTRICAL CONNECTORS
R&R FRONT MODULE COVER
SCREWS
R&R CORE

SECTION SHOWING SCREEN
IN RELATION TO REVEAL MOULDING

1978 Malibu module installation

305 V-8
350 V-8

Heater hose mounting; V6 similar

3. Remove all the right side inner fender panel attaching bolts except those attaching the panel to the radiator support. Pull the panel out, then place a block between the panel and the fender.

4. Remove the screws attaching the blower to the case. On cars equipped with A/C, remove the air cooling hose. Remove the blower assembly.

5. Installation is the reverse of removal.

Heater airflow diagram (© Chevrolet Motor Division)

Heater/defroster assembly

HEATER HOSES
LOOSEN CLAMPS
SLIT HOSE IF NECESSARY

BLACK

SEALER

Heater blower mounting

Heater Core
REMOVAL AND INSTALLATION
1964–67 Except Air Conditioned Cars

1. Disconnect the battery ground cable and drain the radiator.

2. Remove the heater hoses from the core. The top hose connects to the water pump and the lower hose goes to the thermostat housing.

3. Remove the cables and all electrical connections from the heater and defroster assembly.

4. Remove the nuts from the core case studs located on the firewall.

5. From inside the car, remove the case-to-firewall mounting screws and also the heater and defroster assembly.

6. Remove the retaining springs and core.

7. Install the core and retaining spring, making sure the core-to-case sealer is in good shape.

8. Complete the installation by reversing the removal procedure.

1968–77 Except Air Conditioned Cars

1. Disconnect the battery ground cable.
2. Drain the radiator.

3. Disconnect the heater hoses. Plug the core inlet and outlet.

4. Remove the nuts from the air distributor duct studs on the firewall.

5. On post-1969 models remove the glove box and radio, then the defroster duct-to-distributor duct screw.

6. Pull the defroster duct out of the way, and then pull the distributor duct from the firewall mounting. Remove the resistor wires. Lay the duct on the floor.

7. Remove the core assembly from the distributor duct.

8. Reverse the procedure to install. Use new sealer on the duct flange, if necessary.

1978 and later Except Air Conditioned Cars

1. Disconnect the negative battery cable. Drain the radiator. Disconnect heater hoses.

2. Remove the nuts that attach the heater case to the firewall from the firewall side. Then, remove the screws from inside the car.

3. Remove the glovebox and door. Remove the screws attaching the heater outlet duct to the heater case, and remove the duct.

4. Remove the defroster screw. Pull the heater case out. The core may now be pulled out of the case.

5. Reverse the removal procedure to install. Use new seals between the heater case and firewall.

1967 and later Air Conditioned Cars

Removal of the heater core from air conditioned cars requires the opening (evacuation) of the refrigerant lines. These lines contain pressurized Freon gas, capable of inflicting serious injury upon contact. *Do not, under any circumstance, disconnect or loosen any refrigerant hose. This should be attempted only by a qualified refrigeration repairman.* To avoid the possibility of accidents, heater core removal on air-conditioned cars, and all other air-conditioning service procedures have been deleted from this book.

Radio
REMOVAL AND INSTALLATION
1964–72

1. Disconnect the battery ground cable.
2. Remove the ash try and ash tray housing as necessary.
3. Remove the knobs, controls, washers, trim plate, and nuts from radio.
4. Remove the hoses from the center air conditioning duct as necessary.
5. Disconnect all wiring leads.
6. Remove the screw from the radio rear mounting bracket and lower the radio.
7. To install, reverse the above procedure.

Radio mounting details—mounting differs between models and years

1973 and Later

1. Disconnect the battery ground cable.
2. Remove the left air conditioner lap cooler duct.
3. Pull off the knobs and bezels.
4. Remove the control shaft nuts and washers. You will probably need a deep-well socket.
5. Remove the support bracket stud nut. Disconnect the antenna, speaker, and power wires.
6. Move the radio back until the shafts clear the instrument panel. Lower it from behind the panel. On later models, the radio can be removed through the instrument panel opening.
7. Reverse the procedure for installation. Make sure to hook up the speaker leads before turning the radio on; operating without a speaker will damage the transistors.

WINDSHIELD WIPERS

Blade and Arm

REPLACEMENT

If the wiper assembly has a press type release tab at the center, simply depress the tab and remove the blade. If the blade has no release tab, use a screwdriver to depress the spring at the center. This will release the assembly. To install the assembly, position the blade over the pin at the tip of the arm and press until the spring retainer engages the groove in the pin.

To remove the element, either depress the release button or squeeze the spring type retainer clip at the outer end together, and slide the blade element out. Just slide the new element in until it latches.

Removal of the wiper arms requires the use of a special tool, G.M. J8966 or its equivalent. Versions of this tool are generally available in auto parts stores.

1. Insert the tool under the wiper arm and lever the arm off the shaft.

NOTE: *Raising the hood on most later models will facilitate easier wiper arm removal.*

2. Disconnect the washer hose from the arm (if so equipped). Remove the arm.
3. Installation is in the reverse order of re-

The two methods of releasing wiper blade assemblies

Remove the wiper arm with the special tool

moval. The proper park position for the arms is with the blades approximately 2 in. (50 mm) above the lower molding of the windshield. Be sure that the motor is in the park position before installing the arms.

Wiper Motor

REMOVAL AND INSTALLATION

1964–67

1. Make certain that the wiper motor is in the park position.

2. Disconnect the washer hoses and electrical connectors.

3. Remove the three motor bolts. Pull the wiper motor assembly from the cowl opening and loosen the nuts retaining the drive rod ball stud to the crank arm.

4. Reverse the procedure to install, checking the sealing gaskets at the motor. Make sure

Windshield wiper motor mounting—1964–67

the motor is in the park position before installation.

1968–70

1. Make sure that the wiper motor is in the park position.

2. Disconnect the washer hoses and electrical connectors.

3. Remove the plenum chamber grille or access cover. Remove the nut retaining the crank arm to the motor assembly.

4. Remove the retaining screws or nuts and remove the motor. Do not allow the motor to hang by the drive link.

5. Reverse the procedure to install, checking the sealing gaskets at the motor. Make sure the motor is in the park position before installation.

1971 and Later

NOTE: *Your car may be equipped with either a round motor or a rectangular motor.*

1. Remove the screen or grille that covers the cowl area.

2. Working under the hood, disconnect the motor wiring. Then, reach through the cowl opening and loosen, but do not remove, the nuts which attach the transmission drive link to the motor crank arm. Then, disconnect the drive link from the crank arm.

3. Remove the three motor attaching screws, and remove the motor, guiding the crank arm through the hole.

4. Installation is in the reverse order of removal. The motor must be in the park position before assembling the crank arm to the transmission drive link(s).

Linkage

REMOVAL AND INSTALLATION

1964–67

1. Make certain that the wiper motor is in park position. Remove the wiper arm and blade assemblies from the transmission shaft.

2. Remove the plenum chamber grille.

3. Detach the linkage from the wiper crank arm.

4. Remove the transmission retaining screws, lower the assembly into the plenum chamber, and remove the unit.

5. Reverse the procedure to install.

1968 and Later

1. Make sure that the wiper motor is in the park position.

2. Disconnect the battery ground cable.

3. Remove the wiper arm and blade assemblies from the transmission. On the articulated

WINDSHIELD WIPER WASHER PUMP
AND MOTOR ASSEMBLY

VIEW A

ATTACHING BOLTS

Windshield wiper motor mounting—round motor

left arm assemblies, remove the carburetor type clip retaining the pinned arm to the blade arm.

4. Remove the plenum chamber air intake grille or screen.

5. Loosen the nuts retaining the drive rod ball stud to the crank arm and detach the drive rod from the crank arm.

6. Remove the transmission retaining screws. Lower the transmission and drive rod assemblies into the plenum chamber.

7. Remove the transmission and linkage from the plenum chamber through the cowl opening.

8. Reverse the procedure to install, making sure the wiper blade assemblies are installed in the park position. On recessed wiper arms, this occurs at ⅜ in. from the top of the reveal molding.

INSTRUMENT CLUSTER

REMOVAL AND INSTALLATION

1964–65

1. Disconnect the battery ground cable.

2. Remove the upper mast jacket clamp bolt and bend the clamp away from the steering column.

3. Disconnect the speedometer cable. Disconnect the oil pressure line at the gauge on the SS model.

4. Remove the screws that attach the console to the instrument panel and lean the console forward onto the mast jacket. Remove the radio knobs before removing the console from the panel.

5. Disconnect all cluster lamps, harness

SERRATED SHAFT

VIEW "B"

MUST OVERLAP

TRANSMISSION ASSEMBLY

OUTWIPE DIMENSION

B

PAINTED LOWER SECTION OF WINDSHIELD GLASS

A

GASKET

DRIVE LINK

RECTANGULAR MOTOR

CRANKARM

VIEW "A"

Windshield wiper motor mounting—rectangular motor

Instrument cluster—1964-65

connectors, and the two harness retaining clips from the rear of the cluster.

6. Lift the console forward and upward to remove.

7. Unscrew and remove the cluster from the console.

8. Install by reversing the removal procedure.

1966-67

1. Disconnect the battery.

2. Remove the steering coupling bolt and disconnect the steering shaft from the coupling.

3. Loosen the mast jacket lower clamp.

4. On air-conditioned cars, remove the air-conditioning center distribution duct.

Instrument cluster—1966–67

5. Remove the radio rear support bracket screw.

6. Remove the mast jacket trim cover and the support clamp.

7. Loosen the set screw and remove the transmission dial indicator (if so equipped).

8. Disconnect the speedometer shaft at the speedometer head.

9. Remove the instrument panel attaching screws.

10. From under the console, remove the four lower retaining screws from the cluster housing.

11. With the mast jacket padded, pull the instrument panel from the console and lay forward on mast jacket.

12. Disconnect the wiring harness, cluster lamps and wiring terminals from the rear of the cluster assembly.

13. Remove the four screws holding the upper section of the cluster housing to the panel and remove the cluster from the instrument panel.

14. Install by reversing the removal procedure.

1968–69

1. Disconnect the battery ground cable.

2. Remove the ash tray and retainer.

3. Remove the radio knobs, nuts, electrical connectors, and the radio rear support. Remove the radio.

4. Remove the heater control screws, then push the control head out of the instrument panel.

5. Lower the steering column. Remove the automatic transmission indicator cable from the steering column. Protect the steering column with a cloth.

6. Remove the instrument panel retaining screws at the top, bottom, and sides of the panel.

Remove all attachments to the underside of the panel.

7. Lift the panel up and back slightly. Reach behind the cluster to remove the speedometer cable, support the panel on the protected steering column.

8. Remove the clips at the top of the cluster rear cover and remove all connectors at the rear of the cluster. Remove the oil pressure fitting from the rear of the oil pressure gauge, if so equipped.

9. Remove the screws that secure the twin window clusters to the back of the instrument panel and remove the clusters.

10. Install by reversing the procedure.

1970–72

1. Disconnect the battery ground cable.

2. Lower the steering column.

3. Disconnect the parking brake hand release.

4. Disconnect the speedometer cable.

5. Remove the instrument panel pad.

6. Disconnect the radio speaker bracket from the instrument panel. Disconnect the speaker wire from the radio.

7. Disconnect the air conditioning center outlet and the control head.

8. Remove the radio knobs, washers, bezels, and wiring.

9. Unbolt the radio braces. Roll the radio out from under the instrument panel.

10. Remove the six instrument panel bolts and roll out the instrument panel with the help of an assistant.

11. Reverse the procedure for installation.

Instrument cluster—1970–72

1973 and Later

1. Disconnect the battery ground cable.

2. Remove the radio knobs and the clock set stem if so equipped.

3. Remove the instrument bezel retaining screws.

4. Pull the bezel out to disconnect the tail-

gate release or rear defogger switch if so equipped.

5. Remove the instrument bezel.

6. Remove the retaining screws and remove the speedometer head.

7. Remove the retaining screws and remove the fuel gauge and tachometer if so equipped.

8. Remove the clock if so equipped.

9. Disconnect the transmission shift indicator cable from the steering column.

10. Disconnect the wiring and speedometer cable.

11. Remove the instrument cluster case.

12. To install, reverse the removal procedure.

Speedo cable attachment at instrument cluster

Instrument cluster—1973–75

Speedometer cable-to-drive attachment, typical

Instrument cluster—1980–81

Speedometer Cable Replacement

NOTE: *Although not necessary, removing the instrument cluster will give better access to the speedometer cable.*

1. Reach behind the instrument cluster and push the speedometer cable casing toward the speedometer while depressing the retaining spring on the back of the instrument cluster case. Once the retaining spring has released,

hold it in while pulling outward on the casing to disconnect the casing from the speedometer.

2. Remove the cable casing sealing plug from the dash panel. Then, pull the casing down from behind the dash and remove the cable.

3. If the cable is broken and cannot be entirely removed from the top, support the car securely, and then unscrew the cable casing connector at the transmission. Pull the bottom part of the cable out, and then screw the connector back onto the transmission.

4. Lubricate the new cable with a speedometer cable grease. Insert it into the casing until it bottoms. Push inward while rotating it until the square portion at the bottom engages with the coupling in the transmission, permitting the cable to move in another inch or so. Then, reconnect the cable casing to the speedometer and install the sealing plug into the dash panel.

Ignition Switch

NOTE: *All models made in 1969 and later are equipped with ignition switches which are mounted in the steering column. Removal and*

1983 Malibu instrument panel, exploded view

installation procedures for these models can be found in Chapter 8.

REMOVAL AND INSTALLATION

1964–68

1. Disconnect the batter ground cable. Put the ignition switch in the Accessory (ACC) position.

NOTE: *Although not necessary, you may wish to remove the ashtray and radio at this point.*

2. Insert a wire into the small hole in the face of the lock cylinder. Push in on the wire to depress the plunger. Continue turning the key until the cylinder can be removed from the switch.

3. Remove the switch bezel nut, and then pull the switch out from under the dash.

4. Go in from the front of the switch with a screwdriver and unsnap the theft resistant locking tangs on the connector and then unplug the connector.

5. Installation is in the reverse order of removal.

SEAT BELT SYSTEM

Warning Buzzer and Light—1972–73

Beginning January 1, 1972, all cars are required to have a warning system which operates a buzzer and a warning light if either the driver's or the right-hand front passenger's seat belts are not fastened when the seats are occupied and the car is in forward motion.

On Chevrolet products, this system consists of seat belt retractor switches, pressure sensitive front seat switches, a parking brake switch (manual transmission), or a transmission switch (automatic transmission), a warning light, and a buzzer.

The seat belt warning system is wired through the 20 amp "Gauges" fuse.

The warning light is located in the instrument cluster; and the buzzer, which is shared with the ignition key warning system, is taped to the instrument cluster wiring harness.

The warning system is activated when the ignition switch is ON, the front seats are occupied, and the seat belts are left in their retractors. Only when the front seat belts are extended and properly fastened will the warning light and buzzer stop.

Seat Belt/Starter Interlock— 1974–75

As required by law, all 1974 and some 1975 Chevrolet passenger cars cannot be started until the front seat occupants are seated and have fastened their seat belts. If the proper sequence is not followed, the engine cannot be started.

If, after the car is started, the seat belts are unfastened, a warning buzzer and light will be activated in a similar manner to that described above for 1972–73 models.

The shoulder harness and lap belt are permanently fastened together, so that they both must be worn. The shoulder harness uses an inertia-lock reel to allow freedom of movement under normal driving conditions.

NOTE: *This type of reel locks up when the car decelerates rapidly, as during a crash.*

The lap belts use the same rachet-type retractors that the 1972–73 models use.

The switches for the interlock system have been removed from the lap belt retractors and placed in the belt buckles. The seat sensors remain the same as those used in 1972–73.

For ease of service, the car may be started from outside, by reaching in and turning the key, but without depressing the seat sensors.

In case of system failure, an over-ride switch is located under the hood. This is a "one start" switch and it must be reset each time it is used.

DISABLING THE INTERLOCK SYSTEM

Since the requirement for the interlock system was dropped during the 1975 model year, those systems installed on cars built earlier may now be legally disabled. The seat belt warning light is still required.

1. Disconnect the negative battery cable.
2. Locate the interlock harness connector under the left side of the instrument panel on or near the fuse block. It has orange, yellow, and green leads.
3. Cut and tape the ends of the green wire on the body side of the connector.
4. Remove the buzzer from the fuse block or connector.

LIGHTING

Headlights
REMOVAL AND INSTALLATION

1. Unscrew the four retaining screws and remove the headlight bezel.

Headlight bezel and headlamp removal, 1983 Malibu shown

2. Remove the headlight bulb retaining screws. These are the screws which hold the retaining ring for the bulb to the front of the car. Do not touch the two headlight aiming screws, at the top and the side of the retaining ring (these screws will have different heads), or the headlight aim will have to be re-adjusted.
3. Pull the bulb and ring forward and then separate them. Unplug the electrical connector from the rear of the bulb.
4. Plug the new bulb into the electrical connector. Install the bulb into the retaining ring and then install the ring and the bulb. Install the headlight bezel.

HEADLIGHT AIMING

The headlights must be properly aimed to provide the best, safest road illumination. The lights should be checked for proper aim, and adjusted if necessary, after installing a new sealed beam unit or if the front end sheet metal has been replaced. Certain state and local authorities have requirements for headlight aiming; these should be checked before adjustment is made.

Headlight adjustment screw locations. Round headlights similar

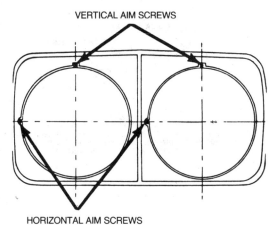

VERTICAL AIM SCREWS

HORIZONTAL AIM SCREWS

Dual headlight adjustment screw location

NOTE: *The car's fuel tank should be about half full when adjusting the headlights. Tires should be properly inflated, and if a heavy load is carried in the trunk or in the cargo area of station wagons, it should remain there.*

Horizontal and vertical aiming of each sealed beam unit is provided by two adjusting screws, which move the mounting ring in the body against the body of the coil spring. There is no adjustment for focus; this is done during headlight manufacturing.

Headlight Switch
REMOVAL AND INSTALLATION

1. Disconnect the battery ground cable.
2. Remove the instrument panel bezel, secured on most model years with six screws (varies among models and years).
3. Pull the headlight control knob to "ON".
4. Remove the screws (usually three) attaching the windshield wiper switch/light switch mounting plate to the instrument cluster and pull the assembly rearward.
4. Depress the shaft retainer on the switch and pull the knob and shaft assembly out.
5. Remove the ferrule nut and switch assembly from the mounting plate.
6. Install the new lighting switch in the reverse order of removal. Connect the battery.

FUSE PANEL

INSTRUMENT PANEL ASM

VIEW A   VIEW B

Headlight switch mounting, typical

CIRCUIT PROTECTION
Fusible Links

A fusible link is a protective device used in an electrical circuit. When the current increases beyond a certain amperage, the fusible metal of the wire link will melt, thus breaking the electrical circuit and preventing further damage to any other components or wiring. Whenever a fusible link is melted because of a short circuit, correct the cause before installing a new one. Most models have four fusible links.

REPLACING FUSIBLE LINKS

1. Disconnect both battery cables. If the link is connected to the junction block or starter solenoid, disconnect it.
2. Cut the wiring harness right behind the link connector(s) and remove.
3. Strip the insulation off the harness wire back ½".
4. Position a clip around the new link and wiring harness or new connector and crimp it securely. Then, solder the connection, using rosin core solder and sufficient heat to guarantee a good connection. Repeat for the remaining connection.
5. Tape all exposed wiring with electrical tape. Where necessary, connect the link to the junction block or starter solenoid. Reconnect battery.

CONNECTOR

FUSIBLE LINK

THOROUGHLY TAPE ALL EXPOSED WIRES

CONNECTOR CRIMPED AND SOLDERED

New fusible links are spliced to the wire

Circuit Breakers

A circuit breaker in the light switch protects the headlight circuit. A separate 30 amp breaker mounted on the firewall protects the power window, seat, and power top circuits. Circuit breakers open and close rapidly to protect the circuit if current is excessive.

Fuses and Flashers

The fusebox is located under the instrument panel on the left side. The turn signal flasher is under the dash to the right of the steering column. The hazard flasher is under the dash, to the left of the steering column. On all 1980 and later models, both the turn signal flasher and the hazard flasher are located at the lower left hand and the upper right hand corners of the

FIGURE 1 labels: SOLENOID STUD, BATTERY CABLE, CUT AS CLOSE AS POSSIBLY, CUT AS CLOSE AS POSSIBLE, ENGINE HARNESS

FIGURE 1
REMOVE BATTERY CABLE & FUSIBLE LINK FROM STARTER SOLENOID AND CUT OFF DEFECTIVE WIRE AS SHOWN TWO PLACES.

FIGURE 2 labels: FUSIBLE LINK (16 GA. BLACK), HEAT SHRINK TUBE, CRIMP SPLICE

FIGURE 2
STRIP INSULATION FROM WIRE ENDS. PLACE HEAT SHRINK TUBE OVER REPLACEMENT LINK. INSERT WIRE ENDS INTO CRIMP SPLICE AS SHOWN. NOTE: PUSH WIRES IN FAR ENOUGH TO ENGAGE WIRE ENDS.

FIGURE 3 label: CRIMP

FIGURE 3
CRIMP SPLICE WITH CRIMPING TOOL TWO PLACES TO BIND BOTH WIRES.

FIGURE 4 labels: 17 N·m (12.5 lb. ft.), HEAT SHRINK TUBE

FIGURE 4
SLIDE TUBE OVER SPLICE WITH SPLICE CENTERED IN TUBE. APPLY LOW TEMPERATURE HEAT TO SHRINK TUBE AROUND WIRES & SPLICE. REASSEMBLE LINKS & BATTERY CABLE.

Fusible link repair

Fuse box—1971–79 (amperage figures may differ with individual models)

Fuse box—1981 and later

fuse block respectively. There is an inline fuse for the underhood/spotlamp circuit. The fusebox is marked to indicate fuse size and the circuit(s) protected on 1971 and later cars. 1978 and later models use the "mini-fuses" shown in the illustration.

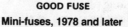

GOOD FUSE   BLOWN FUSE

Mini-fuses, 1978 and later

Fuse Color-Coding

Fuse (Amps)	Color Stripe
3	Violet
5	Tan
7.5	Brown
10	Red
20	Clear
25	White

WIRING DIAGRAMS

Wiring diagrams have been left out of this book. As cars have become more complex, and available with longer and longer option lists, wiring diagrams have grown in size and complexity also. It has become virtually impossible to provide a readable reproduction in a reasonable number of pages. Information on ordering wiring diagrams from the vehicle manufacturer can be found in the owners manual.

Clutch and Transmission

6

MANUAL TRANSMISSION

Understanding the Manual Transmission and Clutch

Because of the way the gasoline engine breathes, it can produce torque, or twisting force, only within a narrow speed range. Most modern engines must turn at about 2,500 rpm to produce their peak torque. By 4,500 rpm they are producing so little torque that continued increases in engine speed produce no power increases.

The transmission and clutch are employed to vary the relationship between engine speed and the speed of the wheels so that adequate engine power can be produced under all circumstances. The clutch allows engine torque to be applied to the transmission input shaft gradually, due to mechanical slippage. The car can, consequently, be started smoothly from a full stop.

The transmission changes the ratio between the rotating speeds of the engine and the wheels by the use of gears. Three-speed or four-speed transmissions are most common. The lower gears allow full engine power to be applied to the rear wheels during acceleration at low speeds.

The clutch driven plate is a thin disc, the center of which is splined to the transmission input shaft. Both sides of the disc are covered with a layer of material which is similar to brake lining and which is capable of allowing slippage without roughness or excessive noise.

The clutch cover is bolted to the engine flywheel and incorporates a diaphragm spring which provides the pressure to engage the clutch. The cover also houses the pressure plate. The driven disc is sandwiched between the pressure plate and the smooth surface of the flywheel when the clutch pedal is released, thus forcing it to turn at the same speed as the engine crankshaft.

The transmission contains a mainshaft which passes all the way through the transmission, from the clutch to the driveshaft. This shaft is separated at one point, so that front and rear portions can turn at different speeds.

Power is transmitted by a countershaft in the lower gears and reverse. The gears of the countershaft mesh with gears on the mainshaft, allowing power to be carried from one to the other. All the countershaft gears are integral with that shaft, while several of the mainshaft gears can either rotate independently of the shaft or be locked to it. Shifting from one gear to the next causes one of the gears to be freed from rotating with the shaft, and locks another to it. Gears are locked and unlocked by internal dog clutches which slide between the center of the gear and the shaft. The forward gears usually employ synchronizers: friction members which smoothly bring gear and shaft to the same speed before the toothed dog clutches are engaged.

The clutch is operating properly if:

1. It will stall the engine when released with the vehicle held stationary.

2. The shift lever can be moved freely between first and reverse gears when the vehicle is stationary and the clutch disengaged.

A clutch pedal free-play adjustment is incorporated in the linkage. If there is about 1–2 in. of motion before the pedal begins to release the clutch, it is adjusted properly. Inadequate free-play wears all parts of the clutch releasing mechanisms and may cause slippage. Excessive free-play may cause inadequate release and hard shifting of gears.

Some clutches use a hydraulic system in place of mechanical linkage. If the clutch fails to release, fill the clutch master cylinder with fluid to the proper level and pump the clutch pedal to fill the system with fluid. Bleed the system in the same way as a brake system. If leaks are located, tighten loose connections or overhaul the master or slave cylinder as necessary.

Identification

See Chapter 1, which lists the basic types of manual transmissions and the various locations of their serial numbers. By finding the serial number on your transmission and comparing its location with the information there, you can readily determine the type of gearbox used.

Linkage Adjustment

COLUMN SHIFT

1964–66

1. Position both transmission levers in Neutral.

2. Position the column selector in Neutral. Align the First/Reverse and Second/Third shifter tube levers on the steering jacket.

3. Install the control rods on the steering jacket levers and secure them with lock clips.

4. Install a swivel on the First/Reverse shifter control rod, and adjust until the swivel can freely enter the transmission shift lever hole (rear). Install a retaining clip on the swivel, and insert the swivel in the lever hole and secure with a nut.

5. Install the Second/Third lower rod to the frame mounted idler lever and in the Second/Third transmission lever and secure with retaining clips.

6. Install the upper Second/Third shifter control rod, in the same manner as the First/Reverse shifter control rod (Step 4), to the frame idler and the jacket shifter lever.

CAUTION: *Ensure that the shifter tube levers stay in alignment.*

7. Check the adjustment by moving the shift lever through all the gear positions.

1967–68

1. Located on the left side of the transmission case are two levers. Manipulate these levers until the transmission is in neutral. Depress the clutch pedal, start the engine, and release the pedal slowly. If the car fails to move and engine is still running with the pedal fully released, the transmission is in neutral. If the car moves, the transmission is in gear and the levers should be repositioned until neutral is found. Loosen the swivel nuts on both shift rods.

2. Move the shift lever (on the column) to the neutral position. Raise the hood and locate the shifter tube levers on the steering column. Align the first and reverse lever with the second and third lever. Using a pin (use a large L-shaped Allen wrench), hold these levers in alignment (most cars have alignment holes in the levers and an alignment plate) until the linkage is connected.

3. Make the final adjustments to align the

Shift linkage (column) adjustment for 1967–69 cars (© Chevrolet Motor Division)

shift rods and levers at the transmission into the neutral position. Road-test the car and check the shifting operation. If the adjustment is correct, the alignment pin should pass freely through all alignment holes. If not, readjustment is necessary.

1969

1. Turn the ignition switch to the "off" position.

2. Loosen the swivel nuts on both shift rods.

3. Place the column-mounted shift lever in the reverse position. There are two levers located on the side of the transmission case. The lever to the front of the transmission controls second and third gears while the other lever controls first and reverse. Place this first and reverse lever into the reverse position. Push up on the first/reverse shift rod until the column lever is in the reverse detent position. Tighten the swivel nut.

4. Place the column lever and the transmission levers (located on the side of the case) in neutral (to determine neutral, see Step One for 1967–68 cars). The shift tube levers are located on the steering column mast jacket. Make sure the column lever is in neutral and hold it in this position by inserting a pin through the alignment holes in the shift tube levers (a $^{3}\!/_{16}$ in. Allen wrench is perfect).

5. Hold the second/third shift rod steady (to prevent a change in adjustment) and tighten the swivel locknut.

6. Remove the alignment pin from the shift tube levers and shift the column shift lever to the reverse position. Turn the ignition key to "lock" and check the ignition interlock control. If it binds, leave the control in "lock" and readjust the first/reverse rod at the swivel.

7. Move the column lever through the gear positions and return it to neutral. The alignment pin should pass freely through the align-

ment holes of the shift tube levers. If it doesn't, loosen the swivel nuts and readjust.

1970–72

1. Place the shift lever (on the column) in reverse and the ignition switch in "off."
2. Raise the car and support it with floor stands.
3. Loosen the locknuts on the shift rod swivels. Pull down slightly on the first/reverse control rod on the lower steering column to remove any slack. Tighten the locknut at the transmission lever.
4. Unlock the ignition switch and shift the column lever into neutral. Position the shift tube levers (located on the lower steering column) in neutral by aligning the lever alignment holes. Hold them in this position by inserting a 3/16 in. Allen wrench through the alignment holes.
5. Hold the second/third shift rod steady and tighten the rod locknut.
6. Remove the alignment tool from the shift tube levers and check the shifting operation.
7. Place the column lever in reverse and check the movement of the ignition key. In reverse and only reverse, the key must turn freely in and out of "lock."

FLOOR SHIFT

Three Speed—1968–72

1. Loosen the locknuts on both shift rod swivels. The shift rods should pass freely through the swivels.
2. Move the floor shift to Neutral and install the locating gauge into the shifter bracket assembly.
NOTE: *The locating gauge is a piece of 1/8 in. thick flat stock 41/64 in. wide and 3 in. long.*
3. Position the levers on the transmission in Neutral. Turn the First/Reverse shift rod nut down against the swivel, and then tighten the locknut against the swivel.

3-speed floor shift linkage (backdrive shown is on 1969–72 models)

4. Turn the Second/Third shift rod nut down against the swivel, and then tighten the locknut against the swivel.
NOTE: *On 1969 and later cars, skip Step 4 and perform Steps 5–8. Step 4 is the final step for 1968 cars.*
5. Remove the locating gauge, and shift into Reverse. Turn the ignition switch to the Lock position.
6. Loosen the swivel locknut on the backdrive control rod. Pull down slightly on the control rod to take up any slack in the column mechanism, and then tighten the clevis jam nut.
7. The ignition switch should move easily in and out of lock. If there is any binding present, keep the switch in Lock and readjust the backdrive control rod.
8. Check the shift pattern for correct operation.

Four-Speed—1964–68

1. Remove the control rods from the transmission levers, and position the levers in Neutral.
2. Move the floor shift lever into Neutral and insert a locating gauge into the bracket assembly (use a 5/16 in. rod on 1964 cars, 1965–74 four-speeds use the same gauge as the three-speed floor shift).
3. Adjust the length of the control rods, and then secure the swivels with the jam nuts and install the clevis pins.
4. Remove the locating gauge, and check the shift pattern.
NOTE: *1965 and later Muncie transmission levers have two control rod holes. Attaching the control rods in the lower holes will result in reduced shift lever travel and allow faster shifting, with increased shifting effort as a minor drawback.*

Muncie 4-speed linkage

Four-Speed—1969 and Later

1. Turn the ignition switch to the Off position, except on 1970 models which should be turned to Lock.

BACK DRIVE LINKAGE

STABILIZER ROD

SAGINAW TRANSMISSION LINKAGE

3RD-4TH
1ST-2ND
REVERSE

MUNCIE TRANSMISSION

Saginaw 4-speed linkage

2. Loosen the swivel lock nuts on the shift rods and backdrive control rod. Position the transmission side cover levers to their Neutral detent positions.

3. Place the floor shift in Neutral and insert a locating gauge (same gauge as three-speed floor shift) into the lever bracket assembly.

4. Adjust all control rods swivels for easy entry into their respective levers.

5. Tighten the shift rod locknuts and remove the gauge.

6. Shift the lever into Reverse and pull down slightly on the backdrive rod to remove the slack. Tighten the locknut.

7. The ignition switch should now be able to be moved easily into Lock, and it must not be possible to turn the key to Lock, when in any other position other than Reverse. Readjust the backdrive rod, if necessary.

8. Check the shift pattern for correctness.

CLUTCH SWITCH ADJUSTMENT AND REPLACEMENT

A clutch-operated neutral safety switch was used beginning in 1970. The ignition switch must be in the "start" position and the clutch must be fully depressed before the car will start. The switch mounts to the clutch pedal arm. Removal of this switch is obvious and simple. This switch cannot be adjusted.

REMOVAL AND INSTALLATION

3 Speed and 4 Speed—1967–69

REMOVAL

1. Raise the car and remove the driveshaft. On floor-shift models, remove the trim plate and shifter boot.

2. On 1968–69 models, it may be necessary to disconnect the exhaust pipe at the manifold.

3. Disconnect the speedometer cable and, on floor-shift models, disconnect the back-up light switch.

4. Remove the crossmember-to-frame bolts. On floor-shift models, remove the bolts holding the control lever support to the crossmember.

5. Remove the transmission mount bolts.

6. Using a suitable jack and a block of wood (to be placed between the jack and the engine), raise the engine slightly and remove or relocate the crossmember.

7. Remove the shift levers from the transmission side cover.

8. On floor-shift models, remove the stabilizer rod (if so equipped) situated between the shift lever assembly and the transmission.

9. Remove the transmission-to-bellhousing bolts. Remove the top bolts first and insert guide pins into the holes, then remove the bottom bolts.

10. Remove the transmission.

INSTALLATION

1. Lift the transmission into position and insert the mainshaft into the bellhousing.

2. Install the transmission-to-bellhousing bolts and lockwashers, and torque them to 50 ft. lbs.

3. Install the transmission shift levers to the side cover. On floor-shift models, install the stabilizer rod (if so equipped).

4. Raise the engine slightly, position the crossmember, and install the bolts.

5. Install the transmission mount bolts. On floor-shift models, install the bolts holding the shift lever support to the crossmember.

CAUTION: *Lubricate the tailshaft bushing before the driveshafts are installed.*

6. Install the driveshaft and, if removed, install the exhaust pipe to manifold.

7. Connect the speedometer cable and, on floor-shift cars, connect the backup light.

8. Fill the transmission with lubricant.

3 Speed and 4 Speed—1970 and Later

REMOVAL

1. On floor-shift models, remove the shift knob and console trim plate.

2. Raise the car and support it with floor stands.

3. Disconnect the speedometer cable and the TCS switch wiring.

4. Remove the driveshaft.

5. Remove the bolts securing the transmission mounts to the crossmember and also those bolts securing the crossmember to the frame. Remove the crossmember.

Typical transmission mounting

6. Remove the shift levers from the side of the transmission.

7. Disconnect the back drive rod from the bellcrank.

8. Remove the bolts from the shift control assembly and carefully lower the assembly until the shift lever clears the rubber shift boot. Remove the assembly from the car.

9. Remove the transmission-to-bellhousing bolts and lift the transmission from the car.

INSTALLATION

1. Lift the transmission and insert the mainshaft into the bellhousing.

2. Install and torque the transmission-to-clutch housing bolts and lockwashers.

3. Install the shift lever.

4. Install the shift levers to the transmission side cover.

5. Connect the back drive rod to the bell-crank.

6. Raise the engine high enough to position the crossmember. Install and tighten the cross-member-to-frame bolts and transmission mounts to crossmember bolts.

7. Install the driveshaft.

8. Connect the speedometer cable and TCS wiring.

9. Fill the transmission with the specified lubricant. If applicable, install the console trim plate and shift knob. Adjust the linkage.

CLUTCH

Understanding the Clutch

The purpose of the clutch is to disconnect and connect engine power from the transmission. A car at rest requires a lot of engine torque to get all that weight moving. An internal-combustion engine does not develop a high starting torque (unlike steam engines), so it must be allowed to operate without any load until it builds up enough torque to move the car. Torque increases with engine rpm. The clutch allows the engine to build up torque by physically disconnecting the engine from the transmission, relieving the engine of any load or resistance. The transfer of engine power to the transmission (the load) must be smooth and gradual; if it weren't, drive line components would wear out or break quickly. This gradual power transfer is made possible by gradually releasing the clutch pedal. The clutch disc and pressure plate are the connecting link between the engine and transmission. When the clutch pedal is released, the disc and plate contact each other (clutch engagement), physically joining the engine and transmission. When the pedal is pushed in, the disc and plate separate (the clutch is disengaged), disconnecting the engine from the transmission.

The clutch assembly consists of the flywheel, the clutch disc, the clutch pressure plate, the throwout bearing and fork, the actuating linkage and the pedal. The flywheel and clutch pressure plate (driving members) are connected to the engine crankshaft and rotate with it. The clutch disc is located between the flywheel and pressure plate, and splined to the transmission shaft. A driving member is one that is attached to the engine and transfers engine power to a driven member (clutch disc) on the transmission shaft. A driving member (pressure plate) rotates (drives) a driven member (clutch disc) on contact and, in so doing, turns the transmission shaft. There is a circular diaphragm spring within the pressure plate cover (transmission side). In a relaxed state (when the clutch pedal is fully released), this spring is convex; that is, it is dished outward toward the transmission. Pushing in the clutch pedal actuates an attached linkage rod. Connected to the other end of this rod is the throwout bearing fork. The throwout bearing is attached to the fork. When the clutch pedal is depressed, the clutch linkage pushes the fork and bearing forward to contact the diaphragm spring of the pressure plate. The outer edges of the spring are secured to the pressure plate and are pivoted on rings so that when the center of the spring is compressed by the throwout bearing, the outer edges bow outward and, by so doing, pull the pressure plate in the same direction—away from the clutch disc. This action separates the disc from the plate, disengaging the clutch and allowing the transmission to be shifted into another gear. A coil type clutch return spring attached to the clutch pedal arm permits full release of the pedal. Releasing the pedal pulls the throwout bearing away from the diaphragm spring resulting in a reversal of spring position. As bearing pressure is gradually released from the spring center, the outer edges of the spring bow outward, pushing the pres-

Clutch and flywheel assembly (exploded view) (© Chevrolet Motor Division)

FLYWHEEL

DRIVEN PLATE ASSY.

PRESSURE PLATE
AND COVER ASSY.

THROWOUT BRG.

CLUTCH HOUSING
COVER

CLUTCH FORK

CLUTCH HOUSING

CLUTCH FORK
BALL STUD

Operation of diaphragm spring clutch (© Chevrolet Motor Division)

DIAPHRAGM
SPRING

PIVOT RINGS

DRIVING PLATE

DIAPHRAGM
SPRING

RELEASE
BEARING

DRIVEN PLATE

PIVOT RING
RETAINING BOLT

RETRACTING
SPRING

ENGAGED

DISENGAGED

sure plate into closer contact with the clutch disc. As the disc and plate move closer together, friction between the two increases and slippage is reduced until, when full spring pressure is applied (by fully releasing the pedal), the speed of the disc and plate are the same. This stops all slipping, creating a direct connection between the plate and disc which results in the transfer of power from the engine to the transmission. The clutch disc is now rotating with the pressure plate at engine speed and, because it is splined to the transmission shaft, the shaft now turns at the same engine speed. Understanding clutch operation can be rather difficult at first; if you're still confused after reading this, consider the following analogy. The action of the diaphragm spring can be compared to that of an oil can bottom. The bottom of an oil can is shaped very much like the clutch diaphragm spring and pushing in on the can bottom and then releasing it produces a similar effect. As mentioned earlier, the clutch pedal return spring permits full release of the pedal and reduces linkage slack due to wear. As the linkage wears, clutch free-pedal travel will increase and free-travel will decrease as the clutch wears. Free-travel is actually throwout bearing lash.

The diaphragm spring type clutches used are available in two different designs: flat diaphragm springs or bent springs. The bent fingers are bent back to create a centrifugal boost ensuring quick reengagement at higher engine speeds. This design enables pressure plate load to increase as the clutch disc wears and makes low pedal effort possible even with a heavy-duty clutch. The throwout bearing used with the bent finger design is 1¼ in. long and is shorter than the bearing used with the flat finger design. These bearings are not interchangeable. If the longer bearing is used with the bent finger clutch, free-pedal travel will not exist. This results in clutch slippage and rapid wear.

The transmission varies the gear ratio between the engine and rear wheels. It can be shifted to change engine speed as driving conditions and loads change. The transmission allows disengaging and reversing power from the engine to the wheels.

CLUTCH CROSS-SHAFT LUBRICATION

Once every 36,000 miles or sooner if necessary, remove the plug, install a fitting and lubricate with a water-resistant EP (Extreme Pressure) chassis lubricant.

LINKAGE INSPECTION

A clutch may have all the symptoms of going bad when the real trouble lies in the linkage.

To avoid the unnecessary replacement of a clutch, make the following linkage checks:

a. Start the engine and depress the clutch pedal until it is about ½ in. from the floor mat and move the shift lever between first and reverse (first and second on a four-speed) several times. If this can be done smoothly without any grinding, the clutch is releasing fully. If the shifting is not smooth, the clutch is not releasing fully and adjustment is necessary.

b. Check the condition of the clutch pedal bushings for signs of sticking or excessive wear.

c. Check the throwout bearing fork for proper installation on the ball stud. The fork could possibly be pulled off the ball if not properly lubricated.

d. Check the cross-shaft levers for distortion or damage.

e. Check the car for loose or damaged motor mounts. Bad motor mounts can cause the engine to shift under acceleration and bind the clutch linkage at the cross-shaft. There must be some clearance between the cross-shaft and motor mount.

f. Check the throwout bearing clearance between the clutch spring fingers and the front bearing retainer on the transmission. If there is no clearance, the fork may be improperly installed on the ball stud or the clutch disc may be worn out.

FREE-PLAY ADJUSTMENT

This adjustment must be made under the vehicle on the clutch operating linkage. Free play is measured at the clutch pedal.

Clutch pedal free-play adjustment—1964–67

1964–67

This adjustment is made from under the car. Free-play is measured at the clutch pedal.

1. Disconnect the spring between the cross-shaft lever and the clutch fork.

2. Loosen the pushrod locknut approximately three turns.

3. If no free travel is present, adjust the pushrod until it is free of the clutch fork.

4. While holding the clutch fork to the rear, adjust the rod until it just touches the fork seat.

5. Turn the locknut until 3/16 in. clearance exists between the nut and the sleeve.

6. Turn the rod until the nut just contacts the sleeve, and hold the rod with a wrench and tighten the nut.

7. Free pedal clearance should be 3/4–1 1/8 in. (1964–65) or 1–1 1/2 in. (1966–67).

1968–70

1. Disconnect the return spring at the clutch operating fork.

2. Use the linkage to push the clutch pedal up against its rubber bumper stop.

3. Loosen the operating rod locknut and lengthen the adjustment rod until it pushes the fork back enough that the release bearing can just be felt to contact the pressure plate fingers.

4. Shorten the rod three turns and tighten the locknut.

5. Replace the spring and check the free play at the pedal pad. It should be about 1 in. or more.

1971 and Later

You can also use this procedure on any earlier models that have a gauge hole in the clutch pivot shaft arm.

1. Disconnect the return spring at the clutch operating fork.

2. Use the linkage to push the clutch pedal up against its rubber bumper stop. On the 1973 Chevelle, more clearance can be obtained by loosening the rubber bumper bracket and moving the bracket.

3. Push the end of the clutch operating fork to the rear until the release bearing can just be felt to contact the pressure plate fingers.

4. Detach the front end of the operating rod from the clutch pivot shaft arm and place it in the gauge hole on the arm.

5. Loosen the locknut and lengthen the rod just enough to take all the play out of the linkage. Tighten the locknut.

6. Replace the operating rod in its original location.

7. Replace the return spring and check the free play at the pedal pad. It should be about 1 in. or more.

REMOVAL

1. Support the engine and remove the transmission.

2. Disconnect the clutch fork push rod and spring.

3. Remove the flywheel housing.

4. Slide the clutch fork from the ball stud and remove the fork from the dust boot. The ball stud is threaded into the clutch housing and may be replaced, if necessary.

5. Install an alignment tool to support the clutch assembly during removal. Mark the flywheel and clutch cover for reinstallation, if they do not already have "X" marks.

6. Loosen the clutch-to-flywheel attaching bolts evenly, one turn at a time, until spring pressure is released. Remove the bolts and clutch assembly.

Clutch release bearing lubrication—flat finger type (top), bent finger type (bottom)

INSTALLATION

1. Clean the pressure plate and flywheel face.

2. Support the clutch disc and pressure plate with an alignment tool. The driven disc is in-

Clutch pedal free-play adjustment—1968–72

stalled with the damper springs on the transmission side. On some 1964–67 6-cylinder engines, the clutch disc is installed in a reverse manner with the damper springs to the flywheel side.

3. Turn the clutch assembly until the mark on the cover lines up with the mark on the flywheel, then install the bolts. Tighten down evenly and gradually to avoid distortion.

4. Remove the alignment tool.

5. Lubricate the ball socket and fork fingers at the release bearing end with high melting-point grease. Lubricate the recess on the inside of the throwout bearing and throwout fork groove with a light coat of graphite grease.

6. Install the clutch fork and dust boot into the housing. Install the throwout bearing to the throwout fork. Install the flywheel housing. Install the transmission.

7. Connect the fork push rod and spring. Lubricate the spring and pushrod ends.

8. Adjust the shift linkage and clutch pedal free-play.

AUTOMATIC TRANSMISSION

Identification

The four types of pan gaskets used on the automatic transmissions used in your car are pictured below for ready identification.

GM Powerglide

GM Turbo Hydra-Matic 200

GM Turbo Hydra-Matic 250, 350, 375B

GM Turbo Hydra-Matic 400

Pan Removal and Installation, Fluid and Filter Change

The fluid should be changed with the transmission warm. A 20 minute drive at highway speeds should accomplish this.

1. Raise and support the vehicle, preferably in a level attitude.

2. With the Turbo Hydra-Matic 250 or 350, support the transmission and remove the support crossmember.

3. Place a large pan under the transmission pan. Remove all the front and side pan bolts. Loosen the rear bolts about four turns.

4. Pry the pan loose and let it drain.

5. Remove the pan and gasket. Clean the pan thoroughly with solvent and air dry it. Be very careful not to get any lint from rags in the pan.

6. Remove the strainer to valve body screws, the strainer, and the gasket. Most 350 transmissions will have a throw-away filter instead of a strainer. On the 400 transmission, remove the filter retaining bolt, filter, and intake pipe O-ring.

7. If there is a strainer, clean it in solvent and air dry.

8. Install the new filter or cleaned strainer with a new gasket. Tighten the screws to 12 ft. lbs. On the 400, install a new intake pipe O-ring and a new filter, tightening the retaining bolt to 10 ft. lbs.

9. Install the pan with a new gasket. Tighten the bolts evenly to 12 ft. lbs. (8 for Powerglide and Torque Drive).

PUMP FILTER TO VALVE BODY   GASKET

Removing the filter on the Turbo 350

FILTER ASSEMBLY

INTAKE PIPE

O-RING SEAL   LOCATOR TABS

Removing the filter, intake pipe and O-ring on the 400

10. Lower the car and add the proper amount of DEXRON® or DEXRON® II automatic transmission fluid through the dipstick tube.

11. Start the engine in Park and let it idle. Do not race the engine. Shift into each shift lever position, shift back into Park, and check the fluid level on the dipstick. The level should be ¼ in. below ADD. Be very careful not to overfill. Recheck the level after the car has been driven long enough to thoroughly warm up the transmission. Add fluid as necessary. The level should then be at FULL.

SHIFT LINKAGE ADJUSTMENT

Powerglide Column Shift

1. The shift tube and lever assembly must be free in the mast jacket.

2. Lift the selector lever toward the steering wheel and allow the selector lever to be positioned in Drive by the transmission detent.

3. Release the selector lever. The lever should be prevented from engaging low, unless the lever is lifted.

4. Lift the selector lever toward the steering wheel and allow the lever to be positioned in Neutral by the transmission detent.

5. Release the selector lever. The selector lever should now be kept from engaging Reverse unless the lever is lifted. If the linkage is adjusted correctly, the selector lever should be prevented from moving beyond both the neutral detent and the Drive detent unless the lever is lifted to pass over the mechanical stop in the steering column.

ROD   CLAMP   TRANS LEVER

SPRING WASHER

SCREW

CROSS SHAFT

Column shift linkage adjustment—Powerglide

If adjustment is necessary, perform the following steps:

6. Adjust the linkage by loosening the adjustment clamp at the cross-shaft. Place the transmission lever in Drive by rotating the lever counterclockwise to the Low detent, and then clockwise one detent to Drive.

7. Place the selector lever in Drive and remove any free-play by holding the cross-shaft up and pulling the shift rod downward.

8. Tighten the clamp and check the adjustment.

On 1969–73 cars, carry out the following additional steps:

9. Place the shift lever in Park and the ignition switch in lock. Loosen the back-drive rod clamp nut. Remove any lash in the column and tighten the clamp nut.

10. When the selector lever is in Park, the ignition key should move freely into lock. Lock position should be obtainable only when the transmission is in Park.

Floor shift linkage adjustment—1964–67 Powerglide

Powerglide Floor Shift—1964–67

1. Loosen the adjustment nuts at the swivel. Place the transmission lever in the Drive position by moving it counterclockwise to the Low detent, and then clockwise one detent position to Drive.

Column shift linkage adjustment—1970 and later Powerglide

2. Place the floorshift lever in Drive. Hold the floorshift unit lower operating lever forward against the shift lever detent.

3. Place a 7/64 in. (0.11) spacer between the rear nut and the swivel. Tighten the rear nut against the spacer.

4. Remove the spacer and tighten the front nut against the swivel, locking the swivel between the nuts.

Powerglide Floor Shift—1968–73

1968 and later cars use a cable-type shift linkage.

1. Place the shift lever in Drive.

2. Disconnect the cable from the transmission lever. Place the transmission lever in Drive by rotating the lever counterclockwise to the Low detent, and then clockwise one detent to Drive.

3. Measure the distance from the rearward face of the attaching bracket to the center of the cable attaching pin. If this distance is not 5.5 in., loosen and move the cable end stud nut to obtain the correct measurement.

NOTE: *1969 and later models require an additional backdrive adjustment.*

4. Place the shift lever in Park and the ignition switch in the Lock position.

5. Loosen and adjust the backdrive rod.

6. With the selector lever in Park, the ignition key should move freely into the Lock position. Lock position should not be obtainable in any transmission position other than Park.

Floor shift linkage adjustment—1968–72 Powerglide

Turbo Hydra-Matic Column and Floor Shift Linkage Adjustment Through 1974

Linkages used on Turbo Hydra-Matic transmissions are similar to those used on Powerglides. Adjustments are the same, except that the transmission lever is adjusted to Drive by moving the lever clockwise to the Low detent, and then counterclockwise two detent positions to Drive.

Column shift linkage components—Turbo Hydra-matic

Column Shift (Except Turbo Hydra-Matic 200)

1. Loosen the swivel at the lower end of the rod that comes from the column.

2. On 1973 and later models, set the transmission lever in the Neutral detent by turning the lever counterclockwise to the L1 detent, then clockwise three positions. On models through 1972, set the lever in the Drive detent by turning the lever counterclockwise to the L1 detent, then clockwise two positions.

3. Put the column lever in Neutral for 1973 and later models, and in Drive for models through 1972. The important thing here is not where the indicator points but that the lever be in the correct position.

4. Tighten the swivel. Readjust the neutral start switch as necessary.

5. Check that the key cannot be removed and that the wheel is not locked with the key in RUN. Check that the key can be removed in LOCK with the lever in Park, and that the steering wheel is locked.

Turbo Hydra-Matic 200

1. Remove the screw and washer from the swivel assembly on the rod which activates the transmission shift lever.

Floor shift linkage—1968–72 Powerglide

2. Put the transmission shift lever in neutral by turning it counterclockwise to L1 detent and then clockwise three detent positions. Put the transmission selector lever in neutral as determined by the mechanical stop in the steering column assembly—do not use the indicator pointer.

3. Turn the swivel until it lines up directly with the hole in the shift lever, and install screw and washer. You should not have to force the transmission lever to move in either direction to install the screw.

4. Adjust the transmission indicator pointer and neutral start switch.

5. Check that the key cannot be removed from the "run" position if the transmission selector is in "Reverse" and that the key can be removed with the selector in "Park." Make sure the lever will not move from "Park" position with key out of ignition.

1975 and Later Cars With Cable Linkage

1. Loosen the swivel at the lower end of the rod that comes from the steering column.

2. Loosen the pin at the transmission end of the cable.

3. Set the floorshift lever in the Drive detent.

4. Set the transmission lever in the Drive detent by moving it counterclockwise to the L1 detent, then clockwise three detent positions.

5. Tighten the nut on the pin at the transmission end of the cable.

6. Put the floorshift lever in Park and the ignition switch in LOCK.

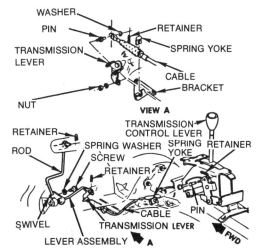

Floor shift linkage adjustment—1973 and later Turbo Hydra-matic

7. Pull down lightly on the rod from the column and tighten its clamp nut.

THROTTLE VALVE LINKAGE ADJUSTMENT

Powerglide—1964–66 V8, 1964–73 Six Cylinder Engines

1. Depress the accelerator pedal.
2. The bellcrank on 6 cylinder engines must be at the wide open throttle position.
3. The dash lever at the firewall must be $1/64$–$1/16$ in. off its lever stop.
4. The transmission lever must be against the transmission internal stop.
5. Adjust the linkage to simultaneously obtain the conditions in Steps 1–4.

Powerglide 1967–73 V8 Engines

1. Remove the air cleaner.
2. Disconnect the accelerator linkage at the carburetor.
3. Disconnect both return springs.
4. Pull the throttle valve upper rod forward until the transmission is through the detent.
5. Open the carburetor to the wide open throttle position. Adjust the swivel on the end of the upper throttle valve rod so that the carburetor reaches wide open throttle position at the same time that the ball stud contacts the end of the slot in the upper throttle valve rod. A tolerance of $1/32$ in. is allowable.

Throttle valve linkage adjustment (© Chevrolet Motor Division)

DETENT CABLE ADJUSTMENT

Turbo Hydra-Matic 250, 350 Through 1972

These transmissions utilize a downshift cable between the carburetor and the transmission.

Detent cable adjustment—Turbo Hydra-matic 350 (250 similar)

1. Pry up on each side of the detent cable snap-lock with a small pry bar to release the lock. On cars equipped with a retaining screw, loosen the detent cable screw.
2. Squeeze the locking tabs and disconnect the snap-lock assembly from the throttle bracket.
3. Place the carburetor lever in the wide open throttle position. Make sure that the lever is against the wide open stop. On cars with Quadrajet carburetors, disengage the secondary lock-out before placing the lever in the wide open position.
NOTE: *The detent cable must be pulled through the detent position.*
4. With the carburetor lever in the wide open position, push the snap-lock on the cable or else tighten the retaining screw.
NOTE: *Do not lubricate the detent cable.*

1973 and Later

The detent cable on these models adjusts itself the first time the accelerator pedal is pushed to the floor.

DETENT SWITCH ADJUSTMENT

Turbo Hydra-Matic 400 transmissions are equipped with an electrical detent, or downshift switch operated by the throttle linkage.

1968

1. Place the carburetor lever in the wide open position.
2. Position the automatic choke so that it is off.
3. Fully depress the switch plunger.
4. Adjust the switch mounting to obtain a distance of 0.05 in. between the switch plunger and the throttle lever paddle.

1969 and Later

1. Pull the detent switch driver rearward until the hole in the switch body aligns with the hole in the driver. Insert a 0.092 in. diam-

Detent (downshift) switch adjustment

eter pin through the aligned holes to hold the driver in position.

2. Loosen the mounting bolt.

3. Press the switch plunger as far forward as possible. This will preset the switch for adjustment, which will occur on the first application of wide open throttle.

4. Tighten the mounting bolt and remove the pin.

Detent switch Adjustment—1968–72 Turbo Hydra-Matic 400 (© Chevrolet Motor Division)

NEUTRAL SAFETY SWITCH REPLACEMENT

The neutral safety switch prevents the engine from being started in any transmission position except Neutral or Park. The switch is located on the upper side of the steering column under the instrument panel on column shift cars, and inside the shift console on floor shift models.

1. Remove the console for access on floor shift models.

2. Disconnect the electrical connectors.

3. Remove the neutral switch.

4. Place 1964–70 column shift lever models

in Drive, and 1971 and later models in neutral. Locate the lever tang against the transmission selector plate on column shift models. Place 1964 through early 1972 floor shift models in Drive, and mid-1972 and later models in Park.

5. Align the slot in the contact support with the hole in the switch. Insert a 3/32 (0.90 in.) pin in place. The switch is now aligned in Drive position.

NOTE: *1973 and later neutral safety switches have a shear-pin installed to aid in proper switch alignment so that insertion of a pin is unnecessary. Moving the shift lever from Neutral shears the pin.*

6. Place the contact support drive slot over the drive tang. Install the switch mounting screws.

7. Remove the aligning pin. Connect the electrical wiring, and replace the console.

8. Set the parking brake and hold your foot on the service brake pedal. Check to see that the engine will start only in Park or Neutral.

NEUTRAL SAFETY SWITCH ADJUSTMENT

NOTE: *1977 and later cars do not have a neutral safety switch. Instead, these cars have an interlock between the lock and the transmission selector, which is nonadjustable.*

1. Place the shift lever in Neutral.

2. Move the switch until you can insert a gauge pin, 0.092 in. into the hole in the switch and through to the alignment hole.

3. Loosen the switch securing screws. Remove the console first, if necessary.

4. Tighten the screws and remove the pin.

5. Step on the brake pedal and check to see that the engine will only start in Neutral or Park.

VIEW A

CONTACT SUPPORT
DRIVE SLOT IN LINE
WITH HOLE IN SWITCH

PAWL

CONTACT POINT B

CONTACT SUPPORT
DRIVE SLOT IN LINE
WITH HOLE IN SWITCH

FLOOR SHIFT

COLUMN SHIFT

Typical neutral safety switch installation (© Chevrolet Motor Division)

.090" GAUGE
PIN

ADJUSTMENT HOLE
IN OUTER COVER

IMPORTANT: EXTREME CARE MUST BE TAKEN NOT
TO OVERTORQUE THE ATTACHING
SCREWS (20 IN. LBS. MAX). IF
THE RETAINER STRIPS, IT MUST
BE REPLACED.

ATTACHING SCREW

RETAINER

Neutral safety switch adjustment

BAND ADJUSTMENTS

There are no band adjustments possible or required for the Turbo Hydra-Matic 200, 350 or 400.

Low Band—Powerglide and Torque Drive

The low band must be adjusted at the first required fluid change or whenever there is slippage.

1. Position the shift lever in Neutral.
2. Remove the protective cap from the adjusting screw on the left side of the transmission.
3. Loosen the locknut ¼ turn and hold it with a wrench during the entire adjusting procedure.
4. Tighten the adjusting nut to 70 in. lbs, using a 7/32 allen wrench.
5. Back off the adjusting nut *exactly* three turns for a band used less than 6,000 miles. Back off *exactly* four turns for a band used 6,000 miles or more.
6. Torque the locknut to 15 ft. lbs. and replace the cap.

Intermediate Band—Turbo Hydra-Matic 250

The intermediate band must be adjusted with every required fluid change or whenever there is slippage.

1. Position the shift lever in Neutral.
2. Loosen the locknut on the right side of the transmission and tighten the adjusting screw to 30 in. lbs.
3. Back the screw out three turns and then tighten the locknut to 15 ft. lbs.

THM 200, 250, 350 detent cable adjustment

DIESEL ENGINE TRANSMISSION LINKAGE ADJUSTMENT

NOTE: *Before making any linkage adjustments, check the injection timing, and adjust if necessary. Also note that these adjustments should be performed together. The vacuum valve adjustment (THM 350s only) requires the use of special tools. If you do not have these tools at your disposal, refer the adjustment to a qualified, professional technician.*

THROTTLE ROD ADJUSTMENT

1. If equipped with cruise control, remove the clip from the control rod, then remove the rod from the bellcrank.

THM 400 downshift switch adjustment

HOLD CARBURETOR IN WIDE OPEN POSITION, PULL CABLE FIRMLY TOWARD FRONT OF CAR. THERE SHOULD BE NO FORWARD MOVEMENT OF THE CABLE.

THROTTLE BRACKET

DETENT CABLE

CABLE SNAP LOCK

POINT "A"

POINT "A" - THERE SHOULD USUALLY BE SOME CLEARANCE AT THIS POINT WHEN PROPERLY ADJUSTED.

POINT "A" - NO CLEARANCE USUALLY INDICATES MIS-ADJUSTED CABLE

THM 200 downshift cable adjustment

THROTTLE CABLE

THROTTLE ROD

BELLCRANK

FAST IDLE SOLENOID AND BRACKET ASSEMBLY

HAIRPIN CLIP

17 FT. LBS.

5 FT. LBS.

BRACKET

17 FT. LBS.

Diesel throttle linkage, V6 and V8 similar

2. Remove the throttle valve cable (THM200) or detent cable (THM350) from the bellcrank.

3. Loosen the locknut on the throttle rod, then shorten the rod several turns.

4. Rotate the bellcrank to the full throttle stop, then lengthen the throttle rod until the injection pump lever contacts the injection pump full throttle stop. Release the bellcrank.

5. Tighten the throttle rod locknut.

6. Connect the throttle valve or detent cable and cruise control rod to the bellcrank. Adjust if necessary.

THROTTLE VALVE (TV) OR DETENT CABLE ADJUSTMENT

Refer to the previous cable adjustment procedures for gas engines. Adjust according to the style of cable which is used.

TRANSMISSION VACUUM VALVE ADJUSTMENT

1. Remove the air cleaner assembly.

2. Remove the air intake crossover from the intake manifold. Cover the intake manifold passages to prevent foreign material from entering the engine.

3. Disconnect the throttle rod from the injection pump throttle lever.

4. Loosen the transmission vacuum valve-to-injection pump bolts.

5. Mark and disconnect the vacuum lines from the vacuum valve.

6. Attach a carburetor angle gauge adapter (Kent-Moore tool J-26701-15 or its equivalent) to the injection pump throttle lever. Attach an angle gauge (J-26701 or its equivalent) to the gauge adapter.

7. Turn the throttle lever to the wide open throttle position. Set the angle gauge to zero degrees.

8. Center the bubble in the gauge level.

9. Set the angle gauge to one of the following settings, according to the year and type of engine:

Year	Engine	Setting
1980	V8	49–50°
1981	V8—Calif.	49–50°
1981	V8—non-Calif.	58°
1982	V8	58°

10. Attach a vacuum gauge to port 2 and a vacuum source (e.g. hand-held vacuum pump) to port 1 of the vacuum valve (as illustrated).

VIEW A

BOTH LOCKING LUGS MUST BE
EXPANDED AND LOCKED IN HOLE

SLIDER RE-ADJUST
DIRECTION

LOCK TAB

T.V./DETENT
CABLE
BRACKET

TERMINAL
VIEW B

LEVER ASSEMBLY

CABLE ADJUSTMENT PROCEDURE

1. Remove pump rod from lever assembly.

2. After installation to transmission, install cable fitting into cable bracket. **CAUTION** Slider must not be adjusted before or during assembly to bracket.

3. Install cable terminal to lever assembly.

4. Rotate the lever assembly to its full throttle stop position to automatically adjust slider on cable to correct setting.

5. Release lever assembly & reconnect the pump rod to lever assembly.

CABLE RE-ADJUSTMENT PROCEDURE

In case re-adjustment is necessary because of inadvertent adjustment before or during assembly, perform the following.

1. Remove pump rod from lever assembly, depress and hold metal lock tab.

2. Move slider through fitting in direction away from lever assembly until slider stops against fitting.

3. Release metal lock tab.

4. Repeat steps 4 & 5 of adjustment procedure.

Diesel transmission vacuum Detent cable adjustment

11. Apply 18–22 in. of vacuum to the valve. Slowly rotate the valve until the vacuum reading drops to one of the following values:

Year	In. Hg.
1980	7
1981 Calif.	7–8
1981 non-Calif.	8½–9
1982–83	10½

12. Tighten the vacuum valve retaining bolts.

13. Reconnect the original vacuum lines to the vacuum valve.

14. Remove the angle gauge and adapter.

15. Connect the throttle rod to the throttle lever.

16. Install the air intake crossover, using new gaskets.

17. Install the air cleaner assembly.

1. Adapter
2. Angle gauge

Angle gauge installation, with adaptor, for diesel vacuum valve adjustment. The gauge is positioned differently, depending on the type of throttle lever used

1980–81

1982 AND LATER

Diesel transmission vacuum valve adjustment

Transmission

REMOVAL AND INSTALLATION

1. Open the hood and place protectors on the fenders. Remove the air cleaner assembly and cover the air intake.

2. Disconnect the detent cable at its upper end.

3. Remove the transmission oil dipstick, and the bolt holding the dipstick tube if it is accessible.

4. Jack up the car and safety support it with jackstands.

NOTE: *If a floor pan reinforcement is used, remove it if it interferes with driveshaft removal or installation.*

6. Disconnect the speedometer cable at the transmission.

7. Disconnect the shift linkage at the transmission.

8. Disconnect all electrical leads at the transmission and any clips that hold these leads to the transmission case.

9. Remove the flywheel cover and match-mark the flywheel and torque converter for later assembly.

10. Remove the torque converter-to-flywheel bolts and/or nuts.

11. On gasoline engined cars, disconnect the catalytic converter support bracket.

12. Remove the transmission support-to-transmission mount bolt and transmission support-to-frame bolts, and any insulators (if used).

Transmission oil cooler lines

Torque converter holding fixture. A C-clamp can also be used

Typical transmission attachment, net-hole design

13. Position a transmission jack under the transmission and raise it slightly.

14. Slide the transmission support rearward.

15. Loosen the transmission enough to gain access to the oil cooler lines and detent cable attachments.

16. Disconnect the oil cooler lines and detent cable. Plug all openings.

17. Support the engine and remove the engine-to-transmission bolts.

18. Disconnect the transmission assembly, being careful not to damage any cables, lines or linkage.

19. Install a C-clamp or torque converter holding tool onto the transmission housing to hold the converter in the housing. Remove the transmission assembly from the car (a hydraulic floor jack is best for this).

20. To install, reverse the removal procedure. When installing the flex plate-to-converter bolts, make sure that the weld nuts on the converter are flush with the flex plate and that the converter rotates freely by hand. Hand-start the three bolts and tighten them finger tight, then torque them evenly.

NOTE Shim must be installed in direction shown.

FWD

TRANS SUPPORT

Some transmission rear mounts are shimmed

Install a new oil seal on the oil filler tube before installing the tube. Torque the fly-wheel-to-converter bolts to 35 ft. lbs. Torque the transmission-to-engine bolts to 35 to 40 ft. lbs. Adjust the shift linkage and detent cable following the procedures in this chapter, and check the transmission fluid if the transmission was not drained previously.

DRIVELINE

Driveshaft and U-joints

Mid-size Chevrolet driveshafts are of the conventional, open type. Located at either end of the driveshaft is a U-joint or universal joint, which allows the driveshaft to move up and down to match the motion of the rear axle. The front U-joint connects the driveshaft to a slip-jointed yoke. This yoke is internally splined, and allows the driveshaft to move in and out on the transmission splines. The rear U-joint is clamped or bolted to a companion flange fastened to the rear axle drive pinion. The rear U-joint is secured in the yoke in one of two ways. Dana and Cleveland design driveshafts use a conventional type snap-ring to hold each bearing cup in the yoke. The snap-ring fits into a groove located in each yoke end, just on top of the bearing cup. A Saginaw design driveshaft secures the U-joints differently. Nylon material is injected through a small hole in the yoke during manufacture, and flows along a circular groove between the U-joint and the yoke creating a non-metallic snap-ring.

There are two methods of attaching the rear U-joint to the rear axle. One method employs a pair of straps, while the other method is a set of bolted flanges. Bad U-joints, requiring replacement, will produce a clunking sound when the car is put into gear and when the transmission shifts from gear to gear. This is due to worn needle bearings or a scored trunnion end possibly caused by improper lubrication during assembly. U-joints require no periodic maintenance and therefore have no lubrication fittings.

Some driveshafts, generally those in heavy-duty applications, use a damper as part of the slip joint. This vibration damper cannot be ser-

SPIDER AND BEARINGS

STRAP

SPIDER AND BEARINGS

STRAP

TORQUE ALL BOLTS TO 14 FT. LBS.

SLIP YOKE

Typical driveshaft and U-joint assembly

viced separately from the slip joint. If either component goes bad, the two must be replaced as a unit.

DRIVESHAFT REMOVAL AND INSTALLATION

1. Raise the vehicle in the air and support it with jackstands.

2. Mark the relationship of the driveshaft to the differential flange so that they can be reassembled in the same position.

3. Disconnect the rear U-joint by removing the U-bolts or retaining straps.

4. To prevent the loss of the needle bearings, tape the bearing caps in place. If you are replacing the U-joint, this is not necessary.

5. Remove the driveshaft from the transmission by sliding it rearward. There will be some oil leakage from the rear of the transmission. It can be contained by placing a small plastic bag over the rear of the transmission and holding it in place with a rubber band.

6. To install the driveshaft, insert the front yoke into the transmission so that the driveshaft splines mesh with the transmission splines.

7. Using the reference marks made earlier, align the driveshaft with the differential flange and secure it with the U-bolts or retaining straps.

Driveshaft flange attachment

Strap-type retainer on driveshaft

U-JOINT OVERHAUL

NOTE: *NEVER clamp a driveshaft in a vise, as the tube is easily dented. Always clamp on one of the yokes, and support the shaft horizontally.*

1. Remove the driveshaft as explained above and remove the snap-rings from the ends of the bearing cup.

2. After removing the snap-rings, place the driveshaft on the floor and place a large diameter socket under one of the bearing cups. Using a hammer and a drift, tap on the bearing opposite this one. This will push the trunnion through the yoke enough to force the bearing cup out of the yoke and into the socket. Repeat this procedure for the other bearing cups. If a hammer doesn't loosen the cups, they will have to be pressed out.

NOTE: *A Saginaw design driveshaft secures its U-joints in a different manner than the conventional snap-rings of the Dana and Cleveland designs. Nylon material is in-*

Replacement U-joint assembly, internal snap-ring type

Replacement U-joint assembly, external snap-ring type

Production (original) type U-joint

Tapping yoke-to-seat retaining ring

Installing retaining ring

Partially inserted bearing cap (top)

jected through a small hole in the yoke and flows along a circular groove between the U-joint and the yoke thus creating a synthetic snap-ring. Disassembly of this Saginaw-type U-joint requires that the joint be pressed from the yoke. If a press is not available, it may be carefully hammered out using the same procedure (Step 2) as the Dana design although it may require more force to break the nylon ring. Either method, press or hammer, will damage the bearing cups and

destroy the nylon rings. Replacement kits include new bearing cups and conventional metal snap-rings to replace the original nylon type rings.

3. Using solvent, thoroughly clean the entire U-joint assembly. Inspect for excessive wear in the yoke bores and on the four ends of the trunnion. The needle bearings should not be scored, broken, or loose in their cups. Bearing cups may suffer slight distortion during removal and should be replaced.

4. Pack the bearings with chassis lube (lithium base) and completely fill each trunnion end with the same lubricant.

5. Place new dust seals on trunnions with cavity of seal toward end of trunnion. Care must be taken to avoid distortion of the seal. A suitable size socket and a vise can be used to press on the seal.

6. Insert one bearing cup about ¼ of the way into the yoke and place the trunnion into yoke and bearing cup. Install another bearing cup and press both cups in and install the snap-rings. Snap-rings on the Dana and Cleveland shafts must go on the outside of the yoke while the Saginaw shaft requires that rings go on the inside of the yoke. The gap in the Saginaw ring must face in toward the yoke. Once installed, the trunnion must move freely in yoke.

NOTE: *The Saginaw shaft uses two different size bearing cups (the ones with the groove) fit into the driveshaft yoke.*

REAR AXLE

IDENTIFICATION

The rear axle number is located in the right or left axle tube adjacent to the axle carrier (differential). See the "Rear Axle Codes" chart at the end of the chapter for information on determining axle ratio from the letter codes. Anti-slip differentials are identified by a tag attached to the lower right section of the axle cover.

Axle Shaft

Two types of axles are used on these models, the C and the non-C type. Axle shafts in the C type are retained by C-shaped locks, which fit grooves at the inner end of the shaft. Axle shafts in the non-C type are retained by the brake backing plate, which is bolted to the axle housing. Bearings in the C type axle consist of an outer race, bearing rollers, and a roller cage retained by snap-rings. The non-C type axle uses a unit roller bearing (inner race, rollers, and outer race), which is pressed onto the shaft up to a shoulder. When servicing C or non-C type axles, it is imperative to determine the axle type before attempting any service. Before

Rear axle identification. Chevrolet manufacturing codes are C Chevrolet-Buffalo; G Chevrolet Gear and Axle

Rear Axle Ratio Chart

Locating the letter prefix of the rear axle serial number in this chart will give you the axle ratio.

Locating the letter prefix of the rear axle serial number in this chart will give you the axle ratio.

1964

3 or 4-Speed (3.08 ratio)	LA, YA, ZA
3 or 4-Speed (3.36 ratio)	LB, YB, ZB
w/Metallic Brakes (3.08 ratio)	ZC
w/Metallic Brakes (3.36 ratio)	ZD
Positraction (3.08 ratio)	LG, YG, ZG
Positraction (3.36 ratio)	LH, YH, ZH
Positraction w/Metallic Brakes (3.08 ratio)	ZE
Positraction w/Metallic Brakes (3.36 ratio)	ZF
w/Overdrive (3.70 ratio)	ZJ
(8 cyl) (3.70 ratio)	ZJ
Positraction (3.70 ratio)	ZK
w/Metallic Brakes (3.70 ratio)	ZL
Positraction w/Metallic Brakes (3.70 ratio)	ZM

1965

327 w/Powerglide (2.73 ratio)	GB
Positraction (2.73 ratio)	GC
Metallic Brakes (2.73 ratio)	GD
Positraction w/Metallic Brakes (2.73 ratio)	GE
(3.08 ratio)	CA
(3.36 ratio)	CB
(3.73 ratio)	CC
Positraction (3.07 ratio)	CD
Positraction (3.08 ratio)	CE
Positraction (3.31 ratio)	CF
Positraction (3.36 ratio)	CG
Positraction (3.70 ratio)	CR
Positraction (3.73 ratio)	CI
w/Metallic Brakes (3.07 ratio)	CJ
Positraction w/Metallic Brakes (3.07 ratio)	CK
w/Metallic Brakes (3.08 ratio)	CL
Positraction w/Metallic Brakes (3.08 ratio)	CM
w/Metallic Brakes (3.31 ratio)	CN
Positraction w/Metallic Brakes (3.31 ratio)	CO
w/Metallic Brakes (3.36 ratio)	CP

1964

Positraction w/Metallic Brakes (3.36 ratio)	CQ
w/Metallic Brakes (3.70 ratio)	CH
Positraction w/Metallic Brakes (3.70 ratio)	CS
w/Metallic Brakes (3.73 ratio)	CT
Positraction w/Metallic Brakes (3.73 ratio)	CU
Overdrive (3.70 ratio)	CV
(3.31 ratio) "327" w/Air Cond	CW
(3.07 ratio) "327"	CX

1966

Positraction w/Metallic Brakes (3.73 ratio)	CU
Overdrive (3.70 ratio)	CV
(3.31 ratio) "396" w/Air Cond	CW
(3.07 ratio) "396" w/Air Cond and PG	CX
w/Metallic Brakes (3.55 ratio)	KF
Positraction w/Metallic Brakes (3.55 ratio)	KG
Positraction (3.55 ratio)	KH
'396" w/PG (2.73 ratio)	KI
(3.55 ratio)	KJ
w/Metallic Brakes (4.10 ratio)	KL
w/Metallic Brakes (4.56 ratio)	KN
w/Metallic Brakes (4.88 ratio)	KP
Positraction (4.10 ratio)	KK
Positraction (4.56 ratio)	KM
Positraction (4.88 ratio)	KO
(3.08 ratio)	CA
(3.36 ratio)	CB
(3.73 ratio)	CC
Positraction (3.07 ratio)	CD
Positraction (3.08 ratio)	CE
Positraction (3.31 ratio)	CF
Positraction (3.36 ratio)	CG
w/Metallic Brakes (3.70 ratio)	CH
Positraction (3.73 ratio)	CI
w/Metallic Brakes (3.07 ratio)	CJ
Positraction w/Metallic Brakes (3.07 ratio)	CK
w/Metallic Brakes (3.08 ratio)	CL
Positraction w/Metallic Brakes (3.08 ratio)	CM
w/Metallic Brakes (3.31 ratio)	CN
Positraction w/Metallic Brakes (3.31 ratio)	CO
w/Metallic Brakes (3.36 ratio)	CP
Positraction w/Metallic Brakes (3.36 ratio)	CQ
Positraction (3.70 ratio)	CR

Rear Axle Ratio Chart (cont.)

Locating the letter prefix of the rear axle serial number in this chart will give you the axle ratio.

Locating the letter prefix of the rear axle serial number in this chart will give you the axle ratio.

1967

Positraction w/Metallic Brakes (3.70 ratio)	CS
w/Metallic Brakes (3.73 ratio)	CT

1967

(3.08 ratio)	CA
(3.36 ratio)	CB
(3.73 ratio)	CC
Positraction (3.07 ratio)	CD
Positraction (3.08 ratio)	CE
Positraction (3.31 ratio)	CF
Positraction (3.36 ratio)	CG
Positraction (2.73 ratio)	CH
Positraction (3.73 ratio)	CI
w/Metallic Brakes (3.07 ratio)	CJ
Positraction w/Metallic Brakes (3.07 ratio)	CK
w/Metallic Brakes (3.31 ratio)	CN
Positraction w/Metallic Brakes (3.31 ratio)	CO
Positraction (3.70 ratio)	CR
w/Metallic Brakes (3.73 ratio)	CT
Positraction w/Metallic Brakes (3.73 ratio)	CU
(3.70 ratio)	CV
(3.31 ratio)	CW
(3.07 ratio)	CX
Positraction (3.55 ratio)	KF
Positraction w/Metallic Brakes (3.55 ratio)	KG
w/Metallic Brakes (3.55 ratio)	KH
(3.55 ratio)	KJ
Positraction (4.10 ratio)	KK
w/Metallic Brakes (4.10 ratio)	KL
Positraction (4.56 ratio)	KM
w/Metallic Brakes (4.56 ratio)	KN
Positraction (4.88 ratio)	KO
w/Metallic Brakes (4.88 ratio)	KP

1968

(3.08 ratio)	CA
(3.36 ratio)	CB
(3.73 ratio)	CC
Positraction (3.07 ratio)	CD
Positraction (3.08 ratio)	CE
Positraction (3.31 ratio)	CF
Positraction (3.36 ratio)	CG
Positraction (2.73 ratio)	CH
Positraction (3.73 ratio)	CI
(2.73 ratio)	CP
Positraction (3.70 ratio)	CR
Positraction w/Metallic Brakes (3.73 ratio)	CU
(3.70 ratio)	CV
(3.31 ratio)	CW
(3.07 ratio)	CX
(3.07 ratio)	CY
(2.73 ratio)	CZ
(2.73 ratio) (small ring gear)	FH
Positraction (2.73 ratio) (small ring gear)	FI
(3.08 ratio)	FJ
Positraction (3.08 ratio)	FK
(3.36 ratio)	FL
Positraction (3.36 ratio)	FM
(3.55 ratio) (small ring gear)	FN
Positraction (3.55 ratio) (small ring gear)	FO
(3.70 ratio)	FP

1968

Positraction (3.70 ratio)	FQ
(3.55 ratio) (small ring gear)	KA
Positraction (3.55 ratio) (small ring gear)	KB
Positraction (2.73 ratio) (small ring gear)	KC
(2.73 ratio) (large ring gear)	KD
Positraction (3.55 ratio) (large ring gear)	KF
(3.55 ratio) (large ring gear)	KJ
Positraction (4.10 ratio)	KK
Positraction (4.56 ratio)	KM
Positraction (4.88 ratio)	KO
w/Metallic Brakes (2.73 ratio)	KW
Positraction (3.07 ratio)	KX
Positraction (3.31 ratio)	KY
(3.31 ratio)	KZ
(3.55 ratio) (large ring gear)	K2
Positraction (3.55 ratio) (large ring gear)	K3
(3.73 ratio)	K4
Positraction (3.73 ratio)	K5
Positraction (4.10 ratio)	K6
Positraction (4.56 ratio)	K7
Positraction (4.88 ratio)	K8

1969

Positraction (2.56 ratio)	CO
(2.73 ratio)	CP
(2.56 ratio)	CQ
Positraction (2.56 ratio)	CS
(2.73 ratio)	CT
(3.31 ratio)	CW
(3.07 ratio)	CX
(3.55 ratio) (small ring gear)	KA
Positraction (2.55 ratio) (small ring gear)	KB
Positraction (2.73 ratio) (small ring gear)	KC
(2.73 ratio) (large ring gear)	KD
Positraction (2.73 ratio) (small ring gear)	KE
Positraction (3.55 ratio) (large ring gear)	KF
(3.08 ratio) (small ring gear)	KG
Positraction (3.08 ratio) (small ring gear)	KH
(3.36 ratio)	KI
(3.55 ratio) (large ring gear)	KJ
Positraction (4.10 ratio)	KK
Positraction (3.36 ratio) (small ring gear)	KL
Positraction (4.56 ratio)	KM
(3.55 ratio) (small ring gear)	KN
Positraction (4.88 ratio)	KO
Positraction (3.55 ratio) (small ring gear)	KP
Positraction (3.07 ratio)	KX
(2.73 ratio)	FH
Positraction (2.73 ratio)	FI
(3.08 ratio)	FJ
Positraction (3.08 ratio)	FK
(3.36 ratio)	FL
Positraction (3.36 ratio)	FM
(3.55 ratio)	FN
Positraction (3.55 ratio)	FO
(3.08 ratio)	CA
(3.36 ratio)	CB
(3.73 ratio)	CC
Positraction (3.07 ratio)	CD
Positraction (3.08 ratio)	CE
Positraction (3.31 ratio)	CF
Positraction (3.36 ratio)	CG

Rear Axle Ratio Chart (cont.)

Locating the letter prefix of the rear axle serial number in this chart will give you the axle ratio.

Locating the letter prefix of the rear axle serial number in this chart will give you the axle ratio.

1969

Positraction (2.73 ratio)	CH
Positraction (3.73 ratio)	CI
(2.56 ratio)	CJ
Positraction (2.56 ratio)	CK
(2.56 ratio)	CL
Positraction (2.56 ratio)	CM
(2.56 ratio)	CN

1970

Positraction (2.73 ratio)	CGD
Positraction (2.73 ratio)	CCH
Positraction (3.07 ratio)	CCD
(2.73 ratio)	CCP
(3.08 ratio)	CCA
(2.56 ratio)	CGA
(2.73 ratio)	CGC
(3.36 ratio)	CGG
Positraction (2.56 ratio)	CGB
Positraction (3.36 ratio)	CGI
(2.56 ratio)	CCN
(2.73 ratio)	CKD
(3.07 ratio)	CCX
(3.31 ratio)	CCW
(3.55 ratio)	CKJ
Positraction (2.56 ratio)	CCO
Positraction (3.31 ratio)	CCF
Positraction (3.55 ratio)	CKF
(4.10 ratio)	CKK
Positraction (2.73 ratio)	CKC
Positraction (3.08 ratio)	CCE
(2.56 ratio)	CRJ
Positraction (2.56 ratio)	CRK
(3.31 ratio)	CRU
Positraction (3.31 ratio)	CRV
(4.10 ratio)	CRW

1971

(3.31)	RU
Positraction (3.31)	RV
(4.10)	RW
(2.73)	GH
(3.08)	GN
Positraction (2.73)	GD
(3.08)	GF

1971

Positraction (2.73)	CH
(2.56)	GA
(2.73)	GC
(3.36)	GG
Positraction (2.56)	GB
Positraction (3.36)	GI
(2.73)	KD
(3.31)	CW
Positraction (3.31)	CF

1972

Positraction (2.73) (G-97, GS1)	GD
(3.08) (G92)	GF
Positraction (2.73)	GH
(2.73)	GC
(3.36)	GG
Positraction (3.36)	GI
(2.73)	GI
(3.31)	CW
Positraction	CF
(3.31)	RU
Positraction (3.31)	RV
(4.10)	RW
(2.73)	GH
(3.08)	GN

1973–74

(2.73)	WB, AC
Positraction (2.73)	XA, XB, CC
(3.08)	WC, XC, AD
Positraction (3.08)	CD
(3.42)	WE, AJ
Positraction (3.42)	XE, CJ

1975–77

(2.56)	CH, AH
(2.73)	WA, XA, CC, AC
(3.08)	WC, XC, CD, AD
(3.42)	WE, XE, CJ, AJ

NOTE: *On 1978 and later axles, the axle numerical ratio is indicated in place of a code.*

attempting any service to the drive axle or axle shafts, remove the axle carrier cover and visually determine if the axle shafts are retained by C-shaped locks at the inner end, or by the brake backing plate at the outer end. If the shafts are *not* retained by C locks, proceed as follows.

REMOVAL AND INSTALLATION

Non C-Type

Design allows for a maximum axle shaft end-play of 0.022 in., which can be measured with a dial indicator. If end-play is found to be excessive, the bearing should be replaced. Shim-ming the bearing is not recommended as this ignores end-play of the bearing itself and could result in improper seating of the bearing.

1. Remove the wheel, tire and brake drum.
2. Remove the nuts holding the retainer plate to the backing plate. Disconnect the brake line.
3. Remove the retainer and install nuts, fingertight, to prevent the brake backing plate from being dislodged.
4. Pull out the axle shaft and bearing assembly, using a slide hammer.
5. Using a chisel, nick the bearing retainer in three or four places. The retainer does not have to be cut, merely collapsed sufficiently,

Axle shaft, cross-section

Removing the axle shaft

Removing axle bearing with bearing puller

Installing axle bearing

to allow the bearing retainer to be slid from the shaft.

6. Press off the bearing and install the new one by pressing it into position.

7. Press on the new retainer.

NOTE: *Do not attempt to press the bearing and the retainer on at the same time.*

8. Assemble the shaft and bearing in the housing being sure that the bearing is seated properly in the housing.

Cutting the bearing retainer, non-C-type

AXLE SHAFT SEAL INSTALLER
J-23771 7-1/2" & 8-1/2" AXLE
J-21128 8-3/4" AXLE

Use a seal installing tool to install axle seal

RING GEAR

BOLT
(PINION SHAFT)

SIDE
BEARING

CASE

PINION
SHAFT

THRUST
WASHER

BOLT
(RING GEAR)

SIDE
GEAR

SIDE
BEARING

THRUST
WASHER

PINION
GEAR

Conventional differential case assembly, all models similar

SHIM

RACE
(OUTER)

CARRIER

SHIM

BEARING

RACE
(OUTER)

CAP (L)

CAP (R)

Conventional differential case and bearings

9. Install the retainer, drum, wheel and tire. Bleed the brakes.

C-Type

If they *are* retained by C-shaped locks, proceed as follows.

1. Raise the vehicle and remove the wheels.
2. The differential cover has already been

RING GEAR
(10 BOLT 8 1/2")

SHIM

BOLT
(PINION SHAFT)

CASE

SPLINED
DISC (3)

PINION
SHAFT

FIXED
DISC (4)

BOLT
(RING GEAR)

SIDE
GEAR

THRUST
WASHER

PINION
GEAR

SIDE
BEARING

PRELOAD
SPRING

Disc-type limited slip rear axle

removed (see Caution note). Remove the differential pinion shaft lock-screw and the differential pinion shaft.

3. Push the flanged end of the axle shaft toward the center of the vehicle and remove the "C" lock from the end of the shaft.

4. Remove the axle shaft from the housing, being careful not to damage the oil seal.

5. Remove the oil seal by inserting the button end of the axle shaft behind the steel case of the oil seal. Pry the seal loose from the bore.

6. Seat the legs of the bearing puller behind the bearing. Seat a washer against the bearing and hold it in place with a nut. Use a slide hammer to pull the bearing.

7. Pack the cavity between the seal lips with wheel bearing lubricant and lubricate a new wheel bearing with same.

8. Use a suitable driver and install the bearing until it bottoms against the tube. Install the oil seal.

9. Slide the axle shaft into place. Be sure that the splines on the shaft do not damage the oil seal. Make sure that the splines engage the differential side gear.

10. Install the axle shaft C-lock on the inner end of the axle shaft and push the shaft outward so that the C-lock seats in the differential side gear counterbore.

11. Position the differential pinion shaft through the case and pinions, aligning the hole in the case with the hole for the lockscrew.

12. Use a new gasket and install the carrier cover. Be sure that the gasket surfaces are clean before installing the gasket and cover.

13. Fill the axle with lubricant to the bottom of the filler hole.

14. Install the brake drum and wheels and lower the car. Check for leaks and road test the car.

Suspension and Steering

8

FRONT SUSPENSION

The front suspension is designed to allow each wheel to compensate for changes in the road surface level without appreciably affecting the opposite wheel. Each wheel is independently connected to the frame by a steering knuckle, ball joint assemblies, and upper and lower control arms. The control arms are specifically designed and positioned to allow the steering knuckles to move in a prescribed three dimensional arc. The front wheels are held in proper relationship to each other by two tie rods which are connected to steering arms on the knuckles and to an intermediate rod.

Coil chassis springs are mounted between the spring housings on the frame or front end sheet metal and the lower control arms. Ride control is provided by double, direct acting, shock absorbers mounted inside the coil springs and attached to the lower control arms by bolts and nuts. The upper portion of each shock absorber extends through the upper control arm frame bracket and is secured with two grommets, two grommet retainers, and a nut.

Side role of the front suspension is controlled by a spring steel stabilizer shaft. It is mounted in rubber bushings which are held to the frame side rails by brackets. The ends of the stabilizer are connected to the lower control arms by link bolts isolated by rubber grommets.

The upper control arm is attacked to a cross shaft through isolating rubber bushings. The cross shaft, in turn, is bolted to frame brackets.

A ball joint assembly is riveted to the outer end of the upper arm. It is pre-loaded by a rubber spring to insure proper seating of the ball in the socket. The upper ball joint is attached to the steering knuckle by a torque prevailing nut.

The inner ends of the lower control arm have pressed-in bushings. Bolts, passing through the bushings, attach the arm to the frame. The lower ball joint assembly is a press fit in the arm and attaches to the steering knuckle with a torque prevailing nut.

Rubber grease seals are provided at ball socket assemblies to keep dirt and moisture from entering the joint and damaging bearing surfaces.

Shock Absorbers

TESTING

Visually inspect the shock absorber. If there is evidence of leakage and the shock absorber is covered with oil, the shock is defective and should be replaced.

If there is no sign of excessive leakage (a small amount of weeping is normal) bounce the car at one corner by pressing down on the fender or bumper and releasing. When you have the car bouncing as much as you can, release the fender or bumper. The car should stop bouncing after the first rebound. If the bouncing continues past the center point of the bounce more than once, the shock absorbers are worn and should be replaced.

REMOVAL AND INSTALLATION

1. Raise the car, and with an open end wrench hold the upper stem of the shock absorber from turning. Remove the upper stem retaining nut, retainer and grommet.

2. Remove the two bolts retaining the lower shock absorber pivot to the lower control arm and then pull the shock out through the bottom of the control arm.

3. With the lower retainer and the rubber grommet in place over the upper stem, install the shock (fully extended) back through the lower control arm.

4. Install the upper grommet, retainer and nut onto the upper stem.

5. Hold the upper stem from turning with

NOTE Hold stud at this point to obtain torque.

Shock absorber mounting locations

an open end wrench and then tighten the retaining nut.

6. Reinstall the retainers on the lower end of the shock.

Coil Springs

CAUTION: *The coil springs are under a considerable amount of tension. Be extremely careful when removing or installing them; they can exert enough force to cause serious injury.*

NOTE: *A coil spring compressor is needed for removal and installation. This tool can usually be rented at tool rental shops.*

REMOVAL AND INSTALLATION

1. Remove the shock absorber. Disconnect the stabilizer bar.

2. Support the car at the frame so the control arms hang free.

3. Support the inner end of the control arm with a floor jack. (Dealers have a device that cradles the inner bushings).

4. Raise the jack enough to take the tension off the lower control arm pivot bolts.

5. Chain the spring to the lower control arm.

THRUST BEARING

3/4" x 10 NUT

Front coil spring removal. Make sure the lock in the top of the spring compressor is in position whenever the tool is used.

NOTE MANDATORY DIRECTION OF BOLT INSTALLATION

STABILIZER BAR

UPPER CENTER ARM

SPRING

STEERING KNACKL

LOWER CONTROL ARM

SHOCK ABSORBER

Front suspension

Spring compressed and ready to install

Spring to be installed with tape at lowest
position. Bottom of spring is coiled helical,
and the top is coiled flat with a gripper
notch near end of wire.

After assembly, end of spring coil must
cover all or part of one inspection drain
hole. The other hole must be partly exposed
or completely uncovered.

**Coil spring positioning, 1983 model shown. Other
years similar installation**

6. Remove first the rear, then the front pivot bolt.

7. Cautiously lower the jack until all spring
tension is released.

8. Note the way in which the spring is installed in relation to the drain holes in the control arm and remove it.

9. On installation, position the spring to the
control arm and raise it into place.

10. Install the pivot bolts and torque the nuts
to 100 ft. lbs. for all 1974 and later models.
Torque all models through 1973 to 85 ft. lbs.

11. Replace the shock absorber and stabilizer bar.

Ball Joints
INSPECTION

NOTE: *Before performing this inspection,
make sure that the wheel bearings are adjusted correctly and that the control arm
bushings are in good condition.*

1. Raise the car by placing the jack under
the lower control arm at the spring seat.

2. Raise the car until there is a 1–2 in.
clearance under the wheel.

3. Insert a bar under the wheel and pry upward. If the wheel raises more than ⅛ in., the
ball joints are worn. Determine whether the
upper or lower ball joint is worn by visual inspection while prying on the wheel.

NOTE: *Due to the distribution of forces in
the suspension, the lower ball joint is usually
the defective joint. Because of this, 1974 and
later models are equipped with wear indicators on the lower ball joint. As long as the
indicator extends below the ball stud seat,
replacement is unnecessary.*

UPPER BALL JOINT REPLACEMENT
1964–70

1. Support the car by placing a jack under
the outer end of the lower control arm.

2. Remove the wheel and tire assembly.

3. Remove the cotter pin and nut from the
stud.

4. Remove the stud from the steering
knuckle.

5. Cut off the ball joint rivets with a chisel.

6. It may be necessary to enlarge the stud
attaching holes in the control arm to accept the
larger ⁵⁄₁₆ in. bolts. Inspect and clean the tapered hole in the steering knuckle. If the hole
is damaged or deformed, the knuckle *must* be
replaced.

7. Install the new joint and connect the stud
to the steering knuckle. When installing the stud
nut, never back off on the nut to align the cotter pin holes; always tighten the nut to the next
hole.

8. Replacement ball joints may not include
the lube fitting. If not, install a self-threading
fitting into the tapped hole.

1971–and later

1. Raise the vehicle and support securely.
Support the lower control arm securely. Remove the tire and wheel.

Steering knuckle cotter pin installation

Drill the upper ball joint rivets—1971 and later

Use a ½ in. drill to drill the upper ball joint rivet heads, 1971 and later

2. Remove the upper ball stud cotter pin and loosen the ball stud nut *just one turn.*

3. Procure a special tool designed to press out '71 and later Chevrolet ball joints. Locate the tool between the upper and lower ball joints and press the joints out of the steering knuckle. Remove the tool.

4. Remove the ball joint stud nut, and separate the joint from the steering knuckle. Lift the upper arm up and place a block of wood between the frame and the arm to support it.

5. With the control arm in the raised posi-

When installing the new upper ball joints, make sure that the nuts are on top (1971 and later)

tion, drill a hole ¼ in. deep into each rivet. Use a ⅛ in. drill bit.

6. Use a ½ in. drill bit and drill off the heads of each rivet.

7. Punch out the rivets using a small punch and then remove the ball joint.

8. Install the new ball joint using fasteners that meet Chevrolet specifications. Bolts should come in from the bottom with the nuts going on top. Torque to 10 ft. lbs.

9. Turn the ball stud cotter pin hole to the fore and aft position. Remove the block of wood from between the upper control arm and frame.

10. Clean and inspect the steering knuckle hole. Replace the steering knuckle if any out of roundness is noted.

11. Insert the ballstud into the steering knuckle, and install and torque the stud nut to 60 ft. lbs. Install a new cotter pin. *If nut must be turned to align cotter pin holes, tighten it further. Do not back off!*

12. Install a lube fitting, and fill the joint with fresh grease.

13. Remove the lower control arm support and lower the car.

LOWER BALL JOINT REPLACEMENT
1964–1970

1. Raise the car and support securely. Support the lower control arm with a floor jack.

2. Remove the wheel. If the vehicle has disc brakes, remove the caliper assembly.

J-9519-10

Pressing out lower ball joint using ball joint tool

3. Remove the lower ball stud. Then, using a tool designed for such work, press the ball stud out of the steering knuckle. Wire the steering knuckle out of the way so you'll have more room.

4. Press the joint out of the control arm with a tool designed for that purpose.

5. Start the replacement joint into the control arm with the air vent in the rubber boot facing inboard.

6. Set the joint in the control arm, pressing it in with a tool designed for that purpose.

7. Install the stud into the steering knuckle, and install the attaching nut and new cotter pin.

8. Reinstall the caliper assembly (as necessary) and wheel remove the jack supporting the control arm, and lower the car.

1971 and later

NOTE: *On models equipped with the wear indicating ball joint, Chevrolet recommends replacement of both upper and lower ball joints if only the lower ball joint is bad.*

1. Raise the vehicle and support it securely. Support the lower control arm with a jack.

2. Remove the lower ball stud cotter pin, and loosen the ball stud nut just one turn.

3. Install a special tool designed for such work between the two ball studs, and press the stud downward in the steering knuckle. Then, remove the stud nut.

4. Pull the tire outward and at the same time upward, with your hands on the bottom

WORN

NEW

SINTERED IRON BEARING

WEAR SURFACES

HOUSING SOCKET

1.27mm (.050")

RUBBER PRESSURE RING

WHEN BALL JOINT WEAR CAUSES THIS SHOULDER TO RETREAT BELOW THE SURFACE, REPLACEMENT IS REQUIRED.

WEAR INDICATOR (OUT WHEN NEW)

Lower ball joint wear indicator—1974 and later

Disconnecting the lower ball joint—1980 shown, others similar

(of the tire), to free the steering knuckle from the ball stud. Then, remove the wheel.

5. Lift up on the upper control arm and place a block of wood between it and the frame. Be careful not to put any tension on the brake hose in doing this.

6. Press the ball joint out of the lower control arm with a tool made for that purpose. You may have to disconnect the tie rod at the steering knuckle to do this.

7. To install, position the new ball joint, with the vent in the rubber boot facing inward, onto the lower control arm. Press the joint fully into the control arm with a tool designed for this.

8. Turn the ball stud cotter pin hole so it is fore and aft.

9. Remove the block of wood holding the upper control arm out of the way, and inspect the tapered hole in the steering knuckle. Remove any dirt from the hole. If the hole is out of round or there is other noticeable damage, replace the entire steering knuckle.

10. Insert the ballstud into the steering knuckle, install the stud nut, and torque it to 83 ft. lbs. Install a new cotter pin, aligning cotter pin holes in the nut and stud *only* through further tightening. *Do not loosen the nut from the torque position.*

11. Install a lube fitting and lube the joint. Reconnect the tie rod (as necessary), install the wheel, remove the jack supporting the lower control arm and lower the car.

Upper Control Arm

REMOVAL AND INSTALLATION

1. Raise the vehicle on a hoist.
2. Support the outer end of the lower control arm with a jack.
3. Remove the wheel.
4. Separate the upper ball joint from the steering knuckle as described above under "Upper Ball Joint Replacement."
5. Remove the control arm shaft-to-frame nuts.

NOTE: *Tape the shims together and identify them so that they can be installed in the positions from which they were removed.*

6. Remove the bolts which attach the control arm shaft to the frame and remove the control arm. Note the positions of the bolts.
7. Install in the reverse order of removal. Make sure that the shaft-to-frame bolts are installed in the same position they were in before removal and that the shims are in their original

Upper control arm components (1983 shown)

Typical upper control arm installation

positions. Use free running nuts (not locknuts) to pull serrated bolts through the frame. Then install the locknuts. Tighten the thinner shim pack first. After the car has been lowered to the ground, bounce the front end to center the bushings and then tighten the bushing collar bolts to 45 ft. lbs. Tighten the shaft-to-frame bolts to 80 ft. lbs. on models through 1973; 1974 and later models require 90 ft. lbs. The control arm shaft nuts are tightened to 65 ft. lbs. through 1974; on 1975 and later models tighten to 75 ft. lbs.

Lower Control Arm
REMOVAL AND INSTALLATION

1. Remove the spring as described earlier.
2. Remove the ball stud from the steering knuckle as described earlier.
3. Remove the control arm pivot bolts and the control arm.
4. To install, reverse the above procedure. If any bolts are to be replaced, do so with bolts of equal strength and quality.

Lower control arm attachment bolts (© Chevrolet Motor Division)

Front End Alignment
CASTER, CAMBER, AND TOE-IN

NOTE: *The procedure for checking and adjusting front wheel alignment requires specialized equipment and professional skills. The following descriptions and adjustment procedures are for general reference only. Also, no attempt to check and/or adjust the front wheel alignment should be made without first making a thorough inspection of the front suspension components.*

Caster is the angle at which the front steering axis tilts either forward or backward from a vertical position. Positive caster is a backward tilt while a forward tilt is negative caster. Caster angle cannot be seen with the eye, it requires the use of instruments. Caster angle can, however, be visualized. If you look down from the top of the upper control arm to the ground, you notice that the upper and lower ball joints do not line up (unless a 0 degree caster angle existed). With any angle (other than 0 degrees), one ball joint would be slightly ahead or slightly to the rear of the other. If you had a positive angle, the lower ball joint would be slightly ahead (more to the front of the car) of the upper ball joint.

The front wheels will tilt outward or inward at the top depending on whether the camber is positive or negative. Camber angle then is the amount (in degrees) that a wheel tilts from a perfectly vertical position. When the wheels tilt outward at the top, it has positive camber; camber is negative when the wheel tilts inward at the top.

Toe-in, measured in fractions of an inch, is the turning in of the front of the front wheels. The front wheels must roll parallel to each other; if they don't uneven tire wear will result.

When performing a front wheel alignment, the mechanic checks all three of these measurements and makes any necessary adjustments. Since one adjustment affects each of the others, they must be adjusted in a specific order: caster, camber, and then toe-in. Proper wheel alignment is necessary for ease and stability of steering and controlling tire wear.

Adjustment of caster and camber is carried out by adding or subtracting shims between the upper control arm shaft and the frame bracket. Camber is adjusted by adding or subtracting shims from both the front and rear of the shaft. Adding shims decreases positive camber. Caster is adjusted by adding or subtracting shims from one end of the shaft. Moving one shim to the front bolt from the rear bolt will decrease positive caster. To adjust, loosen the shaft-to-frame nuts and add or subtract shims as necessary. Torque the nuts to 55 ft. lbs. when the adjustment is final. At least two bolt threads should be protruding from the shim pack. The difference between the front and rear shim pack should never exceed ⅖ in.

Toe-in is adjusted after the caster and camber adjustments are carried out. Adjust the toe-in by loosening the clamps on the tie-rod sleeves, and turning the sleeves in equal amount in the opposite direction, to maintain wheel spoke alignment while adjusting.

REAR SUSPENSION

The rear axle assembly is attached to the frame through a link-type suspension system. Two rubber bushed lower control arms mounted

Wheel Alignment Specifications

Year	Model	Caster Range (deg)	Caster Pref Setting (deg)	Camber Range (deg)	Camber Pref Setting (deg)	Toe-in (in.)	Steering Axis Inclination (deg)	Wheel Pivot Ratio Inner Wheel	Wheel Pivot Ratio Outer Wheel
1964	All	¼N to ¾P	¼P	¼ to 1¼P	¾P	0 to ⅛	8¼	20	18¾
1965	All	1½ to ½N	1N	¼N to ¾P	¼P	¹⁄₁₆ to ³⁄₁₆	8	20	18¾
1966	All	1½ to ½N	1N	0 to 1P	½P	⅛ to ¼	8	20	18¾
1967	All	1½ to ½N ①	1N	0 to 1P	½P	⅛ to ¼	8¼	20	18¾
1968–69	All	1½ to ½N ①	1N	0 to 1P	½P	⅛ to ¼	8¼	20	18½
1970–71	Chevelle, Monte Carlo	1½ to ½N ①	1N	0 to 1P	½P	⅛ to ¼	7¾ to 8¾	20	NA
1972	Chevelle	1½ to ½N	1N	¼ to 1¼P	¾P	⅛ to ¼	7¾ to 8¾	NA	NA
	Monte Carlo	½N to ½P	0	¼ to 1¼P	¾P	⅛ to ¼	7¾ to 8¾	NA	NA
1973	Chevelle	1¾ to ¾N	1¼N	½ to 1½P	1P ②	⅛ to ¼	9½	NA	NA
	Monte Carlo	4¼ to 5¼P	4¾P	½ to 1½P	1P ②	0 to ⅛	9½	NA	NA
1974	Chevelle ③	1½ to ½N	1N	½ to 1½P	1P	0 to ⅛	10½	NA	NA
	Chevelle ④	½N to ½P	0	½ to 1½P	1P	0 to ⅛	10½	NA	NA
	Monte Carlo	4½ to 5½P	5	½ to 1½P	1P	0 to ⅛	10½	NA	NA
1975–77	Chevelle	1½ to 2½P	2P ⑤	½ to 1½P ②	1P	0 to ⅛	9¾	NA	NA
	Monte Carlo	4½ to 5½P	5P	¼ to 1½P ②	1P	0 to ⅛	9¾	NA	NA
1978–81	Malibu, Monte Carlo	½ to 1½P	1P	0 to 1P	½P	¹⁄₁₆ to ³⁄₁₆	7.86	NA	NA
1983–84	Malibu, El Camino Monte Carlo	½ to 1½P ⑥	1P	0 to 1P	½P	¹⁄₁₆ to ³⁄₁₆	7.86	NA	NA

① SS 396 and El Camino—0 to 1P
② Left wheel given; right wheel is ½P ± ½
③ Manual steering
④ Power steering
⑤ Radial tires—1P ± ½ with belted tires
⑥ Power steering: 2½P to 3½P, 3P
N Negative   P Positive
NA Not available

Camber, caster, and toe-in (© Chevrolet Motor Division)

PIVOT SHAFT INBOARD OF FRAME

Caster and camber adjustment (© Chevrolet Motor Division)

between the axle assembly and the frame maintain fore and aft relationship of the axle assembly to the chassis. Two rubber bushed upper control arms, angularly mounted with respect to the centerline of the car, control driving and braking torque and sideways movement of the axle assembly. The rigid axle holds the rear wheels in proper alignment.

The upper control arms are shorter than the lower arms, causing the differential housing to "rock" or tilt forward on compression. This rocking or tilting lowers the rear propeller shaft to make possible the use of a lower tunnel in the rear floor pan area.

The rear upper control arms control drive forces, side sway and pinion nose angle. Pinion angle adjustment can greatly affect car smoothness and most be maintained as specified.

The rear chassis springs are located between brackets on the axle tube and spring seats in the frame. The springs are held in the seat pilots by the weight of the car and by the shock absorbers which limit axle movement during rebound.

Ride control is provided by two identical direct double acting shock absorbers angle-mounted between brackets attached to the axle housing and the rear spring seats. Shock ab-

Rear suspension

sorbers are located behind the axle housing on pre-1968 models. Beginning in 1968, the shock absorbers were staggered to resist axle hop; the right shock in front of the axle and the left behind the axle.

Springs

REMOVAL AND INSTALLATION

1964–1972

1. Raise the car and support it at the frame with stands.
2. Position a hydraulic jack under the axle and support it.
3. Disconnect the shock absorber at the bottom on the side where the spring is being replaced.
4. Lower the axle to the bottom of its travel, and then pry the lower end of the spring over the axle retainer.
5. Remove the spring and its insulator.
NOTE: *On 1964–66 cars, the spring retainer must be removed to remove the spring. It is fastened to the housing with a nut and bolt.*
6. Install the spring in the frame seat with its rubber insulation.
7. Pry the spring into the axle housing retainer. Install the retainer on 1964–66 cars and torque the bolt to 45–55 ft. lbs.
8. Raise the axle and install the shock absorber. Tighten the shock absorber nuts to 12 ft. lbs.

1973–81

1. Raise the car and support it at the frame with stands.
2. Position a hydraulic jack under the axle and support it.
3. Disconnect the shock absorber at the bottom on the side where the spring is being replaced.
4. Disconnect the brake hydraulic line at the junction block located on the axle housing.
5. Disconnect the upper control arm at the axle.
6. Lower the axle to the bottom of its travel, then pry the lower end of the spring over the axle retainer and remove the spring and its insulator.
7. Install the spring in its frame seat with its rubber insulator.
8. Pry the lower end of the spring over the vertical flange of the axle bracket spring seat.
9. Position the spring so that the end of the upper coil points toward the right-side of the car.
10. Raise the axle and install the shock absorber. Tighten the nut to 12 ft. lbs.

11. Connect the upper control arm to the axle housing.
12. Connect the brake hydraulic lines and bleed the brakes.
13. Remove the jack and lower the car.

Shock Absorbers

TESTING

If the ride of your car has become increasingly bouncy or fluid leakage can be observed on the shock absorber, it's time to replace them. Push up and down on the rear bumper several times and then let go. If the car continues to move up and down the shocks aren't doing their job.

REMOVAL AND INSTALLATION

1. Jack the rear of the car up and support the axle.
2. Remove the two upper mounting bolts and disconnect the air line if equipped with superlift shock absorbers.
3. While holding the stud hex with a wrench, remove the lower mounting nut.
4. Remove the shock absorber from the car.
5. Install the upper mounting bolts hand-tight.
6. Install the lower stud into the housing bracket and loosely install the nut.
7. Tighten the two upper bolts to 12 ft. lbs.
8. While holding the stud hex, tighten the lower nut to 60 ft. lbs.
9. On superlift equipped cars, install the air hose and add approximately 10 psi of air.
10. Lower the car.

STATION WAGON AND PICKUP

Rear shock absorber mounting

STEERING

All models have recirculating ball type steering. Forces are transmitted from a worm to a sector gear through ball bearings. Relay type steering linkage is used with a pitman arm connected to one end of the relay rod. The other end of the relay rod is connected to an idle arm which is attached to the frame. The relay rod is connected to the steering arms by two adjustable tie rods. Most models are equipped with a collapsible steering column designed to collapse on impact, thereby reducing possible chest injuries during accidents. When making any repairs to the steering column or steering wheel, excessive pressure or force capable of collapsing the column must be avoided. Beginning 1969, the ignition lock, ignition switch, and an antitheft system were built into each column. The key cannot be removed unless the transmission is in "Park" (automatic) or Reverse (manual) with the switch in the "Lock" position. Placing the lock in the "Lock" position activates a rod within the column which locks the steering wheel and shift lever. On floorshift models, a back drive linkage between the floorshift and the column produces the same effect.

Steering Wheel

CAUTION: *Most steering columns are collapsible. When replacing the wheel, do not hammer or exert any force against the column.*

STANDARD WHEEL

Chevelle—1964–69

1. Pry out the center cap and retainer.
2. Remove the three receiving cup screws and remove the cup, belleville spring, bushing, and pivot ring.
3. Remove the steering wheel nut and washer.
4. Mark the wheel-to-shaft relationship, and then remove the wheel with a puller.

Steering wheel puller in position

5. Install the wheel on the shaft, aligning the previously made marks. Tighten the nut to 35 ft. lbs.
6. Install the belleville spring (dished side up), pivot ring, bushing, and receiving cup. Install the center cap and reconnect the battery.

NOTE: *Removal of the 1970 padded steering wheel is similar to the above.*

Chevelle—1969 Deluxe Wheel and All Models Standard Wheel—1970 and Later

1. Remove the four trim retaining screws from behind the wheel.
2. Lift the trim off and pull the horn wires from the signal cancelling cam.
3. On 1975 models, remove the snap ring.
4. Remove the steering wheel nut.
5. Mark the wheel-to-shaft relationship, and then remove the wheel with a puller.
6. Install the wheel on the shaft, aligning the previously made marks. Tighten the nut to 30 ft. lbs.
7. On 1975 models, install the snap-ring.
8. Insert the horn wires into the cancelling cam.

Steering wheel and horn components—1964–69

1969 deluxe and 1970–72 standard steering wheel

Steering wheel and horn—1973–74

Steering wheel—1975

9. Install the center trim and reconnect the battery cable.

NOTE: *The 1967–69 simulated wood wheel does not require pulling for removal. Remove the center cap and horn contact assembly. The wheel is held to the hub by phillips screws. Reverse the disassembly procedure to install the wheel.*

CUSHIONED RIM WHEEL

1971—and later

1. Disconnect the battery ground cable.
2. Remove the horn button cap. Remove the snap ring.
3. Remove the steering wheel nut.
4. Remove the upper horn insulator. receiver, and belleville spring.
5. Install the wheel puller, turn the puller bolt clockwise, and remove the wheel.
6. Place the turn signal lever in a Neutral position, position the wheel to the shaft, and tighten the nut.
7. Position the horn lower insulator, eyelet, and spring in the horn contact tower. Install the belleville spring, receiver, and horn upper insulator.
8. Install the horn button cap and connect the battery cable.

1971 and later cushioned rim wheel (© Chevrolet Motor Division)

1980 and later standard steering wheel, installation

Turn Signal Switch

REPLACEMENT

Chevelle—1964–66

1. Remove the steering wheel as outlined above.

2. On column shift cars, remove the shift lever retaining pin and the lever.

3. Disconnect the column wiring harness from the chassis harness.

4. Remove the lower trim plate and the up-per mast jacket clamp. On automatic cars, remove the indicator retaining screw and the pointer.

5. Remove the three turn signal-to-housing screws.

6. Remove the turn signal switch, housing, and shift bowl from the steering column. Separate the switch from the wiring harness.

7. Install using the reverse of the removal procedure.

NOTE: *Two different switch assemblies are used. Removal procedures are the same, but they are not interchangeable.*

1967–68

1. Disconnect the battery ground cable.

2. Disconnect the signal switch wiring from the wiring harness under the instrument panel.

3. Remove the steering wheel.

4. If applicable, remove the shift lever.

5. Remove the four-way flasher lever arm.

6. If equipped with an automatic transmission, remove the dial indicator housing and lamp assembly from the column.

7. Remove the mast jacket lower trim cover.

8. Remove the C-ring and washers from the upper steering shaft.

9. Loosen the signal switch screws, move the switch counterclockwise, and remove it from the mast jacket.

10. Remove the upper support bracket assembly.

CAUTION: *Support the column; do not allow it to be suspended by the lower reinforcement only.*

11. Remove the wiring harness protector and clip, and then reinstall the support bracket and finger-tighten the bolts.

12. Remove the shift lever bowl from the mast jacket and disconnect it from the wiring harness.

13. Remove the three lockplate screws, being careful not to lose the three springs.

14. Disassemble the switch and upper bearing housing from the switch cover.

15. Insert the upper bearing housing assembly and switch assembly into the switch cover.

16. Align the switch and bearing housing with the mounting holes in the cover and install the three mounting screws.

17. Slide the springs onto the screws and install the lockplate over the springs. Tighten the screws three turns into the lockplate.

18. Position the switch wire through the shift lever bowl and place the upper end assembly on top of the bowl.

19. Place the shift lever bowl and signal switch assembly on top of the jacket, inserting the lockplate tangs into the slots.

1. Cancelling cam
2. Attaching screw
3. Switch assembly
4. Switch housing
5. Lever
6. Harness wiring

Turn signal assembly—1964–66

Turn signal switch removal, standard steering column—1980 shown

Turn signal switch removal, adjustable column

20. Push down on the cover assembly and turn clockwise to lock the assembly into position.

21. Tighten the signal mounting screws.

22. Remove the mast jacket support bracket, then install the wiring, wiring cover and clip, and install and tighten the support bracket.

23. Install a C-ring onto the shaft.

24. Install the dial indicator and lamp assembly on the column if so equipped.

25. Install the mast jacket lower trim cover if so equipped.

26. Install the four-way flasher knob and the turn signal lever.

27. Install the shift lever.

28. Install the steering wheel.

29. Connect the wiring and battery cable.

1969—and later

1. Remove the steering wheel.

2. Remove the trim cover from the column.

3. Remove the steering column cover from the shaft by removing the three screws or by prying it out with a screwdriver (1976 and later models).

4. Using a compressing tool, compress the lockplate. With the plate compressed, pry out the snap-ring from its shaft groove and throw it away.

5. Slide the cancelling cam, spring, and washer off the shaft.

6. Remove the turn signal lever.

7. Push the four-way flasher knob in and unscrew it.

8. Remove the three switch mounting screws.

9. Pull the switch connector out of the bracket and wrap it with tape to prevent it from snagging.

10. If applicable, place tilt columns in the low and remove the harness cover.

11. Remove the switch.

12. To install, reverse the removal procedure, being sure to use only the specified nuts and bolts. Using screws that are slightly too long could prevent the column from collapsing during a collision.

13. When installing the cancelling cam, spring, and washer, make sure that the switch is in neutral and that the flasher knob is out.

14. Use a compressing tool to compress the lockplate and install a new snap-ring.

Lock Cylinder

REMOVAL AND INSTALLATION

1968—and later

1. Remove the steering wheel and the directional signal switch. It is not necessary to pull the wiring harness out of the column. See the applicable procedures above.

Using a special tool to remove the lockplate retaining ring on 1969 and later cars (© Chevrolet Motor Division)

Depressing the lock cylinder retainer (1969 and later cars) (© Chevrolet Motor Division)

Removing the turn signal switch assembly (© Chevrolet Motor Division)

ADAPTER   ANTI-THEFT RING

WAVE WASHER

LOCK CYLINDER SLEEVE

IGNITION LOCK CYLINDER

Exploded view of ignition lock assembly (© Chevrolet Motor Division)

DISASSEMBLE

1. Place lock in "run".

2. Remove lock plate, turn signal switch and buzzer switch (see service manual.)

3. Remove screw & lock cylinder. **CAUTION:** *If screw is dropped on removal, it could fall into the column, requiring complete disassembly to retrieve the screw.*

ASSEMBLE

1. Rotate as shown, align cylinder key with keyway in housing.

2. Push lock all the way in.

3. Install screw. Tighten to 4.5 N·m for regular columns— 2.5 N·m for adjustable columns.

LOCK CYLINDER SET

To assemble — Rotate to stop while holding cylinder.

HOUSING

CYLINDER KEY

LOCK RETAINING SCREW

Lock cylinder removal—1979 shown, others similiar

2. Place the lock cylinder in "Lock" (up to 1970), or "Run" (1971–and later).

3. Insert a smll screwdriver into the turn signal housing slot. Keeping the screwdriver to the right side of the slot, break the housing flash loose and depress the spring latch at the lower end of the lock cylinder. Remove the lock cylinder.

NOTE: *Considerable force may be necessary to break this casting flash, but be careful not to damage any other parts. When ordering a new lock cylinder, specify a cylinder assembly. This will save assembling the cylinder washer, sleeve, and adaptor.*

4. To install, hold the lock cylinder sleeve and rotate the knob clockwise against the stop. Insert the cylinder into the housing, aligning the key and keyway. On 1969–76 cars hold a 0.070 in. drill between the lock bezel and the housing. On 1977–and later cars, push the cylinder into abutment of cylinder and sector. Rotate the cylinder counterclockwise, maintaining a light pressure until the drive section of the cylinder mates with the sector. Push in until the snap-ring pops into the grooves. Remove the drill. Check the operation of the cylinder. Install the direction signal switch and steering wheel.

Manual Steering Gear
REMOVAL AND INSTALLATION

NOTE: *On 1964–67 models, remove the stabilizer bar-to-frame mounting brackets. Unbolt the left front bumper bracket and brace from the frame after marking their location.*

1. Disconnect the steering shaft coupling.

LASH ADJUSTER SCREW

ALIGNMENT MARKS

LOCK NUT

WORM BEARING ADJUSTER

Typical steering gear mounting

2. Remove the pitman arm with a puller after marking the arm-to-shaft relationship.

3. Remove the steering gear-to-frame mounting bolts and remove the steering gear.

4. Reverse the removal steps to install the steering gear. Tighten the frame mounting bolts to 70 ft. lbs. Tighten the pitman shaft nut to 180 ft. lbs. and the steering coupling nuts to 20 ft. lbs.

Power Steering Gear
REMOVAL AND INSTALLATION

Installation and removal of power steering gears is the same as that described for manual steering gears above, with the addition of disconnecting and reconnecting the hydraulic lines. Cap both hoses and steering gear outlets to prevent foreign material from entering the system.

Power Steering Pump
REMOVAL AND INSTALLATION

1. Remove the hoses at the pump and tape the openings shut to prevent contamination. Position the disconnected lines in a raised position to prevent leakage.
2. Remove the pump belt.
3. Loosen the retaining bolts and any braces, and remove the pump.
4. Install the pump on the engine with the retaining bolts hand-tight.
5. Connect and tighten the hose fittings.
6. Refill the pump with fluid and bleed by turning the pulley counterclockwise (viewed from the front). Stop the bleeding when air bubbles no longer appear.
7. Install the pump belt on the pulley and adjust the tension as described in Chapter 1.

SYSTEM BLEEDING

1. Fill the fluid reservoir.
2. Let the fluid stand undisturbed for two minutes, then crank the engine for about two seconds. Refill reservoir if necessary.
3. Repeat Steps 1 and 2 above until the fluid level remains constant after cranking the engine.
4. Raise the front of the car until the wheels are off the ground, then start the engine. Increase the engine speed to about 1,500 rpm.
5. Turn the wheels to the left and right, checking the fluid level and refilling if necessary. If the oil is extremely foamy, allow the car to stand a few minutes with the engine off, then repeat the above procedure.

Steering Linkage
TIE-ROD REMOVAL AND INSTALLATION

1. Remove the cotter pins and nuts from the tie-rod end studs.
2. Tap on the steering arm near the tie-rod end (use another hammer as backing) and pull down on the tie-rod, if necessary, to free it.
3. Remove the inner stud in the same manner as the outer.
4. Loosen the clamp bolts and unscrew the ends if they are being replaced.
5. Lubricate the tie-rod end threads with chassis grease if they were removed. Install each end assembly an equal distance from the sleeve.
6. Ensure that the tie-rod end stud threads and nut are clean. Install new seals and install the studs into the steering arms and relay rod.
7. Install the stud nuts. Tighten the inner and outer end nuts to 35 ft. lbs.
8. Adjust the toe-in to specifications.
NOTE: *Before tightening the sleeve clamps, ensure that the clamps are positioned so that adjusting sleeve slot is covered by the clamp.*

Disconnecting steering linkage using puller (arrow) or ball joint tool

IDLER ARM REMOVAL AND INSTALLATION

1. Remove the idler arm-to-frame nut, washer, and bolt.
2. Remove the cotter pin and nut from the idler arm-to-relay rod ball end stud.
3. Tap the relay rod with a hammer, using

Power steering pump and lines, all models similar

STEERING GEAR

(35 FT. LBS.)

OUTER TIE ROD

IDLER ARM

(60 FT. LBS.)

ADJUSTER SLEEVE

STEERING KNUCKLE

PITMAN ARM

(185 FT. LBS.)

* AFTER REACHING TORQUE REQUIRED, NUT MUST ALWAYS BE TIGHTENED (UP TO 1/6 TURN) FURTHER. NEVER BACK NUT OFF TO INSERT COTTER PIN.

Steering linkage, all models similar

another hammer as backing, to remove the relay rod from the idler arm.

4. Remove the idler arm.

5. Place the idler arm on the frame and install the retaining bolts and nuts. Tighten the nuts to 35 ft. lbs.

6. Position the relay rod on the idler arm. Ensure that the seal is on the stud. Install the nut and tighten to 35 ft. lbs. Install a cotter pin.

RELAY ROD (INTERMEDIATE ROD) REMOVAL AND INSTALLATION

1. Remove the inner tie-rod ends from the relay rod as outlined under "Toe-Rod Removal and Installation."

2. On 1974 models with manual steering, remove the damper from the relay rod.

3. Remove the relay rod stud nut and cotter pin from the pitman arm. Free the relay rod from the pitman arm, moving the steering linkage if necessary. Repeat this operation to remove the relay rod from the idler arm and remove the relay rod from the car.

4. Install the relay rod on the idler arm. Tighten the nut to 35 ft. lbs.

5. Raise the relay and install it on the pitman arm. Tighten the nut to 45 ft. lbs.

6. Install the tie-rod ends to the relay rod.

7. Install the damper on 1974 models.

8. Adjust the toe-in as previously described.

PITMAN ARM REMOVAL AND INSTALLATION

1. Remove the pitman arm stud nut and cotter pin.

2. Tap the relay rod off the pitman arm, using another hammer as backing. Pull the relay rod off the pitman arm stud.

3. Remove the pitman arm nut and mark the arm-to-shaft relationship.

4. Remove the pitman arm using a puller.

5. Install the pitman arm on the shaft, aligning the previously made marks. Install the pitman shaft nut and tighten it to 180 ft. lbs.

6. Install the relay rod on the pitman arm. Tighten the nut to 45 ft. lbs. and install a cotter pin.

HYDRAULIC SYSTEM

Master Cylinder

REMOVAL AND INSTALLATION

1. Disconnect the hydraulic line(s) at the master cylinder.

2. Remove the two retaining nuts and lockwashers that hold the cylinder to firewall.

NOTE: *Starting in 1967, disconnect the pushrod at the brake pedal.*

3. Remove the master cylinder, gasket and rubber boot.

4. Position the master cylinder on the firewall, making sure that the pushrod goes through the rubber boot into the piston.

NOTE: *Starting in 1967, reconnect pushrod clevis to brake pedal.*

5. Install nuts and lockwashers.

6. Install hydraulic line(s), then check the brake pedal free-play.

7. Bleed the brakes, as described later in this chapter.

NOTE: *Cars having disc brakes do not have a check valve in the front outlet port of the master cylinder. If one is installed, front discs will immediately wear out due to residual hydraulic pressure holding pads against rotor.*

OVERHAUL

1964–66

1. Secure the master cylinder in a vise and remove the pushrod assembly and protective boot. This exposes the lock ring which, when removed, allows extraction of the piston stop, secondary cup, and piston.

2. Remove the cylinder end plug and push out the primary cup, spring, valve assembly, and seat.

3. Wash the component parts with denatured alcohol.

Master cylinder mounting

4. Carefully inspect the washed metal parts and the cylinder bore. A corroded cylinder must be replaced. Discoloration or stains can be removed with crocus cloth. When doing this, wrap

1. Reservoir cover	7. Spring
2. Bail wire	8. Primary cup
3. Seal	9. Piston
4. Body	10. Secondary cup
5. Valve seat	11. Lock ring
6. Valve assembly	12. Boot

Cutaway view of typical master cylinder—1964–66

the cloth around your finger and rotate the cylinder around the cloth.

CAUTION: *Do not polish the bore lengthwise, as this can cause a fluid leak.*

5. To reassemble, moisten the cylinder bore with brake fluid and replace the valve seat, valve assembly, and spring.

CAUTION: *Be sure that the valve and seat are properly installed before proceeding. An incorrectly assembled check valve will distort and fail to provide a check valve seal, which will result in a reduction of brake pedal travel with a corresponding loss in braking.*

6. Moisten the primary cup with brake fluid and install it, flat side out, and seated over the spring. The primary cup is distinguished by a brass support ring at its base.

7. Dip the secondary cup in brake fluid and slip it over the end of the piston.

8. Insert the completed assembly, with the bleeder brake end of the piston installed first. Secure the parts with the piston stop and the snap-ring, and install the end plug.

9. Attach the rubber boot and pushrod, and install the master cylinder.

10. Attach the brake pedal clevis and adjust the pushrod-to-piston clearance. Correct adjustment calls for a barely perceptible free pedal before piston/pushrod contact.

NOTE: *Overhaul of the main cylinder portion of power brake master cylinders is the same as that for manual master cylinders.*

1967 and Later

1. Remove the master cylinder from the car.

2. Remove the mounting gasket and boot, and the main cover. Empty the cylinder of all fluid.

Typical master cylinder mounting for cars equipped with power brakes

3. Place the cylinder in a vise and remove the pushrod retainer and the secondary piston stop bolt that are found inside the front reservoir.

4. Remove the retaining ring and primary piston assembly.

5. Direct compressed air into the piston stop screw hole to force the secondary piston, spring, and retainer from the cylinder bore. If compressed air isn't available, use a hooked wire to pull out the secondary piston.

6. Check the brass tube fitting inserts and, if damaged, remove them; if not, leave them in place.

7. If insert replacement is necessary, thread a No. 6-32 x ⅝ in. self-tapping screw into the insert. Hook the end of the screw with a claw hammer and pull out the insert.

8. An alternative (but more troublesome) way to remove the inserts is to drill out the outlet holes with a ¹³⁄₆₄ in. drill and then thread

Cross section of a master cylinder

1. Spring	10. Spring	18. Secondary piston stop
2. Check valve	11. Retainer	19. Spring
3. Valve seat	12. Seal	20. Spring retainer
4. Bleeder valve	13. Seal protector	21. Seal
5. Bail wire	14. Primary piston	22. Seal protector
6. Cover	15. Seal	23. Secondary piston
7. Diaphragm	16. Seal	24. Seal
8. Stopscrew	17. Piston extension screw	25. Retaining ring
9. Body		

Exploded view of a master cylinder. Some 1980 and all 1981 and later models no longer use the bails to retain the reservoir cap.

them with a ¼ in.-20 tap. Position a thick washer over the hole to serve as a spacer and then thread a ¼ in.-20 x ¾ in. hex-head bolt into the insert and tighten the bolt until the insert is free.

9. Use only *denatured alcohol* or brake fluid and compressed air to clean the parts. Slight rust may be removed with crocus cloth.

CAUTION: *Do not polish the aluminum bore of type "A" cylinders with any type of abrasive. Never use any mineral-based solvents (gasoline, kerosene, etc.) for cleaning. It will quickly deteriorate rubber parts.*

10. Replace the brass tube inserts by positioning them in their holes and threading a brake line tube nut into the outlet hole. Turn down the nut until the insert is seated.

11. Check the piston assemblies for correct identification and, when satisfied, position the replacement secondary seals in the twin grooves of the secondary piston.

12. The outside seal is correctly placed when its lips face the flat end of the piston.

13. Slip the primary seal and its protector over the end of the secondary piston opposite the secondary seals. The flat side of this seal

Master cylinder with plastic removable reservoir

Moraine cast iron master cylinder with integral reservoir as used on 350 diesel models

should face the piston's compensating hole flange.

14. Replace the primary piston assembly with the assembled piece in the overhaul kit.

15. Coat the cylinder bore and the secondary piston's inner and outer seals with brake fluid. Assemble the secondary piston spring to its retainer and place them over the end of the primary seal.

16. Insert the combined spring and piston assembly into the cylinder and, using a pencil, seat the spring against the end of the bore.

17. Coat the primary piston seals with brake fluid and push it (push rod receptacle end out) into the cylinder.

18. Hold the piston in and snap the retaining ring into place.

19. Continue to hold the piston down to

make sure that all components are seated and insert the secondary piston stop screw in its hole in the bottom of the front reservoir. Torque the screw to 25–40 in. lbs.

20. Install the reservoir diaphragm and cover.

21. It will save time to bleed the cylinder before installing it in the car. Do so in the following manner:

a. Install plugs in the outlet ports

b. Place the unit in a vise with the front end tilted slightly downward. *DO NOT OVERTIGHTEN* the vise.

c. Fill both reservoirs with clean fluid

d. Using a smooth, round rod (try the eraser end of a pencil), push in on the primary piston.

e. Release the pressure on the rod and watch for air bubblies in the fluid. Keep repeating this until the bubbles disappear.

f. Loosen the vise and position the cylinder so the front end if tilted slightly upward. Repeat steps "d" and "e."

g. Place the diaphragm cover on the reservoir.

NOTE: *Master cylinder overhaul on cars with power brakes is the same as above.*

Combination Valve

REMOVAL AND INSTALLATION

1. Disconnect the negative battery cable.

2. Disconnect the electrical lead from the switch.

3. Place rags under the unit to absorb any spilled brake fluid.

4. Clean any dirt from the hydraulic lines and the switch/valve assembly. Disconnect the hydraulic lines from the assembly. If necessary, loosen the line connections at the master cylinder. Tape the open line ends to prevent the entrance of dirt.

5. Remove the mounting screws and remove the switch/valve assembly.

6. Make sure that the new unit is clean and free of dust and line. If in doubt, wash the new unit in clean brake fluid.

Combination valve mounting on front frame member

Power booster mounting

Have an assistant pump the brake pedal slowly while you bleed each wheel

7. Place the new unit in position and install it to its mounting bracket with screws.

8. Remove the tape from the hydraulic lines and connect them to the unit. If necessary, tighten the line connections at the master cylinder.

9. Connect the electrical lead.

10. Connect the negative battery cable.

11. Bleed the brake systems.

Power Booster
REMOVAL AND INSTALLATION

1. Disconnect the booster pushrod from the brake pedal arm by removing the retaining clip, and sliding the eyelet end of the pushrod off of the pin on the brake arm.

2. Disconnect the master cylinder from the booster.

3. Remove the attaching nuts and remove the booster from the firewall.

4. Installation is the reverse of removal. Tighten the booster-to-firewall attaching nut to 22 – 33 ft. lbs.

Brake Bleeding

The hydraulic brake system must be bled any time one of the lines is disconnected or any time air enters the system. If the brake pedal feels spongy upon application, and goes almost to the floor but regains height when pumped, air has entered the system. It must be bled out. Check for leaks that would have allowed the entry of air and repair them before bleeding the system. The correct bleeding sequence is: right rear wheel cylinder, left rear, right front, and left front. If the master cylinder is equipped with bleeder valves, bleed them first then go to the wheel cylinder nearest the master cylinder (left front) followed by the right front, left rear, and right rear.

MANUAL BLEEDING

This method of bleeding requires two people, one to depress the brake pedal and the other to open the bleeder screws.

1. Clean the top of the master cylinder, remove the cover and fill the reservoirs with clean fluid. To prevent squirting fluid, replace the cover.

IMPORTANT: *On cars with front disc brakes, it will be necessary to hold in the metering valve pin during the bleeding procedure. The metering valve is located beneath the master cylinder and the pin is situated under the rubber boot on the end of the valve housing. This may be taped in or held by an assistant.*

CAUTION: *Never reuse brake fluid which has been bled from the system.*

2. Fill the master cylinder with brake fluid.

3. Install a box-end wrench on the bleeder screw on the right rear wheel.

4. Attach a length of small diameter, clear vinyl tubing to the bleeder screw. Submerge the other end of the rubber tubing in a glass jar partially filled with clean brake fluid. Make sure the rubber tube fits on the bleeder screw

Wrench and plastic tubing fit on the bleeder nipple on each caliper

snugly or you may be squirted with brake fluid when the bleeder screw is opened.

5. Have your friend slowly depress the brake pedal. As this is done, open the bleeder screw half a turn and allow the fluid to run through the tube. Close the bleeder screw, then return the brake pedal to its fully released position.

6. Repeat this procedure until no bubbles appear in the jar. Refill the master cylinder.

7. Repeat this procedure on the left rear, right front, and left front wheels, in that order. Periodically refill the master cylinder so it does not run dry.

8. If the brake warning light is on, depress the brake pedal firmly. If there is no air in the system, the light will go out.

FRONT DISC BRAKES

Disc Brake Pads

INSPECTION

Brake pads should be inspected once a year or at 7,500 miles, whichever occurs first. Check both ends of the outboard shoe, looking in at each end of the caliper; then check the lining thickness on the inboard shoe, looking down through the inspection hole. Lining should be more than .020″ thick above the rivet (so that the lining is thicker than the metal backing). Keep in mind that any applicable state inspection standards that are more stringent take precedence. All four pads must be replaced if one shows excessive wear.

NOTE: *All 1979 and later models have a wear indicator that makes a noise when the linings wear to a degree where replacement is necessary. The spring clip is an integral part of the inboard shoe and lining. When the brake pad reaches a certain degree of wear, the clip will contact the rotor and produce a warning noise.*

REMOVAL AND INSTALLATION

1966−68

1. Siphon off about two-thirds of the brake fluid from a full master cylinder.

CAUTION: *The insertion of the thicker replacement pads will push the caliper pistons back into their bores and will cause a full master cylinder to overflow causing paint damage. In addition to siphoning fluid, it would be wise to keep the cylinder cover on during pad replacement.*

2. Raise the car and support it with jack stands. Remove the wheels.

NOTE: *Replacing the pads on just one wheel will result in uneven braking. Always replace the pads on both wheels.*

3. Extract and discard the pad retaining pin cotter key.

Disc brake pad inspection

Front disc brake pad wear indicator—1979 and later

New and worn brake pads

4. Remove the retaining pin and, while removing one pad, insert its replacement before the piston has time to move outward. If you were too slow and the pistons were too fast, it will be necessary to use a wide-bladed putty knife to hold in the pistons while inserting the new pads. If this gives you difficulty open the bleeder screw on that caliper and release some of the fluid, but do not allow the fluid to drain from the master cylinder. This may reduce the pressure and make it easier to push in on the pistons. After removing the outboard pad, inspect it and compare it with the inboard pad. They may be slightly different; if so, make sure that the replacement pads are installed correctly.

5. After installing the new pads, install the retaining pin and insert a new cotter pin.

6. Refill the master cylinder and bleed the system if necessary.

1969—and later

1. Siphon off about two-thirds of the brake fluid from a full master cylinder.

CAUTION: *The insertion of the thicker replacement pads will push the piston back into its bore and will cause a full master cylinder to overflow causing paint damage. In addition to siphoning off fluid it would be wise to keep the cylinder cover on during pad replacement.*

2. Raise the car and support it with jackstands. Remove the wheels.

NOTE: *Replacing the pads on just one wheel*

Use a C-clamp to seat the caliper piston

Installing the shoe support spring—1970–8

will result in uneven braking. Alwo place the pads on both wheels.

3. Install a C-clamp on the calipe the solid side of the clamp rests agains of the caliper and so the screw end r the metal part (shoe) of the outboa

4. Tighten the clamp until the enough to bottom the piston i move the clamp.

5. Remove the two al' mounting bolts enough to al' be pulled off the disc.

6. Remove the inboard outboard pad. Place the ca' strain the brake hose. It we it out of the way.

7. Remove the pad sup the piston.

8. Remove the two bol four rubber bushings from

9. Brake pads should be are worn to within 1/32 in.

10. Check the inside of age and the condition of th

11. Lubricate the two r bushings with a silicone sp

12. Install the bushing Install the two sleeves in td

13. Install the pad supu the old pad into the centon will then push this pad d

CALIPER HOUSING

Install inboard brake shoe

SHOE RETAINER SPRING

INBOARD SHOE AND LINING

er retaining spring installation

PRY AGAINST STEERING
KNUCKLE ATTACHING
BOLT

OVE CALIPER
SSEMBLY OUT TO
EE OUTSIDE SHOE

MOVE CALIPER
ASSEMBLY IN TO
FREE INBOARD SHOE

essing caliper with pry bar

END OF BOLT
S UNDER
ING EAR

must go under the pad retaining
rolet Motor Division).

caliper. This part of the job is a
uires an assistant. While the as-
e caliper and loosens the bleeder
pressure, you get a pry bar and
old pad into make the piston
cl aliper surface. When it is flush,
the r valve so that no air gets into
N

*models with wear sensors, make
the sensor is toward the rear of*

CHANNEL LOCK
PLIERS (12")

UPPER SHOE EAR

SMALL NOTCH

Use pliers to fit the brake pad to the caliper housing

14. Place the outboard pad in the caliper with its top ears over the caliper ears and the bottom tab engaged in the caliper cutout.

15. After both pads are installed, lift the caliper and place the bottom edge of the outboard pad on the outer edge of the disc to make sure that there is no clearance between the tab on the bottom of the shoes and the caliper abutment.

16. Place the caliper over the disc, lining up the hole in the caliper ears with the hole in the mounting bracket. Make sure that the brake hose is not kinked.

17. Start the caliper-to-mounting bracket bolts through the sleeves in the inboard caliper ears and through the mounting bracket making sure that the ends of the bolts pass under the retaining ears of the inboard shoe.

18. Push the mounting bolts through to engage the holes in the outboard shoes and the outboard caliper ears and then threading them into the mounting bracket.

19. Torque the mounting bolts to 35 ft. lbs. Pump the brake pedal to seat the linings against the rotors.

20. With a pair of channel lock pliers placed on the notch on the caliper housing, bend the caliper upper ears until no clearance exists between the shoe and the caliper housing.

21. Install the wheels, lower the car, and refill the master cylinder with fluid. Pump the brake pedal to make sure that it is firm. If it is not, bleed the brakes.

CALIPER REPLACEMENT AND OVERHAUL

1966–68

1. Raise the car and support it on jackstands.

2. Remove the tire and wheel assembly from the side on which the caliper is being removed.

MOUNTING BOLT
SLEEVE
BUSHING
BLEEDER SCREW
BUSHING
PISTON SEAL
PISTON
BOOT
SHOE RETAINER SPRING
INBOARD SHOE AND LINING
OUTBOARD SHOE AND LINING

Exploded view of the brake caliper. Single piston type shown

3. Disconnect the brake hose at the support bracket. Tape the end of the line to prevent contamination.

4. Remove the cotter pin from the brake pad and retaining pin and remove the pin.

5. Remove the brake pads and identify them as inboard or outboard if they are being reused.

6. Remove the U-shaped retainer from the hose fitting and pull the hose from the bracket.

7. Remove the two caliper retaining bolts and also the caliper from its mounting bracket.

8. Separate the caliper halves. Remove the two O-rings from the fluid transfer holes in the caliper.

9. Push the piston all the way down into the caliper. Using the piston as a fulcrum, place a screwdriver under the steel ring in the boot and pry the boot from the caliper half.

10. Remove the pistons and springs, being careful not to damage the seal.

11. Remove the boot and seal from the piston.

12. Clean all metal components with clean brake fluid or denatured alcohol.

CAUTION: *Do not use gasoline, kerosene, or any other mineral-based solvent for cleaning. These solvents form an oily film on the parts which leads to fluid contamination and the deterioration of rubber parts.*

13. Blow out all fluid passages with an air hose.

14. Discard and replace all rubber parts.

15. Inspect all bores for scoring and pitting and replace if necessary. Minor flaws can be removed with very fine crocus cloth but do so with a circular motion.

16. Using a feeler gauge, check the clearance of the piston in its bore. If the bore is not damaged and the clearance exceeds the maximum limit below, then the piston must be replaced.

Bore Diameter	Clearance
2$\frac{1}{16}$ in.	0.0045–0.010 in.
1$\frac{7}{8}$ in.	0.0045–0.010 in.
1$\frac{3}{8}$ in.	0.0035–0.009 in.

17. Insert the seal in the piston groove nearest the flat end of the piston. The seal lip must face the large end of the piston. The lips must be in the groove and may not extend beyond.

18. Place the spring in the piston bore.

19. Coat the seal with clean brake fluid.

20. Install the piston assembly into the bore, being careful not to damage the seal lip on the edge of the bore.

21. Install the boot into the piston groove closest to the concave end of the piston.

22. The fold in the boot must face the seal end of the piston.

23. Push the pistons to the bottom of the bore and check for smooth piston movement. The end of the piston must be flush with the end of the bore. If it is not, check the installation of the seal.

24. Seat the piston boot so that its metal ring is even in the counterbore. The ring is even in the counterbore. The ring must be flush or below the machined face of the caliper. If the ring is seated unevenly dirt and moisture could get into the bore.

25. Insert the O-rings around the fluid transfer holes at both ends of the caliper halves.

26. Lubricate the bolts with brake fluid, connect the caliper halves, and torque the bolts to 130 ft. lbs.

27. While holding in the brake pistons with a putty knife, mount the caliper over the disc. Be careful not to damage the piston boots on the edge of the disc.

28. Install the two mounting bolts and torque them to 130 ft. lbs.

29. Install the brake pads. If the same pads are being reused, return them to their original places (outboard or inboard) as marked during removal. New pads will usually have an arrow on the back indicating the direction of disc rotation. See "Brake Pad Replacement" for details.

30. Install the brake hose into the caliper, passing the female end through the support bracket.

31. Make sure that the tube line is clean and connect the brake line nut to the caliper.

32. Install the hose fitting into the support bracket and install the U-shaped retainer. Turn the steering wheel from side to side to make sure that the hose doesn't interfere with the tire. If it does, turn the hose end one or two points in the bracket until the interference is eliminated.

33. After performing the above check, install the steel tube connector and tighten it.

34. Bleed the brakes as instructed earlier in this chapter.

35. Install the wheels and lower the car.

1969 and later

1. Perform the removal steps for pad replacement.

2. Disconnect the brake hose and plug the line.

3. Remove the U-shaped retainer from the fitting.

4. Pull the hose from the frame bracket and remove the caliper with the hose attached.

5. Clean the outside of the caliper with denatured alcohol.

Piston removal using compressed air. Keep fingers out of the way of the piston when the air is applied

6. Remove the brake hose and discard the copper gasket.

7. Remove the brake fluid from the caliper.

8. Place clean rags inside the caliper opening to catch the piston when it is released.

9. Apply compressed air to the caliper fluid inlet hole and force the piston out of its bore. Do not blow the piston out; use just enough pressure to ease it out.

10. Use a screwdriver to pry the boot out of the caliper. Avoid scratching the bore.

11. Remove the piston seal from its groove in the caliper bore. *Do not use a metal tool of any type for this operation.*

NOTE: *Replace (do not reuse) the boot, piston seal, rubber bushings, and sleeves.*

12. Blow out all passages in the caliper and bleeder valve. Clean the piston and piston bore with fresh brake fluid.

13. Examine the piston for scoring, scratches, or corrosion. If any of these conditions exist, the piston must be replaced because it is plated and cannot be refinished.

14. Examine the bore for the same defects. Light rough spots may be removed by rotating crocus cloth, using finger pressure, in the bore. Do not polish with an in-and-out motion or use any other abrasive.

15. Lubricate the piston bore and the new rubber parts with fresh brake fluid. Position the seal in the piston bore groove.

16. Lubricate the piston with brake fluid and assemble the boot into the piston groove so that the fold faces the open end of the piston.

17. Insert the piston into the bore, taking care not to unseat the seal.

18. Force the piston to the bottom of the bore (this will require a force of 40–100 lbs). Seat the boot lip around the caliper counterbore. Proper seating of the boot is very important for sealing out contaminants.

19. Install the brake hose into the caliper with a new copper gasket.

20. Lubricate the new sleeves and rubber bushings. Install the bushings in the caliper ears. Install the sleeves so that the end toward the disc pad is flush with the machined surface.

NOTE: *Lubrication of the sleeves and bushings is essential to insure the proper operation of the sliding caliper design.*

21. Install the shoe support spring in the piston.

22. Install the disc pads in the caliper and remount the caliper on the hub (see "Disc Pad Replacement").

23. Reconnect the brake hose to the steel brake line. Install the retainer clip. Bleed the brakes (see "Brake Bleeding").

24. Replace the wheels, check the brake fluid level, check the brake pedal travel, and road-test the vehicle.

Brake Disc

DISC INSPECTION

1. Tighten the spindle nut to remove all wheel bearing play.

2. Install a dial indicator on the caliper so that its feeler will contact the disc about 1 in. below its outer edge.

3. Turn the disc and observe the runout reading. If the reading exceeds 0.002 in. (.004 in. total reading), the disc should be replaced.

4. Measure the thickness of the rotor at 5

Use a dial indicator to determine brake disc runout

points around the circumference. Tolerance is .0005 in.

5. Minimum thickness dimensions are cast into the caliper for reference.

DISC REPLACEMENT

1. Raise the car, support it with jackstands, and remove the wheel and tire assembly.

Exploded view of the disc brake assembly

Discard dimension (.965) stamped on disc hub

2. Remove the brake caliper as previously outlined.

3. Drill out the five rivets holding the disc to the hub.

4. Remove the disc.

5. Remove the rivet stubs from the hub.

6. Install the disc on the hub, aligning the lug bolts with the holes in the disc.

7. Install the brake caliper and shoes as previously outlined.

8. Bleed the brakes, install the wheel, and lower the car. Adjust front wheel bearings as described at the end of this chapter.

Wheel Bearings

Properly adjusted bearings have a slightly loose feeling. Wheel bearings must never be preloaded. Preloading will damage the bearings and eventually the spindles. If the bearings are too loose, they should be cleaned, inspected, and then adjusted.

Hold the tire at the top and bottom and move the wheel in and out of the spindle. If the movement is greater than 0.008 in. (0.005 in. 1974 and later), the bearings are too loose.

ADJUSTMENT

1. Raise and support the car by the lower control arm.

2. Remove the hub cap, then remove the dust cap from the hub.

3. Remove the cotter pin and spindle nut.

4. Spin the wheel forward by hand. Tighten the nut until snug to fully seat the bearings.

5. Back off the nut ¼–½ turn until it is just loose, then tighten it finger-tight.

6. Loosen the nut until either hole in the spindle lines up with a slot in the nut and then insert the cotter pin. This may appear to be too loose, but it is the correct adjustment. The spindle nut should not be even fingertight.

Wheel bearing adjustment

7. Proper adjustment creates 0.001–0.008 in (0.001–0.005 in. 1974 and later) of endplay.

REMOVAL AND INSTALLATION

1964–69

1. Remove the wheel and tire assembly, and the brake drum or brake caliper.

2. On those cars with disc brakes, remove the hub and disc as an assembly. Remove the caliper mounting bolts and insert a block between the brake pads as the caliper is removed. Remove the caliper and wire it out of the way.

3. Pry out the grease cap, cotter pin, spindle nut, and washer, then remove the hub. Do not drop the wheel bearings.

4. Remove the outer roller bearing assembly from the hub. The inner bearing assembly will remain in the hub and may be removed after prying out the inner seal. Discard the seal.

5. Clean all parts in solvent (air dry) and check for excessive wear or damage.

6. Using a hammer and drift, remove the bearing cups from the hub. When installing new cups, make sure they are not cocked and that they are fully seated against the hub shoulder.

7. Using a high melting point bearing lubricant, pack both inner and outer bearings.

8. Place the inner bearing in the hub and install a new inner seal, making sure the seal flange faces the bearing cup.

9. Carefully install the wheel hub over the spindle.

10. Using your hands, firmly press the outer bearing into the hub. Install the spindle washer and nut, and adjust as instructed above.

1970—and later

1. Remove the hub and disc assembly as described in Steps 1–63 above.

2. Remove the outer roller bearing assembly from the hub. The inner bearing assembly can be removed after prying out the inner seal. Discard the seal.

3. Wash all parts in solvent and check for excessive wear or damage.

4. To replace the outer or inner race, knock out the old race with a hammer and brass drift. New races must be installed squarely and evenly to avoid damage.

5. Pack the bearings with a high melting-point bearing lubricant.

6. Lightly grease the spindle and the inside of the hub.

7. Place the inner bearing in the hub race and install a new grease seal.

8. Carefully install the hub and disc assembly.

9. Install the outer wheel bearing.

10. Install the washer and nut and adjust the bearings according to the procedure outlined above.

11. Install the caliper and torque the mounting bolts to 35 ft. lbs.

12. Install the dust cap and the wheel and tire assembly, then lower the car to the ground.

PACKING

Clean the wheel bearings thoroughly with solvent and check their condition before installation.

CAUTION: *Do not blow the bearing dry with compressed air as this would allow the bearing to turn without lubrication.*

Apply a sizable daub of lubricant to the palm of one hand. Using your other hand, work the bearing into the lubricant so that the grease is pushed through the rollers and out the other side. Keep rotating the bearing while continuing to push the lubricant through it.

FRONT AND REAR DRUM BRAKES

Brake Drum

REPLACEMENT

1. Raise and support the car.

2. Remove the wheel or wheels.

3. Pull the brake drum off. It may be necessary to gently tap the rear edges of the drum to start it off the studs.

4. If extreme resistance to removal is encountered, it will be necessary to retract the

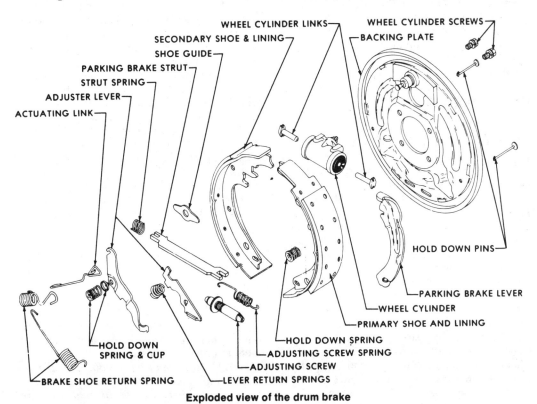

WHEEL CYLINDER LINKS
SECONDARY SHOE & LINING
SHOE GUIDE
PARKING BRAKE STRUT
STRUT SPRING
ADJUSTER LEVER
ACTUATING LINK
WHEEL CYLINDER SCREWS
BACKING PLATE
HOLD DOWN PINS
PARKING BRAKE LEVER
WHEEL CYLINDER
PRIMARY SHOE AND LINING
HOLD DOWN SPRING
ADJUSTING SCREW SPRING
ADJUSTING SCREW
LEVER RETURN SPRINGS
HOLD DOWN SPRING & CUP
BRAKE SHOE RETURN SPRING

Exploded view of the drum brake

BACKING PLATE

TOOL J-4735

INSERT SMALL SCREWDRIVER OR AWL THROUGH BACKING PLATE SLOT AND HOLD ADJUSTER LEVER AWAY FROM SPROCKET BEFORE BACKING OFF BRAKE SHOE ADJUSTMENT

Brake adjustment

adjusting screw. Knock out the access hole in the brake drum and turn the adjuster to retract the linings away from the drum.

5. Install a replacement hole cover before reinstalling drum.

6. Install the drums in the same position on the hub as removed. Adjust front wheel bearings as described at the end of this chapter.

DRUM INSPECTION

1. Check the drums for any cracks, scores, grooves, or an out-of-round condition. Replace if cracked. Slight scores can be removed with fine emery cloth while extensive scoring requires turning the drum on a lathe.

2. Never have a drum turned more than 0.060 in.

Brake Shoes

ADJUSTMENT

1. Raise the car and support it with safety stands.

2. Remove the rubber plug from the adjusting slot on the backing plate.

3. Insert a brake adjusting spoon into the slot and engage the lowest possible tooth on the starwheel. Move the end of the brake spoon downward to move the starwheel upward and expand the adjusting screw. Repeat this operation until the brakes lock the wheel.

4. Insert a small screwdriver or piece of firm fire (coat-hanger wire) into the adjusting slot and push the automatic adjuster lever out and free of the starwheel on the adjusting screw.

5. Holding the adjusting lever out of the way, engage the topmost tooth possible on the starwheel with a brake adjusting spoon. Move the end of the adjusting spoon upward to move the adjusting screw starwheel downward and con-

tract the adjusting screw. Back off the adjusting screw starwheel until the wheel spins freely with a minimum of drag. Keep track of the number of turns the starwheel is backed off.

6. Repeat this operation for the other side. When backing off the brakes on the other side, the adjusting lever must be backed off the same number of turns to prevent side-to-side brake pull.

7. Repeat this operation on the other set of brakes (front or rear).

8. When all 4 brakes are adjusted, make several stops, while backing the car, to equalize all of the wheels.

9. Road-test the car.

REMOVAL AND INSTALLATION

1. Raise the car and support it on jackstands.

2. Slacken the parking brake cable.

3. Remove the rear wheel and brake drum. The front wheel and drum may be removed as a unit by removing the spindle nut and cotter pin.

4. Free the brake shoe return springs, actuator pull-back spring, hold-down pins and springs, and actuator assembly.

NOTE: *Special tools available from auto supply stores will ease removal of the spring and anchor pin, but the job may still be done with common hand tools.*

5. On the rear wheels, disconnect the adjusting mechanism and spring, and remove the primary shoe. The primary shoe has a shorter lining than the secondary and is mounted at the front of the wheel.

6. Disconnect the parking brake lever from the secondary shoe and remove the shoe. Front wheel shoes may be removed together.

7. Clean and inspect all brake parts.

8. Check the wheel cylinders for seal condition and leaking.

9. Repack wheel bearings and replace the seals.

10. Inspect the replacement shoes for nicks or burrs, lubricate the backing plate contact points, brake cable and levers, and adjusting screws and then assemble.

11. Make sure that the right and left-hand adjusting screws are not mixed. You can prevent this by working on one side at a time. This will also provide you with a reference for reassembly. The star wheel should be nearest to the secondary shoe when correctly installed.

12. To install, reverse the removal procedure. When completed, make an initial adjustment as previously described.

NOTE: *Maintenance procedures for the metallic lining option are the same as those for standard linings. Do not substitute these lin-*

ings in standard drums, unless they have been honed to a 20 micro-inch finish and equipped with special heat-resistant springs.

Wheel Cylinders

OVERHAUL

As is the case with master cylinders, overhaul kits for wheel cylinders are readily available. It is a good idea to replace the cylinders on both sides when you replace one (when one side leaks or fails, the other side is usually in the same shape). When rebuilding and installing wheel cylinders, avoid getting any contaminants into the system. Always install clean, new high-quality brake fluid. If dirty or improper fluid has been used, it will be necessary to drain the entire system, flush the system with proper brake fluid, replace all rubber components, refill, and bleed the system.

1. Remove the rubber boots from the cylinder ends with pliers. Discard the boots.
2. Remove and discard the pistons and cups.
3. Wash the cylinder and metal parts in denatured alcohol or clean brake fluid.

NOTE: *Crocus cloth may be used to remove light corrosion and stains. Replace the wheel cylinder assembly if crocus cloth does not remove corrosion or if bore is scored.*

CAUTION: *Never use a minieral-based solvent such as gasoline, kerosene, or paint thinner for cleaning purposes. These solvents will swell rubber components and quickly deteriorate them.*

4. Allow the parts to air dry or use compressed air. Do not use rags for cleaning since lint will remain in the cylinder bore.
5. Inspect the piston and replace it if it shows scratches.
6. Lubricate the cylinder bore and counterbore with clean brake fluid.
7. Install the rubber cups (flat side out) and then the pistons (flat side in).
8. Insert new boots into the counterbores by hand. Do not lubricate the boots.

9. Install the wheel cylinder to the backing plate and connect all push rods and springs. Connect the brake line, install the brake drum, and bleed the brakes.

REMOVAL AND INSTALLATION

1. Clean away all dirt, crud and foreign material from around wheel cylinder. It is important that dirt be kept away from the brake line when the cylinder is disconnected.
2. Disconnect the inlet tube line.
3. Wheel cylinders are retained by two types of fasteners. One type uses a round retainer with locking clips, which attaches to the wheel cylinder on the back side of the brake backing plate. The other type simply uses two bolts, which screw into the wheel cylinder from the back side of the backing plate.
4. To remove the round retainer-type cylinders, insert two awls or pins into the access slots between the wheel cylinder pilot and the retainer locking tabs. Bend both tabs away simultaneously. The wheel cylinder can be removed, as the retainer is released.

Wheel cylinder secured by retainer

Exploded view of a typical wheel cylinder (© Chevrolet Motor Division)

Bend retainer stubs using awls

Use a socket and extension to seat the new retainer

Bolt-type wheel cylinder

5. To remove the cylinders, loosen and remove the bolts from the back side of the backing plate, and remove the cylinder.

6. To install the retainer-type cylinder, position the wheel cylinder and hold it in place with a wooden block between the cylinder and axle flange. Install a new retainer clip, using a 1⅛ in., 12-point socket and socket extension as shown in the illustration. This tool will seat the retainer evenly.

7. On the bolt-type cylinder, position the cylinder and install the bolts.

8. On both types of cylinders, torque the inlet type nuts to 120 ft. lbs.

9. Assemble the remaining brake components. Bleed the brakes.

Wheel Bearings

Refer to the "Front Disc Brakes—Wheel Bearings" section for removal and installation, adjustment and packing procedures.

PARKING BRAKE

All models are equipped with a foot-operated ratchet-type parking brake. A cable assembly connects this pedal to an intermediate cable by means of an equalizer. Adjustment is made at the equalizer. The intermediate cable connects with two rear cables and each of these cables enters a rear wheel.

Cable

ADJUSTMENT

1964–72

1. Jack the rear of the car up and support with jackstands.

Brake Specifications

Year	Lug Nut Torque (ft. lb.)	Master Cylinder Bore	Brake Disc		Brake Drum			Minimum Lining Thickness	
			Minimum Thickness	Maximum Run-Out	Diameter	Max Machine O/S	Max Wear Limit	Front	Rear
1964–65	80	1.0	NA	NA	9.5	9.560	9.590	2/32	2/32
1964–65 ②	80	.875	NA	NA	9.5	9.560	9.590	2/32	2/32
1966–68	80	11.125 (disc) 1.0 (drum)		.004	9.5	9.560	9.590	2/32	2/32
1969	80	1.0		.004	9.5	9.560	9.590	2/32	2/32
1970–77	80	1.125	.980	.002	9.5 ①	9.560	9.590	2/32	2/32
1978–83	80	1.125 (power) .9375 (manual)	.980	.002	9.5	9.560	9.590	2/32	2/32

① 11.0 inches for 1973–75 station wagons
② Metallic Linings
NOTE: *Minimum lining thickness is as recommended by the manufacturer. Because of variations in state inspection regulations, the minimum allowable thickness may be different than recommended by the manufacturer.*

Parking brake cable assembly, all models similar

Parking brake cable adjustment

2. Pull the parking brake on two notches from the fully released position.

3. Loosen the forward equalizer check nut, and adjust the rear nut as necessary to obtain a light drag when the rear wheel is turned.

4. Tighten both check nuts.

5. Release the parking brake lever and check to see that there is no drag present when the wheel is turned.

6. Lower the car.

1973 and Later

1. Raise the rear of the car and support it with jackstands.

2. Push down on the parking brake pedal so that it is two notches (clocks) from the fully released position.

3. Loosen the forward equalizer check nut and adjust the rear nut as necessary to obtain a light drag when the rear wheel is turned forward.

4. Tighten both check nuts.

5. Fully release the parking brake lever and check to see that there is no drag present when the rear wheel is turned forward.

6. Lower the car.

7. If the parking brake has to be forcibly released, clean and lubricate the cables and equalizer, and also the parking brake assembly, then check the cables for straightness and kinks.

Troubleshooting

This section is designed to aid in the quick, accurate diagnosis of automotive problems. While automotive repairs can be made by many people, accurate troubleshooting is a rare skill for the amateur and professional alike.

In its simplest state, troubleshooting is an exercise in logic. It is essential to realize that an automobile is really composed of a series of systems. Some of these systems are interrelated; others are not. Automobiles operate within a framework of logical rules and physical laws, and the key to trouble-shooting is a good understanding of all the automotive systems.

This section breaks the car or truck down into its component systems, allowing the problem to be isolated. The charts and diagnostic road maps list the most common problems and the most probable causes of trouble. Obviously it would be impossible to list every possible problem that could happen along with every possible cause, but it will locate MOST problems and eliminate a lot of unnecessary guesswork. The systematic

format will locate problems within a given system, but, because many automotive systems are interrelated, the solution to your particular problem may be found in a number of systems on the car or truck.

USING THE TROUBLESHOOTING CHARTS

This book contains all of the specific information that the average do-it-yourself mechanic needs to repair and maintain his or her car or truck. The troubleshooting charts are designed to be used in conjunction with the specific procedures and information in the text. For instance, troubleshooting a point-type ignition system is fairly standard for all models, but you may be directed to the text to find procedures for troubleshooting an individual type of electronic ignition. You will also have to refer to the specification charts throughout the book for specifications applicable to your car or truck.

TOOLS AND EQUIPMENT

The tools illustrated in Chapter 1 (plus two more diagnostic pieces) will be adequate to troubleshoot most problems. The two other tools needed are a voltmeter and an ohmmeter. These can be purchased separately or in combination, known as a VOM meter.

In the event that other tools are required, they will be noted in the procedures.

Tach-dwell hooked-up to distributor

Troubleshooting Engine Problems
See Chapters 2, 3, 4 for more information and service procedures.

Index to Systems

System	To Test	Group
Battery	Engine need not be running	1
Starting system	Engine need not be running	2
Primary electrical system	Engine need not be running	3
Secondary electrical system	Engine need not be running	4
Fuel system	Engine need not be running	5
Engine compression	Engine need not be running	6
Engine vacuum	Engine must be running	7
Secondary electrical system	Engine must be running	8
Valve train	Engine must be running	9
Exhaust system	Engine must be running	10
Cooling system	Engine must be running	11
Engine lubrication	Engine must be running	12

Index to Problems

Problem: Symptom	Begin at Specific Diagnosis, Number
Engine Won't Start:	
Starter doesn't turn	1.1, 2.1
Starter turns, engine doesn't	2.1
Starter turns engine very slowly	1.1, 2.4
Starter turns engine normally	3.1, 4.1
Starter turns engine very quickly	6.1
Engine fires intermittently	4.1
Engine fires consistently	5.1, 6.1
Engine Runs Poorly:	
Hard starting	3.1, 4.1, 5.1, 8.1
Rough idle	4.1, 5.1, 8.1
Stalling	3.1, 4.1, 5.1, 8.1
Engine dies at high speeds	4.1, 5.1
Hesitation (on acceleration from standing stop)	5.1, 8.1
Poor pickup	4.1, 5.1, 8.1
Lack of power	3.1, 4.1, 5.1, 8.1
Backfire through the carburetor	4.1, 8.1, 9.1
Backfire through the exhaust	4.1, 8.1, 9.1
Blue exhaust gases	6.1, 7.1
Black exhaust gases	5.1
Running on (after the ignition is shut off)	3.1, 8.1
Susceptible to moisture	4.1
Engine misfires under load	4.1, 7.1, 8.4, 9.1
Engine misfires at speed	4.1, 8.4
Engine misfires at idle	3.1, 4.1, 5.1, 7.1, 8.4

Sample Section

Test and Procedure	Results and Indications	Proceed to
4.1—Check for spark: Hold each spark plug wire approximately ¼" from ground with gloves or a heavy, dry rag. Crank the engine and observe the spark.	If no spark is evident:	4.2
	If spark is good in some cases:	4.3
	If spark is good in all cases:	4.6

Specific Diagnosis

This section is arranged so that following each test, instructions are given to proceed to another, until a problem is diagnosed.

Section 1—Battery

Test and Procedure	Results and Indications	Proceed to
1.1—Inspect the battery visually for case condition (corrosion, cracks) and water level. Inspect the battery case	If case is cracked, replace battery:	**1.4**
	If the case is intact, remove corrosion with a solution of baking soda and water (**CAUTION:** *do not get the solution into the battery*), and fill with water:	**1.2**
1.2—Check the battery cable connections: Insert a screwdriver between the battery post and the cable clamp. Turn the headlights on high beam, and observe them as the screwdriver is gently twisted to ensure good metal to metal contact. TESTING BATTERY CABLE CONNECTIONS USING A SCREWDRIVER	If the lights brighten, remove and clean the clamp and post; coat the post with petroleum jelly, install and tighten the clamp:	**1.4**
	If no improvement is noted:	**1.3**
1.3—Test the state of charge of the battery using an individual cell tester or hydrometer.	If indicated, charge the battery. **NOTE:** *If no obvious reason exists for the low state of charge (i.e., battery age, prolonged storage),* proceed to:	**1.4**

ADD THIS NUMBER TO THE HYDROMETER READING TO OBTAIN THE CORRECTED SPECIFIC GRAVITY

SUBTRACT THIS NUMBER FROM THE HYDROMETER READING TO OBTAIN THE CORRECTED SPECIFIC GRAVITY

Specific Gravity (@ 80° F.)

Minimum	Battery Charge
1.260	100% Charged
1.230	75% Charged
1.200	50% Charged
1.170	25% Charged
1.140	Very Little Power Left
1.110	Completely Discharged

The effects of temperature on battery specific gravity (left) and amount of battery charge in relation to specific gravity (right)

1.4—Visually inspect battery cables for cracking, bad connection to ground, or bad connection to starter.	If necessary, tighten connections or replace the cables:	
		2.1

Section 2—Starting System
See Chapter 3 for service procedures

Test and Procedure	Results and Indications	Proceed to
Note: Tests in Group 2 are performed with coil high tension lead disconnected to prevent accidental starting.		
2.1—Test the starter motor and solenoid: Connect a jumper from the battery post of the solenoid (or relay) to the starter post of the solenoid (or relay).	If starter turns the engine normally:	2.2
	If the starter buzzes, or turns the engine very slowly:	2.4
	If no response, replace the solenoid (or relay).	3.1
	If the starter turns, but the engine doesn't, ensure that the flywheel ring gear is intact. If the gear is undamaged, replace the starter drive.	3.1
2.2—Determine whether ignition override switches are functioning properly (clutch start switch, neutral safety switch), by connecting a jumper across the switch(es), and turning the ignition switch to "start".	If starter operates, adjust or replace switch:	3.1
	If the starter doesn't operate:	2.3
2.3—Check the ignition switch "start" position: Connect a 12V test lamp or voltmeter between the starter post of the solenoid (or relay) and ground. Turn the ignition switch to the "start" position, and jiggle the key.	If the lamp doesn't light or the meter needle doesn't move when the switch is turned, check the ignition switch for loose connections, cracked insulation, or broken wires. Repair or replace as necessary:	3.1
	If the lamp flickers or needle moves when the key is jiggled, replace the ignition switch.	3.3

Checking the ignition switch "start" position

STARTER RELAY (IF EQUIPPED)

Test and Procedure	Results and Indications	Proceed to
2.4—Remove and bench test the starter, according to specifications in the engine electrical section.	If the starter does not meet specifications, repair or replace as needed:	3.1
	If the starter is operating properly:	2.5
2.5—Determine whether the engine can turn freely: Remove the spark plugs, and check for water in the cylinders. Check for water on the dipstick, or oil in the radiator. Attempt to turn the engine using an 18″ flex drive and socket on the crankshaft pulley nut or bolt.	If the engine will turn freely only with the spark plugs out, and hydrostatic lock (water in the cylinders) is ruled out, check valve timing:	9.2
	If engine will not turn freely, and it is known that the clutch and transmission are free, the engine must be disassembled for further evaluation:	Chapter 3

Section 3—Primary Electrical System

Test and Procedure	Results and Indications	Proceed to
3.1—Check the ignition switch "on" position: Connect a jumper wire between the distributor side of the coil and ground, and a 12V test lamp between the switch side of the coil and ground. Remove the high tension lead from the coil. Turn the ignition switch on and jiggle the key.	If the lamp lights:	**3.2**
	If the lamp flickers when the key is jiggled, replace the ignition switch:	**3.3**
	If the lamp doesn't light, check for loose or open connections. If none are found, remove the ignition switch and check for continuity. If the switch is faulty, replace it:	**3.3**

Checking the ignition switch "on" position

3.2—Check the ballast resistor or resistance wire for an open circuit, using an ohmmeter. See Chapter 3 for specific tests.	Replace the resistor or resistance wire if the resistance is zero. **NOTE: *Some ignition systems have no ballast resistor.***	**3.3**

RESISTOR BLOCK

CALIBRATED RESISTANCE LEAD

Two types of resistors

3.3—On point-type ignition systems, visually inspect the breaker points for burning, pitting or excessive wear. Gray coloring of the point contact surfaces is normal. Rotate the crankshaft until the contact heel rests on a high point of the distributor cam and adjust the point gap to specifications. On electronic ignition models, remove the distributor cap and visually inspect the armature. Ensure that the armature pin is in place, and that the armature is on tight and rotates when the engine is cranked. Make sure there are no cracks, chips or rounded edges on the armature.	If the breaker points are intact, clean the contact surfaces with fine emery cloth, and adjust the point gap to specifications. If the points are worn, replace them. On electronic systems, replace any parts which appear defective. If condition persists:	**3.4**

Test and Procedure	Results and Indications	Proceed to
3.4—On point-type ignition systems, connect a dwell-meter between the distributor primary lead and ground. Crank the engine and observe the point dwell angle. On electronic ignition systems, conduct a stator (magnetic pickup assembly) test. See Chapter 3.	On point-type systems, adjust the dwell angle if necessary. **NOTE:** *Increasing the point gap decreases the dwell angle and vice-versa.*	**3.6**
	If the dwell meter shows little or no reading;	**3.5**
	On electronic ignition systems, if the stator is bad, replace the stator. If the stator is good, proceed to the other tests in Chapter 3.	

Dwell is a function of point gap

3.5—On the point-type ignition systems, check the condenser for short: connect an ohmeter across the condenser body and the pigtail lead.	If any reading other than infinite is noted, replace the condenser	**3.6**

Checking the condenser for short

3.6—Test the coil primary resistance: On point-type ignition systems, connect an ohmmeter across the coil primary terminals, and read the resistance on the low scale. Note whether an external ballast resistor or resistance wire is used. On electronic ignition systems, test the coil primary resistance as in Chapter 3.	Point-type ignition coils utilizing ballast resistors or resistance wires should have approximately 1.0 ohms resistance. Coils with internal resistors should have approximately 4.0 ohms resistance. If values far from the above are noted, replace the coil.	**4.1**

Check the coil primary resistance

Section 4—Secondary Electrical System
See Chapters 2–3 for service procedures

Test and Procedure	Results and Indications	Proceed to
4.1—Check for spark: Hold each spark plug wire approximately ¼″ from ground with gloves or a heavy, dry rag. Crank the engine, and observe the spark.	If no spark is evident:	**4.2**
	If spark is good in some cylinders:	**4.3**
	If spark is good in all cylinders:	**4.6**

Check for spark at the plugs

4.2—Check for spark at the coil high tension lead: Remove the coil high tension lead from the distributor and position it approximately ¼″ from ground. Crank the engine and observe spark. **CAUTION: This test should not be performed on engines equipped with electronic ignition.**	If the spark is good and consistent:	**4.3**
	If the spark is good but intermittent, test the primary electrical system starting at 3.3:	**3.3**
	If the spark is weak or non-existent, replace the coil high tension lead, clean and tighten all connections and retest. If no improvement is noted:	**4.4**
4.3—Visually inspect the distributor cap and rotor for burned or corroded contacts, cracks, carbon tracks, or moisture. Also check the fit of the rotor on the distributor shaft (where applicable).	If moisture is present, dry thoroughly, and retest per 4.1:	**4.1**
	If burned or excessively corroded contacts, cracks, or carbon tracks are noted, replace the defective part(s) and retest per 4.1:	**4.1**
	If the rotor and cap appear intact, or are only slightly corroded, clean the contacts thoroughly (including the cap towers and spark plug wire ends) and retest per 4.1:	
	If the spark is good in all cases:	**4.6**
	If the spark is poor in all cases:	**4.5**

CORRODED OR LOOSE WIRE

EXCESSIVE WEAR OF BUTTON

HIGH RESISTANCE CARBON

ROTOR TIP BURNED AWAY

Inspect the distributor cap and rotor

CHILTON'S
AUTO BODY
REPAIR TIPS

Tools and Materials • Step-by-Step Illustrated Procedures
How To Repair Dents, Scratches and Rust Holes
Spray Painting and Refinishing Tips

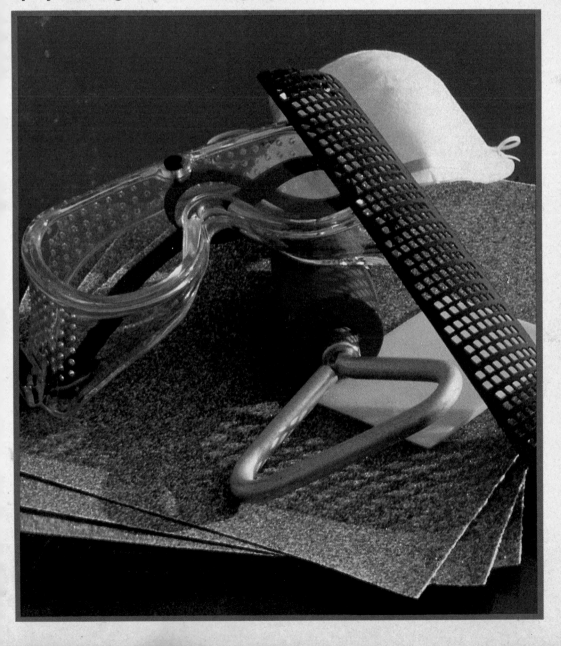

With a little practice, basic body repair procedures can be mastered by any do-it-yourself mechanic. The step-by-step repairs shown here can be applied to almost any type of auto body repair.

TOOLS & MATERIALS

You may already have basic tools, such as hammers and electric drills. Other tools unique to body repair — body hammers, grinding attachments, sanding blocks, dent puller, half-round plastic file and plastic spreaders — are relatively inexpensive and can be obtained wherever auto parts or auto body repair parts are sold. Portable air compressors and paint spray guns can be purchased or rented.

Auto Body Repair Kits

The best and most often used products are available to the do-it-yourselfer in kit form, from major manufacturers of auto body repair products. The same manufacturers also merchandise the individual products for use by pros.

Kits are available to make a wide variety of repairs, including holes, dents and scratches and fiberglass, and offer the advantage of buying the materials you'll need for the job. There is little waste or chance of materials going bad from not being used. Many kits may also contain basic body-working tools such as body files, sanding blocks and spreaders. Check the contents of the kit before buying your tools.

BODY REPAIR TIPS

Safety

Many of the products associated with auto body repair and refinishing contain toxic chemicals. Read all labels before opening containers and store them in a safe place and manner.

• Wear eye protection (safety goggles) when using power tools or when performing any operation that involves

the removal of any type of material.

• Wear lung protection (disposable mask or respirator) when grinding, sanding or painting.

Sanding

1 Sand off paint before using a dent puller. When using a non-adhesive sanding disc, cover the back of the disc with an overlapping layer or two of masking tape and trim the edges. The disc will last considerably longer.

2 Use the circular motion of the sanding disc to grind *into* the edge of the repair. Grinding or sanding away from the jagged edge will only tear the sandpaper.

3 Use the palm of your hand flat on the panel to detect high and low spots. Do not use your fingertips. Slide your hand slowly back and forth.

WORKING WITH BODY FILLER

Mixing The Filler

Cleanliness and proper mixing and application are extremely important. Use a clean piece of plastic or glass or a disposable artist's palette to mix body filler.

1 Allow plenty of time and follow directions. No useful purpose will be served by adding more hardener to make it cure (set-up) faster. Less hardener means more curing time, but the mixture dries harder; more hardener means less curing time but a softer mixture.

2

2 Both the hardener and the filler should be thoroughly kneaded or stirred before mixing. Hardener should be a solid paste and dispense like thin toothpaste. Body filler should be smooth, and free of lumps or thick spots.

Getting the proper amount of hardener in the filler is the trickiest part of preparing the filler. Use the same amount of hardener in cold or warm weather. For contour filler (thick coats), a bead of hardener twice the diameter of the filler is about right. There's about a 15% margin on either side, but, if in doubt use less hardener.

2

2

3 Mix the body filler and hardener by wiping across the mixing surface, picking the mixture up and wiping it again. Colder weather requires longer mixing times. Do not mix in a circular motion; this will trap air bubbles which will become holes in the cured filler.

3

Applying The Filler

1 For best results, filler should not be applied over ¼" thick.

Apply the filler in several coats. Build it up to above the level of the repair surface so that it can be sanded or grated down.

The first coat of filler must be pressed on with a firm wiping motion.

Apply the filler in one direction only. Working the filler back and forth will either pull it off the metal or trap air bubbles.

REPAIRING DENTS

Before you start, take a few minutes to study the damaged area. Try to visualize the shape of the panel before it was damaged. If the damage is on the left fender, look at the right fender and use it as a guide. If there is access to the panel from behind, you can reshape it with a body hammer. If not, you'll have to use a dent puller. Go slowly and work the metal a little at a time. Get the panel as straight as possible before applying filler.

1 This dent is typical of one that can be pulled out or hammered out from behind. Remove the headlight cover, headlight assembly and turn signal housing.

2 Drill a series of holes ½ the size of the end of the dent puller along the stress line. Make some trial pulls and assess the results. If necessary, drill more holes and try again. Do not hurry.

3 If possible, use a body hammer and block to shape the metal back to its original contours. Get the metal back as close to its original shape as possible. Don't depend on body filler to fill dents.

4 Using an 80-grit grinding disc on an electric drill, grind the paint from the surrounding area down to bare metal. Use a new grinding pad to prevent heat buildup that will warp metal.

5 The area should look like this when you're finished grinding. Knock the drill holes in and tape over small openings to keep plastic filler out.

6 Mix the body filler (see Body Repair Tips). Spread the body filler evenly over the entire area (see Body Repair Tips). Be sure to cover the area completely.

7 Let the body filler dry until the surface can just be scratched with your fingernail. Knock the high spots from the body filler with a body file ("Cheese-grater"). Check frequently with the palm of your hand for high and low spots.

8 Check to be sure that trim pieces that will be installed later will fit exactly. Sand the area with 40-grit paper.

9 If you wind up with low spots, you may have to apply another layer of filler.

10 Knock the high spots off with 40-grit paper. When you are satisfied with the contours of the repair, apply a thin coat of filler to cover pin holes and scratches.

11 Block sand the area with 40-grit paper to a smooth finish. Pay particular attention to body lines and ridges that must be well-defined.

12 Sand the area with 400 paper and then finish with a scuff pad. The finished repair is ready for priming and painting (see Painting Tips).

Materials and photos courtesy of Ritt Jones Auto Body, Prospect Park, PA.

REPAIRING RUST HOLES

There are many ways to repair rust holes. The fiberglass cloth kit shown here is one of the most cost efficient for the owner because it provides a strong repair that resists cracking and moisture and is relatively easy to use. It can be used on large and small holes (with or without backing) and can be applied over contoured areas. Remember, however, that short of replacing an entire panel, no repair is a guarantee that the rust will not return.

1 Remove any trim that will be in the way. Clean away all loose debris. Cut away all the rusted metal. But be sure to leave enough metal to retain the contour or body shape.

2 Grind away all traces of rust with a 24-grit grinding disc. Be sure to grind back 3-4 inches from the edge of the hole down to bare metal and be sure all traces of paint, primer and rust are removed.

3 Block sand the area with 80 or 100 grit sandpaper to get a clear, shiny surface and feathered paint edge. Tap the edges of the hole inward with a ball peen hammer.

4 If you are going to use release film, cut a piece about 2-3" larger than the area you have sanded. Place the film over the repair and mark the sanded area on the film. Avoid any unnecessary wrinkling of the film.

5 Cut 2 pieces of fiberglass matte to match the shape of the repair. One piece should be about 1" smaller than the sanded area and the second piece should be 1" smaller than the first. Mix enough filler and hardener to saturate the fiberglass material (see Body Repair Tips).

6 Lay the release sheet on a flat surface and spread an even layer of filler, large enough to cover the repair. Lay the smaller piece of fiberglass cloth in the center of the sheet and spread another layer of filler over the fiberglass cloth. Repeat the operation for the larger piece of cloth.

7 Place the repair material over the repair area, with the release film facing outward. Use a spreader and work from the center outward to smooth the material, following the body contours. Be sure to remove all air bubbles.

8 Wait until the repair has dried tack-free and peel off the release sheet. The ideal working temperature is 60°-90° F. Cooler or warmer temperatures or high humidity may require additional curing time. Wait longer, if in doubt.

9

Sand and feather-edge the entire area. The initial sanding can be done with a sanding disc on an electric drill if care is used. Finish the sanding with a block sander. Low spots can be filled with body filler; this may require several applications.

10

10 When the filler can just be scratched with a fingernail, knock the high spots down with a body file and smooth the entire area with 80-grit. Feather the filled areas into the surrounding areas.

11

11 When the area is sanded smooth, mix some topcoat and hardener and apply it directly with a spreader. This will give a smooth finish and prevent the glass matte from showing through the paint.

12

12 Block sand the topcoat smooth with finishing sandpaper (200 grit), and 400 grit. The repair is ready for masking, priming and painting (see Painting Tips).

Materials and photos courtesy Marson Corporation, Chelsea, Massachusetts

PAINTING TIPS

Preparation

1 SANDING — Use a 400 or 600 grit wet or dry sandpaper. Wet-sand the area with a ¼ sheet of sandpaper soaked in clean water. Keep the paper wet while sanding. Sand the area until the repaired area tapers into the original finish.

2 CLEANING — Wash the area to be painted thoroughly with water and a clean rag. Rinse it thoroughly and wipe the surface dry until you're sure it's completely free of dirt, dust, fingerprints, wax, detergent or other foreign matter.

3 MASKING — Protect any areas you don't want to overspray by covering them with masking tape and newspaper. Be careful not get fingerprints on the area to be painted.

4 PRIMING — All exposed metal should be primed before painting. Primer protects the metal and provides an excellent surface for paint adhesion. When the primer is dry, wet-sand the area again with 600 grit wet-sandpaper. Clean the area again after sanding.

4

Painting Techniques

P aint applied from either a spray gun or a spray can (for small areas) will provide good results. Experiment on an old piece of metal to get the right combination before you begin painting.

SPRAYING VISCOSITY (SPRAY GUN ONLY) — Paint should be thinned to spraying viscosity according to the directions on the can. Use only the recommended thinner or reducer and the same amount of reduction regardless of temperature.

AIR PRESSURE (SPRAY GUN ONLY) — This is extremely important. Be sure you are using the proper recommended pressure.

TEMPERATURE — The surface to be painted should be approximately the same temperature as the surrounding air. Applying warm paint to a cold surface, or vice versa, will completely upset the paint characteristics.

THICKNESS — Spray with smooth strokes. In general, the thicker the coat of paint, the longer the drying time. Apply several thin coats about 30 seconds apart. The paint should remain wet long enough to flow out and no longer; heavier coats will only produce sags or wrinkles. Spray a light (fog) coat, followed by heavier color coats.

DISTANCE — The ideal spraying distance is 8″-12″ from the gun or can to the surface. Shorter distances will produce ripples, while greater distances will result in orange peel, dry film and poor color match and loss of material due to overspray.

OVERLAPPING — The gun or can should be kept at right angles to the surface at all times. Work to a wet edge at an even speed, using a 50% overlap and direct the center of the spray at the lower or nearest edge of the previous stroke.

RUBBING OUT (BLENDING) FRESH PAINT — Let the paint dry thoroughly. Runs or imperfections can be sanded out, primed and repainted.

Don't be in too big a hurry to remove the masking. This only produces paint ridges. When the finish has dried for at least a week, apply a small amount of fine grade rubbing compound with a clean, wet cloth. Use lots of water and blend the new paint with the surrounding area.

WRONG

Thin coat. Stroke too fast, not enough overlap, gun too far away.

CORRECT

Medium coat. Proper distance, good stroke, proper overlap.

WRONG

Heavy coat. Stroke too slow, too much overlap, gun too close.

Test and Procedure	Results and Indications	Proceed to
4.4—Check the coil secondary resistance: On point-type systems connect an ohmmeter across the distributor side of the coil and the coil tower. Read the resistance on the high scale of the ohmmeter. On electronic ignition systems, see Chapter 3 for specific tests.	The resistance of a satisfactory coil should be between 4,000 and 10,000 ohms. If resistance is considerably higher (i.e., 40,000 ohms) replace the coil and retest per 4.1. **NOTE:** *This does not apply to high performance coils.*	

Testing the coil secondary resistance

4.5—Visually inspect the spark plug wires for cracking or brittleness. Ensure that no two wires are positioned so as to cause induction firing (adjacent and parallel). Remove each wire, one by one, and check resistance with an ohmmeter.	Replace any cracked or brittle wires. If any of the wires are defective, replace the entire set. Replace any wires with excessive resistance (over 8000 Ω per foot for suppression wire), and separate any wires that might cause induction firing.	**4.6**

Misfiring can be the result of spark plug leads to adjacent, consecutively firing cylinders running parallel and too close together

On point-type ignition systems, check the spark plug wires as shown. On electronic ignitions, do not remove the wire from the distributor cap terminal; instead, test through the cap

Spark plug wires can be checked visually by bending them in a loop over your finger. This will reveal any cracks, burned or broken insulation. Any wire with cracked insulation should be replaced

4.6—Remove the spark plugs, noting the cylinders from which they were removed, and evaluate according to the color photos in the middle of this book.	See following.	**See following.**

Test and Procedure	Results and Indications	Proceed to
4.7—Examine the location of all the plugs.	The following diagrams illustrate some of the conditions that the location of plugs will reveal.	4.8

Two adjacent plugs are fouled in a 6-cylinder engine, 4-cylinder engine or either bank of a V-8. This is probably due to a blown head gasket between the two cylinders

The two center plugs in a 6-cylinder engine are fouled. Raw fuel may be "boiled" out of the carburetor into the intake manifold after the engine is shut-off. Stop-start driving can also foul the center plugs, due to overly rich mixture. Proper float level, a new float needle and seat or use of an insulating spacer may help this problem

An unbalanced carburetor is indicated. Following the fuel flow on this particular design shows that the cylinders fed by the right-hand barrel are fouled from overly rich mixture, while the cylinders fed by the left-hand barrel are normal

If the four rear plugs are overheated, a cooling system problem is suggested. A thorough cleaning of the cooling system may restore coolant circulation and cure the problem

Finding one plug overheated may indicate an intake manifold leak near the affected cylinder. If the overheated plug is the second of two adjacent, consecutively firing plugs, it could be the result of ignition cross-firing. Separating the leads to these two plugs will eliminate cross-fire

Occasionally, the two rear plugs in large, lightly used V-8's will become oil fouled. High oil consumption and smoky exhaust may also be noticed. It is probably due to plugged oil drain holes in the rear of the cylinder head, causing oil to be sucked in around the valve stems. This usually occurs in the rear cylinders first, because the engine slants that way

Test and Procedure	Results and Indications	Proceed to
4.8—Determine the static ignition timing. Using the crankshaft pulley timing marks as a guide, locate top dead center on the compression stroke of the number one cylinder.	The rotor should be pointing toward the No. 1 tower in the distributor cap, and, on electronic ignitions, the armature spoke for that cylinder should be lined up with the stator.	4.8
4.9—Check coil polarity: Connect a voltmeter negative lead to the coil high tension lead, and the positive lead to ground (**NOTE:** *Reverse the hook-up for positive ground systems*). Crank the engine momentarily. Checking coil polarity	If the voltmeter reads up-scale, the polarity is correct: If the voltmeter reads down-scale, reverse the coil polarity (switch the primary leads):	5.1 5.1

Section 5—Fuel System
See Chapter 4 for service procedures

Test and Procedure	Results and Indications	Proceed to
5.1—Determine that the air filter is functioning efficiently: Hold paper elements up to a strong light, and attempt to see light through the filter.	Clean permanent air filters in solvent (or manufacturer's recommendation), and allow to dry. Replace paper elements through which light cannot be seen:	5.2
5.2—Determine whether a flooding condition exists: Flooding is identified by a strong gasoline odor, and excessive gasoline present in the throttle bore(s) of the carburetor.	If flooding is not evident: If flooding is evident, permit the gasoline to dry for a few moments and restart. If flooding doesn't recur: If flooding is persistent:	5.3 5.7 5.5

If the engine floods repeatedly, check the choke butterfly flap

Test and Procedure	Results and Indications	Proceed to
5.3—Check that fuel is reaching the carburetor: Detach the fuel line at the carburetor inlet. Hold the end of the line in a cup (not styrofoam), and crank the engine.	If fuel flows smoothly: If fuel doesn't flow (**NOTE:** *Make sure that there is fuel in the tank*), or flows erratically:	5.7 5.4

Check the fuel pump by disconnecting the output line (fuel pump-to-carburetor) at the carburetor and operating the starter briefly

Test and Procedure	Results and Indications	Proceed to
5.4—Test the fuel pump: Disconnect all fuel lines from the fuel pump. Hold a finger over the input fitting, crank the engine (with electric pump, turn the ignition or pump on); and feel for suction.	If suction is evident, blow out the fuel line to the tank with low pressure compressed air until bubbling is heard from the fuel filler neck. Also blow out the carburetor fuel line (both ends disconnected):	5.7
	If no suction is evident, replace or repair the fuel pump: **NOTE:** *Repeated oil fouling of the spark plugs, or a no-start condition, could be the result of a ruptured vacuum booster pump diaphragm, through which oil or gasoline is being drawn into the intake manifold (where applicable).*	5.7
5.5—Occasionally, small specks of dirt will clog the small jets and orifices in the carburetor. With the engine cold, hold a flat piece of wood or similar material over the carburetor, where possible, and crank the engine.	If the engine starts, but runs roughly the engine is probably not run enough. If the engine won't start:	5.9
5.6—Check the needle and seat: Tap the carburetor in the area of the needle and seat.	If flooding stops, a gasoline additive (e.g., Gumout) will often cure the problem:	5.7
	If flooding continues, check the fuel pump for excessive pressure at the carburetor (according to specifications). If the pressure is normal, the needle and seat must be removed and checked, and/or the float level adjusted:	5.7
5.7—Test the accelerator pump by looking into the throttle bores while operating the throttle.	If the accelerator pump appears to be operating normally:	5.8
	If the accelerator pump is not operating, the pump must be reconditioned. Where possible, service the pump with the carburetor(s) installed on the engine. If necessary, remove the carburetor. Prior to removal:	5.8

Check for gas at the carburetor by looking down the carburetor throat while someone moves the accelerator

Test and Procedure	Results and Indications	Proceed to
5.8—Determine whether the carburetor main fuel system is functioning: Spray a commercial starting fluid into the carburetor while attempting to start the engine.	If the engine starts, runs for a few seconds, and dies:	5.9
	If the engine doesn't start:	6.1

Test and Procedure	Results and Indications	Proceed to
5.9—Uncommon fuel system malfunctions: See below:	If the problem is solved:	6.1
	If the problem remains, remove and recondition the carburetor.	

Condition	Indication	Test	Prevailing Weather Conditions	Remedy
Vapor lock	Engine will not restart shortly after running.	Cool the components of the fuel system until the engine starts. Vapor lock can be cured faster by draping a wet cloth over a mechanical fuel pump.	Hot to very hot	Ensure that the exhaust manifold heat control valve is operating. Check with the vehicle manufacturer for the recommended solution to vapor lock on the model in question.
Carburetor icing	Engine will not idle, stalls at low speeds.	Visually inspect the throttle plate area of the throttle bores for frost.	High humidity, 32–40° F.	Ensure that the exhaust manifold heat control valve is operating, and that the intake manifold heat riser is not blocked.
Water in the fuel	Engine sputters and stalls; may not start.	Pump a small amount of fuel into a glass jar. Allow to stand, and inspect for droplets or a layer of water.	High humidity, extreme temperature changes.	For droplets, use one or two cans of commercial gas line anti-freeze. For a layer of water, the tank must be drained, and the fuel lines blown out with compressed air.

Section 6—Engine Compression
See Chapter 3 for service procedures

6.1—Test engine compression: Remove all spark plugs. Block the throttle wide open. Insert a compression gauge into a spark plug port, crank the engine to obtain the maximum reading, and record.	If compression is within limits on all cylinders:	7.1
	If gauge reading is extremely low on all cylinders:	6.2
	If gauge reading is low on one or two cylinders: (If gauge readings are identical and low on two or more adjacent cylinders, the head gasket must be replaced.)	6.2

Checking compression

6.2—Test engine compression (wet): Squirt approximately 30 cc. of engine oil into each cylinder, and retest per 6.1.	If the readings improve, worn or cracked rings or broken pistons are indicated:	**See Chapter 3**
	If the readings do not improve, burned or excessively carboned valves or a jumped timing chain are indicated:	7.1
	NOTE: *A jumped timing chain is often indicated by difficult cranking.*	

Section 7—Engine Vacuum
See Chapter 3 for service procedures

Test and Procedure	Results and Indications	Proceed to
7.1—Attach a vacuum gauge to the intake manifold beyond the throttle plate. Start the engine, and observe the action of the needle over the range of engine speeds.	See below.	**See below**

INDICATION: normal engine in good condition

Proceed to: 8.1

Normal engine
Gauge reading: steady, from 17–22 in./Hg.

INDICATION: sticking valves or ignition miss

Proceed to: 9.1, 8.3

Sticking valves
Gauge reading: intermittent fluctuation at idle

INDICATION: late ignition or valve timing, low compression, stuck throttle valve, leaking carburetor or manifold gasket

Proceed to: 6.1

Incorrect valve timing
Gauge reading: low (10–15 in./Hg) but steady

INDICATION: improper carburetor adjustment or minor intake leak.

Proceed to: 7.2

Carburetor requires adjustment
Gauge reading: drifting needle

INDICATION: ignition miss, blown cylinder head gasket, leaking valve or weak valve spring

Proceed to: 8.3, 6.1

Blown head gasket
Gauge reading: needle fluctuates as engine speed increases

INDICATION: burnt valve or faulty valve clearance. Needle will fall when defective valve operates

Proceed to: 9.1

Burnt or leaking valves
Gauge reading: steady needle, but drops regularly

INDICATION: choked muffler, excessive back pressure in system

Proceed to: 10.1

Clogged exhaust system
Gauge reading: gradual drop in reading at idle

INDICATION: worn valve guides

Proceed to: 9.1

Worn valve guides
Gauge reading: needle vibrates excessively at idle, but steadies as engine speed increases

White pointer = steady gauge hand | Black pointer = fluctuating gauge hand

Test and Procedure	Results and Indications	Proceed to
7.2—Attach a vacuum gauge per 7.1, and test for an intake manifold leak. Squirt a small amount of oil around the intake manifold gaskets, carburetor gaskets, plugs and fittings. Observe the action of the vacuum gauge.	If the reading improves, replace the indicated gasket, or seal the indicated fitting or plug: If the reading remains low:	8.1 7.3
7.3—Test all vacuum hoses and accessories for leaks as described in 7.2. Also check the carburetor body (dashpots, automatic choke mechanism, throttle shafts) for leaks in the same manner.	If the reading improves, service or replace the offending part(s): If the reading remains low:	8.1 6.1

Section 8—Secondary Electrical System
See Chapter 2 for service procedures

Test and Procedure	Results and Indications	Proceed to
8.1—Remove the distributor cap and check to make sure that the rotor turns when the engine is cranked. Visually inspect the distributor components.	Clean, tighten or replace any components which appear defective.	8.2
8.2—Connect a timing light (per manufacturer's recommendation) and check the dynamic ignition timing. Disconnect and plug the vacuum hose(s) to the distributor if specified, start the engine, and observe the timing marks at the specified engine speed.	If the timing is not correct, adjust to specifications by rotating the distributor in the engine: (Advance timing by rotating distributor opposite normal direction of rotor rotation, retard timing by rotating distributor in same direction as rotor rotation.)	8.3
8.3—Check the operation of the distributor advance mechanism(s): To test the mechanical advance, disconnect the vacuum lines from the distributor advance unit and observe the timing marks with a timing light as the engine speed is increased from idle. If the mark moves smoothly, without hesitation, it may be assumed that the mechanical advance is functioning properly. To test vacuum advance and/or retard systems, alternately crimp and release the vacuum line, and observe the timing mark for movement. If movement is noted, the system is operating.	If the systems are functioning: If the systems are not functioning, remove the distributor, and test on a distributor tester:	8.4 8.4
8.4—Locate an ignition miss: With the engine running, remove each spark plug wire, one at a time, until one is found that doesn't cause the engine to roughen and slow down.	When the missing cylinder is identified:	4.1

Section 9—Valve Train
See Chapter 3 for service procedures

Test and Procedure	Results and Indications	Proceed to
9.1—Evaluate the valve train: Remove the valve cover, and ensure that the valves are adjusted to specifications. A mechanic's stethoscope may be used to aid in the diagnosis of the valve train. By pushing the probe on or near push rods or rockers, valve noise often can be isolated. A timing light also may be used to diagnose valve problems. Connect the light according to manufacturer's recommendations, and start the engine. Vary the firing moment of the light by increasing the engine speed (and therefore the ignition advance), and moving the trigger from cylinder to cylinder. Observe the movement of each valve.	Sticking valves or erratic valve train motion can be observed with the timing light. The cylinder head must be disassembled for repairs.	**See Chapter 3**
9.2—Check the valve timing: Locate top dead center of the No. 1 piston, and install a degree wheel or tape on the crankshaft pulley or damper with zero corresponding to an index mark on the engine. Rotate the crankshaft in its direction of rotation, and observe the opening of the No. 1 cylinder intake valve. The opening should correspond with the correct mark on the degree wheel according to specifications.	If the timing is not correct, the timing cover must be removed for further investigation.	**See Chapter 3**

Section 10—Exhaust System

Test and Procedure	Results and Indications	Proceed to
10.1—Determine whether the exhaust manifold heat control valve is operating: Operate the valve by hand to determine whether it is free to move. If the valve is free, run the engine to operating temperature and observe the action of the valve, to ensure that it is opening.	If the valve sticks, spray it with a suitable solvent, open and close the valve to free it, and retest. If the valve functions properly: If the valve does not free, or does not operate, replace the valve:	**10.2** **10.2**
10.2—Ensure that there are no exhaust restrictions: Visually inspect the exhaust system for kinks, dents, or crushing. Also note that gases are flowing freely from the tailpipe at all engine speeds, indicating no restriction in the muffler or resonator.	Replace any damaged portion of the system:	**11.1**

Section 11—Cooling System
See Chapter 3 for service procedures

Test and Procedure	Results and Indications	Proceed to
11.1—Visually inspect the fan belt for glazing, cracks, and fraying, and replace if necessary. Tighten the belt so that the longest span has approximately ½″ play at its midpoint under thumb pressure (see Chapter 1).	Replace or tighten the fan belt as necessary:	**11.2**

Checking belt tension

11.2—Check the fluid level of the cooling system.	If full or slightly low, fill as necessary:	**11.5**
	If extremely low:	**11.3**
11.3—Visually inspect the external portions of the cooling system (radiator, radiator hoses, thermostat elbow, water pump seals, heater hoses, etc.) for leaks. If none are found, pressurize the cooling system to 14–15 psi.	If cooling system holds the pressure:	**11.5**
	If cooling system loses pressure rapidly, reinspect external parts of the system for leaks under pressure. If none are found, check dipstick for coolant in crankcase. If no coolant is present, but pressure loss continues:	**11.4**
	If coolant is evident in crankcase, remove cylinder head(s), and check gasket(s). If gaskets are intact, block and cylinder head(s) should be checked for cracks or holes.	
	If the gasket(s) is blown, replace, and purge the crankcase of coolant:	**12.6**
	NOTE: *Occasionally, due to atmospheric and driving conditions, condensation of water can occur in the crankcase. This causes the oil to appear milky white. To remedy, run the engine until hot, and change the oil and oil filter.*	
11.4—Check for combustion leaks into the cooling system: Pressurize the cooling system as above. Start the engine, and observe the pressure gauge. If the needle fluctuates, remove each spark plug wire, one at a time, noting which cylinder(s) reduce or eliminate the fluctuation.	Cylinders which reduce or eliminate the fluctuation, when the spark plug wire is removed, are leaking into the cooling system. Replace the head gasket on the affected cylinder bank(s).	

Pressurizing the cooling system

Test and Procedure	Results and Indications	Proceed to
11.5—Check the radiator pressure cap: Attach a radiator pressure tester to the radiator cap (wet the seal prior to installation). Quickly pump up the pressure, noting the point at which the cap releases.	If the cap releases within ± 1 psi of the specified rating, it is operating properly:	**11.6**
	If the cap releases at more than ± 1 psi of the specified rating, it should be replaced:	**11.6**

Checking radiator pressure cap

11.6—Test the thermostat: Start the engine cold, remove the radiator cap, and insert a thermometer into the radiator. Allow the engine to idle. After a short while, there will be a sudden, rapid increase in coolant temperature. The temperature at which this sharp rise stops is the thermostat opening temperature.	If the thermostat opens at or about the specified temperature:	**11.7**
	If the temperature doesn't increase: (If the temperature increases slowly and gradually, replace the thermostat.)	**11.7**
11.7—Check the water pump: Remove the thermostat elbow and the thermostat, disconnect the coil high tension lead (to prevent starting), and crank the engine momentarily.	If coolant flows, replace the thermostat and retest per 11.6:	**11.6**
	If coolant doesn't flow, reverse flush the cooling system to alleviate any blockage that might exist. If system is not blocked, and coolant will not flow, replace the water pump.	

Section 12—Lubrication
See Chapter 3 for service procedures

Test and Procedure	Results and Indications	Proceed to
12.1—Check the oil pressure gauge or warning light: If the gauge shows low pressure, or the light is on for no obvious reason, remove the oil pressure sender. Install an accurate oil pressure gauge and run the engine momentarily.	If oil pressure builds normally, run engine for a few moments to determine that it is functioning normally, and replace the sender.	—
	If the pressure remains low:	**12.2**
	If the pressure surges:	**12.3**
	If the oil pressure is zero:	**12.3**
12.2—Visually inspect the oil: If the oil is watery or very thin, milky, or foamy, replace the oil and oil filter.	If the oil is normal:	**12.3**
	If after replacing oil the pressure remains low:	**12.3**
	If after replacing oil the pressure becomes normal:	—

Test and Procedure	Results and Indications	Proceed to
12.3—Inspect the oil pressure relief valve and spring, to ensure that it is not sticking or stuck. Remove and thoroughly clean the valve, spring, and the valve body.	If the oil pressure improves: If no improvement is noted:	— **12.4**
12.4—Check to ensure that the oil pump is not cavitating (sucking air instead of oil): See that the crankcase is neither over nor underfull, and that the pickup in the sump is in the proper position and free from sludge.	Fill or drain the crankcase to the proper capacity, and clean the pickup screen in solvent if necessary. If no improvement is noted:	**12.5**
12.5—Inspect the oil pump drive and the oil pump:	If the pump drive or the oil pump appear to be defective, service as necessary and retest per 12.1: If the pump drive and pump appear to be operating normally, the engine should be disassembled to determine where blockage exists:	**12.1** **See Chapter 3**
12.6—Purge the engine of ethylene glycol coolant: Completely drain the crankcase and the oil filter. Obtain a commercial butyl cellosolve base solvent, designated for this purpose, and follow the instructions precisely. Following this, install a new oil filter and refill the crankcase with the proper weight oil. The next oil and filter change should follow shortly thereafter (1000 miles).		

TROUBLESHOOTING EMISSION CONTROL SYSTEMS

See Chapter 4 for procedures applicable to individual emission control systems used on specific combinations of engine/transmission/model.

TROUBLESHOOTING THE CARBURETOR

See Chapter 4 for service procedures

Carburetor problems cannot be effectively isolated unless all other engine systems (particularly ignition and emission) are functioning properly and the engine is properly tuned.

Condition	Possible Cause
Engine cranks, but does not start	1. Improper starting procedure 2. No fuel in tank 3. Clogged fuel line or filter 4. Defective fuel pump 5. Choke valve not closing properly 6. Engine flooded 7. Choke valve not unloading 8. Throttle linkage not making full travel 9. Stuck needle or float 10. Leaking float needle or seat 11. Improper float adjustment
Engine stalls	1. Improperly adjusted idle speed or mixture **Engine hot** 2. Improperly adjusted dashpot 3. Defective or improperly adjusted solenoid 4. Incorrect fuel level in fuel bowl 5. Fuel pump pressure too high 6. Leaking float needle seat 7. Secondary throttle valve stuck open 8. Air or fuel leaks 9. Idle air bleeds plugged or missing 10. Idle passages plugged **Engine Cold** 11. Incorrectly adjusted choke 12. Improperly adjusted fast idle speed 13. Air leaks 14. Plugged idle or idle air passages 15. Stuck choke valve or binding linkage 16. Stuck secondary throttle valves 17. Engine flooding—high fuel level 18. Leaking or misaligned float
Engine hesitates on acceleration	1. Clogged fuel filter 2. Leaking fuel pump diaphragm 3. Low fuel pump pressure 4. Secondary throttle valves stuck, bent or misadjusted 5. Sticking or binding air valve 6. Defective accelerator pump 7. Vacuum leaks 8. Clogged air filter 9. Incorrect choke adjustment (engine cold)
Engine feels sluggish or flat on acceleration	1. Improperly adjusted idle speed or mixture 2. Clogged fuel filter 3. Defective accelerator pump 4. Dirty, plugged or incorrect main metering jets 5. Bent or sticking main metering rods 6. Sticking throttle valves 7. Stuck heat riser 8. Binding or stuck air valve 9. Dirty, plugged or incorrect secondary jets 10. Bent or sticking secondary metering rods. 11. Throttle body or manifold heat passages plugged 12. Improperly adjusted choke or choke vacuum break.
Carburetor floods	1. Defective fuel pump. Pressure too high. 2. Stuck choke valve 3. Dirty, worn or damaged float or needle valve/seat 4. Incorrect float/fuel level 5. Leaking float bowl

Condition	Possible Cause
Engine idles roughly and stalls	1. Incorrect idle speed 2. Clogged fuel filter 3. Dirt in fuel system or carburetor 4. Loose carburetor screws or attaching bolts 5. Broken carburetor gaskets 6. Air leaks 7. Dirty carburetor 8. Worn idle mixture needles 9. Throttle valves stuck open 10. Incorrectly adjusted float or fuel level 11. Clogged air filter
Engine runs unevenly or surges	1. Defective fuel pump 2. Dirty or clogged fuel filter 3. Plugged, loose or incorrect main metering jets or rods 4. Air leaks 5. Bent or sticking main metering rods 6. Stuck power piston 7. Incorrect float adjustment 8. Incorrect idle speed or mixture 9. Dirty or plugged idle system passages 10. Hard, brittle or broken gaskets 11. Loose attaching or mounting screws 12. Stuck or misaligned secondary throttle valves
Poor fuel economy	1. Poor driving habits 2. Stuck choke valve 3. Binding choke linkage 4. Stuck heat riser 5. Incorrect idle mixture 6. Defective accelerator pump 7. Air leaks 8. Plugged, loose or incorrect main metering jets 9. Improperly adjusted float or fuel level 10. Bent, misaligned or fuel-clogged float 11. Leaking float needle seat 12. Fuel leak 13. Accelerator pump discharge ball not seating properly 14. Incorrect main jets
Engine lacks high speed performance or power	1. Incorrect throttle linkage adjustment 2. Stuck or binding power piston 3. Defective accelerator pump 4. Air leaks 5. Incorrect float setting or fuel level 6. Dirty, plugged, worn or incorrect main metering jets or rods 7. Binding or sticking air valve 8. Brittle or cracked gaskets 9. Bent, incorrect or improperly adjusted secondary metering rods 10. Clogged fuel filter 11. Clogged air filter 12. Defective fuel pump

TROUBLESHOOTING FUEL INJECTION PROBLEMS

Each fuel injection system has its own unique components and test procedures, for which it is impossible to generalize. Refer to Chapter 4 of this Repair & Tune-Up Guide for specific test and repair procedures, if the vehicle is equipped with fuel injection.

TROUBLESHOOTING ELECTRICAL PROBLEMS

See Chapter 5 for service procedures

For any electrical system to operate, it must make a complete circuit. This simply means that the power flow from the battery must make a complete circle. When an electrical component is operating, power flows from the battery to the component, passes through the component causing it to perform its function (lighting a light bulb), and then returns to the battery through the ground of the circuit. This ground is usually (but not always) the metal part of the car or truck on which the electrical component is mounted.

Perhaps the easiest way to visualize this is to think of connecting a light bulb with two wires attached to it to the battery. If one of the two wires attached to the light bulb were attached to the negative post of the battery and the other were attached to the positive post of the battery, you would have a complete circuit. Current from the battery would flow to the light bulb, causing it to light, and return to the negative post of the battery.

The normal automotive circuit differs from this simple example in two ways. First, instead of having a return wire from the bulb to the battery, the light bulb returns the current to the battery through the chassis of the vehicle. Since the negative battery cable is attached to the chassis and the chassis is made of electrically conductive metal, the chassis of the vehicle can serve as a ground wire to complete the circuit. Secondly, most automotive circuits contain switches to turn components on and off as required.

Every complete circuit from a power source must include a component which is using the power from the power source. If you were to disconnect the light bulb from the wires and touch the two wires together (don't do this) the power supply wire to the component would be grounded before the normal ground connection for the circuit.

Because grounding a wire from a power source makes a complete circuit—less the required component to use the power—this phenomenon is called a short circuit. Common causes are: broken insulation (exposing the metal wire to a metal part of the car or truck), or a shorted switch.

Some electrical components which require a large amount of current to operate also have a relay in their circuit. Since these circuits carry a large amount of current, the thickness of the wire in the circuit (gauge size) is also greater. If this large wire were connected from the component to the control switch on the instrument panel, and then back to the component, a voltage drop would occur in the circuit. To prevent this potential drop in voltage, an electromagnetic switch (relay) is used. The large wires in the circuit are connected from the battery to one side of the relay, and from the opposite side of the relay to the component. The relay is normally open, preventing current from passing through the circuit. An additional, smaller, wire is connected from the relay to the control switch for the circuit. When the control switch is turned on, it grounds the smaller wire from the relay and completes the circuit. This closes the relay and allows current to flow from the battery to the component. The horn, headlight, and starter circuits are three which use relays.

It is possible for larger surges of current to pass through the electrical system of your car or truck. If this surge of current were to reach an electrical component, it could burn it out. To prevent this, fuses, circuit breakers or fusible links are connected into the current supply wires of most of the major electrical systems. When an electrical current of excessive power passes through the component's fuse, the fuse blows out and breaks the circuit, saving the component from destruction.

Typical automotive fuse

A circuit breaker is basically a self-repairing fuse. The circuit breaker opens the circuit the same way a fuse does. However, when either the short is removed from the circuit or the surge subsides, the circuit breaker resets itself and does not have to be replaced as a fuse does.

A fuse link is a wire that acts as a fuse. It is normally connected between the starter relay and the main wiring harness. This connection is usually under the hood. The fuse link (if installed) protects all the

Most fusible links show a charred, melted insulation when they burn out

The test light will show the presence of current when touched to a hot wire and grounded at the other end

chassis electrical components, and is the probable cause of trouble when none of the electrical components function, unless the battery is disconnected or dead.

Electrical problems generally fall into one of three areas:

1. The component that is not functioning is not receiving current.

2. The component itself is not functioning.

3. The component is not properly grounded.

The electrical system can be checked with a test light and a jumper wire. A test light is a device that looks like a pointed screwdriver with a wire attached to it and has a light bulb in its handle. A jumper wire is a piece of insulated wire with an alligator clip attached to each end.

If a component is not working, you must follow a systematic plan to determine which of the three causes is the villain.

1. Turn on the switch that controls the inoperable component.

2. Disconnect the power supply wire from the component.

3. Attach the ground wire on the test light to a good metal ground.

4. Touch the probe end of the test light to the end of the power supply wire that was disconnected from the component. If the component is receiving current, the test light will go on.

NOTE: *Some components work only when the ignition switch is turned on.*

If the test light does not go on, then the problem is in the circuit between the battery and the component. This includes all the switches, fuses, and relays in the system. Follow the wire that runs back to the battery. The problem is an open circuit between the battery and the component. If the fuse is blown and, when replaced, immediately blows again, there is a short circuit in the system which must be located and repaired. If there is a switch in the system, bypass it with a jumper wire. This is done by connecting one end of the jumper wire to the power supply wire into the switch and the other end of the jumper wire to the wire coming out of the switch. If the test light lights with the jumper wire installed, the switch or whatever was bypassed is defective.

NOTE: *Never substitute the jumper wire for the component, since it is required to use the power from the power source.*

5. If the bulb in the test light goes on, then the current is getting to the component that is not working. This eliminates the first of the three possible causes. Connect the power supply wire and connect a jumper wire from the component to a good metal ground. Do this with the switch which controls the component turned on, and also the ignition switch turned on if it is required for the component to work. If the component works with the jumper wire installed, then it has a bad ground. This is usually caused by the metal area on which the component mounts to the chassis being coated with some type of foreign matter.

6. If neither test located the source of the trouble, then the component itself is defective. Remember that for any electrical system to work, all connections must be clean and tight.

Troubleshooting Basic Turn Signal and Flasher Problems
See Chapter 5 for service procedures

Most problems in the turn signals or flasher system can be reduced to defective flashers or bulbs, which are easily replaced. Occasionally, the turn signal switch will prove defective.

F = Front   R = Rear   ● = Lights off   ○ = Lights on

Condition		Possible Cause
Turn signals light, but do not flash		Defective flasher
No turn signals light on either side		Blown fuse. Replace if defective. Defective flasher. Check by substitution. Open circuit, short circuit or poor ground.
Both turn signals on one side don't work		Bad bulbs. Bad ground in both (or either) housings.
One turn signal light on one side doesn't work		Defective bulb. Corrosion in socket. Clean contacts. Poor ground at socket.
Turn signal flashes too fast or too slowly		Check any bulb on the side flashing too fast. A heavy-duty bulb is probably installed in place of a regular bulb. Check the bulb flashing too slowly. A standard bulb was probably installed in place of a heavy-duty bulb. Loose connections or corrosion at the bulb socket.
Indicator lights don't work in either direction		Check if the turn signals are working. Check the dash indicator lights. Check the flasher by substitution.
One indicator light doesn't light		On systems with one dash indicator: See if the lights work on the same side. Often the filaments have been reversed in systems combining stoplights with taillights and turn signals. Check the flasher by substitution. On systems with two indicators: Check the bulbs on the same side. Check the indicator light bulb. Check the flasher by substitution.

Troubleshooting Lighting Problems
See Chapter 5 for service procedures

Condition	Possible Cause
One or more lights don't work, but others do	1. Defective bulb(s) 2. Blown fuse(s) 3. Dirty fuse clips or light sockets 4. Poor ground circuit
Lights burn out quickly	1. Incorrect voltage regulator setting or defective regulator 2. Poor battery/alternator connections
Lights go dim	1. Low/discharged battery 2. Alternator not charging 3. Corroded sockets or connections 4. Low voltage output
Lights flicker	1. Loose connection 2. Poor ground. (Run ground wire from light housing to frame) 3. Circuit breaker operating (short circuit)
Lights "flare"—Some flare is normal on acceleration—If excessive, see "Lights Burn Out Quickly"	High voltage setting
Lights glare—approaching drivers are blinded	1. Lights adjusted too high 2. Rear springs or shocks sagging 3. Rear tires soft

Troubleshooting Dash Gauge Problems
Most problems can be traced to a defective sending unit or faulty wiring. Occasionally, the gauge itself is at fault. See Chapter 5 for service procedures.

Condition	Possible Cause
COOLANT TEMPERATURE GAUGE	
Gauge reads erratically or not at all	1. Loose or dirty connections 2. Defective sending unit. 3. Defective gauge. To test a bi-metal gauge, remove the wire from the sending unit. Ground the wire for an instant. If the gauge registers, replace the sending unit. To test a magnetic gauge, disconnect the wire at the sending unit. With ignition ON gauge should register COLD. Ground the wire; gauge should register HOT.
AMMETER GAUGE—TURN HEADLIGHTS ON (DO NOT START ENGINE). NOTE REACTION	
Ammeter shows charge Ammeter shows discharge Ammeter does not move	1. Connections reversed on gauge 2. Ammeter is OK 3. Loose connections or faulty wiring 4. Defective gauge

Condition	Possible Cause

OIL PRESSURE GAUGE

Condition	Possible Cause
Gauge does not register or is inaccurate	1. On mechanical gauge, Bourdon tube may be bent or kinked. 2. Low oil pressure. Remove sending unit. Idle the engine briefly. If no oil flows from sending unit hole, problem is in engine. 3. Defective gauge. Remove the wire from the sending unit and ground it for an instant with the ignition ON. A good gauge will go to the top of the scale. 4. Defective wiring. Check the wiring to the gauge. If it's OK and the gauge doesn't register when grounded, replace the gauge. 5. Defective sending unit.

ALL GAUGES

Condition	Possible Cause
All gauges do not operate All gauges read low or erratically All gauges pegged	1. Blown fuse 2. Defective instrument regulator 3. Defective or dirty instrument voltage regulator 4. Loss of ground between instrument voltage regulator and frame 5. Defective instrument regulator

WARNING LIGHTS

Condition	Possible Cause
Light(s) do not come on when ignition is ON, but engine is not started Light comes on with engine running	1. Defective bulb 2. Defective wire 3. Defective sending unit. Disconnect the wire from the sending unit and ground it. Replace the sending unit if the light comes on with the ignition ON. 4. Problem in individual system 5. Defective sending unit

Troubleshooting Clutch Problems

It is false economy to replace individual clutch components. The pressure plate, clutch plate and throwout bearing should be replaced as a set, and the flywheel face inspected, whenever the clutch is overhauled. See Chapter 6 for service procedures.

Condition	Possible Cause
Clutch chatter	1. Grease on driven plate (disc) facing 2. Binding clutch linkage or cable 3. Loose, damaged facings on driven plate (disc) 4. Engine mounts loose 5. Incorrect height adjustment of pressure plate release levers 6. Clutch housing or housing to transmission adapter misalignment 7. Loose driven plate hub
Clutch grabbing	1. Oil, grease on driven plate (disc) facing 2. Broken pressure plate 3. Warped or binding driven plate. Driven plate binding on clutch shaft
Clutch slips	1. Lack of lubrication in clutch linkage or cable (linkage or cable binds, causes incomplete engagement) 2. Incorrect pedal, or linkage adjustment 3. Broken pressure plate springs 4. Weak pressure plate springs 5. Grease on driven plate facings (disc)

Troubleshooting Clutch Problems (cont.)

Condition	Possible Cause
Incomplete clutch release	1. Incorrect pedal or linkage adjustment or linkage or cable binding 2. Incorrect height adjustment on pressure plate release levers 3. Loose, broken facings on driven plate (disc) 4. Bent, dished, warped driven plate caused by overheating
Grinding, whirring grating noise when pedal is depressed	1. Worn or defective throwout bearing 2. Starter drive teeth contacting flywheel ring gear teeth. Look for milled or polished teeth on ring gear.
Squeal, howl, trumpeting noise when pedal is being released (occurs during first inch to inch and one-half of pedal travel)	Pilot bushing worn or lack of lubricant. If bushing appears OK, polish bushing with emery cloth, soak lube wick in oil, lube bushing with oil, apply film of chassis grease to clutch shaft pilot hub, reassemble. NOTE: Bushing wear may be due to misalignment of clutch housing or housing to transmission adapter
Vibration or clutch pedal pulsation with clutch disengaged (pedal fully depressed)	1. Worn or defective engine transmission mounts 2. Flywheel run out. (Flywheel run out at face not to exceed 0.005″) 3. Damaged or defective clutch components

Troubleshooting Manual Transmission Problems
See Chapter 6 for service procedures

Condition	Possible Cause
Transmission jumps out of gear	1. Misalignment of transmission case or clutch housing. 2. Worn pilot bearing in crankshaft. 3. Bent transmission shaft. 4. Worn high speed sliding gear. 5. Worn teeth or end-play in clutch shaft. 6. Insufficient spring tension on shifter rail plunger. 7. Bent or loose shifter fork. 8. Gears not engaging completely. 9. Loose or worn bearings on clutch shaft or mainshaft. 10. Worn gear teeth. 11. Worn or damaged detent balls.
Transmission sticks in gear	1. Clutch not releasing fully. 2. Burred or battered teeth on clutch shaft, or sliding sleeve. 3. Burred or battered transmission mainshaft. 4. Frozen synchronizing clutch. 5. Stuck shifter rail plunger. 6. Gearshift lever twisting and binding shifter rail. 7. Battered teeth on high speed sliding gear or on sleeve. 8. Improper lubrication, or lack of lubrication. 9. Corroded transmission parts. 10. Defective mainshaft pilot bearing. 11. Locked gear bearings will give same effect as stuck in gear.
Transmission gears will not synchronize	1. Binding pilot bearing on mainshaft, will synchronize in high gear only. 2. Clutch not releasing fully. 3. Detent spring weak or broken. 4. Weak or broken springs under balls in sliding gear sleeve. 5. Binding bearing on clutch shaft, or binding countershaft. 6. Binding pilot bearing in crankshaft. 7. Badly worn gear teeth. 8. Improper lubrication. 9. Constant mesh gear not turning freely on transmission mainshaft. Will synchronize in that gear only.

Condition	Possible Cause
Gears spinning when shifting into gear from neutral	1. Clutch not releasing fully. 2. In some cases an extremely light lubricant in transmission will cause gears to continue to spin for a short time after clutch is released. 3. Binding pilot bearing in crankshaft.
Transmission noisy in all gears	1. Insufficient lubricant, or improper lubricant. 2. Worn countergear bearings. 3. Worn or damaged main drive gear or countergear. 4. Damaged main drive gear or mainshaft bearings. 5. Worn or damaged countergear anti-lash plate.
Transmission noisy in neutral only	1. Damaged main drive gear bearing. 2. Damaged or loose mainshaft pilot bearing. 3. Worn or damaged countergear anti-lash plate. 4. Worn countergear bearings.
Transmission noisy in one gear only	1. Damaged or worn constant mesh gears. 2. Worn or damaged countergear bearings. 3. Damaged or worn synchronizer.
Transmission noisy in reverse only	1. Worn or damaged reverse idler gear or idler bushing. 2. Worn or damaged mainshaft reverse gear. 3. Worn or damaged reverse countergear. 4. Damaged shift mechanism.

TROUBLESHOOTING AUTOMATIC TRANSMISSION PROBLEMS

Keeping alert to changes in the operating characteristics of the transmission (changing shift points, noises, etc.) can prevent small problems from becoming large ones. If the problem cannot be traced to loose bolts, fluid level, misadjusted linkage, clogged filters or similar problems, you should probably seek professional service.

Transmission Fluid Indications

The appearance and odor of the transmission fluid can give valuable clues to the overall condition of the transmission. Always note the appearance of the fluid when you check the fluid level or change the fluid. Rub a small amount of fluid between your fingers to feel for grit and smell the fluid on the dipstick.

If the fluid appears:	It indicates:
Clear and red colored	Normal operation
Discolored (extremely dark red or brownish) or smells burned	Band or clutch pack failure, usually caused by an overheated transmission. Hauling very heavy loads with insufficient power or failure to change the fluid often result in overheating. Do not confuse this appearance with newer fluids that have a darker red color and a strong odor (though not a burned odor).
Foamy or aerated (light in color and full of bubbles)	1. The level is too high (gear train is churning oil) 2. An internal air leak (air is mixing with the fluid). Have the transmission checked professionally.
Solid residue in the fluid	Defective bands, clutch pack or bearings. Bits of band material or metal abrasives are clinging to the dipstick. Have the transmission checked professionally.
Varnish coating on the dipstick	The transmission fluid is overheating

TROUBLESHOOTING DRIVE AXLE PROBLEMS

First, determine when the noise is most noticeable.

Drive Noise: Produced under vehicle acceleration.

Coast Noise: Produced while coasting with a closed throttle.

Float Noise: Occurs while maintaining constant speed (just enough to keep speed constant) on a level road.

External Noise Elimination

It is advisable to make a thorough road test to determine whether the noise originates in the rear axle or whether it originates from the tires, engine, transmission, wheel bearings or road surface. Noise originating from other places cannot be corrected by servicing the rear axle.

ROAD NOISE

Brick or rough surfaced concrete roads produce noises that seem to come from the rear axle. Road noise is usually identical in Drive or Coast and driving on a different type of road will tell whether the road is the problem.

TIRE NOISE

Tire noise can be mistaken as rear axle noise, even though the tires on the front are at fault. Snow tread and mud tread tires or tires worn unevenly will frequently cause vibrations which seem to originate elsewhere; *temporarily, and for test purposes only,* inflate the tires to 40–50 lbs. This will significantly alter the noise produced by the tires, but will not alter noise from the rear axle. Noises from the rear axle will normally cease at speeds below 30 mph on coast, while tire noise will continue at lower tone as speed is decreased. The rear axle noise will usually change from drive conditions to coast conditions, while tire noise will not. Do not forget to lower the tire pressure to normal after the test is complete.

ENGINE/TRANSMISSION NOISE

Determine at what speed the noise is most pronounced, then stop in a quiet place. With the transmission in Neutral, run the engine through speeds corresponding to road speeds where the noise was noticed. Noises produced with the vehicle standing still are coming from the engine or transmission.

FRONT WHEEL BEARINGS

Front wheel bearing noises, sometimes confused with rear axle noises, will not change when comparing drive and coast conditions. While holding the speed steady, lightly apply the footbrake. This will often cause wheel bearing noise to lessen, as some of the weight is taken off the bearing. Front wheel bearings are easily checked by jacking up the wheels and spinning the wheels. Shaking the wheels will also determine if the wheel bearings are excessively loose.

REAR AXLE NOISES

Eliminating other possible sources can narrow the cause to the rear axle, which normally produces noise from worn gears or bearings. Gear noises tend to peak in a narrow speed range, while bearing noises will usually vary in pitch with engine speeds.

Noise Diagnosis

The Noise Is:	Most Probably Produced By:
1. Identical under Drive or Coast	Road surface, tires or front wheel bearings
2. Different depending on road surface	Road surface or tires
3. Lower as speed is lowered	Tires
4. Similar when standing or moving	Engine or transmission
5. A vibration	Unbalanced tires, rear wheel bearing, unbalanced driveshaft or worn U-joint
6. A knock or click about every two tire revolutions	Rear wheel bearing
7. Most pronounced on turns	Damaged differential gears
8. A steady low-pitched whirring or scraping, starting at low speeds	Damaged or worn pinion bearing
9. A chattering vibration on turns	Wrong differential lubricant or worn clutch plates (limited slip rear axle)
10. Noticed only in Drive, Coast or Float conditions	Worn ring gear and/or pinion gear

Troubleshooting Steering & Suspension Problems

Condition	Possible Cause
Hard steering (wheel is hard to turn)	1. Improper tire pressure 2. Loose or glazed pump drive belt 3. Low or incorrect fluid 4. Loose, bent or poorly lubricated front end parts 5. Improper front end alignment (excessive caster) 6. Bind in steering column or linkage 7. Kinked hydraulic hose 8. Air in hydraulic system 9. Low pump output or leaks in system 10. Obstruction in lines 11. Pump valves sticking or out of adjustment 12. Incorrect wheel alignment
Loose steering (too much play in steering wheel)	1. Loose wheel bearings 2. Faulty shocks 3. Worn linkage or suspension components 4. Loose steering gear mounting or linkage points 5. Steering mechanism worn or improperly adjusted 6. Valve spool improperly adjusted 7. Worn ball joints, tie-rod ends, etc.
Veers or wanders (pulls to one side with hands off steering wheel)	1. Improper tire pressure 2. Improper front end alignment 3. Dragging or improperly adjusted brakes 4. Bent frame 5. Improper rear end alignment 6. Faulty shocks or springs 7. Loose or bent front end components 8. Play in Pitman arm 9. Steering gear mountings loose 10. Loose wheel bearings 11. Binding Pitman arm 12. Spool valve sticking or improperly adjusted 13. Worn ball joints
Wheel oscillation or vibration transmitted through steering wheel	1. Low or uneven tire pressure 2. Loose wheel bearings 3. Improper front end alignment 4. Bent spindle 5. Worn, bent or broken front end components 6. Tires out of round or out of balance 7. Excessive lateral runout in disc brake rotor 8. Loose or bent shock absorber or strut
Noises (see also "Troubleshooting Drive Axle Problems")	1. Loose belts 2. Low fluid, air in system 3. Foreign matter in system 4. Improper lubrication 5. Interference or chafing in linkage 6. Steering gear mountings loose 7. Incorrect adjustment or wear in gear box 8. Faulty valves or wear in pump 9. Kinked hydraulic lines 10. Worn wheel bearings
Poor return of steering	1. Over-inflated tires 2. Improperly aligned front end (excessive caster) 3. Binding in steering column 4. No lubrication in front end 5. Steering gear adjusted too tight
Uneven tire wear (see "How To Read Tire Wear")	1. Incorrect tire pressure 2. Improperly aligned front end 3. Tires out-of-balance 4. Bent or worn suspension parts

HOW TO READ TIRE WEAR

The way your tires wear is a good indicator of other parts of the suspension. Abnormal wear patterns are often caused by the need for simple tire maintenance, or for front end alignment.

Excessive wear at the center of the tread indicates that the air pressure in the tire is consistently too high. The tire is riding on the center of the tread and wearing it prematurely. Occasionally, this wear pattern can result from outrageously wide tires on narrow rims. The cure for this is to replace either the tires or the wheels.

This type of wear usually results from consistent under-inflation. When a tire is under-inflated, there is too much contact with the road by the outer treads, which wear prematurely. When this type of wear occurs, and the tire pressure is known to be consistently correct, a bent or worn steering component or the need for wheel alignment could be indicated.

Feathering is a condition when the edge of each tread rib develops a slightly rounded edge on one side and a sharp edge on the other. By running your hand over the tire, you can usually feel the sharper edges before you'll be able to see them. The most common causes of feathering are incorrect toe-in setting or deteriorated bushings in the front suspension.

When an inner or outer rib wears faster than the rest of the tire, the need for wheel alignment is indicated. There is excessive camber in the front suspension, causing the wheel to lean too much putting excessive load on one side of the tire. Misalignment could also be due to sagging springs, worn ball joints, or worn control arm bushings. Be sure the vehicle is loaded the way it's normally driven when you have the wheels aligned.

Cups or scalloped dips appearing around the edge of the tread almost always indicate worn (sometimes bent) suspension parts. Adjustment of wheel alignment alone will seldom cure the problem. Any worn component that connects the wheel to the suspension can cause this type of wear. Occasionally, wheels that are out of balance will wear like this, but wheel imbalance usually shows up as bald spots between the outside edges and center of the tread.

Second-rib wear is usually found only in radial tires, and appears where the steel belts end in relation to the tread. It can be kept to a minimum by paying careful attention to tire pressure and frequently rotating the tires. This is often considered normal wear but excessive amounts indicate that the tires are too wide for the wheels.

Over-inflation

Under-inflation

Feathering

One side wear

Cupping

Second-rib wear

Troubleshooting Disc Brake Problems

Condition	Possible Cause
Noise—groan—brake noise emanating when slowly releasing brakes (creep-groan)	Not detrimental to function of disc brakes—no corrective action required. (This noise may be eliminated by slightly increasing or decreasing brake pedal efforts.)
Rattle—brake noise or rattle emanating at low speeds on rough roads, (front wheels only).	1. Shoe anti-rattle spring missing or not properly positioned. 2. Excessive clearance between shoe and caliper. 3. Soft or broken caliper seals. 4. Deformed or misaligned disc. 5. Loose caliper.
Scraping	1. Mounting bolts too long. 2. Loose wheel bearings. 3. Bent, loose, or misaligned splash shield.
Front brakes heat up during driving and fail to release	1. Operator riding brake pedal. 2. Stop light switch improperly adjusted. 3. Sticking pedal linkage. 4. Frozen or seized piston. 5. Residual pressure valve in master cylinder. 6. Power brake malfunction. 7. Proportioning valve malfunction.
Leaky brake caliper	1. Damaged or worn caliper piston seal. 2. Scores or corrosion on surface of cylinder bore.
Grabbing or uneven brake action—Brakes pull to one side	1. Causes listed under "Brakes Pull". 2. Power brake malfunction. 3. Low fluid level in master cylinder. 4. Air in hydraulic system. 5. Brake fluid, oil or grease on linings. 6. Unmatched linings. 7. Distorted brake pads. 8. Frozen or seized pistons. 9. Incorrect tire pressure. 10. Front end out of alignment. 11. Broken rear spring. 12. Brake caliper pistons sticking. 13. Restricted hose or line. 14. Caliper not in proper alignment to braking disc. 15. Stuck or malfunctioning metering valve. 16. Soft or broken caliper seals. 17. Loose caliper.
Brake pedal can be depressed without braking effect	1. Air in hydraulic system or improper bleeding procedure. 2. Leak past primary cup in master cylinder. 3. Leak in system. 4. Rear brakes out of adjustment. 5. Bleeder screw open.
Excessive pedal travel	1. Air, leak, or insufficient fluid in system or caliper. 2. Warped or excessively tapered shoe and lining assembly. 3. Excessive disc runout. 4. Rear brake adjustment required. 5. Loose wheel bearing adjustment. 6. Damaged caliper piston seal. 7. Improper brake fluid (boil). 8. Power brake malfunction. 9. Weak or soft hoses.

Troubleshooting Disc Brake Problems (cont.)

Condition	Possible Cause
Brake roughness or chatter (pedal pumping)	1. Excessive thickness variation of braking disc. 2. Excessive lateral runout of braking disc. 3. Rear brake drums out-of-round. 4. Excessive front bearing clearance.
Excessive pedal effort	1. Brake fluid, oil or grease on linings. 2. Incorrect lining. 3. Frozen or seized pistons. 4. Power brake malfunction. 5. Kinked or collapsed hose or line. 6. Stuck metering valve. 7. Scored caliper or master cylinder bore. 8. Seized caliper pistons.
Brake pedal fades (pedal travel increases with foot on brake)	1. Rough master cylinder or caliper bore. 2. Loose or broken hydraulic lines/connections. 3. Air in hydraulic system. 4. Fluid level low. 5. Weak or soft hoses. 6. Inferior quality brake shoes or fluid. 7. Worn master cylinder piston cups or seals.

Troubleshooting Drum Brakes

Condition	Possible Cause
Pedal goes to floor	1. Fluid low in reservoir. 2. Air in hydraulic system. 3. Improperly adjusted brake. 4. Leaking wheel cylinders. 5. Loose or broken brake lines. 6. Leaking or worn master cylinder. 7. Excessively worn brake lining.
Spongy brake pedal	1. Air in hydraulic system. 2. Improper brake fluid (low boiling point). 3. Excessively worn or cracked brake drums. 4. Broken pedal pivot bushing.
Brakes pulling	1. Contaminated lining. 2. Front end out of alignment. 3. Incorrect brake adjustment. 4. Unmatched brake lining. 5. Brake drums out of round. 6. Brake shoes distorted. 7. Restricted brake hose or line. 8. Broken rear spring. 9. Worn brake linings. 10. Uneven lining wear. 11. Glazed brake lining. 12. Excessive brake lining dust. 13. Heat spotted brake drums. 14. Weak brake return springs. 15. Faulty automatic adjusters. 16. Low or incorrect tire pressure.

Condition	Possible Cause
Squealing brakes	1. Glazed brake lining. 2. Saturated brake lining. 3. Weak or broken brake shoe retaining spring. 4. Broken or weak brake shoe return spring. 5. Incorrect brake lining. 6. Distorted brake shoes. 7. Bent support plate. 8. Dust in brakes or scored brake drums. 9. Linings worn below limit. 10. Uneven brake lining wear. 11. Heat spotted brake drums.
Chirping brakes	1. Out of round drum or eccentric axle flange pilot.
Dragging brakes	1. Incorrect wheel or parking brake adjustment. 2. Parking brakes engaged or improperly adjusted. 3. Weak or broken brake shoe return spring. 4. Brake pedal binding. 5. Master cylinder cup sticking. 6. Obstructed master cylinder relief port. 7. Saturated brake lining. 8. Bent or out of round brake drum. 9. Contaminated or improper brake fluid. 10. Sticking wheel cylinder pistons. 11. Driver riding brake pedal. 12. Defective proportioning valve. 13. Insufficient brake shoe lubricant.
Hard pedal	1. Brake booster inoperative. 2. Incorrect brake lining. 3. Restricted brake line or hose. 4. Frozen brake pedal linkage. 5. Stuck wheel cylinder. 6. Binding pedal linkage. 7. Faulty proportioning valve.
Wheel locks	1. Contaminated brake lining. 2. Loose or torn brake lining. 3. Wheel cylinder cups sticking. 4. Incorrect wheel bearing adjustment. 5. Faulty proportioning valve.
Brakes fade (high speed)	1. Incorrect lining. 2. Overheated brake drums. 3. Incorrect brake fluid (low boiling temperature). 4. Saturated brake lining. 5. Leak in hydraulic system. 6. Faulty automatic adjusters.
Pedal pulsates	1. Bent or out of round brake drum.
Brake chatter and shoe knock	1. Out of round brake drum. 2. Loose support plate. 3. Bent support plate. 4. Distorted brake shoes. 5. Machine grooves in contact face of brake drum (Shoe Knock). 6. Contaminated brake lining. 7. Missing or loose components. 8. Incorrect lining material. 9. Out-of-round brake drums. 10. Heat spotted or scored brake drums. 11. Out-of-balance wheels.

Troubleshooting Drum Brakes (cont.)

Condition	Possible Cause
Brakes do not self adjust	1. Adjuster screw frozen in thread. 2. Adjuster screw corroded at thrust washer. 3. Adjuster lever does not engage star wheel. 4. Adjuster installed on wrong wheel.
Brake light glows	1. Leak in the hydraulic system. 2. Air in the system. 3. Improperly adjusted master cylinder pushrod. 4. Uneven lining wear. 5. Failure to center combination valve or proportioning valve.

Mechanic's Data

General Conversion Table

Multiply By	To Convert	To	
		LENGTH	
2.54	Inches	Centimeters	.3937
25.4	Inches	Millimeters	.03937
30.48	Feet	Centimeters	.0328
.304	Feet	Meters	3.28
.914	Yards	Meters	1.094
1.609	Miles	Kilometers	.621
		VOLUME	
.473	Pints	Liters	2.11
.946	Quarts	Liters	1.06
3.785	Gallons	Liters	.264
.016	Cubic inches	Liters	61.02
16.39	Cubic inches	Cubic cms.	.061
28.3	Cubic feet	Liters	.0353
		MASS (Weight)	
28.35	Ounces	Grams	.035
.4536	Pounds	Kilograms	2.20
—	To obtain	From	Multiply by

Multiply By	To Convert	To	
		AREA	
.645	Square inches	Square cms.	.155
.836	Square yds.	Square meters	1.196
		FORCE	
4.448	Pounds	Newtons	.225
.138	Ft./lbs.	Kilogram/meters	7.23
1.36	Ft./lbs.	Newton-meters	.737
.112	In./lbs.	Newton-meters	8.844
		PRESSURE	
.068	Psi	Atmospheres	14.7
6.89	Psi	Kilopascals	.145
		OTHER	
1.104	Horsepower (DIN)	Horsepower (SAE)	.9861
.746	Horsepower (SAE)	Kilowatts (KW)	1.34
1.60	Mph	Km/h	.625
.425	Mpg	Km/1	2.35
—	To obtain	From	Multiply by

Tap Drill Sizes

National Coarse or U.S.S.

Screw & Tap Size	Threads Per Inch	Use Drill Number
No. 5	40	39
No. 6	32	36
No. 8	32	29
No. 10	24	25
No. 12	24	17
1/4	20	8
5/16	18	F
3/8	16	5/16
7/16	14	U
1/2	13	27/64
9/16	12	31/64
5/8	11	17/32
3/4	10	21/32
7/8	9	49/64

National Coarse or U.S.S.

Screw & Tap Size	Threads Per Inch	Use Drill Number
1	8	7/8
1 1/8	7	63/64
1 1/4	7	1 7/64
1 1/2	6	1 11/32

National Fine or S.A.E.

Screw & Tap Size	Threads Per Inch	Use Drill Number
No. 5	44	37
No. 6	40	33
No. 8	36	29
No. 10	32	21

National Fine or S.A.E.

Screw & Tap Size	Threads Per Inch	Use Drill Number
No. 12	28	15
1/4	28	3
6/16	24	1
3/8	24	Q
7/16	20	W
1/2	20	29/64
9/16	18	33/64
5/8	18	37/64
3/4	16	11/16
7/8	14	13/16
1 1/8	12	1 3/64
1 1/4	12	1 11/64
1 1/2	12	1 27/64

Drill Sizes In Decimal Equivalents

Inch	Decimal	Wire	mm
1/64	.0156		.39
	.0157		.4
	.0160	78	
	.0165		.42
	.0173		.44
	.0177		.45
	.0180	77	
	.0181		.46
	.0189		.48
	.0197		.5
	.0200	76	
	.0210	75	
	.0217		.55
	.0225	74	
	.0236		.6
	.0240	73	
	.0250	72	
	.0256		.65
	.0260	71	
	.0276		.7
	.0280	70	
	.0292	69	
	.0295		.75
	.0310	68	
1/32	.0312		.79
	.0315		.8
	.0320	67	
	.0330	66	
	.0335		.85
	.0350	65	
	.0354		.9
	.0360	64	
	.0370	63	
	.0374		.95
	.0380	62	
	.0390	61	
	.0394		1.0
	.0400	60	
	.0410	59	
	.0413		1.05
	.0420	58	
	.0430	57	
	.0433		1.1
	.0453		1.15
3/64	.0465	56	
	.0469		1.19
	.0472		1.2
	.0492		1.25
	.0512		1.3
	.0520	55	
	.0531		1.35
	.0550	54	
	.0551		1.4
	.0571		1.45
	.0591		1.5
	.0595	53	
	.0610		1.55
1/16	.0625		1.59
	.0630		1.6
	.0635	52	
	.0650		1.65
	.0669		1.7
	.0670	51	
	.0689		1.75
	.0700	50	
	.0709		1.8
	.0728		1.85

Inch	Decimal	Wire	mm
	.0730	49	
	.0748		1.9
	.0760	48	
	.0768		1.95
5/64	.0781		1.98
	.0785	47	
	.0787		2.0
	.0807		2.05
	.0810	46	
	.0820	45	
	.0827		2.1
	.0846		2.15
	.0860	44	
	.0866		2.2
	.0886		2.25
	.0890	43	
	.0906		2.3
	.0925		2.35
	.0935	42	
3/32	.0938		2.38
	.0945		2.4
	.0960	41	
	.0965		2.45
	.0980	40	
	.0981		2.5
	.0995	39	
	.1015	38	
	.1024		2.6
	.1040	37	
	.1063		2.7
	.1065	36	
	.1083		2.75
7/64	.1094		2.77
	.1100	35	
	.1102		2.8
	.1110	34	
	.1130	33	
	.1142		2.9
	.1160	32	
	.1181		3.0
	.1200	31	
	.1220		3.1
1/8	.1250		3.17
	.1260		3.2
	.1280		3.25
	.1285	30	
	.1299		3.3
	.1339		3.4
	.1360	29	
	.1378		3.5
	.1405	28	
9/64	.1406		3.57
	.1417		3.6
	.1440	27	
	.1457		3.7
	.1470	26	
	.1476		3.75
	.1495	25	
	.1496		3.8
	.1520	24	
	.1535		3.9
	.1540	23	
5/32	.1562		3.96
	.1570	22	
	.1575		4.0
	.1590	21	
	.1610	20	

Inch	Decimal	Wire & Letter	mm
	.1614		4.1
	.1654		4.2
	.1660	19	
	.1673		4.25
	.1693		4.3
	.1695	18	
11/64	.1719		4.36
	.1730	17	
	.1732		4.4
	.1770	16	
	.1772		4.5
	.1800	15	
	.1811		4.6
	.1820	14	
	.1850	13	
	.1850		4.7
	.1870		4.75
3/16	.1875		4.76
	.1890		4.8
	.1890	12	
	.1910	11	
	.1929		4.9
	.1935	10	
	.1960	9	
	.1969		5.0
	.1990	8	
	.2008		5.1
	.2010	7	
13/64	.2031		5.16
	.2040	6	
	.2047		5.2
	.2055	5	
	.2067		5.25
	.2087		5.3
	.2090	4	
	.2126		5.4
	.2130	3	
	.2165		5.5
7/32	2188		5.55
	.2205		5.6
	.2210	2	
	.2244		5.7
	.2264		5.75
	.2280	1	
	.2283		5.8
	.2323		5.9
	.2340	A	
15/64	.2344		5.95
	.2362		6.0
	.2380	B	
	.2402		6.1
	.2420	C	
	.2441		6.2
	.2460	D	
	.2461		6.25
	.2480		6.3
1/4	.2500	E	6.35
	.2520		6.
	.2559		6.5
	.2570	F	
	.2598		6.6
	.2610	G	
	.2638		6.7
17/64	.2656		6.74
	.2657		6.75
	.2660	H	
	.2677		6.8

Inch	Decimal	Letter	mm
	.2717		6.9
	.2720	I	
	.2756		7.0
	.2770	J	
	.2795		7.1
	.2810	K	
9/32	.2812		7.14
	.2835		7.2
	.2854		7.25
	.2874		7.3
	.2900	L	
	.2913		7.4
	.2950	M	
	.2953		7.5
19/64	.2969		7.54
	.2992		7.6
	.3020	N	
	.3031		7.7
	.3051		7.75
	.3071		7.8
	.3110		7.9
5/16	.3125		7.93
	.3150		8.0
	.3160	O	
	.3189		8.1
	.3228		8.2
	.3230	P	
	.3248		8.25
21/64	.3281		8.33
	.3307		8.4
	.3320	Q	
	.3346		8.5
	.3386		8.6
	.3390	R	
	.3425		8.7
11/32	.3438		8.73
	.3445		8.75
	.3465		8.8
	.3480	S	
	.3504		8.9
	.3543		9.0
	.3580	T	
	.3583		9.1
23/64	.3594		9.12
	.3622		9.2
	.3642		9.25
	.3661		9.3
	.3680	U	
	.3701		9.4
	.3740		9.5
3/8	.3750		9.52
	.3770	V	
	.3780		9.6
	.3819		9.7
	.3839		9.75
	.3858		9.8
	.3860	W	
	.3898		9.9
25/64	.3906		9.92
	.3937		10.0
	.3970	X	
	.4040	Y	
13/32	.4062		10.31
	.4130	Z	
	.4134		10.5
27/64	.4219		10.71

Inch	Decimal	mm
	.4331	11.0
7/16	.4375	11.11
	.4528	11.5
29/64	.4531	11.51
15/32	.4688	11.90
	.4724	12.0
31/64	.4844	12.30
	.4921	12.5
1/2	.5000	12.70
	.5118	13.0
33/64	.5156	13.09
17/32	.5312	13.49
	.5315	13.5
35/64	.5469	13.89
	.5512	14.0
9/16	.5625	14.28
	.5709	14.5
37/64	.5781	14.68
	.5906	15.0
19/32	.5938	15.08
39/64	.6094	15.47
	.6102	15.5
5/8	.6250	15.87
	.6299	16.0
41/64	.6406	16.27
	.6496	16.5
21/32	.6562	16.66
	.6693	17.0
43/64	.6719	17.06
11/16	.6875	17.46
	.6890	17.5
45/64	.7031	17.85
	.7087	18.0
23/32	.7188	18.25
	.7283	18.5
47/64	.7344	18.65
	.7480	19.0
3/4	.7500	19.05
49/64	.7656	19.44
	.7677	19.5
25/32	.7812	19.84
	.7874	20.0
51/64	.7969	20.24
	.8071	20.5
13/16	.8125	20.63
	.8268	21.0
53/64	.8281	21.03
27/32	.8438	21.43
	.8465	21.5
55/64	.8594	21.82
	.8661	22.0
7/8	.8750	22.22
	.8858	22.5
57/64	.8906	22.62
	.9055	23.0
29/32	.9062	23.01
	.9219	23.41
59/64	.9252	23.5
15/16	.9375	23.81
	.9449	24.0
61/64	.9531	24.2
	.9646	24.5
31/64	.9688	24.6
	.9843	25.0
63/64	.9844	25.0
1	1.0000	25.4

Index

A

Air cleaner, 8
Air conditioning, 19
Air injection, 173
Alternator, 83, 88, 98
Antifreeze, 17, 264
Automatic transmission, 269
   Adjustment, 270
   Filter change, 269
   Pan removal, 269
Axle
   Fluid recommendations, 29
   Identification, 285
   Lubricant level, 24
Axle ratio, 286
Axle shaft, 288
   Bearings and seals, 289

B

Ball joints, 293
Battery, 13, 82, 96
   Jump starting, 38
   Maintenance, 13, 26
Belt tension adjustments, 15, 88
Bolts, 117
Brakes, 309
   Adjustment, 322
   Bleeding, 313
   Caliper, 316
   Discs, 319
   Drums, 321
   Fluid level, 23
   Fluid recommendations, 37
   Front brakes, 314
   Master cylinder, 309
   Parking brake, 33, 324
   Rear brakes, 321
Breaker points, 57

C

C-4 system, 184
Camber, 297
Camshaft and bearings, 145
Capacities, 34
Carburetor, 69, 203
   Adjustment, 70, 205
   Overhaul, 203
   Replacement, 203
Caster, 297
Catalytic converter, 194
CCC system, 185
Charging system, 83
Chassis lubrication, 37
Choke, 203
Clutch, 261, 265
   Adjustment, 267
   Replacement, 268

Coil (ignition), 66
Coil springs, 292, 300
Condenser, 57
Connecting rod and bearings, 153
Control arm
   Upper, 296
   Lower, 297
Cooling system, 17, 164
Crankcase ventilation (PCV), 10, 11
Crankshaft, 155
Cylinder head, 118
   Removal and installation, 118
   Service, 136
   Torque sequence, 119

D

Diesel fuel injection, 79
Differential, 33, 285
   Fluid change, 24
   Ratios, 286
Distributor, 84
   Removal and installation, 84
   Breaker points, 57
Door hinges, 33
Drill sizes, 361
Drive axle, 33, 285
Driveshaft, 283
Dwell angle, 60
Dwell meter, 60

E

EGR valve, 180, 198
Electrical
   Chassis, 245
   Engine, 46, 82
Electronic ignition, 62, 84
Electronic spark timing, 194
Emission controls, 19, 167
   Diesel, 197
Engine, 95
   Camshaft, 145
   Cylinder head torque sequence, 119
   Exhaust manifold, 130
   Front cover, 139
   Identification, 5
   Ignition timing, 67
   Intake manifold, 127
   Oil recommendations, 29
   Pistons and rings, 111, 149
   Rebuilding, 82, 115
   Removal and installation, 113
   Rocker arm (or shaft), 123
   Specifications, 101
   Timing chain (or gears), 143
   Tune-up, 48
Evaporative canister, 12, 169
Exhaust manifold, 130